Coping with Overloaded Criminal Justice Systems

Jörg-Martin Jehle · Marianne Wade

Coping with Overloaded Criminal Justice Systems

The Rise of Prosecutorial Power Across Europe

With contributions by
Bruno Aubusson de Cavarley, Martine Blom,
Teodor Bulenda, Beatrix Elsner, Beate Grusczynska,
Jörg-Martin Jehle, Andrzej Kremplewski,
Christopher Lewis, Julia Peters, Paul Smit,
Piotr Sobota, Marianne Wade, Josef Zila

Springer

Professor Dr. Jörg-Martin Jehle
Dr. Marianne Wade

Universität Göttingen
Institute for Criminal Law
& Criminal Justice
Department of Criminology
Platz der Göttinger Sieben 6
37073 Göttingen
Germany

abtkrim@gwdg.de
mwade@jura.uni-goettingen.de

The publication of the book was sponsored by the European Commision (AGIS Programm 2005).
The research project was funded by the Fritz Thyssen Stiftung.

Cataloging-in-Publication Data

ISBN 978-3-642-07048-8 e-ISBN 978-3-540-33963-2

Springer is a part of Springer Science+Business Media

springeronline.com

Hardcover-Design: Erich Kirchner, Heidelberg

Preface

The comparative study documented here was supported by the Fritz Thyssen Stiftung and the European Commission. It examined prosecution services in different European countries intending to understand their national role and function within the respective criminal justice system and thereby to highlight common features and important differences between European systems. The prosecution service is regarded as a part of the criminal justice system; a coherent system under pressure to deal with high numbers of cases. Within this system the prosecution level is increasingly becoming the decisive stage reducing its workload by means of simplified methods and proceedings.

The research was carried out by a network of experts from England and Wales, France, Germany, the Netherlands, Poland and Sweden in order to develop common questions and data collection concepts and to gather the country-specific information required to allow comparison. The study deals with an area in which little research has been done and which is increasingly becoming the central, decision-making level of evolving criminal justice systems, with far-reaching consequences for society and the fundamental principles of criminal law.

The roots of our study lie in a project which generated the European Sourcebook of Crime and Criminal Justice Statistics. In 1996 the Council of Europe commissioned a group of specialists chaired by Martin Kilias to prepare a collection of criminal justice data for the whole of Europe; since then the European Sourcebook has been established and published in several editions. The production of the chapter on public prosecution for which Jörg-Martin Jehle and Bruno Aubusson de Cavarlay had particular responsibility highlighted a lack of comparable statistical and legal information. Thus the idea for this indepth study was born.

Our project partners are criminal justice system experts and experienced comparative researchers, e.g. through their membership of the European Sourcebook group and other international committees: They are Chris Lewis for England and Wales, Bruno Aubusson de Cavarlay for France, Paul Smit and Martine Blom for the Netherlands, Beata Grusczynska together with Teodor Bulenda, Andrzej Kremplewski and Piotr Sobota for Poland, Josef Zila for Sweden and the German project management and research team consisting of Beatrix Elsner, Jörg-Martin Jehle, Julia Peters and Marianne Wade.

Due to the extraordinary commitment of all the partners to our joint venture, the research instruments could be developed and the outcome be validated in intensive sessions and bilateral discussions. All results presented in this volume are the product of the joint efforts of the group as a whole. We are deeply grateful for such unusually close partnership and friendship growing increasingly in the course of cooperation. We would also like to express our gratitude to the Fritz Thyssen Foundation which generously supported the completion of our project.

The project results were presented and discussed at an international conference held at Göttingen University in October 2005. We are very much obliged to Mazen Houssami, Hans-Jürgen Kerner, Harald Range, Andrew Sanders, Henk-Marquardt Scholz, Peter Tak and Thomas Weigend for their additional papers reflecting on and complementing the study results. We are indebted to the European Commission for funding the conference and the publication of this volume through the AGIS Programme.

Concerning the preparation of the print publication Beatrix Elsner and Julia Peters made invaluable contributions to the production of the synoptic tables and graphs. Thies Doerpmund and Axel Litty did an excellent job mastering the difficult technical setting work. We also like to thank our publisher Springer for good cooperation. Last, but not least, we express our gratitude to all the staff at the Göttingen Department of Criminology, especially to Heike Amouei and Marion Heinze. Their help was a great contribution to the success of this project.

Göttingen, in May 2006 Jörg-Martin Jehle, Marianne Wade

Contents

Part III: Appendix

Part I

Varying Structures and Convergent Trends in Prosecution within Europe

A European Six-Country Comparison

The Function of Public Prosecution within the Criminal Justice System

Aim, Approach and Outcome of a European Comparative Study

Jörg-Martin Jehle

1 Aim and Approach

The study supported by the Fritz-Thyssen Foundation and the European Commission examined prosecution services in different European countries with the intention to understand their national role and function within the criminal justice system and thereby to highlight common features and important differences. By this means convergent trends in dealing with high criminal justice system workloads can be identified.

In order to achieve these aims the project examined the prosecution services from two perspectives:

1. From a criminological point of view the prosecution service is regarded as a part of the criminal justice system as a whole. A system under pressure to deal with ever rising numbers of cases in which the prosecution level is increasingly becoming the decisive (de-)criminalisation stage. An organisational-sociological point of view is integral to this; investigating how the prosecution services manage to deal with the rising number of cases and proceedings in terms of reducing their workload by means of simplified methods and proceedings.
2. A critical analysis of the shift of competences to the prosecutorial level made from a legal viewpoint. Raising questions concern the principles of legality and opportunity, procedural guarantees and the protection provided for the accused person's human rights.

The research was carried out by a network of experts from different European countries and lead by the Department of Criminology of the University of Göttingen's Law Faculty. Researchers there worked with partner institutions in England and Wales, France, the Netherlands, Poland and Sweden in order to develop the common questions and data collection concepts and to gather the country-specific information required to allow a comparison. The study draws on experience gained in producing the European Sourcebook of Crime and Criminal Justice Statistics. In this way it provides for the development of European harmonisation suggestions and future supra-national solutions where these are regarded as necessary. At the same time the study deals with an area in which far too little research has been done and which is increasingly becoming the central, decision-making level of the evolving justice system, with far-reaching consequences for society and the fundamental principles of states bound by the rule of law.

2 Basic Concepts and Assumptions of the Study

2.1 The Function and Structures of Prosecution

In the history of criminal law the institution of a prosecuting authority is a relatively new feature. It first appeared in the wake of the French revolution after which it, step by step, took up its position as a central institution in the legal systems of continental European law. It is only in the past few decades that it has become established as a feature of common law systems. In modern day Europe all prosecuting authorities have a statutory basis and in some countries, e.g. Belgium, Hungary, Poland, Spain, and France, their existence is constitutionally based. They are frequently connected to the executive through the ministry of justice or are seen as part of the judiciary. The majority of countries, however, allow prosecutors to be given both general and specific instructions by the head of the prosecution authority hierarchy in order to direct the country's general criminal policy. At the same time prosecuting authorities have a duty to ensure that proceedings are fair for all parties, the common law countries being the exception.[1]

Naturally the prosecuting authorities' specific structures and functions differ greatly from country to country. In order to facilitate comparison, especially of a statistical nature, the term prosecution is used pragmatically; defined as an intermediary stage between the police and court levels. The process as a whole usually begins with an offence being reported to the police and the identification, sooner or later, of a suspect. Once this has happened, in almost all of the criminal justice systems dealt with here a decision has to be made whether or not the case should be brought before a court, i.e. whether to prosecute or not. Making this decision is the main task of the legal body known as the prosecuting authority, which is to be found either in the form of a public prosecutor and/or an investigating judge.

There are, however, some deviations from the ideal type of a separate prosecution authority.

In some countries this intermediary stage is not (always) easily discernible as the police themselves make prosecution related decisions. From beginning (pre-

[1] For information on prosecuting authorities within Europe see: The report of the Committee of Experts on the role of the Public Prosecution in the Criminal Justice System commissioned by the European Committee on Crime Problems. Strasbourg PC-PR (97) 1 Rev. 3.

charge) to end (case brought before a court) responsibility for a case rests with the police, e.g. in Norway in particular minor cases and in England and Wales prior to the introduction of the Crown Prosecution Service. Furthermore the police may also have the ability to end a case by imposing some kind of sanction, e.g. cautioning in England and Wales.

In some countries the prosecuting function is not carried out by one prosecuting authority alone, but is divided between e.g. a public prosecutor's office and, for certain cases, investigating judges (juge d'instruction). The responsibility for the decision to prosecute or not lies either with the public prosecutor or the juge d'instruction.

Independent of this, even in cases where a prosecution authority in the classic form of a public prosecutor is in charge of a case, the courts have a role to play in cases where the prosecuting authority uses certain investigative measures, namely in protecting the suspect's civil rights. With regards to the central topic of this study, namely decisions about the progression or the disposal of cases, this overlapping of competence is of minor importance.

2.2 High Workload as a Challenge Facing Criminal Justice Systems

If one looks at the numbers of offences and suspects recorded one can observe that for decades an enormous rise in crime has taken place in Western Europe, even if in some countries the crime rates have stabilized or are slightly declining in the last years. Increasing crime figures can also be seen in Central and Eastern European countries for the last 15 years. In particular the so-called mass-crimes, i.e. traffic offences and thefts, have risen strongly. How does the criminal justice system react to this growth? It is obvious that the prosecution services and criminal courts cannot deal with the increased load unless the number of staff or the working mechanisms are changed. In principle there are three possible ways of dealing with the increased number of criminal proceedings:

1. In accordance with the principle of legality all cases are, as before, prosecuted by the prosecution service and brought to charge in front of a criminal court and the judge deals with all cases in an oral hearing. In this case, however, the prosecution service and court personnel will have to be considerably increased. Understandably this option, which is connected with considerable additional costs, is not the one chosen. Realistically there are only two alternatives.
2. A decriminalisation of material law. In this case the threat of a criminal sanction is removed for less serious breaches of the law. Either minor offences, especially traffic offences, are defined as "administrative" offences and a reaction ensues by administrative proceedings and fines; this was the partial solution used, for example, in Germany and the Netherlands. Alternatively or in addition minor offences in the "classic" field are decriminalised. For example a 100 Euro minimum could be introduced for thefts; only above this boundary will the theft be defined as behaviour, which has to be crimi-

nally sanctioned. Below this boundary non-criminal sanctions are made available. This option was in part chosen by the Central and Eastern European countries. In Western Europe, on the other hand, predominantly the third option was chosen:

3. Discretion used by the police or prosecution service and simplified criminal procedure rules. Today criminal proceedings can be dropped, e.g. if the accused's guilt is of a minor nature and there is no public interest in a prosecution, without an oral hearing before a criminal court. The flood of criminal proceedings is mastered by procedural short cuts and simplifications. In this case the prosecution service often plays the central role and becomes the "judge before the judge".

Thus it is clear that prosecution services are gaining increasing importance within Europe and playing a vital role in the criminal justice systems as they are given more responsibility to decide how to deal with suspected criminals.

2.3 PPS as Part of Criminal Justice as a Coherent System

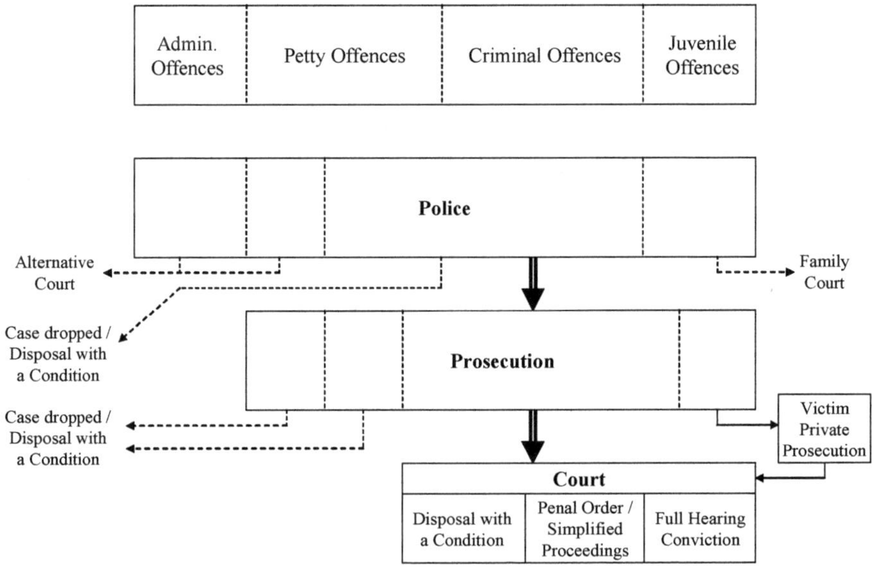

Fig. 1. Stages of Diversion and Discretion within the Criminal Justice System – Fictional Model –

In order to understand the different national criminal justice systems (cjs) and to establish a basis for comparison it is necessary not only to consider the prosecution service level, but to regard the criminal justice system as a unit and to evaluate the role and competence of the prosecution service within the system as a whole. The options available to reduce the number of cases dealt with by a court can be seen in Fig. 1.

This diagram is a fictional model made up of the various decriminalisation and de-penalisation options and the possibilities of discretion at police and prosecution service level as we find them in various countries. Naturally the detail of national legal systems cannot be depicted. But at least the rough, ideal-type structures can be compared. The number of cases to be dealt with by the prosecution service is decisive. If a large proportion of cases is decriminalised, subject to a final decision by the police or dealt with outside of the criminal justice system, the prosecution service can concentrate on more serious offences and thus requires less discretionary powers. If – on the other hand – the police hand all offences on to the prosecution service, the criminal justice system will have to create "vents" at the prosecution level and allow considerable discretion.

3 Previous Studies

So far there have been only a few attempts to view the prosecutorial level comparatively in Europe. A legal comparison of western European countries was carried out in the early 1970's (Jescheck 1979) which dealt with the different legal structures for prosecution. It did not include any details of practice and is, naturally, no longer up to date.

A similar attempt can be seen in the recent study by Tak (2005) in which the legal structures of different European countries are described according to a standardised pattern. Detailed information on working rules, cases dealt with by the PPS and disposals as well as statistical data are not included. The same is true of further studies by *inter alia* Ambos (2000) and Vander Beken (2000).

In 1998 the Council of Europe collated the results of a questionnaire on prosecution services which posed a number of questions about the positions, structures and working practices of prosecution services. Unfortunately answers were not received from many countries and the detail provided also varied considerably. Furthermore the relationship between legal and practical aspects was also not taken into consideration.

3.1 Data from the European Sourcebook of Crime and Criminal Justice

An empirically oriented attempt has been made by the project "European Sourcebook of Crime and Criminal Justice Statistics". At its 45th plenary session in June 1996 the European Committee on Crime Problems commissioned the group of specialists[2] which had previously produced the "European Sourcebook of Crime and Criminal Justice Statistics: Draft Model" to prepare a collection of criminal justice data for the whole of Europe, presenting data for the years 1990–1996. Data were collected by use of a network of national correspondents who provided data from national statistical sources. Thus one person, required to be an expert in crime and criminal justice statistics, was responsible for the collection and initial checking of the data. This structure was reinforced by certain members acting as regional co-ordinators overseeing collection and double checking the data. The questionnaires used to collect the figures, which were completed by 36 countries, not only requested statistical data but also required information as to legal and statistical definitions to be provided. The data were checked and corrected and then put onto a database. The final version was published in 1999. A further edition based upon the same procedure of data collection was published in 2003, the third edition is in print.[3]

Prosecution Data

Despite the challenges of doing so, the European Sourcebook group dedicates the second chapter of the European Sourcebook to comparing the structures of prosecution in Europe. Chapter 2 of the Sourcebook for which the author has a special responsibility attempts to show the differences as well as the common features of the prosecution services of the Council of Europe member states. In order to do so the following five categories of statistics are collected:

1. the total number of cases the prosecuting authority recorded as having been dealt with within a particular year,
2. the number of cases brought before a court,
3. the number of cases dropped,
4. the number of cases dropped conditionally,
5. the number of cases ended by the imposition of a sanction.

Workload and Disposals of PPS

The term workload is used here, deviating from the common definition, to describe the total number of cases disposed of by the prosecution authority per 100 000 of the population. In other words, we attempt to measure the workload of the entire prosecutorial system in a given country in relation to its population. Naturally the workload an institution can deal with depends upon how many employees

---

[2] Members were: G. Barclay and C. Lewis (England and Wales), P. Tournier, later B. Aubusson de Cavarlay (France), J.-M. Jehle (Germany), I. Kertesz (Hungary), H. von Hofer (Sweden), M. Kommer, later P. Smit (the Netherlands), M. Killias (Switzerland, Chairman) as well as W. Rau from the Council of Europe; at a later stage the group was enlarged by M. Aebi (Spain), A. Ahven (Estonia), U. Gatti (Italy), Z. Karabec (Czech Rebublic), V. V. Kembowski (Macedonia), A. Arozola (Spain), C.Spinnellis (Greece).

[3] Authors are: M. Aebi, K. Aromaa, B. Aubusson de Carvalay, G. Barclay, B. Gruszcynska, H. v. Hofer , V. Hysi, J.-M. Jehle, M. Killias, P. Smit, C. Tavares.

it has and what individual workload they have to process. Presumably the following will be true: the more cases a single prosecutor has to deal with, the sooner he will search for ways to lessen the work he puts into each individual case. Therefore he will presumably prefer to utilise the simpler and less time consuming alternatives to going to court, i.e. to drop cases, than the complicated and drawn out process of a trial, i.e. of taking a case to court. This presumption can, however, not be proved or disproved with the available material because exact numbers as to the employees of prosecuting authorities are not available for many European countries.

The number of cases disposed of on the prosecutorial level depends on two main factors: firstly on the amount of crimes known to the police and secondly on the question as to whether the police are obliged to hand all cases over to the public prosecutor or are able to dispose of some cases independently. As a consequence of the different input levels in the individual countries the workload varies considerably.

The workload of the prosecuting authorities measured by the output of prosecuting authorities shows massive differences across Europe. In some East European countries the figures of prosecutorial disposals are low and this is matched by a growing number of pending cases. The caseload development (from 1995 to 2000) also differs greatly: In many (western) countries the rates of all cases disposed of by the prosecuting authorities appear to be stable on a high level (i.e. increase or decrease in case numbers of less than 10%), in other countries there is a remarkable increase of between 10% and 50% (Armenia, Latvia, Lithuania, Moldova, Norway, Poland, Romania, Slovenia) and in some Central and Eastern European countries there is a high increase of more than 50% (Estonia, Slovakia).

Regarding the reaction of the prosecutorial system it is decisive whether the case is brought before a court, i.e. if the disposal could lead to a formal conviction by the court or if the disposal means a formal conviction does not ensue. The rate of cases brought before a court is an important indicator. The underlying assumption is: The higher the prosecution service's workload, the more cases will be disposed of without court involvement, in other words, the less cases will be brought to court. The table indicates that a relationship of this kind exists:

Table 1. Percentage of cases brought before a court by rate of all cases disposed of

		Cases brought before a court		
		low: below 33 % of total cases disposed of	middle: from 33 % to under 66 % of total cases disposed of	high: 66 % and above of total cases disposed of
Cases disposed of per 100,000 population in 1999	low 33 %: below 1200	Slovenia	Albania[a] Croatia Slovakia	Armenia Czech Republic[a] Hungary[a] Latvia Lithuania
	middle 33 %: from 1200 to under 2800	France Moldova Romania[a] Poland	Netherlands	Finland (1998) England & Wales
	high 33 %: 2800 and above	Estonia[a] Germany Portugal[a] Switzerland	Austria Scotland	

Source: The European Sourcebook of Crime and Criminal Justice Statistics 2003, p. 91

[a] Cases disposed of include proceedings against unknown offenders.

The table shows the rate of all cases disposed of and the percentage of cases brought before court in 1999. Several countries were excluded, as they could not provide this information. It illustrates the relationship between the two factors (the trend runs from the top right to the bottom left). More specifically, where a prosecution authority has to deal with a relatively low number of cases, the percentage of cases brought before a court will be high (e.g. in Hungary), while, where the total of cases disposed of is high, the percentage of cases brought before a court tends to be low (e.g. in Germany).

4 Design of the Study

The study was based on two methodological means: an international comparison of the prosecution service functions on the one hand, also considering the factual (supported by statistical data) functional equivalents contained in the respective system. Building upon the relatively rough European Sourcebook chapter, our aim was to develop a finer data collection instrument which allows the identification of similarities as well as of the respective national peculiarities. On the other hand an analysis of the (changing) legal framework was necessary including its effect upon the principles of legality and opportunity as well as the rule of law guarantees relating to the prosecutors decision-making.

These national research and international comparison tasks required a network of experts with representatives from each country to be formed and the creation of a working structure which provided for continuous electronic contact and an exchange of thoughts partly in bi-lateral meetings, partly in conferences involving all parties.

The following were necessary in order to provide for a comparative basis:

1. a common catalogue of questions to be studied
2. suitable common criteria, categories and instruments to collect statistical and informational data which on the one hand display national peculiarities whilst providing a basis for comparative conclusions.

The agreement upon common categories and criteria is decisive for a fruitful comparison, at the same time, however, a very complex and difficult task. If one chooses English as the working language, as we did, difficulties arise on two levels: when describing national systems the English legal language can often not offer a technical term for an exact translation because certain legal concepts known in most of the continental European countries do not exist in the English legal system. On the international comparison level for the legal systems studied a specific institution is named by the same English term, but has a (slightly) different meaning in the national context. Therefore we had to search thoroughly for adequate categories, in order to find precise definitions and to develop descriptions of the meaning of the terms used. Nevertheless, in many cases, remarks and footnotes explaining the deviations are necessary.

The categories and criteria developed together with the partners were incorporated in a questionnaire which was designed to comprehensively capture the legal and factual conditions.[4]

The data collected related mainly to the following complexes:

- legal regulation of procedures, competences and – focally – decisions at the prosecutorial level
- organisational prosecution structures including the police and court levels
- statistical information concerning the personnel and material capacities, the procedures, procedural mechanisms and, in particular, the case-ending decisions at the prosecution level
- as well as the important question as to how the cjs input is determined or rather which offences or offenders are dealt with outside of it as a consequence of decriminalisation.

The evaluation of the data and information collected in this way results in an international, comparative synthesis which deals particularly with the following questions in relation to the convergent trends:

1. In how far are the common law systems adapting to become more like the continental systems?

[4] The content of the questionnaire can be seen in the appendix and completed questionnaires are available online under *www.kriminologie.uni-goettingen.de/pps.*

2. In how far are the continental European countries breaking away from the principle of legality and developing the principle of opportunity?
3. Are the Eastern European countries adapting towards western practices?

This synthesis provides a basis for dealing with ideas for European harmonisation and supra-national regulation, in particular decision-making competence of the prosecution service.

5 The National Criminal Justice Systems Studied

The German project management and team worked with a network of partners in England & Wales, France, the Netherlands, Poland and Sweden in order to gather the information needed and to collate these in a suitable comparative synthesis. The partners are experts for the criminal justice system in the respective country; they are researchers with international experience, e.g. through their membership of the European Sourcebook group and other international committees. They represent countries which provide a fairly representative picture of the prosecution services in Europe. In this way large, small, eastern and western as well as the different prosecution service types are represented:

England (also covering Wales) provides an insight into a common law system which has only recently introduced a prosecution service and which is fairly stringently bound to the principle of legality, i.e. is required to bring a large number of cases to court. On the other hand the police have discretion to deal with cases themselves, that means a lower input on prosecutorial level than other countries.

France not only provides an opportunity to study the oldest prosecution service in Europe, but is exemplary for Romanic legal cultures, with their special feature of having not only a prosecuting service, but also including a Jugé d'Instruction (examining Judge).

The Netherlands provide an excellent example of a smaller western European country which is the most advanced in terms of dealing with cases informally, that is without a court hearing. The prosecution service there can be regarded as the "judge before the judge", due to its role in ending cases.

Sweden is included as representative of the Scandinavian legal culture which differs from the rest of Europe in several ways in particular in relation to the police role.

Poland provides an example of the eastern European legal culture, with a tradition of binding its prosecution services strictly to the principle of legality and a far-reaching decriminalisation of less serious offences.

Finally Germany has a legal culture known for a traditional binding to the principle of legality and of mandatory prosecution which has, however, allowed increasing breaches of these during the past decades so that the legislative ideal type is now the exception in reality.

The following sections present the rough structures of the different national cjs in simplified form. Exact descriptions can be found in the country reports in part 2 of this volume.

5.1 Simplified Model of the Criminal Justice System in England and Wales

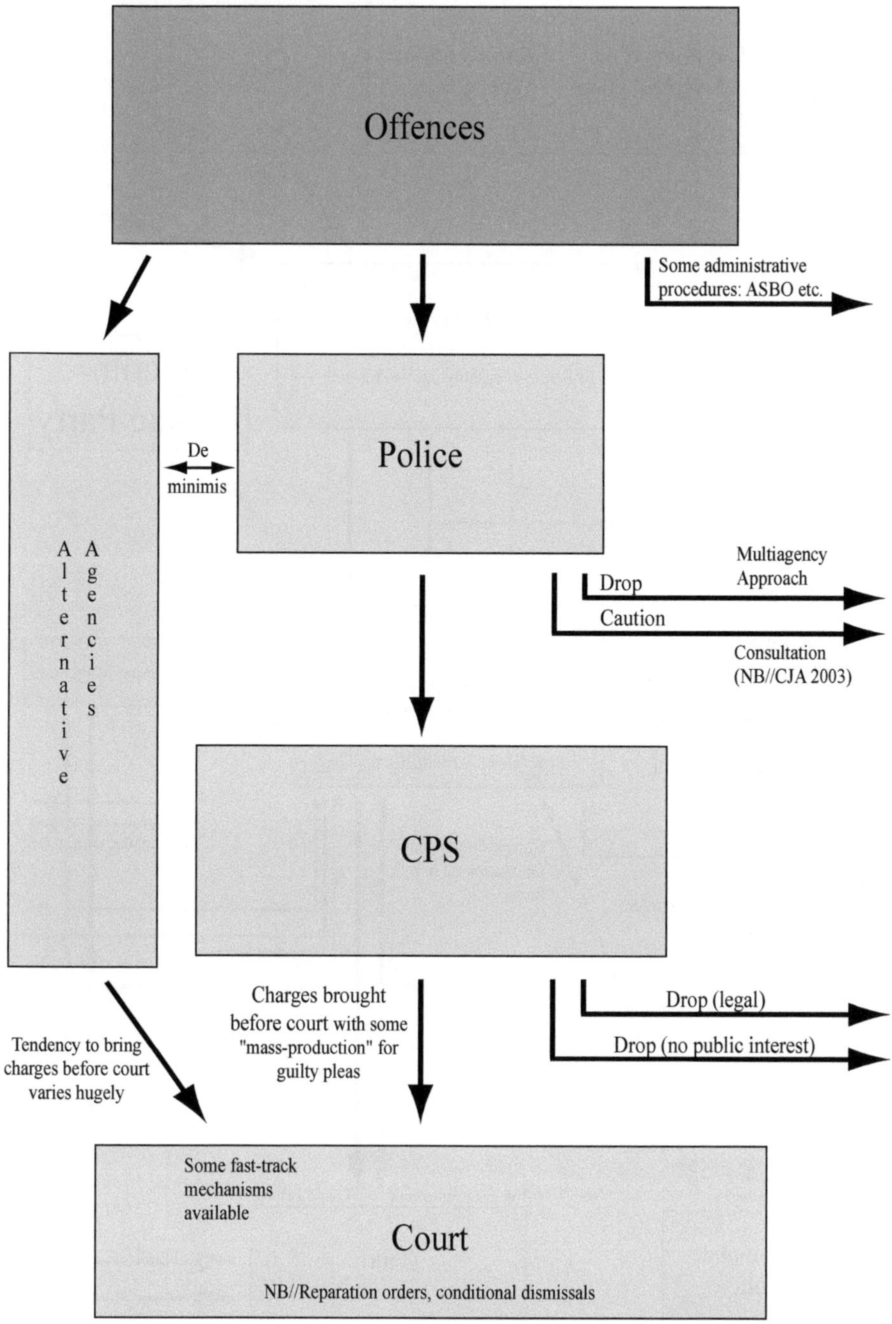

5.2 Simplified Model of the Criminal Justice System in France

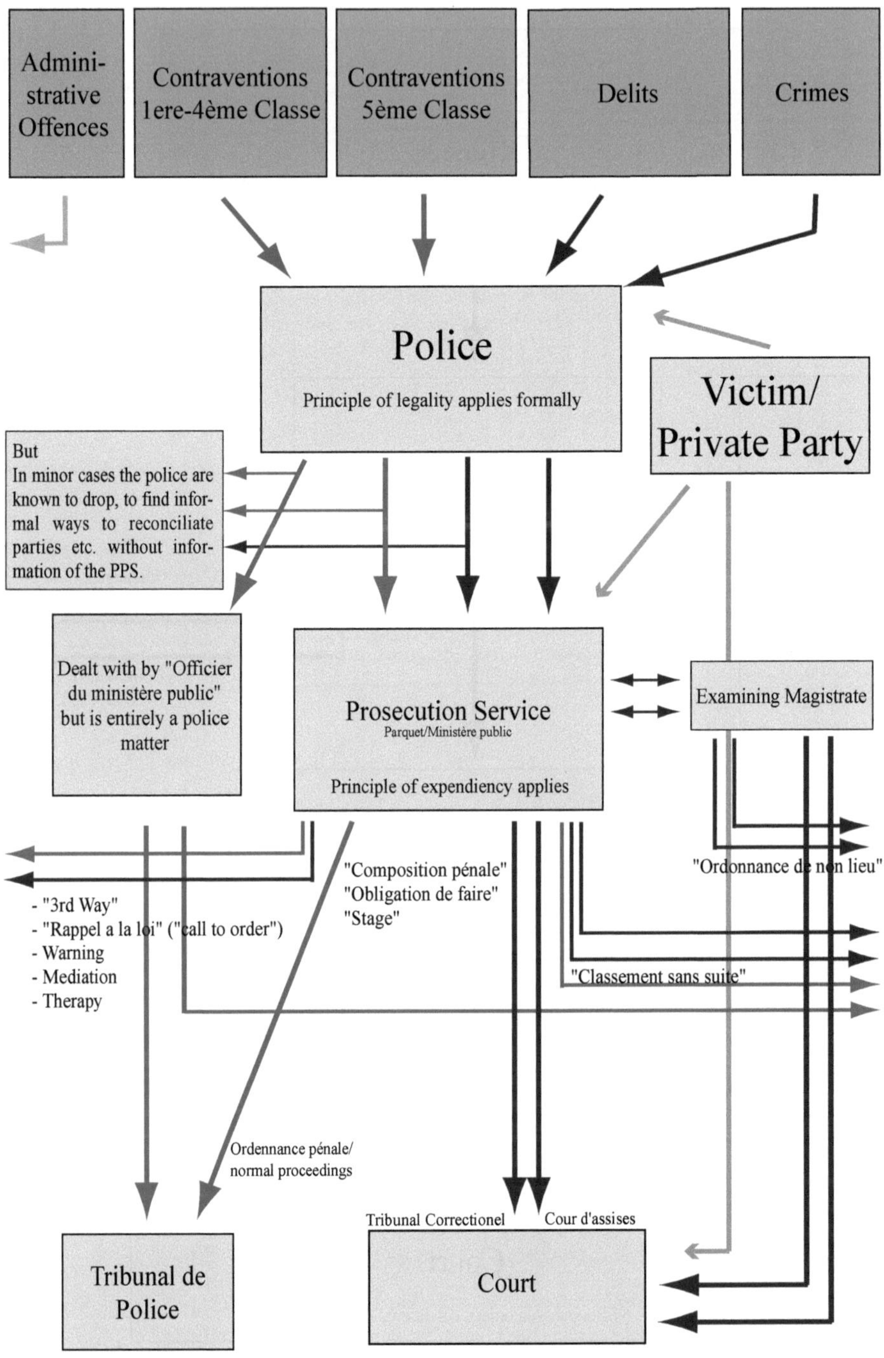

5.3 Simplified Model of the Criminal Justice System in the Netherlands

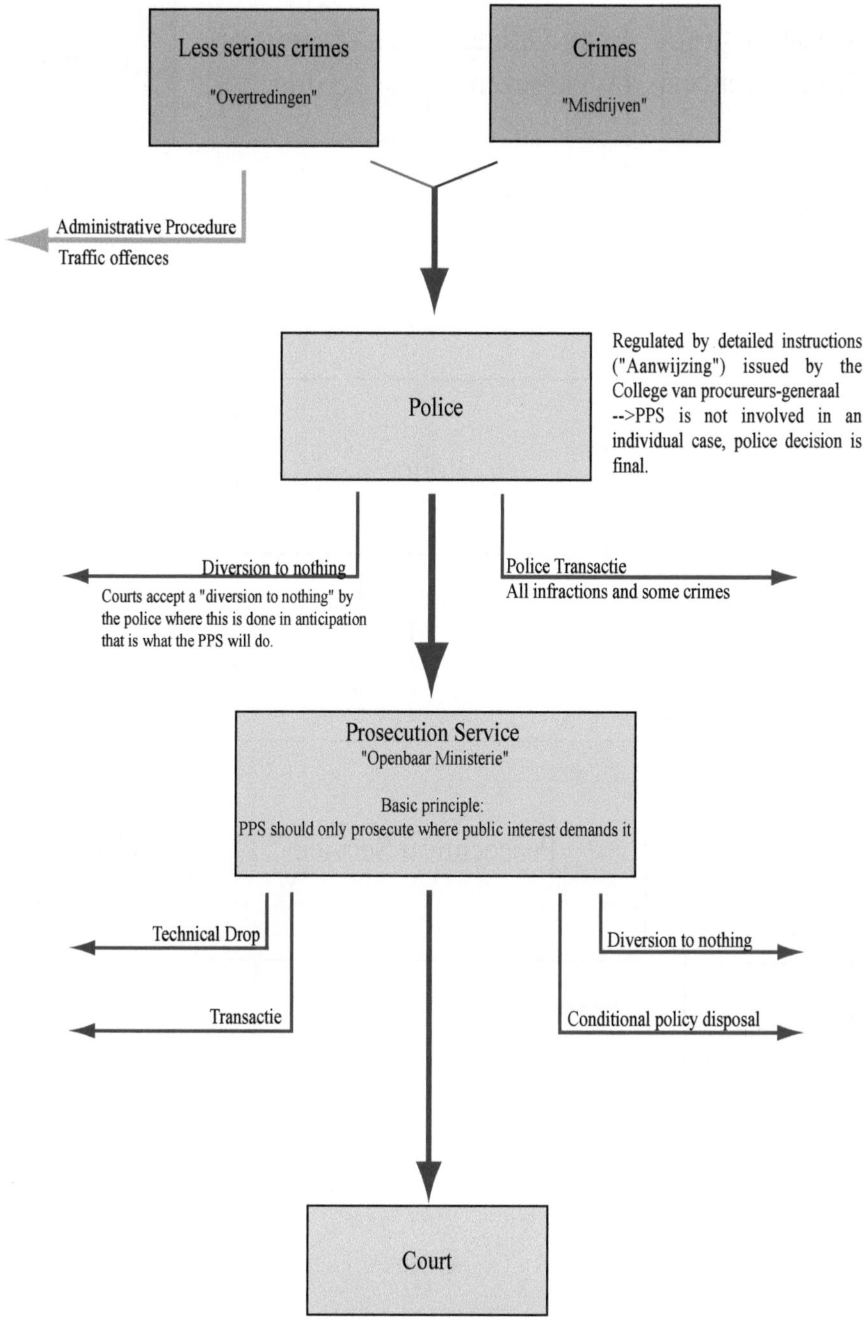

5.4 Simplified Model of the Criminal Justice System in Poland

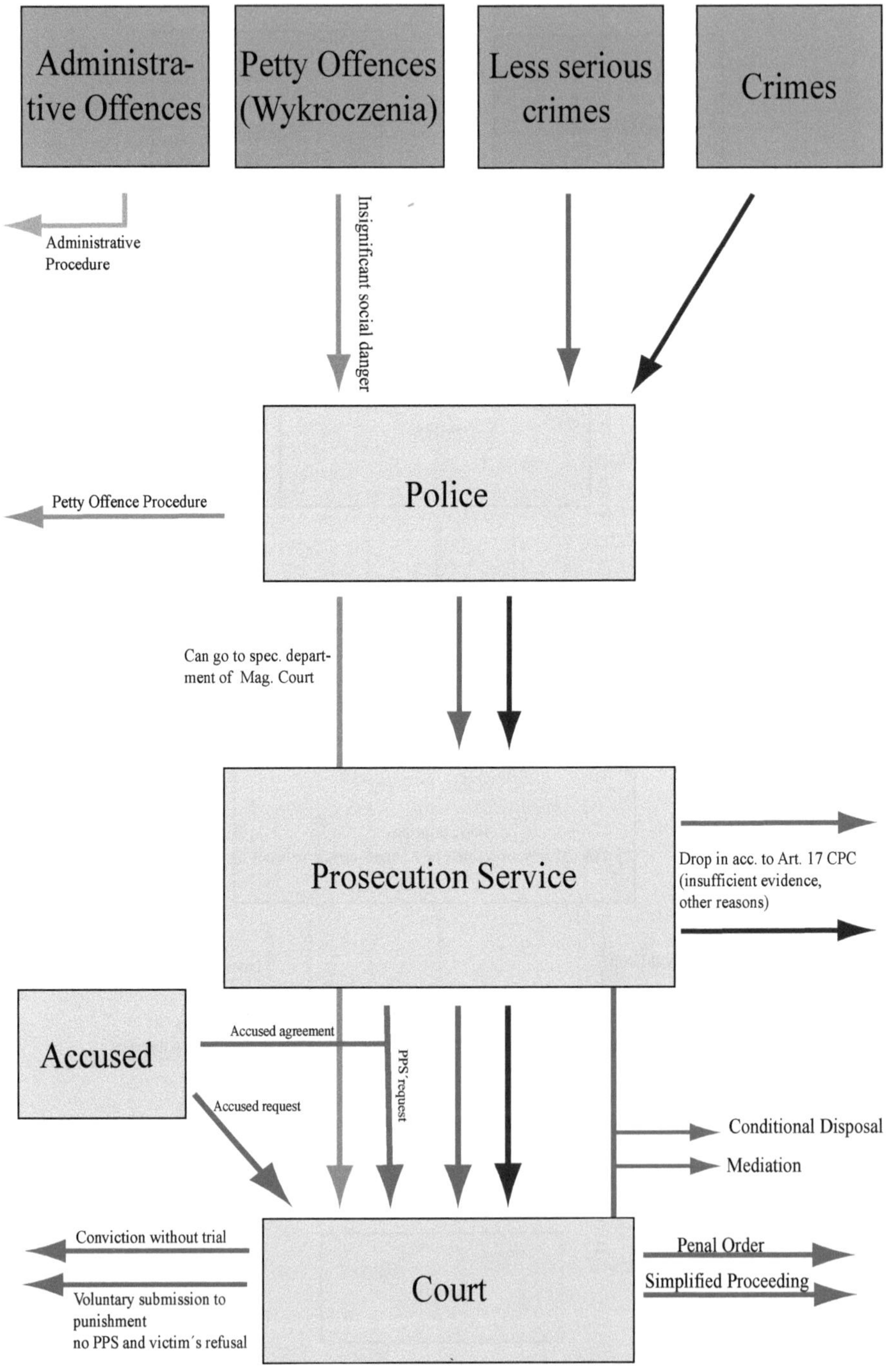

5.5 Simplified Model of the Criminal Justice System in Sweden

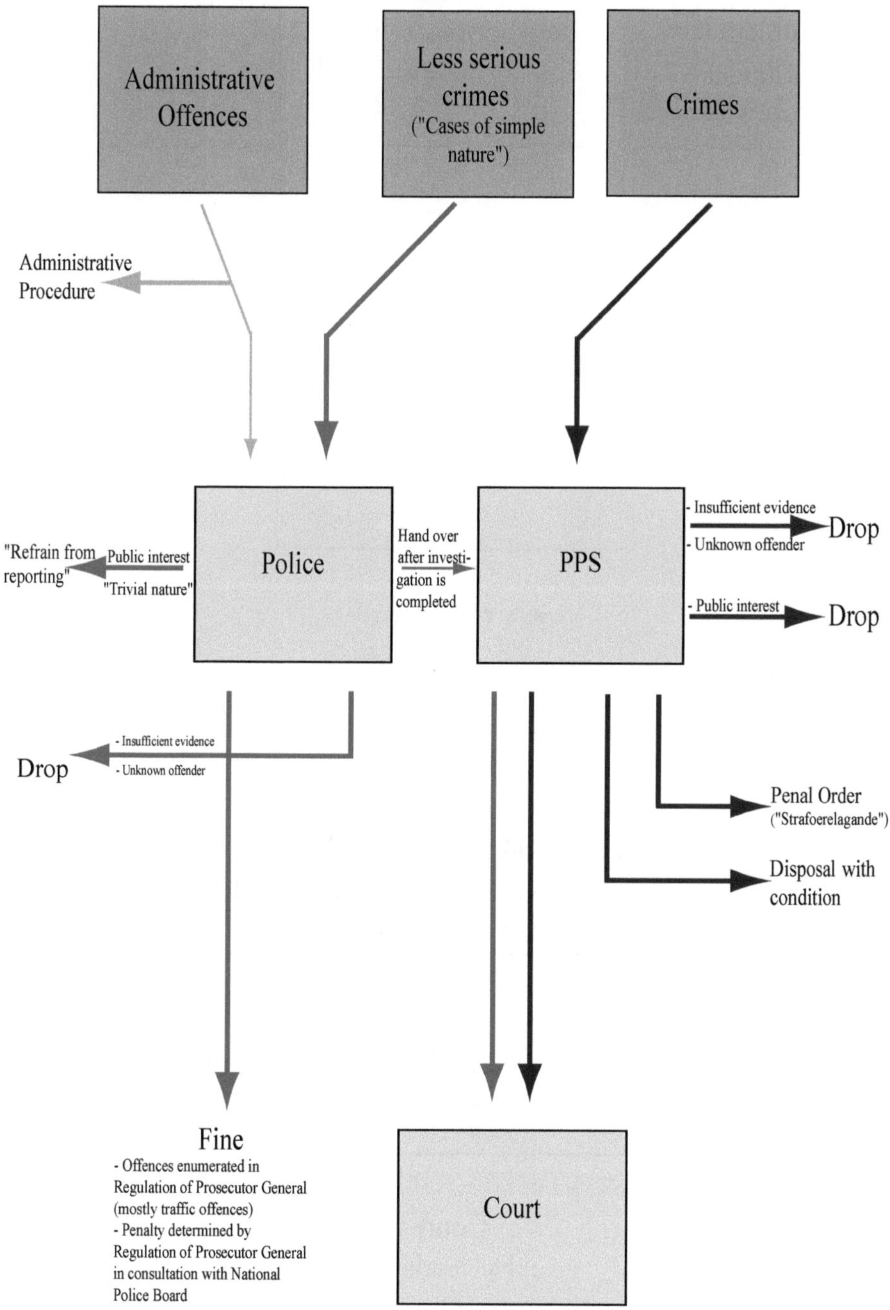

5.6 Simplified Model of the Criminal Justice System in Germany

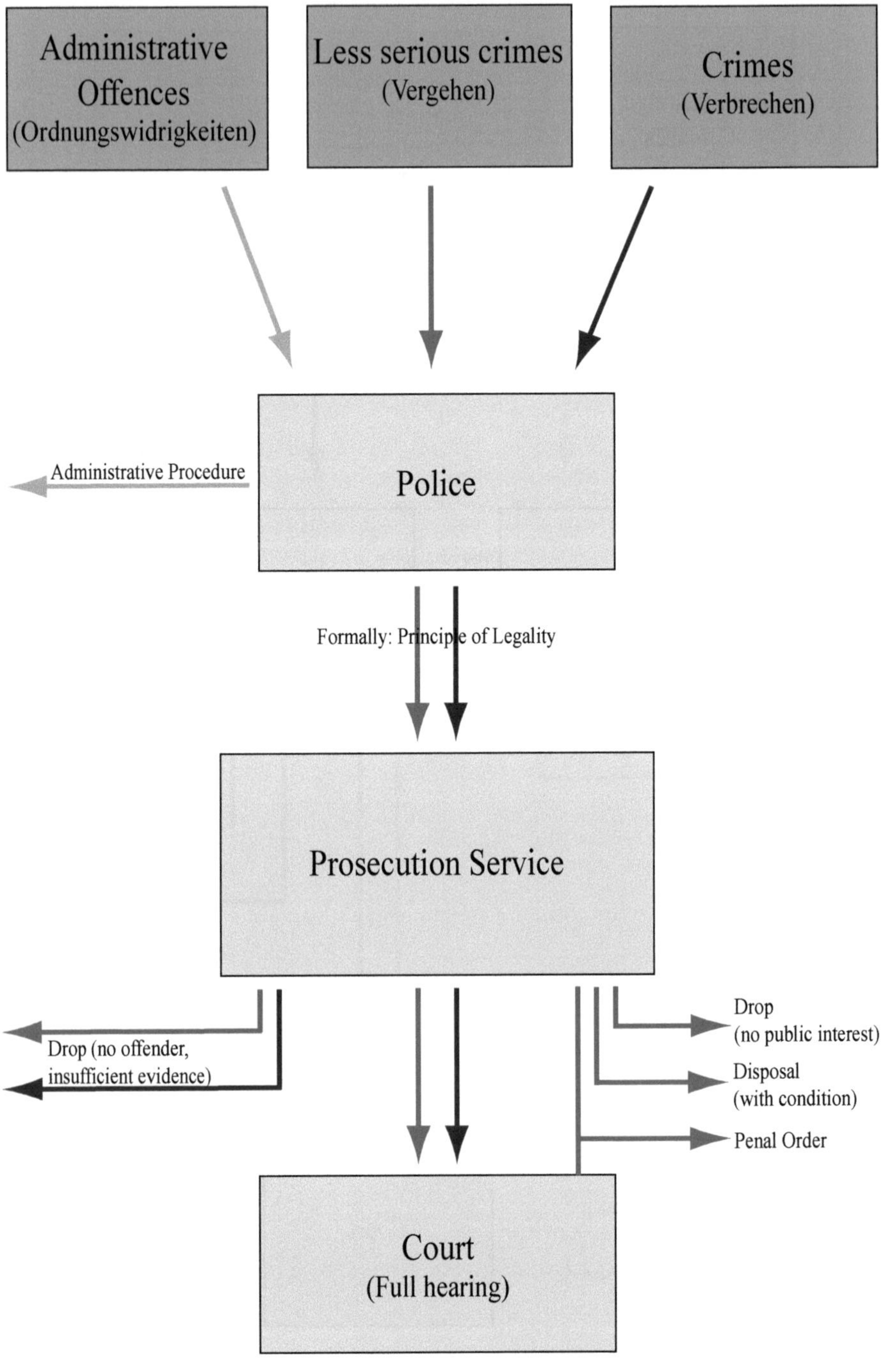

6 Outcome of the Comparative Study – Patterns of Selection and Discretion

The national questionnaires and reports as well as the multidimensional comparisons offer a huge variety of interesting results (see Wade in this volume). Here only the main trends and dominating patterns can be described following the stages of diversion and discretion within the cjs.

6.1 Decriminalisation

Where courts are overloaded and no additional resources available, the obvious solution is to reduce the number of cases getting to the courts. But, discretion at prosecution level is not the only option available. As mentioned previously, this can also be achieved by decriminalisation (see diagram 1 – first stage –).

Certain forms of behaviour are decriminalised; they are either no longer considered as requiring a reaction by the criminal justice system at all or are defined as a special sort of offence, requiring a reaction from another system, such as an administrative authority. This often happens in relation to minor traffic offences. For example, we have the Ordnungswidrigkeiten (administrative offences) regulation in Germany. Similar regulations exist in many European countries.

The same effect can, of course, also be achieved if the offences, small thefts for example, remain technically criminal, but are subject to different procedural paths and different forms of sanctions. One can count the procedures in former socialist countries to this category, which gave the so called social courts jurisdiction over certain forms of petty offences. Today the situation requires differentiation: in part there is still the possibility to divert these kinds of cases from the criminal justice system into the jurisdiction of a special court or committee (as e.g. Poland) and in part this system was abolished.

Another form of diversion can be seen in France. The so-called contraventions of the 1st–4th class include traffic offences and very minor cases of assault and are dealt with in summary proceedings by the police and the police court. In these cases categories of sanctionable behaviour are diverted from the criminal justice system and its institutions as a whole or in part.

In addition, some countries treat offences committed by juveniles outside of the criminal justice system. With the exception of serious crimes, the police do not hand cases over to the prosecution service, but to special (non-criminal) courts. This applies to Central and Eastern European Countries in particular. In Poland the family court takes charge of the investigation and decides upon the appropriate reaction.

All of these modes of decriminalisation and diversion involve the police, but not as part of the criminal justice system. Therefore they are not usually controlled by the prosecution service in this respect.

6.2 Police level

The Police – Prosecution Service Relationship

Although the prosecution service is often regarded as the head of the investigative stage, meaning that prosecutors should be controlling the steps taken by police officers in investigating offences, the reality in European criminal justice systems is that prosecutors are involved only very superficially, if at all, in all but the most serious or politically sensitive cases. This reflects the pressure on resources and police expertise in the investigatory field.

However, particularly if it is necessary that priorities be set as to which offences are investigated, it appears problematic for the police to make such decisions independently. An efficient criminal justice system requires the police to deliver adequate evidence to the prosecution service, but also to do so in line with the rule of law. Thus the reduced prosecution service involvement in the investigatory stage is, for example in the Netherlands, complemented with clear guidelines and priority setting for police actions as well as close co-operation between the police and the prosecution service at a more local level to establish general working rules the police will consistently apply.

Police Discretion

If the offence is defined as criminal, usually the police are strictly bound by the *principle of legality* and be required to pass all cases known to them on to the prosecution level. This is the case in almost all Central and Eastern European countries and most Western European Countries. But the police may be allowed to end cases in line with the principle of legality, i.e. to drop a case regarded as evidentially insufficient etc., but not on any other grounds.

The police may additionally be allowed to end cases in line with the principle of opportunity, i.e. to make a *discretionary decision* as to whether to pass a case on or not. In England and Wales, the police can stop proceedings and attach a legal consequence to their decision not to pass on – this is called a caution which is regarded by some as equivalent to a conviction (a local record is made). This anomaly can be explained by the common law system which traditionally differed greatly from continental law in this respect. Until recently, it was the police who brought cases to court because there was no prosecution service. Only in the mid 1980's was the Crown Prosecution Service introduced. A strong police position in making decisions as to what should happen to cases, now in co-operation with the Prosecution Service, remains evident.

In the Netherlands the so called transactie system has been established. It applies to the prosecution level, but allows the police to end cases, in accordance with general guidelines of the prosecutor-generals, by imposing a condition, this being a "voluntary" fine of up to 350 Euro. Despite the prosecution service having control in a general manner, this could be seen as a sort of discretion at police level; and the police's binding to the principle of legality is loosened, at least as far as minor offences are concerned. Whether this is the right way to deal with the mass crimes is the subject of controversial discussion.

The Police as (Part of) the Prosecution Service

The police may themselves carry out the function of a prosecuting authority for minor offences; they decide on which of these cases to investigate and which to bring before a court. In this case the police will be controlled by the Ministry of Justice. Two decades ago this was the case in the UK. Nowadays procedures of this kind exist very rarely, e.g. in Norway.

6.3 Discretionary Powers on Prosecution Service Level

The prosecution service's workload depends on the input from the police level. How a prosecution service can deal with the cases falling into its mandate is a subject of great variation within Europe. Three basic structures are possible:

Strict Principle of Legality

There are countries (e.g. Poland) in which the prosecuting authority has neither the discretion to drop a case nor the ability to impose conditions / sanctions upon an offender; in accordance with a strict principle of legality the prosecuting authority merely has the function of preparing a case for court. Here the input is identical to the output; all cases have to be brought before a court (except evidentially insufficient cases etc. which can, of course, be dropped in accordance with the principle of legality).

Decision to Drop

In some European countries the prosecuting authority doesn't only drop cases in accordance with the principle of legality, but additionally has discretion whether or not to prosecute (i.e. to drop a case completely if there is no public interest in prosecution). This decision cannot be combined with any form of condition or sanction. The court alone has an ability to punish or impose a condition or legal consequence. On the prosecutorial level it is only possible to end cases in one of two ways: a case can be dropped – meaning nothing more happens and no consequences ensue for the suspect – or it has to be brought before a court.

Conditional Disposal

In some countries the prosecuting authority has not only a discretion whether to prosecute or not, but also the ability to conditionally drop the case, i.e. to bind or sanction the suspected offender, e.g. to pay a sort of fine as in Germany and the Netherlands. This is only possible if s/he agrees to the measure (otherwise the case will go to court). As the condition is "voluntarily" fulfilled, this sort of "sanction" is not seen as a conviction.

There is of course great variation in the degree of independence granted to a prosecuting authority in exercising such discretion. Sometimes the prosecution service is allowed to make a decision of this kind independently, i.e. on its own authority. In other cases a final check or formal consent by the courts may be required. Whether this kind of control by the court is in fact exercised effectively will depend on everyday practice. Particularly where courts are overloaded, one can easily imagine judges making decisions under time pressure and thus tending to rely strongly on prosecution service suggestions.

There are of course boundaries to this discretion. Thus in Germany a conditional disposal is only possible in proceedings in which the minimum punishment is less than a year of imprisonment. The transactie in the Netherlands can only be used for offences punishable with up to 6 years imprisonment. This of course means that in Germany and most certainly in the Netherlands most mass crimes are subject to prosecutorial discretion. The considerable flexibility is reduced legislatively by unspecific legal concepts such as the defendant's guilt being of a minor nature or a lack of public interest in the prosecution. In practice, however, guidelines issued either by the Ministry of Justice or Prosecutor-General are of great importance in limiting discretion and defining which cases may be disposed of regularly. Thus if one wishes to compare two countries one must look not only at legislation, but additionally analyse the guidelines issued.

To sum up, discretionary power on prosecution service level provides an alternative: on the one hand there are formal charges, on the other proceedings can end on the prosecution level, with or without a condition.

Other Forms of Diversion

In some countries further options are available: For example, there is what is called private prosecution in Germany. If the prosecution service decides there is no public interest in a prosecution, certain types of cases can be ended leaving the victim the choice whether to pursue the prosecution personally. This demonstrates that alongside the state and the accused there is also a "third" party which should be considered. How the victim's interests can be taken into consideration varies greatly from one criminal justice system to another. It is a point which cannot be addressed here.

6.4 Prosecution Service Influence on Court Level

If our only concern were prosecution services' discretionary powers, we could stop here. However, if we observe the interdependencies within criminal justice systems, we must also consider the court level. This is because there are procedural forms which formally lead to a sanction prescribed by a court, but which are pre-formed strongly by the prosecution service. In many ways they can be regarded as a functional equivalent of a conditional prosecution disposal.

The German Strafbefehl and French ordonnance/composition penale are good examples. Here the prosecution service does all the preparatory work and requests a certain sanction (usually a fine). The prosecution service files for court approval in summary, i.e. written, proceedings. The court can only entirely reject the application and this happens very rarely. Functionally this can be understood as a prosecution service decision which is checked and approved by the court. But unlike a conditional disposal it is formally a conviction.

In other countries there may be similar proceedings which end in a formal court sentence, but are in fact determined by the prosecution service. Simplifications such as not having an oral hearing of the accused and other witnesses will mean that the information provided by the prosecution service is decisive.[5]

In how far a prosecution service influence plays a role in conditional disposals/dismissals made by a court is another factor worth considering. In many cases this formal court decision may simply be "rubber stamping" a prosecution proposal. Many systems require prosecution agreement to such disposals as a minimum so that one can often reckon with certain prosecution service influence on how a significant proportion of cases are ended in court.

Furthermore, recent reforms have seen prosecutors being given a true adjudicatory function in order to increase criminal justice system efficiency. This can be observed in three forms: firstly in their established powers to drop less serious charges against an offender accused of multiple-offences because they are regarded as relatively insignificant, secondly in variations of the guilty plea proceedings tradition stemming from common law jurisdictions. Originally an offender pleading guilty profited from a sentence reduction because his or her confession lead to procedural simplifications. Some newer procedural forms emerging see prosecutors agreeing to deals in which the courts are requested to impose a lower sanction than the prosecutor would usually have asked for. The defendant usually makes the application to court (e.g. "voluntary submission to punishment" in Poland). A third form is plea-bargaining proceedings in which negotiations take place between the prosecutor and defence and the charge brought is reduced (e.g. the new French "guilty plea" proceedings). These types of proceedings see a prosecutor negotiating with the defendant in order to achieve a non-contested trial. This agreement has to be accepted by a judge, but this is usually done in shortened proceedings and in the vast majority of cases the prosecutor plays the decisive role. These alternatives are available for more serious offences and offer significant potential to increase the efficiency of criminal justice systems. It will be interesting to see in how far practice is able to exploit this potential in accordance with the rule of law in the next few years.

[5] A similar effect can be achieved without special procedural forms in systems in which a guilty plea changes the content of a trial such as in England and Wales. Again the prosecution service can exert a considerable influence upon the information a court gets about a case in this way.

7 Closing Comments related to the Principles of Legality and Opportunity

The closing comments try to summarise the findings described above. They go, however, a little beyond a pure analysis and consider the prosecution service's function with regard to the principles of legality and opportunity. Hereby they refer to thoughts reflected by the Council of Europe in its recommendation on the simplification of criminal justice.[6]

1. *There is almost no country in Europe which follows the principle of legality without any exception.* Almost nowhere are all criminal offenders prosecuted in order to be convicted by a court. Mostly one finds either diversion from the criminal justice system or discretion at police and/or prosecution service level.
2. *Specific forms of deviation from the principles of legality have to be considered in the framework of national legal culture and of the criminal justice system as a whole.* An isolated comparison of the specific prosecution service discretionary powers in any two countries is misleading because it ignores the varying impact of the powers and any possible functional equivalents.
3. *Where possible, material decriminalisation should be preferred to procedural diversion.* One should avoid drawing minor cases into the criminal justice system if one doesn't want a criminal justice response to them. The path chosen by several countries in using administrative offences and fines should be used increasingly. This would simultaneously be an important step in limiting the range of discretion in line with the principle of opportunity.
4. *The police have to be bound by the principle of legality.* Otherwise there is a higher liability to corruption and influence by politicians and citizens. If diversion at police level is considered necessary for a functioning criminal justice system, then this must at least be restricted to very minor cases and subjected to final control by the prosecution service.
5. *On prosecution level a certain, but limited range of discretionary power is necessary.* A criterion of pettiness should apply where there is no public interest in a prosecution. This cannot be achieved exclusively by decriminalisation, for it is difficult to define a fixed legal boundary for many criminal offences, such as theft or assault, above which criminal liability should ensue and below which a criminal consequence is not necessary. Therefore a certain amount of flexibility in the form of the principle of opportunity is required. However, discretionary decisions by the prosecution service should concern only less serious offences. They should be given a clear profile by general rules, preferably legal provisions, and be subject to examination by the court. Crimes above a medium level of seriousness must be subject to mandatory prosecution.

---

[6] See: The precise considerations of the Council of Europe, The Simplification of Criminal Justice, Recommendation No. R. (87) 18 and explanatory Memorandum.

6. *Disposals by the prosecution service, even if connected to conditions (fines), cannot be equivalent to a conviction.* The imposition of conditions must not be coercive for the suspect; s/he must be free to fulfil the condition voluntarily. In any case these decisions should be subject to judicial examination/agreement.
7. *Legality and opportunity are not alternatives, but two principles which limit or rather complement each other.*

References

Aebi M et al (2005) European Sourcebook of Crime and Criminal Justice Statistics (3rd edn). WODC, The Hague. Also available online under *http://www.europeansourcebook.org/esb/*

Ambos K, Arbour L, Eser A, Sanders A (2000) The Prosecutor of a Permanent International Criminal Court. International workshop in co-operation with the Office of the Prosecutor of the International Criminal Tribunals (ICTY and ICTR). Freiburg im Breisgau, May 1998, Freiburg i. Br., 708 pp.

Council of Europe (1987) The Simplification of Criminal Justice. Recommendation No. R. (87) 18 and explanatory Memorandum. Strasbourg

Council of Europe (1997) Report of the Committee of Experts on the role of the Public Prosecution in the Criminal Justice System commissioned by the European Committee on Crime Problems. Strasbourg PC-PR (97) 1 Rev. 3.

Council of Europe (2000) The Role of Public Prosecution in the Criminal Justice System. Recommendation Rec. (2000) 19 and explanatory Memorandum. Strasbourg

European Journal of Crime, Criminal Law and Criminal Justice (2000) Volume 8 Number 3 (Special Issue: Public Prosecution Service in Europe), Brill Academic Publishers, Dordrecht

Jehle JM (2000) Prosecution in Europe: Varying Structures, Convergent Trends. European Journal of Criminal Policy and Research 8: 27–42

Jehle JM (2004) The Prosecution Service Function in Relation to the Principles of Legality and Opportunity. Available online under *http://www.coe.int/t/e/legal_affairs/legal_co-operation/conferences_and_high-level_meetings/european_public_prosecutors/2004(Celle).asp#TopOfPage*

Jehle JM (2005) Criminal Justice in Germany: Facts and Figures (5th edn) Federal Ministry of Justice (ed). Forum Verlag Godesberg, Mönchengladbach. Available online: *http://www.bmj.de/media/archive/961.pdf*

Jescheck HH (ed) (1979) Funktion und Tätigkeit der Anklagebehörde im ausländischen Recht. Nomos, Baden-Baden

Tak P (2004) Introduction. In: Tak P (ed) Tasks and Powers of the Prosecution Services in the EU Member States. Wolf Legal Publishers, Nijmegen, pp 1–15.

Vander Beken T, Kilchling M (eds) (2000) The Role of the Public Prosecutor in the European Criminal Justice Systems. VWK, Brussels

The Power to Decide – Prosecutorial Control, Diversion and Punishment in European Criminal Justice Systems Today

Marianne Wade

Content

1 Aim and Methodology

The study set out to explore and compare the function of the prosecution services in six European legal jurisdictions. The countries: England & Wales, France, Germany, the Netherlands, Sweden and Poland were chosen as representatives of distinct European legal and/or cultural traditions or social circumstances (the transitional period for Central and Eastern European countries). The basic idea was that the prosecution service has a core function; to decide whether a case should be taken to court or not. Traditionally its task was restricted to a legal judgement of this but as the pressures on criminal justice systems have increased, it has been widened to include discretionary powers involving a certain value judgement as to the worth of or public interest in taking a case to court. This study aimed to find out exactly to what extent this had occurred, what further powers (if any) had been coupled with this discretion and on what basis such decisions are factually taken. Our presumption is that these are fundamentally prosecution service tasks in Europe. However, as there is great variety in the structuring of criminal justice systems across Europe, we were aware that in some countries, for a variety of reasons, this is a function, which may factually be carried out by the police and other agencies. Thus the primary aim of the study required exploration of other instances within the criminal justice systems, at least with regard to such powers.

Based on the impression gained from the European Sourcebook of Crime and Criminal Justice Statistics (see Jehle in this volume), the study premise also went beyond this. There were indications that the prosecution influence and therefore what we refer to as its function, extended beyond even these powers to end cases formally assigned explicitly to it and that it had gained significant influence upon how courts process and evaluate cases through special procedural forms. For this reason the collection of empirical and informational data from the court stage, as well as in relation to certain special topics was regarded as necessary.

In order to truly understand the systems being studied it was regarded as necessary to have national experts with experience in comparative research involved in the project. For this reason a project network involving 11 partners from 6 countries was created. Furthermore agreement upon a few terms used within the project was regarded as necessary to facilitate true comparison: frequently studies use certain vocabulary, often in English and is taken as given that all partners are using them to describe the same thing. We were aware from an early stage that whilst there were common terms used in this context, what one means by them is not necessarily uniform. For this reason, one study step was to develop certain basic common definitions and concepts.

To facilitate this, initial research into each of the systems to be studied was undertaken. On this basis a draft questionnaire was developed containing definitions and concepts to be applied uniformly. These did not necessarily reflect all the aspects of the individual national systems but they reflect core features (see 1.2 and 1.3). This draft questionnaire was then discussed during a first partner meeting. This was altered as required and then sent to the partners for an initial data collection round.

The questionnaire spanned 168 pages as a word document, but was converted into and augmented in a more stable format and sent as an electronic instrument to be filled in by computer. It was, for the most part, a structured questionnaire requiring the partners to tick one of a range of standardised answers provided. There was always room to provide further comments and/or explanations. In addition, statistical information was requested for 1993–2002. Partners were asked to trace any legislative and policy changes during this period. Much of the detailed statistical information requested was, however, not available in any of the jurisdictions studied.

1.1 Questionnaire Structure

The questionnaire was divided into the following 13 sections:

- I. Offence Definition
- II. Investigative Stage
- III. Control by the Prosecution Service in the Investigative Stage
- IV. Police Decisions
- V. Unknown Offenders and Police Output
- VI. Prosecution Stage: Input
- VII. Prosecution Decision-making
- VIII. Court Stage
- IX. Prosecution Service's Legal Role
- X. Control of the Prosecution Service and Individual Public Prosecutor (PP) Decisions
- XI. Juveniles
- XII. Victims
- XIII. Basic Principles

Each section contained a number of questions aimed at discovering legal provisions for or information as to guidelines and other regulations of practice as well as any formal or informal provisions for working practice relevant to exploring the study's subject matter.[1]

After the initial data collection phase was completed, the questionnaires were reviewed by the project management. Where necessary requests for clarification or additional information were made. For the rest of the project period bi-lateral discussions and meetings took place to ensure high quality, comparable data were attained. Simultaneously an initial evaluation of all six country responses was undertaken and comparative tables to reflect the situation in all study countries prepared. These were then discussed at a second partner meeting with all project partners attending. During this discussion, misunderstandings, inaccurate comparisons, problems etc. were identified and solutions explored. The correction process followed to ensure that the comparative conclusions to be drawn were correct, but also that the national information to be published corresponded with these conclusions. Once the data validation process was completed, the partners met to decide which results to present and discuss with practitioners, policy-makers and other academics. The wish was to further validate the study results in doing so.

The second partner meeting was also used to agree the design for a country report to complement the information provided in the questionnaire. It was neces-

[1] The content of the questionnaire can be seen in appendix and completed questionnaires are available online under *www.kriminologie.uni-goettingen.de/pps/*.

sary to agree a common structure to provide an overview of all the systems concerned as well as providing an opportunity to trace individual developments and features which the partners did not feel adequately highlighted in the common, standardised questionnaire. Those are the country reports which make up the second section of this book. The common structure and view developed: of systems through which cases flow and are dealt with at certain stages, is borne out in these. The conclusions drawn in this chapter are based on information provided by the partners in the questionnaires or those chapters.

The core results were presented at a conference held in Göttingen in October 2005, which this volume documents. They were discussed there with further participants including practitioners and policy-makers. It is hoped in this way to reflect the systems studied beyond mere legal comparison reflecting within the bounds of a study evaluating at national level actual working practices.

1.2 Offence Categories

A division of offences according to seriousness took place: Systems are regarded as potentially containing the following offence categories:

Administrative offences: These are offences which are dealt with outside of the criminal justice system. An action is defined as socially undesirable and worthy of a state reaction but not of one enforced by the criminal justice system (CJS). They are dealt with by standardised form, in writing. The payment of an administrative fine is the usual penalty. They may be administered by the police and, in appeal by other CJS agencies, but their nature is non-criminal. The state reaction is not considered a "true" punishment or sanction and the person accused is not given a criminal record.

Minor Offences: These are the least serious offences prosecuted within the criminal justice system. The boundary between them and administrative offences is a matter of great variation among the jurisdictions studied. They may be dealt with using different, simplified procedures compared to more serious offence categories. They are still considered to be crimes and usually – but not always – a person found guilty of them will have this fact registered and so have a criminal record as a consequence.

Less serious offences: an intermediate category of offences inherent in some systems, these are offences which are "real offences" in that a person found guilty of them will have a criminal record and face a "real" sanction. They may be easiest to define procedurally because they can be dealt with differently than the most serious category of offences but this is the consequence of the fact that they are felt to be less serious or alternative solutions are regarded as acceptable in response to them.

Serious offences: the most severe offences dealt with by the criminal justice system.

For the specific explanation of the differentiation between serious and less serious cases see table 1 in the annex.

1.3 Typology of Procedures and Case-ending Decisions

The following typology of procedures and case-ending decisions (by which a procedural step after which proceedings are considered finished by the institutions involved is meant) was agreed upon:

Administrative Reaction: refers to the kinds pf proceedings described above to deal with administrative offences. Non-CJS reactions, usually imposing the obligation to pay a financial penalty, with little evidence presented and no necessity for the accused to be heard, carried out in writing only.

Paper Reaction: A CJS reaction, involving a judge but evidence is presented in a summary form and in writing. The police or PPS send a minimal account of the offence to a court requesting a certain punishment. There is no formal hearing unless a party entitled to do so demands one. They lead to a conviction (meaning a sanction and a criminal record, the French system has one category exceptional to this, as we shall see below) and so are concentrated criminal proceedings, which take place solely on paper in the majority of cases. They are a procedurally less strenuous reaction because they apply lesser standards to the evidence upon which the deciding institution bases its judgement; more to the point the written evidence provided by the preparing institution is valued higher than it would be in full proceedings.

Drop (evidence/factual): A pre-court CJS institution halts criminal proceedings because there is insufficient evidence to support a prosecution or because some legal ground bars it.

Drop (public interest): A pre-court CJS institution halts criminal proceedings and there is no further consequence for the suspect although he or she is presumed to be guilty of the offence (i.e. the case, if taken to court is categorised as being likely to have lead to a conviction) because in weighing all aspects of the case and surrounding circumstances, considerations overweigh which mean the case is not worth prosecuting. Such a case ending may be subject to court approval.

Conditional disposal: a pre-court CJS institution disposes of a case where it does not merely halt the proceedings but attaches some kind of consequence or condition to doing so. Often it requires some activity by the suspected offender. If s/he accepts and fulfils the condition attached, this disposal spends the state's right to prosecute for the offence the person is suspected of. There is a presumption (but not a finding) of guilt, with which the offender is regarded as agreeing. Such a case ending may be subject to court approval.

Penal order: this is the classic CJS paper reaction. The pre-court CJS institution issues an application for a punishing order to be made, it is in writing and the court approves or refuses it. Where it is issued, affected parties have the right to appeal during a certain time period after which, if they do not do so, they are convicted of the offence and subject to the punishment stated. It is a particularly efficient CJS procedure for achieving certain punishments for certain offences.

Accelerated proceedings: This category contains other procedural forms which involve the court in deciding whether a suspect is guilty of an offence or not but they allow certain procedural short cuts either before the case is taken to court or in the way it is presented to court in comparison to a full-trial.

Negotiated settlement: This is a new type of proceedings emerging in the jurisdictions studied which involves an agreement being made between two parties in the criminal process as to how and with what punishment an offence is to be dealt with. There is court involvement but it is cursory. A conviction and sanction ensues. The rights of parties to appeal against the resulting judgement are strongly limited.

Full/Normal Trial: the CJS path which the respective system holds as the path which should represent the norm in dealing with criminal offences. A conviction and sanction results for a suspect found guilty of an offence tried in a public trial with evidence being presented fully. It is the legally "normal" path; the classic proceedings for which the system was conceived.

1.4 Further Terms

Beyond the definitions above, the following terms are key:

- *Principle of legality* – or the principle of mandatory prosecution. It is a principle which requires full criminal proceedings to be brought against every person suspected of an offence where there is sufficient evidence to do so. They should then face a similar penalty to that faced by others who have committed similar offences.
- The *principle of opportunity* – exists where CJS institutions are given discretion to break with the principle of legality
- *Sanction* – a true sanction is a punishment imposed as the result of criminal proceedings in which a person has been found guilty and for which a criminal record ensues.

The following abbreviations are used in the course of this paper

- CJS – criminal justice system
- PP – public prosecutor
- PPS – public prosecution service
- N.a. – not available, meaning the matter referred to is not an option available in that jurisdiction.
- N.d.a. – means no data is available for the category dealt with even though it exists in the jurisdiction under discussion.

2 Potential Paths to "Punishment"

2.1 Reactions Available

In order to explore the PPS role within the criminal justice system, it is necessary, first of all, to understand the criminal justice system's role. Naturally our assumption was that a criminal justice system is created in order to deal with forms of behaviour subject to a criminal sanction. This is also the case in all of our study's jurisdictions. However, just because a form of behaviour is regarded as undesirable, and indeed even where the legislative considers it worthy of a state-imposed penalty, this by no means causes a modern European state to recourse automatically to the criminal law and the CJS in order to deal with it; as is appropriate considering the criminal law's status as an ultimo ratio. It also means, however, that a conscious decision must be made as to what falls within the ambit of the CJS and what does not. This is the first major variable of our study. If a system is considered to be overloaded, one of the easiest solutions at hand is to decrease the parameters of its responsibility, i.e. to decriminalise and to react to certain offences by alternative means. Figure 1 below shows the theoretical options available. These are material decriminalisation and "procedural decriminalisation" – meaning that an offence, which remains criminal formally, is dealt with by non-criminal justice system institutions. A third option is depenalisation; an offence remains criminal and within CJS jurisdiction but is factually never punished. This is an option within the system, which will be dealt with at a later stage.

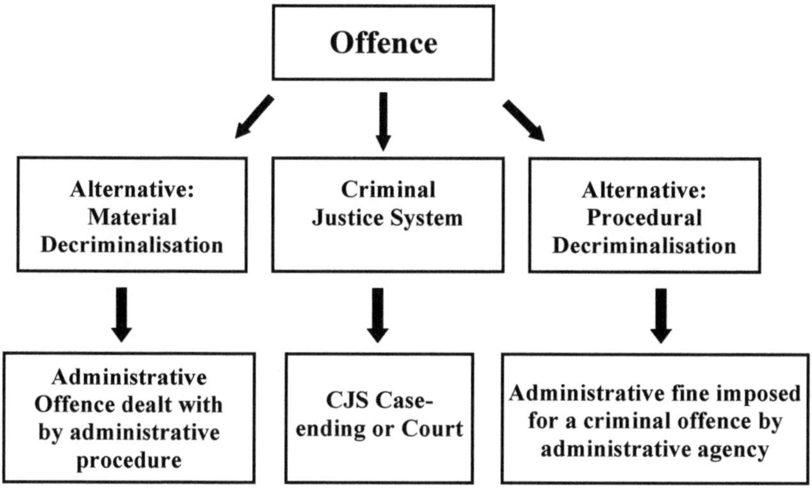

Fig. 1. Alternatives to the Criminal Justice Route

2.2 Proceedings Outside the Criminal Justice System

The systems studied include all of the theoretical options explored. They all feature materially decriminalised offence forms referred to as administrative offences, contraventions, offences against order or petty offences. These are formally de-criminalised and dealt with outside the criminal justice system.[2] All of the systems studied have used and use this option to relieve the pressure on their system, to varying extents. Thus it is important to bear in mind when comparing the systems, in particular statistically, that precisely where the jurisdictional, criminal justice boundary is drawn is subject to variation. As is indeed the clarity with which this boundary is drawn; in some countries it is difficult to determine precisely the status of offences and their treatment. The status of the Polish wykrocenia or petty offences, for example, has long been the subject of academic discussion. The status of offences in England and Wales is not clearly defined. It is more correct to speak of procedural decriminalisation there.

The following tables 1 and 2 display the kinds of procedure available in the study countries and what offences they are used for. Not surprisingly, decriminalising options are frequently used across Europe for minor offence forms of high numerical relevance. Primarily these are traffic offences but tax offences and some special cases, e.g. in France very light forms of bodily injury, in Poland thefts of below € 50 value, are also included.

[2] Although it should be noted that some criminal justice system institutions are often involved in these kind of simplified "sanctioning" proceedings but in a different, non-CJS function.

Table 1. How the Jurisdictions Categorise and Process Less Serious Offences

	EW[a]	FR	DE	NL	PL	SE
Offences categorisation	Minor criminal offences most likely motoring/traffic offences	Minor criminal offences *(contravention 1–4 classe)*	Admin. Offences (*Ordnungswidrigkeiten*), primarily concerning traffic offences	Minor criminal offences (most likely traffic offences) of which the handling is regulated in a special law (*WAHV*)	Minor criminal offences (*wykroczenia*) determined in Petty Offences Procedure Code 2001	Admin. offences (kind of unlawful behaviour)
Procedure	Mixed procedural possibility: simplified court procedure at mag. court or fixed penalty imposed by an alternative admin. agency	Mixed procedural possibility: dealt with either administratively by imposing a fine or by taking the case to court (Tribunal de Police)	Admin. procedure: police are investigative agency, local admin. agency imposes fine	Admin. procedure: police are investigative agency, central admin. agency imposes fine	Mixed procedural possibility: police (or PPS) can impose a fine or bring the case before special court department	Admin. procedure: admin. fine (sanctions fee) imposed by an admin. body. Regulation is unsystematic and represents an ad hoc solution

[a] Abbreviation for England and Wales.

Table 2. Types of Reaction Available (by Law)

	Admin. offence	Minor crime	Less serious crime	Serious crime
Admin. reaction by purely admin. authority	FR, DE, SE, NL	NL[a] (tax invasions/ overtredingen), EW	NL[a] (tax invasions)	NL[a] (tax invasions)
Admin. reaction by police	DE, FR[b], SE, NL	EW[c], FR[b], PL	EW[d]	EW[d]
Admin. reaction by PPS	/	/	/	/
Drop or disposal by police		EW, FR[e], NL[f], SE	EW, NL[g]	EW
Drop or disposal by PPS		EW, DE, NL[h], PL, SE[i]	EW, FR[j], DE , NL, PL, SE[i]	EW, NL
Paper reaction by police to court		EW[k], FR[a], PL	EW[k]	
Paper reaction by police, not to court		FR[a] , SE[l]		
Police prosecution		FR[a], SE[m]		
Paper reaction by PPS to court		DE	DE, FR[l], PL	
Paper reaction by PPS not to court		Se[n]	SE[n]	
Full court reaction		EW[o], DE, NL , SE[m]	EW, DE FR[m], NL, PL, SE[m]	EW, DE , FR, NL, PL, SE[m]

[a] Can lead to a fine.
[b] Can lead to a fine and other reactions as i.e. driving licence ban.
[c] Possible reaction in this case is a caution.
[d] Caution as possible reaction.
[e] Drop only.
[f] Can lead to a Transactie or a Halt-Reaction (juvenile program). Only informal drop possible.
[g] Can lead to a Transactie or a Halt-Reaction (juvenile program).
[h] Can lead to a fine or a community service; pay compensation.
[i] Condition to fulfil.
[j] Can lead to a fine or any other reaction as for instance CSO, mediation, compensation.
[k] A possible reaction might be a fine or a community penalty.
[l] Only leads to a fine.
[m] Can lead to a prison sentence or a fine.
[n] Leads to a fine or a conditional sentence.
[o] Possible reactions are prison sentence, fine, community penalty.

Where a decision is made that a system is no longer able to deal with all the offences assigned to it and therefore that no formal CJS reaction will in fact ensue to certain categories of offences, material decriminalisation is the logical consequence. However, it is an option rarely taken today in the countries studied. The experts involved refer to an unwillingness to use this option and indeed a contrary trend. This can be observed in certain contexts: the offences against order in England & Wales, the recent developments for some offences in the public/moral domain in France and in Poland in relation to the Wykrocenia which have been brought back into CJS jurisdiction, with special divisions of the criminal courts now responsible for judging them (as of 2003). Whilst legally and logically the more attractive option, decriminalisation is regarded as politically unattractive and is currently not a likely solution to the universal system over-loading problem. Figure 2 gives a rough idea, however, of how much difference decriminalisation can make by displaying the proportion of offences reacted to which are decriminalised. Unfortunately data are not comparable and so the largest differences between the countries are explained by the inclusion or exclusion of traffic offences. The diagrams are intended solely to give a very rough guide. The French example, however, which includes traffic offences, shows what a small proportion of sanctioned behaviour is in fact dealt with by the criminal justice system as such. Many types of behaviour, considered undesirable and worthy of a state reaction, are not regarded as worthy of CJS time at all.

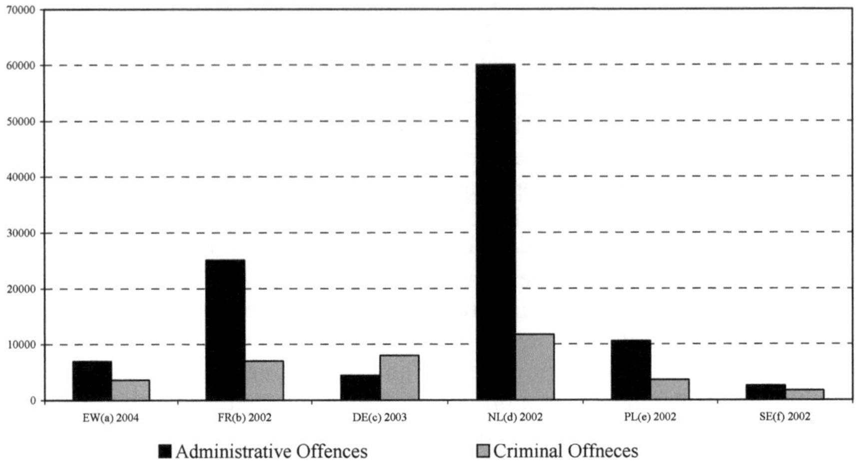

Fig. 2. Proportion of Offences dealt with by the CJS and Outside of it per 100,000 of the population

Sources: EW: Global Numbers 2004 (Questionnaire Annex) and The Prosecution Service Function within the English Criminal Justice System; FR: The Prosecution Service Function within the French Criminal Justice System and Questionnaire Tab. V.1; DE: Polizeiliche Kriminalstatistik and Statist. Mitteilungen des Kraftfahrtbundesamts; NL: The Prosecution Service Function within the Dutch Criminal Justice System; PL: The Prosecution Service Function within the Polish Criminal Justice System and Questionnaire Table V.1; SE: Swedish Official statistics and Questionnaire Table V.1

[a] Administrative Offences (including traffic offences): FPN (n=3,600,000) [2002] and PND (n=50,000); Criminal Offences (including traffic offences): n=1,896,000; of which: 984,000 bulk proceedings.

[b] Administrative Offences (including traffic offences): n=14,800,000; Criminal Offences (including traffic offences): n= 4,113,882; of which: Contraventions 5/délits: n=3,538,989; Contraventions 1-4 full trial: n=151,084; Contraventions 1-4 ordonnance pénale: n=423,809.

[c] Administrative Offences (NB this includes only traffic offences for which points are noted on licences, i.e. only the most serious, the total number of administrative offences is far higher but not available statistically): n=3,629,000; Criminal Offences: n=6,572,135 (without traffic offences).

[d] Administrative Offences: n=9,536,864 (Mulder Law, traffic offences only); Criminal Offences (including traffic offences): n=1,865,900 (Dutch data concerns offences recorded).

[e] Administrative Offences (including traffic offences): n=4,087,000 (wykroczenia and other adm. offences); Criminal Offences: n=1,404,229.

As these findings indicate, decriminalisation bears huge potential to relieve pressure upon a criminal justice system. There can be little doubt that the systems studied, now reputed to be overloaded, would cease to function were they expected to deal with all of the offences for which a state reaction ensues. A more pragmatic solution is found. A clear statement is made that certain forms of behaviour, whilst considered undesirable and worthy of a state reaction, are not serious enough to warrant treatment by the CJS. There is an honest statement that such offences are to be dealt with differently. The CJS is reserved for a smaller group of acts, to be used only when this is really required.

The negative side of this is that the state effectively imposes a sanction of sorts upon its citizens without the protection of full criminal proceedings and thus the chances of incorrect treatment are raised. All of the systems allow for an appeal procedure to counter this. In some cases, however, there is some risk for the suspect in raising objections; the appeal instance is likely to impose a higher penalty fine if it considers the person guilty. In other words, as the penalty is only a sanction and no criminal record follows, there may be a higher chance that factually innocent suspects comply with the procedure to avoid a higher risk or because they do not understand that they are in fact not liable for punishment. The risk of this infringement is, arguably, to be weighed against the practicalities of dealing with the offences as well as the benefits of decriminalisation to the „offenders." The counter argument is that human rights principles do not allow a pragmatic approach such as this: wherever the state claims a right to intervene with a citizen´s rights by imposing a sanction, it is required to prove guilt.

A further issue is the question as to where the line between criminal and noncriminal offences should be drawn. As has been indicated above, factors of political viability are also relevant here. This may mean that the line is drawn controversially. Furthermore, in as far as the line is drawn pragmatically, guided merely by the number of cases: meaning that more frequently committed offences will be decriminalised in order to provide CJS relief, this may lead to a very strange situation indeed in as far as determining principles behind the criminal law are concerned. Equivalently culpable conduct (however this is determined) may face very different state reactions. The boundaries of decriminalisation are reached because the law does not stand alone from society: it reflects and influences the values within it. Action de-criminalised will, at least with time, come to be seen as less stigmatised than that subject to criminal sanctions.

---

[f] Administrative Offences: n=228,429 (*brotsförelaggande* issued by police; it is difficult to categorise these offences. The Swedish system does not regard them as administrative and because of the powers associated with them, much speaks for categorising them differently (see also 3.2. below). However, because this procedure is used for offences (mostly traffic offences) that in other countries are treated as administrative and is indeed a procedure so simplified that one could argue it as being administrative, it is treated as such here to display in how far the system has found relief by procedural means. The data used here concern traffic offences only and are therefore shown here as administrative; Criminal Offences: n=150,310.

This may not be justified morally[3] although decriminalisation might appear desirable to provide for a functioning CJS. Even where an offence so rarely provokes a factual CJS reaction that it might be regarded as factually decriminalised, general prevention arguments may prevail against those for material decriminalisation.

With less stigma and less resources being dedicated to the prosecution of such offences – that after all is the point of de-criminalisation – issues of equality before the law are raised unless clear moral boundaries are drawn. Decriminalised offences may, in addition, no longer be investigated quite as intensely, making it more a matter of luck whether one is caught or not. This is not less true, however, if they remain criminalised and insufficient resources are dedicated to them – in which case the question of legal inequality and unfairness may be regarded as having more serious consequences. Decriminalisation and the resulting less intensive stigma and investigation – made officially known to the public – may also cause the offence to be committed more frequently. Arguments for legal clarity speak for decriminalisation, more pragmatic social control issues may well speak against it (whether such considerations are legitimate for a CJS is a question which goes beyond the scope of this paper).

The reader is merely asked to bear in mind that the systems examined draw their jurisdictional lines in different places; that there are arguments for seeking solutions quite different to those which form the focus of this study. Creating a legally clear and robust model is not a simple task. The question as to where the material line should be drawn is a complex one. Nevertheless, it is impossible to imagine European systems today without a category of offences subject to treatment outside of the CJS.

3 The Investigative Stage

3.1 The PPS Role

In civilian systems at least, the PPS is traditionally considered to have a controlling role in the investigative stage. In all the study countries except England & Wales (where the police are legally independent, even for this function), the police are directly responsible to the PPS in relation to investigative functions. In some cases (Germany, the Netherlands), the PPS is legally the "ruler" of the investigative stage. This is true in Sweden only for those offences for which the PPS is declared as being in charge of the investigation.

---

3 See for example criticism of where these lines are drawn in the British system, leaving work-related deaths outside of the CJS (Sanders & Young, 2000, p. 365).

3.1.1 PPS-Police Relationship

In all countries, however, we are dealing with legally independent institutions and, in terms of organisation, the police have an entirely independent structure. It is perhaps also interesting to note that in Sweden the police and PPS are considered equal institutions and are both answerable to one institution, namely the Ministry of Justice. In other jurisdictions the PPS answers to the Ministry of Justice whilst the police is directed by the Ministry of the Interior;[4] England & Wales having quite different structures.[5] If the police are considered subservient, then only in relation to the prosecution of offences. It is not difficult to imagine this legal PPS superiority being hampered by reality. After all police services have more specific investigative competence and the PPS is dependent upon the police to carry out investigative actions in all of the countries studied; no PPS has an own investigative unit and it is the police who are "on the ground", doing the work.

In most systems the PPS furthermore has no direct powers to influence the police, although in France disciplinary measures will be used in serious cases of disobedience. Only in the Netherlands and in England & Wales do we see what is classified as means of indirect influence; the Dutch sharing personnel and discussing policy during "tripartite consultations" whilst the British exercise influence by placing PPS personnel in police stations. The French "real-time treatment", which sees prosecutors in constant telephonic communication with investigating officers, would seem to bear potential for such influence, but it is not reported as doing so. A deeper look at the day-to-day dynamics of the modern PPS/police relationship would be of great interest in all jurisdictions.

PPS influence upon this stage is regarded as necessary because it is concerned with the gathering of evidence to be used before court. The PPS's role is to ensure the necessary rules are stuck to and the evidence gathered in such a way to be of maximum use to the court. With systems being reported as increasingly overloaded, perhaps not surprisingly, accounts of the police working more and more independently of the PPS in this stage became frequent.

---

[4] Except in France in its function as police judicière.

[5] See the country reports in part II.

Table 3. General Guidance Issued by the PPS Deal with

	EW[a]	FR	DE	NL[b]	PL[c]	SE[d]
PPS directs police use of resources				X	X	
PPS guidance of evidence collection by general guidelines		X[e]	X	X[f]	X	
PPS specifies what should be done during the investigation of offence types		X[g]	X	X	X	X[h]
PPS only has indirect means of influencing Police investigation						X[i]
Local co-operation has an on-going influence on police work	X[j]	X[k]				X[l]

[a] There are no general directions by PPS but only local police decisions how to investigate under rules set down by parliament. There is also a lot of consultation about what to do about a particular case between police and CPS and there are several guidelines which have been drawn up between those two.

[b] These are also well observed in practice.

[c] Those guidelines are legally binding; all actions of police have to be approved by PPS. But some official decisions are generally regulated and issued by PPS.

[d] There are only guidelines which determine the relationship between PPS and police in general (issued by Prosecutor General) that is which cases are of simple nature and which cases the PPS leads as the head of investigation. Moreover the PPS has no means to direct police investigative actions. They may play an active part (presence during interrogation), but that does not mean that the PPS takes over the investigation as a whole.

[e] Issued by the ministry of justice (formal head of PPS). PPS has influence at local level through unwritten agreements with the police according to which the PPS can only instruct in specific, individual cases.

[f] Takes place at national as well as district level, at the district level this is developed in consultation with the police.

[g] Has influence via local unwritten agreement, instruction ensues only in specific from during individual cases.

[h] The Office of the Prosecutor General has issued a certain number of guidelines concerning special types of offences, which also contain instructions regarding the way to properly organize investigation(s), what kinds of facts should be presented in court, and what kind of sentence should be proposed in court. There are also corresponding guidelines with instructions for the police (issued by the National Police Board). All regulations are relatively wide-ranging, which means that there is enough space left for local regulations as well.

[i] The PPS cannot issue any guidelines which directly address the police, but those issued for PPS itself may indirectly concern also polices` activity in preliminary investigation. In that case these guidelines are either adopted in consultation with the National Police Board, or the National Police Board issues own guidelines identical to the guidelines of the PPS.

[j] Shared personnel.

[k] Intense, case-specific communication during "real-time" treatment has general influence.

[l] The Guidelines are issued by the Office of the Prosecutor General, in consultation with the National Police Board. The division of competence is regulated by the CJP and the Guidelines of the Prosecutor General (in consultation with the National Police Board). The legal regulation is very vague and the guidelines are not binding.

Table 4. Factual Standing PPS/Police[a]

	EW	FR	DE	NL	PL	SE[b]
PPS factually involved in investigations		•/••	•	•/••	•/••	•/••
Police factually solely responsible for investigations	••••	•••[c]	•••	•••	•••/••	•••
Police factually conducts investigation until the end and then hand the file on to the PPS	••••[d]	•••[e]	•••/••	•••/••	•••/••	•••

• = in serious cases •• = in moderately serious cases ••• = minor offences •••• = all

[a] How this is regulated is explained in table 2 in the annex.
[b] Differentiation is other than as a in the other countries; police conducts the investigation solely and is responsible for the investigation of cases of a simple nature. Of course these will mostly be less serious cases (for further information see tables above).
[c] Contraventions 1–4. classe.
[d] The police can issue a caution or a final warning. Increasingly the decision on what to do is taken following a discussion between the police and the PPS.
[e] In case of C 1–4; it is also possible to take the case to the Tribunal de Police by themselves.

This study attempted to chart the current legal and factual position of the PPS in the countries studied. As table 3 shows, in all the countries studied, bar England & Wales and Sweden, the PPS has powers to exercise considerable influence generally as to how investigations should be carried out.[6] In Sweden, the PPS has some influence upon such issues because the (ruling body of the) service co-ordinates its work with the police ruling body, via guidelines issued in both their names. Only in England and Wales, not surprisingly considering the PPS's youth and the tradition of a very strong police force, is its influence in this matter restricted to local exchange. It will be interesting to see how the highly dynamic situation there develops during the next few years.

Table 4 shows that in systems in which the PPS is regarded as being in charge of investigations legally, factually its involvement is limited. Not unexpectedly, in England & Wales, where the PPS was given no competence in this area, we see no factual involvement and the police in charge of all investigations. The prosecution service will receive a file once the police decide it is ready to be handed over. The PPS can naturally request further investigative action at that point. Where the police turn to the PPS for advice during an investigation, there will be some factual PPS involvement; but this is still reported to be the exception rather than the rule.[7]

---

[6] The form in which this is exercised is documented by table 2 in the annex.

[7] With the PPS having been given the statutory power (as of October 2005) to determine which charge is to be brought, the police's tendency to consult the PPS would seem likely to grow stronger.

In Germany, were the PPS is the declared ruler of the investigative stage, we see factual PPS involvement only in investigations into serious offences. Moderately serious and minor cases will be handled by the police alone unless coercive measures are planned which require PPS or court agreement. In all the other study countries, there is PPS involvement in serious cases and in some of the moderately serious cases, presumably depending upon the individual characteristics of the case. In minor and simpler and less invasive moderately serious cases, the police conduct investigations independently, guided only by more general provisions and rules the PPS may have made and set down.

Our study indicates a European trend of far-reaching police independence in the investigatory stage as far as minor offences are concerned and to some extent in moderately serious cases. The legal differences between civilian and common law jurisdictions can only be seen in practice in relation to serious offences where the PPS is active in civilian systems. Time will tell whether this divergence will remain. If the civilian systems accept lesser PPS involvement and the British police seek legal advice more often (and this seems most likely in serious cases), we may witness further factual convergence.

3.1.2 PPS Tasks during the Investigative Stage

Table 5 shows the tasks performed by the PPS during the investigative stage and that this is fairly unitary in the countries studied (bar England & Wales where there is no involvement). In Poland and Sweden it is limited to more serious cases – or rather, to the cases for which the PPS has jurisdiction. During the investigatory stage the PPS may initiate the investigation; they will plan it and direct the collection of evidence. In all countries bar France, members of the PPS may also be present during or conduct interrogations as necessary.

Table 5. PPS Role in the Investigative Stage

	EW		FR		DE		NL		PL		SE	
Seriousness of cases[a]	Sc	Lsc	Sc	Lsc	Sc	Lsc	Sc	Lsc	Sc	Lsc	Sc	Lsc
Direct evidence collection			X[b]		X		X[c]		X[d]		X[e]	
Be present at/conduct interrogation					X[f]		X[g]		X[d]		X[h]	
Co-ordinate and plan investigation			X		X		X		X[d]		X[i]	
Initiate investigation/case			X		X		X		X[d]		X	
Other												

Sc = serious cases Lsc = less serious cases

[a] For an explanation of this differentiation between serious and less serious cases see explanation-table above.

[b] *In serious cases*: for flagrants delits (only after the suspect is arrested) if not transmitted to EM for during judicial investigation; *in less serious cases*: For flagrants delits (only after the suspect is arrested), together with EM during judicial investigation.

[c] Leads the investigation and has therefore the final responsibility for all required measures within criminal investigations.

[d] This is possible in any investigation, but usually only done in serious cases.

[e] If the PPS is in charge of/the head of investigation, it can require assistance from the police and in that case the PPS may guide police evidence collection. This is not true if the police head the investigation. If the PPS receives the case from the police after that the investigation has been completed, the PPS may ask for further complementing evidence to be sought.

[f] § 163 a III 2/161 a StPO.

[g] Usually done by an assistant-PP.

[h] The question is not regulated by law. However, considering that the PPS may take over the investigation at any time, the possibility to be present in this case is of course open for the PP.

[i] In cases in which PPS is head of investigation and asks for police assistance.

Table 6. Legal Requirements and Factual Information Flow between the Police and PPS*

	EW[a]		FR		DE		NL		PL		SE	
	Leg.	Fact.	Leg.	Fact.	Leg.	Fact.	Leg.	Fact.	Leg.	Fact.	Leg.	Fact.
As soon as offence discovered			••••	•••[b]	••••	•	••••[c]	•	••••	••••	•[d]	•/••
When 1st investigatory action undertaken				••••[e]					••••		••••[f]	••••[g]
Shortly after investigation begins				••[h]					••••[i]	••••[j]		
When suspect found				••[k]					••••[l]		••••[m]	
Particular action required	••••[n]	••••[n]	••••[o]	••••				••••[p]	••••[q]		••••[r]	••••

• = in serious cases •• = in moderately serious cases ••• = minor offences •••• = all Leg. = legally Fact. = factually
* footnotes in annex 5

Table 7. When do the Police Inform the PPS about a Case during the Investigation?

	EW[a]		FR		DE		NL		PL		SE	
	Leg.	Fact.	Leg.	Fact.	Leg.	Fact.	Leg.	Fact.	Leg.	Fact.	Leg.	Fact.
Police believe they have sufficient evidence[b]	••••[c]	••••[d]		••[e]		••/•••		•••[f]	••••		••••[g]	••••[h]
When clear that no offender will be found						••••			••••			

• = in serious cases •• = in moderately serious cases ••• = minor offences only •••• = all Leg. = Legally Fact. = Factually

[a] The police have complete discretion about when to inform PPS about a case, but they tend to follow the guidelines set down by CPS. The police also inform the CPS when it is asked to carry out some non-prosecution functions.
[b] No drop/disposal/sanction by police are possible/wanted.
[c] If they decide to go ahead with taking the case to court.
[d] The police report a case to PPS if there is some concern about evidence, what charge or whether the case should be prosecuted; otherwise a case is also reported to PPS when the investigation is over. Not officially but in practice the PPS will be informed by police about cases of sensitive investigation or in serious cases of murder or terrorism. Increasingly the police and CPS are co-located and discuss offences at an earlier stage.
[e] For less serious crime, delits and minor cases and contraventions 5. classe.
[f] Three tracked division of police handling a case more or less independently is a result of working tradition.
[g] In all those cases which shall be brought before court and which cannot be treated by police alone.
[h] Where the police lead the investigation – as laid down in guidelines.

Tables 6 and 7 reflect the actual possibilities for control between the two agencies during the investigative stage in illustrating what information the PPS will factually have been given, at what point in time, by the police. Declaring the PPS in charge of this stage is rather hollow because factually, it remains dependent upon the police who are "on the ground" and factually in control of information about a case[8] and concerning what steps have been taken. This situation creates a natural PPS dependency upon the police, unless the law stipulates that the PPS must receive this information and this ensues in practice. Only an agency which knows about an investigation, is in a position to exercise any control over it.

Given the study findings shown here, it is not surprising that the PPS's factual involvement is limited to serious cases: all countries (England & Wales being left out because there is no such expectation there) except Sweden, legally require the PPS to be given information about all cases immediately. Factually in Germany and the Netherlands this only occurs in serious cases. Beyond that the picture appears varied, with information often flowing when first investigatory actions are taken or when the PPS's active involvement is required (e.g. because it has to apply for a permit to allow certain investigatory actions). Information flows where certain hard criteria are met and the law requires it to flow as a consequence. It is not difficult to imagine that the police have some independence and leeway in controlling the information flow and that they thus factually have a strong position. It should be noted that the PPS has the legal power to change this, should it desire to do so. The situation reflected is thus likely to tell us not only of an independent police running free of factual PPS control but of a factual agreement between PPS and police that the former only be informed at such points of the investigation. Usually written guidelines provide for this end. Naturally this requires PPS knowledge of the situation, which cannot be comprehensive in this case. It is, however, no less difficult to imagine that an overloaded PPS is grateful to receive selective information only.

This study regards the CJS as a chain with competencies being passed down as the pressure on the level above mounts. These findings are compatible with the PPS leaving the police to get on with those tasks it believes the investigators capable of and only insisting upon becoming involved where this is really necessary. Just as we see the British police involving the PPS where their competence is required, we see civilian PPSs leaving the police to work independently where they do not consider their skills required.

As it stands this does, however, leave the police with the power to define when this is the case, which is fundamentally contrary to the balance desired by civilian systems in principle. During the early 1990's precisely this situation caused wide-scale reform and the PPS to be strengthened in the Netherlands because the police there were perceived as working too freely (Tak, 2003, 27 & 28). Whether other systems feel the current balance to be correct or move towards more factual PPS control or legally-anchored police independence, remains to be seen.

---

[8] Unless, of course, it was initiated by or reported directly to the PPS – the latter is often the case in Sweden, in such cases the PPS will at least be aware that an investigation has begun.

Table 8 again confirms this more pragmatic approach to PPS involvement in all but the most serious cases. The PPS takes over responsibility for only the most serious cases from the very beginning. In others it varies from system to system, but one can basically conclude that fairly specific actions and stages are legally supposed to trigger PPS involvement and that, usually, they factually also do.[9]

Table 9 gives an overview over which agencies are required to approve or even permit (by which a more formal, active allowing procedure required in advance is meant) which steps during the investigatory stage. This is also a fairly good measure of the agency's status.

Thus in England and Wales we see strong signs of police independence and court control; the PPS having an applicant function, if one at all. In France we see the strength of the judicially trained investigatory agencies with most powers divided between a strong PPS or the examining magistrate required to take its place in the most serious investigations. In Germany we see the formal manifestation of the PPS as a mere preparatory body, with court control still regarded as necessary. PPS strength is very evident in the Dutch system with almost all measures being dependent upon their approval there. Poland is a mixture of court control and police independence, the PPS hardly featuring, reflective of the recent political will that it should not be a powerful body. The situation in Sweden gives some indication of a strong PPS but the mixed nature of the system is perhaps reflected in this assignment of tasks. All in all, significant diversity is still to be seen very clearly in relation to which institution a system entrusts with decisions interfering with citizen's rights.

[9] For the forms in which this is regulated, see table 2 in the annex.

Table 8. When is a Case (file and responsibility) Handed over within an Investigation?*

	EW		FR		DE		NL[a]		PL		SE	
	Leg.	Fact.	Leg.	Fact.	Leg.	Fact.	Leg.	Fact.	Leg.	Fact.	Leg.	Fact.
As soon as offence discovered			•	•	••••	•	••••	•	••••	••••	•[b]	•[b]
When 1st investigatory action undertaken												
Shortly after investigation begins			••[c]	••[c]					••••[d]	••••[d]		
When suspect found			••[e]	••[e]		••/•••	••••				•/••[f]	•/••
Particular action required		••••[g]	••••[h]	••••[i]	••••	••••	••••	••••			••••[j]	••••
Police believe they have sufficient evidence		••••		••/•••[k]		••/•••		••/•••			•••[l]	•••
When clear that no offender will be found		[m]		••••	••••							

• = in serious cases only •• = in moderately serious cases ••• = minor offences only •••• = all offences Leg. = legally Fact. = factually
* footnotes in annex 6

Table 9. Which Actions Require Whose Approval[*] during the Investigative Stage?[**]

Act	EW	FR	DE	NL	PL	SE
Search of premises	Court	PPS/EM[a]	Court	PPS[b]/EM	PPS	P indep./PPS/Court[c]
Confiscation / Forfeiture	PPS[d]/Court	EM/Court	Court	P indep.[e]	PPS[f] post facto	P. indep./Court[g]
Assets frozen	PPS[d]/Court	EM	Court	Court	Court permit	Court permit[h]
Visual surveillance (recording)	Home Office	P indep.	Court	PPS	Court	Court permit
DNA-test	P. independent[i]	PPS[j]	Court	PPS/EM[k]	PPS	P indep.
Telephone taps	Home Office	EM permit	Court	EM permit[l]	Court	Court permit
Police detention < 6 hours	P independent	PPS[m]	PPS/later Court	PPS or assistant[n]	P indep.	P indep./PPS[o]
Police detention < 12 hours	P independent		PPS/later Court	PPS or assistant[p]	P indep.	PPS
Police detention < 24 hours	P independent		PPS/Court	PPS or assistant[p]	P indep.	PPS permit
Police detention < 36/48	PPS[d]/Court	PPS[q]		PPS or assistant[p]	P indep. up to 48 hours/then Court	PPS permit[r]
Travel ban	Court permit[s]					PPS permit
Obligation to report	Court permit[t]					PPS permit
Pre-trial detention	PPS[d]/Court permit	Judicial permit[u]	Court permit	EM[v]/Court permit	Court permit	Court permit[w]

[*] Permit where explicitly stated EM= Examining Magistrate P= Police
[**] footnotes in annex 7

3.1.3 Conclusion

The study shows quite clearly that across Europe the PPS role in the investigatory stage is reduced to extensive involvement only in serious cases, a certain participation in some moderately serious cases in some jurisdictions, more often than not, a greater or lesser degree of more general guidance being given in such, as well as in minor cases. Beyond that, the PPS frequently plays a part in allowing or seeking-allowance for certain – in human rights terms – interventionary investigatory actions. In other words, where a step of higher legal relevance is taken, this will often be subject to PPS scrutiny. The degree to which the PPS plays this role, however, varies considerably within the study countries.

In this stage of the CJS differences between civilian and the British common law tradition are strongly visible. There are some indications that these differences may be more legal in nature as reports of what is increasingly British practice indicate a stronger PPS role emerging, but the fundamental, legal difference remains.

3.2 The End of the Investigatory Stage

The end of the investigatory stage is a defining moment for the PPS role as it is key in determining what cases the PPS deals with at all in so far as it defines what input is made into the PPS workload.

Table 10. Police Action upon Investigation Completion

	EW	FR	DE	NL	PL	SE
Hand over to PPS	••••	•/••[a]	••••	••••	••••	••••[b]
but can drop because evidence insufficient	••••[c]	•••[d]		••••[e]		••••[f]
but can drop a case if offender unknown	••••[g]	•••[h]		••••[e]	••••	••••[f]
Can drop a case *(no public interest)*	••••	•••		•••[i]	••••[j]	
by fixed penalty	••••[k]	•••[l]		•••[m]		•••[n]
Can sanction/dispose *by other means*						

• = in serious cases •• = in moderately serious cases ••• = minor offen. •••• = all offen.

[a] All crimes, delits, contraventions 5 classe.

[b] Normal proceeding when the police are in charge of investigation and it is over (cases of simple nature) or when certain circumstances require PPS leading the investigation (in case of medial interest). Furthermore a hand over takes place in all cases PPS is in charge of the investigation at the moment a suspect has been found.

[c] Police have full discretion. They would usually drop such a case after consultation with the CPS but could do so on their own. They would tend to use the same criteria as in the CPS code of practice. They can do this for all offences. It is regulated by guidelines that are issued by the Home Office in consultation with the police chiefs ACPO. PPS can influence their decision to drop by being present at police stations where it can give a great deal of informal advice.

[d] The reason for dropping a case may be a lack of evidence, which is seen as a legal factor (regulated by law).

[e] Police drop has no legal basis, but police may drop (according to guidelines and a verdict from the Supreme Court). Exception: very serious violent offences or offences with dead victims. In that case the police have to make an official report (summary) and send it to the PPS. At least the police inform the PP of dropped cases by keeping a list of all shelved cases. This list comes up to the regular consultation between police and PPS, so that the latter has a control about police` dropping.

[f] In all cases where the police is in charge of the investigation (cases of simple nature), this is regulated by law and guidelines issued by police at national level; PPS might only influence this decision to drop by taking over the investigation immediately.

[g] The decision no longer to look actively for an offender is made by police and CPS together.

[h] There is no legal provision, but in practice the decision to drop a case because no offender can be found is a police decision. This because PPS theoretically has the right to decide if the police drop of further investigation was correct or if the investigation shall be continued because its PPS which decides about the final drop of the case. But in practice PPS almost never does so. It will not check the decision of dropping the case because of unknown offender in a very detailed way but mostly follow police advice to do so.

[i] No legislative basis but allowed by Supreme Court.

[j] PPS and/or court approval necessary.

Table 10 shows the options the police have and that in all countries studied but France – where this is the case only for serious and moderately serious offences – the police will hand all *types* of cases over to the PPS; i.e. the PPS has jurisdiction for all cases. However, in England & Wales, in the Netherlands and in Sweden, as well as in France as far as minor cases are concerned, the police will drop the case (i.e. not hand it on to the PPS) if it considers the evidence to be insufficient. This includes cases in which the offender is unknown for which the Polish police have equivalent powers. In England & Wales and the Netherlands, where PPS personnel work in police stations (and particularly in the former as of 2005 with the introduction of PPS statutory charging responsibilities) may well have some influence on deciding whether this will be the case or not. However, it is clear that with this defining power, the police gains key influence upon what work the PPS gets. The police evaluate what is worthy of PPS attention.

In some jurisdictions this power goes further because the police are entitled to do the same where they regard public interest in a prosecution to be lacking. In England & Wales this is true for all offences, in France and the Netherlands this is the case only for minor offences. In France this refers to the police jurisdiction for and the option to opt for non-criminal proceedings for the contraventions 1–4th class. In Poland the police have powers to suggest a drop of this kind and thus to prepare it but it is subject to PPS and court approval. In England and Wales and France these powers are flanked by an ability to impose a fixed penalty sanction. In the Netherlands the police drop a case if a fixed sum of money is paid. This means the police can impose a sanction, at least of sorts, but its nature and the conditions of impositions are strongly defined in law or guidelines. In Sweden the police have independent sanctioning power. Interestingly Swedish police officers have no powers to drop but a particularly strong one to sanction because they concurrently impose a status of guilt upon the suspected offender. The German police emerge as comparatively weak legally.

Table 11 shows a summary of the findings as to the legal and factual situation at the end of the investigative stage. Table 12 lists more closely the police powers available. Table 13 is a summary of the legal competence available.

As can be seen, practice tends to follow legal requirements except as far as handing over cases in which no offender has been found are concerned. In all of the countries studied the police are considered subject to the principle of legality, meaning they are formally obliged to hand all evidentially sufficient cases over to

---

[k] By caution/ warnings. There are no rules. The police can drop any case, but this is usually done where there is no evidence or no evidence that crime has really been committed or they don't believe the victim. In many cases the police discuss the case with the prosecutor before dropping the case, or before issuing a caution.

[l] Contraventions 1–4, police can impose a fine.

[m] Transactie (up to 350 Euro).

[n] Summary fine possible (imposed by "ordningsbotsföreläggande", Art 48 CJP)); in case of simple nature (possible offences are listed in the Regulation of the Prosecutors General Board).

the PPS. Table 11 gives some indication of in how far they are allowed to define evidential viability themselves. In practice, although the law requires all such cases to be subject to PPS scrutiny, this does not happen for minor cases. In England & Wales and, under much more limited circumstances, Germany (where the law does not foresee this, and it happens in practice for a very restricted category of cases only, subject to guidelines), the police dispose of cases/impose sanctions. In France and the Netherlands the police drop cases without legal provision for them to do so. The latter is of particular relevance to this study because it occurs in a larger number of cases. It is an example of workload pressures shaping widespread and more or less accepted practice, without the law being changed to provide for it. In the Netherlands, however, this practice is stringently provided for in guidelines because it is intended to be anticipatory of PPS decisions, in France, real-time treatment should ensure effective PPS control. This practice may be regarded as less objectionable there than in jurisdictions in which the law/practice divide gives grounds for fears of uncontrolled practice. The question why legal regulation is not seen to be appropriate remains.

Once a case is handed over to the PPS, it truly passes into a new domain in which it is the central, decision-making instance. This is indicative of strong PPS status in this intermediary stage between the police and court, as one would expect (see annex 3 for regulatory modalities).

Tables 14 and 15 give an indication of the legal regulation and describe the competences found in this area. Only England & Wales have regulation for drops and together with the Netherlands have legal regulation for police disposals.

Only the Swedish police have formal sanctioning powers for offences within the criminal justice system with the level of sanctions closely defined by law and the offender considered guilty.

Table 11. Action upon Investigation Completion

Police hand over:	EW Leg.	EW Fact.	FR Leg.	FR Fact.	DE Leg.	DE Fact.	NL Leg.	NL Fact.	PL Leg.	PL Fact.	SE Leg.	SE Fact.
All cases - even where suspect unknown			••••[a]	•••	••••	••••	••••[b]		••••	••••		
Only where suspect is known	••••[c]	•/••[d]	••••	•/••		•/••	••••	•/••[e]			••••[f]	••••[g]

• = in serious cases •• = in moderately serious cases ••• = minor offences •••• = all offences Leg. = legally Fact. = factually

[a] Except in case of C. 1–4, that they can take to court themselves.
[b] In the Netherlands it is not a case but an offender who is handed over; a case is not actually handed over, it remains on both police and PPS level.
[c] There is no legal provision, it depends on the case and whether a caution can be given or not. However, if the investigation is over and the police have enough evidence to take the case to court they have to hand it over to the PPS because they can't bring the case to court by themselves.
[d] Depends on the case. See above.
[e] Informal working tradition.
[f] In all cases except those which can be ended by a fine by police themselves.
[g] The police shall hand over the cases that are not of simple nature as soon as a suspect has been found. The PPS shall also take over the investigation in other cases, if there are special reasons for it.

Table 12. Police Options at the End of the Investigatory Stage

	EW		FR		DE		NL		PL		SE	
	Leg.	Fact.	Leg.	Fact.	Leg.	Fact.	Leg.	Fact.	Leg.	Fact.	Leg.	Fact.
Can dispose/ sanction	••••	•••[a]				•••[b]	•••	•••[c]			•••[d]	•••[d]
Can drop	••••	••••		•••[e]		•••		••••[f]			•••[g]	•••[h]
Can hand the case over to court									•••	•••		

• = in serious cases •• = in moderately serious cases ••• = minor offences only •••• = all offences

[a] Possible in all cases but there are guidelines about what to do, so clearly they will not do this for serious offences. A caution is mostly used for less serious offences like shoplifting.

[b] Some guidelines exist in several federal states giving the police the competence to prepare a PPS disposal.

[c] This happens not only in minor cases because in some moderately serious cases a police-transaction is possible. In practice the police drop cases and often only hand over cases when a suspect and enough evidence for a prosecution are found.

[d] In cases of simple nature.

[e] Drop is possible for all offences, only for C 1–4 without PPS involvement (but those offences are not included here in this table because they are treated by police completely independently); but in practice police might do an informal drop in less serious cases involving known offenders and reported by victims.

[f] No legal provision, but happens in practice when the offender is unknown or there is not sufficient evidence for a prosecution (except for very serious cases). This is only done with prior general approval given with the PPS (guidelines). For which cases the police can do so depends on the reason the cases is dropped for: On grounds of insufficient evidence and unknown offender police can generally drop every case but will not do so in very serious cases (dead victim etc.); in cases where there seems to be no public interest police can also drop a case in minor offences.

[g] In cases where the police is in charge of investigation (cases of simple nature), regulated by law and guidelines.

[h] Possible for all cases where the police is head of the investigation.

Table 13. Police Legal Case-ending Competence

EW	Caution: final warning of the offender done by a police officer, (formal criminal record?) Reprimand: same as above but for juveniles, (formal criminal record?) Fixed penalty: mostly fixed summary fine
FR	In case of contraventions 1–4 classe: Fixed summary fine: administrative sanction, no criminal record <u>or</u> Competence to bring the case before court (Tribunal de Police): no criminal record if only a fine in the sanction given by court.
DE	No competence existing.
NL	Politietransactie: in case of all overtredingen and some misdrijven: kind of disposal with the condition of payment to the treasury, no criminal record) Drop: no legal provision, but in practice done by police and accepted by courts since 1950 provided police are anticipating PPS decision.
PL	Fixed summary fine <u>or</u> Competence to bring a case before (special dept. of criminal) court: criminal record
SE	Fixed summary fine: kind of criminal sanction, results in a criminal record.

Table 14. Regulation of Police Drops (no Public Interest)

Police drop…	EW	FR	DE	NL	PL	SE
is considered an admission of guilt	X			Happens in practice – no legal provision		
leads to an informal record	X					
cannot be used on lack of public interest basis		X	X		X	X

Table 15. Regulation of Police Disposal with a Condition

A police disposal with a condition…	EW	FR	DE	NL	PL	SE
is considered an admission of guilt				X		
leads to an informal record	X			X		
is subject to agreement by the suspect	X			X		
leads to a conviction	[a]					
is not available		X	X		X	X

[a] A local record is made. Some categorise this as a conviction.

3.3 Conclusion

Whilst the situation does not allow one to speak of a clear European trend reflected by the countries studied, there can be little doubt that a tendency towards greater police powers, also to make case-ending decisions, is apparent. Above all, practice is creating this reality and it would not be unexpected for the law to follow in due course. As all systems complain of over-loading, allowing police to make case-ending decisions in minor cases is an attractive option in order to relieve the PPS.

There is nothing of course to prevent systems deciding against this option. Civilian systems fundamentally tend against this as shown by their desire to control the investigatory agencies through legal inspection by the PPS via guidelines issued by the PPS. In all but the Swedish case, the police are not enforcing a formal finding of guilt and so not a "true" sanction. There can be little doubt, however, that a citizen told to pay a certain sum of money to settle a case will feel punished. Thus this must be regarded as the imposition of a quasi-sanction at least. If this is done by the police there is no formal provision for trained legal evaluation and so less guarantee of a legally correct decision. Any argument that provision can be made for this by further training or PPS involvement will have to be measured against the fundamental motivation (for the granting of such powers in the first place) of using fewer resources for such case settlements. Unless such practices are very clearly provided for and some effective form of inspection created, a danger of lacking transparency, legal correctness and control remains.

Another consideration is the unity of case ending decision maker with investigatory power. If one and the same force or even officer becomes responsible for both, the ability and possibly temptation to apply greater pressure upon suspects increase. The issues for the separation of powers and the danger of corruption are considerable. With regard to the fact that police always retain the discretion to "look the other way", one must additionally concede that the principle of equality before the law becomes endangered further, the more options individual police officers have.

Establishing such powers is also a clear breach of the principle of legality, fundamental to many of the systems.

However, precisely because the police will always retain an uncontrollable discretion to "look the other way", in a situation of system over-loading, there may be a strong need to regulate this kind of practice closely in order to provide some control and equality before the law of any sort. If a system is unable to cope with its workload, ways will be found to do so. If no other is provided, individual members of the system "looking the other way" whenever their subjective instinct tells them it would not be so bad to do so, may remain the only option. It is only really the police who are in a position to do so. Given this possibility, it is surely understandable that officers do not continue completing cases, they presume will meet no response anyway. In other words, all the objections listed above may apply equally, if not more strongly, to unregulated reality. Where further resources are not (made) available in order to deal with all offences, the legislature or the controlling institutions providing more pragmatic solutions to deal with the problems faced, will probably end up with a better controlled, more equal and principled response than would result from sticking rigidly to legal fundamentals, to which practice is paying lip-service at most. Good police training and some form of PPS control of these measures must, however, be provided for. If this option is taken, only overt provision can ensure effective regulation.

As legally ambiguous as these kind of "quasi-punishing" procedures may be, they do provide the CJS with a wider range of more flexible and faster responses to deal with suspects informally as a first step and to send a warning signal without imposing the full stigma and stress of a full criminal trial and ensuing record.

4 Prosecution Power and the Use of Discretion

As has been seen in the previous section, some discretion has been given to police forces in some jurisdictions in order to be able to deal with cases more effectively. This study set out to analyse the prosecutorial role; the police powers examined may provide a substitute and are certainly a pre-determinant in relation to this role. The central premise of this study is that prosecution services across Europe are becoming increasingly powerful; legally and/or factually. This premise was based upon observations made within the European Sourcebook framework, which indicated a shift of case-ending decisions from the court to the prosecution level . The basic idea is that stated in the introduction of this paper (see also Jehle in this volume); that the CJS is a chain and if one level is over-loaded, the level before will logically exercise discretion in what is passing on. The system is hydraulic; more pressure from above will force greater cracks (through which cases are passed out of the system) further down. The plausibility of this idea is confirmed by our observations at the police stage, where certain powers previously ascribed to the PPS can now be seen in police use in many jurisdictions. The European Sourcebook findings indicated a trend towards cases being ended by PPS discretion rather than public charges being brought. This is what is often called for in order to counter CJS over-loading (see e.g. Tak, 2005). If responsibility is passed down to a lower level in the CJS one would assume that this will be restricted to less serious cases because only so much responsibility is passed down to ensure the upper levels, and thus the system as a whole, can function.

It should be stated that this study never saw prosecutorial discretion as the only or natural solution to the problems systems claim to be facing; as documented by Jehle (2000) three potential paths for overloaded systems to find relief are recognised: the alternatives material decriminalisation and increased resources being made available are, however, the less likely options in the current west European contexts. Despite the use of a certain degree of decriminalisation in most jurisdictions as illustrated above, this study identifies a trend, if any, towards further, not less, criminalisation in European legal systems today (see developments surrounding the Wykrozenia in Poland and public order disturbances in England and Wales and France). The only politically viable option appears to be the expansion of prosecutorial power. The study premise is that this can potentially happen through two paths: directly through increased prosecutorial power to end cases directly itself or increased power to influence court decisions. The latter can be aided legally by creating special procedural paths on which evidence prepared by the prosecutor becomes central, but a factual shift of power can also occur in that the courts simply lend prosecution service's evidence more weight. Both of these paths were examined.

4.1 Prosecutorial Power to End Cases

As one would expect, all of the prosecution services studied have the power to decide not to take a case to court if they regard it as evidentially insufficient. Such a power is the very point of having a prosecution service and entirely in line with the principle of legality. Where there is not sufficient evidence or grounds to believe that a court may find a person guilty of the offence s/he is accused of, the prosecution service sees to it, that the case is not brought to court. The prosecution service acts as the courts' filter.

As can be seen in table 16, however, the prosecution service performs this task beyond simply evaluating the sufficiency of evidence. It is the PPS which drops a case in which no offender has been found in all countries but in the Netherlands (where the case remains open), which ensures that a prosecution does not fall foul to a statute of limitation (i.e. that the time in which a prosecution may be brought has not expired), in Germany and Poland the PPS will check that no amnesty has been granted and in all study countries it is the PPS which is responsible for ensuring that the "ne bis in idem" rule is observed. Where a victim's agreement is required to proceed (this may be the case in all jurisdictions but England and Wales), it is the PPS who will halt a case, if this is not provided. In all the jurisdictions examined therefore, the PPS has the basic role of ensuring the parameters for a court decision are present. If it judges evidence not to be strong enough, or if there is any other technical, legal impediment to a court making a convicting judgement, it is the PPS' role to ensure court time is not spent on the case.

Going beyond this central task, all except the Polish PPS have powers to consider dropping a case on what we refer to as public interest or policy grounds. In fact, the British PPS is obliged to consider dropping a case on these grounds. As can be seen in the national reports, the grounds upon which and the extent to which cases are dropped upon such grounds is a matter of considerable variation. How such powers are used in practice will be subject to more intense scrutiny below. The fact is, however, that such considerations go beyond the principle of legality and the core prosecution function. Immediately we can see that across Europe – excepting Poland and its criminal procedure code as it currently stands (previously it was not exceptional in this regard) – the PPS has been given discretionary powers to stop a prosecution, i.e. to end a case on grounds beyond a technical or legal judgement as to its suitability for a court judgement.

Table 16. Prosecution Power

PPS can/must drop because	EW	FR	DE	NL	PL	SE
No offender found[a]	Must[b] ▲	Must ■ ▲	Must ■	N.a.	Must	Can ■
Insufficient evidence	Must[b] ▲	Must ■ ▲	Must[c] ■	Can[d] ■	Must	Must ■ ▲
Statute of limitation	Must	Must	Must	Must	N.a.	Must
Amnesty	[e]	[f]	Must		Must	N.a.
Ne bis in idem	Must	Must	Must	Must	Must	Must[g]
No victim agreement (required by law)		Must ■	Can/Must[h] ■ ▲[i]	Must	Must	Must ■
Public interest	Must[b*] ▲	Can ■ ▲	Can[j] ■[k]	Can	N.a.	Can[l] ■ ▲
Policy	Must[b*] ▲	Can ▲	Can[m]	Can	N.a.	[n]
A private prosecution without PPS-reference is	Possible	Possible	Possible[o]	Not possible		Not possible[p]

■ case can be reopened ▲ alternative prosecution possible by victim
[*] within the boundaries defined in guidelines

[a] General explanation: in the Netherlands there is no case ending decision as such: an investigation is stopped because it cannot proceed any further, the case is not actively dropped, this is also true for EW. In France this is an official drop made by an active decision. In Sweden the legal status isn't clear and an investigation can remain open. If someone was identified as a suspect but later regarded as innocent, the PPS in the Netherlands may and sometimes does go to court because it is in the person's interest to be found "not guilty". This is possible because the system fundamentally says that only a judge can decide whether evidence is insufficient or not. In such cases the PPS pleads not guilty. In all other systems charges would not be brought in such cases.

[b] An alternative prosecution is possible by other.

[c] In accordance with § 170 StPO the PPS brings a public charge when investigations provide sufficient grounds to do so. I.e. when the evidence available to support the act the suspect is accused of is such that a conviction is to be expected. Otherwise the PPS will drop the case (§ 170 II StPO) in accordance with the principle of legality.

[d] Legally the PPS can bring the case before court, but normally the PPS will drop.

[e] The PPS doesn't have to apply a test of this kind.

[f] PPS doesn't apply a test of this kind. Amnesty is generally linked to the actual sentence.

[g] If the prosecuted person was sentenced for the offence in question in a foreign country, prosecution in Sweden is possible under certain circumstances.

[h] It is basically irrelevant whether or not the victim agrees to a prosecution. The so-called "Antragsdelikte" (application offences) are an exception to this. If no application is made for prosecution/charges to be pressed in relation to one of the absolute application offences, the PPS is not permitted to prosecute. In cases of relative application offences the PPS can nevertheless bring charges if it regards this as justified due to the strength of public interest.

The question as to what criteria form the basis for public interest or policy-related decisions is a complex one with a variety of answers. We do, however, group these powers in one category because they are fundamentally an exception or limitation to the principle of legality, which allow the PPSs to bring non-evidential criteria into the decision to take a case to court or not. In Sweden, the law explicitly includes a PPS consideration as to whether it is worth bringing a case to court – in terms of the economic cost of a trial in relation to the harm done to society by the offence –, other jurisdictions are a long way from explicitly condoning such a role. With the exception of Poland, however, all the jurisdictions studied have made an overt declaration that they expect their prosecution services not only to examine a case's legal merits in deciding whether it should be brought to court, but also to consider certain factors which may lead to a decision that it is not *worth* bringing a case before court. This may be subject to strong limitations,

---

[i] Even when the victim doesn't press charges where this is a pre-condition for a public prosecution, this doesn't necessarily exclude a prosecution by the victim by other means. In accordance with § 374 StPO the victim can pursue a private prosecution without involving the PPS beforehand. This path is, however, available only for the following offences: trespass, defamation/breach of postal secrecy, bodily injury, threat, corruption or bribery in a business context, criminal damage. This list is not restricted to the application offences, as it was previously (it includes, e.g., threat) but the majority are such offences.

[j] The basic assumption is that there is public interest in a prosecution. Therefore proceedings may only exceptionally be dropped/disposed of, namely only when it is a case of a less serious crime ("Vergehen"), the perpetrator's guilt is of a minor nature and there is no public interest in prosecution (§ 153 I StPO).

[k] By law, in exceptional cases, no court approval is necessary if the case is of a "Vergehen" for which the minimum punishment is not heightened and the consequences of the act are minor (§ 153 I 2 StPO). In practice, this is the normal case.

[l] Must – or may – be tested only concerning the offences where the legislator decided that the public interest is a pre-requisite for prosecution, i.e. these provisions are to be found in substantive criminal law, not as a general rule for a certain category of offences, but as an ad hoc rule for a number of offences. The public interest (or lack of public interest) is obviously the reason behind some of the provisions that allow a prosecution to be dropped.

[m] Political orders can cause the PPS to drop/dispose but the PPS cannot be forced not to press charges. The finality of this decision depends on the norm in accordance to which it is made and whether court approval is necessary.

[n] Reference to a private prosecution is a drop/disposal of the proceedings because the public interest is denied in the prosecution of an offence for which a private prosecution is possible (§ 376 StPO), i.e. the need for a public trial is denied. Nevertheless the PPS can take over the proceedings at any stage, § 377 I. In this case the private prosecutor loses this role and can participate only as a "Nebenkläger", should s/he attach proceedings in accordance with § 396 StPO and be among those entitled to do so as listed in § 395.

[o] Policy issued is considered as part of the public interest test.

[p] The PPS does not have to refer a case actively. Where the PPS drops a case, the victim is generally allowed to prosecute. The only exception is insult, which is only prosecutable by private prosecution.

may be closely defined, but it is nevertheless a fundamental step, a decision to require the PPS to make a *value*-judgement, which we regard as a decision considering wider criteria as to what is in the *public's best interest* and so we refer to such decisions as "public interest" ones. This vocabulary might not fit easily in all systems, but it is used to describe the PPS balancing the interest in going to court, with other factors relevant to the good of society. It should be a decision which is in the public's interest. This is the first step to creating a judge before the judge and a far more pragmatic approach to criminal justice.

Table16 also lends us some idea of the faith placed in the PPS and thus of the status of it's decisions. In several cases, where the PPS has decided a case should no longer be pursued, it has the final word. The PPS is trusted to make final, legally binding judgements. This status is strengthened in the Netherlands and Sweden in that the PPS has an absolute monopoly over taking cases to court. It is not possible for any other party to attempt to bring a case the PPS has decided to drop to court. The deciding power lent to the PPS is considerable. In England and Wales – generally –, France and Germany – in relation to certain offences –, private parties retain the right to bring cases to court themselves where they feel the PPS has made a mistake in deciding not to do so. This at least tells us that the legal system is not resting its faith solely in the PPS to ensure all cases which should be, are, in fact, brought to court. However, as the study reports show (see also table 17), a right to bring a case by no means enables a private party to bring a successful prosecution. It is the PPS which decides whether to devote public resources to bringing a case to court. If a private party wishes to bring a case independently, s/he bears the financial risk of doing so and faces a sometimes Herculean task in attempting to gather enough evidence for a successful prosecution. Thus we see PPS drops with a referral to private prosecution – i.e. even those cases which the PPS regards as fundamentally worthy of a prosecution, but judges the interests being such that not the public, but only those personally affected have an interest in further pursuing the case – as being a case-ending decision in the vast majority of cases. Whether or not it has the legal monopoly over prosecutions, it appears fair to conclude that the PPS, at least factually, has the monopoly to decide whether a prosecution with any real chance of a resulting conviction, will be brought in the vast majority of cases. The prosecution service makes the key decision as to whether certain behaviour or events are to be regarded as potentially criminally sanctionable.

Where the PPS has discretionary powers to drop or dispose of cases (in all countries studies except Poland) this is regulated by law, and in more detail, by guidelines. In England & Wales, the Netherlands and Sweden, these are issued by the operational heads of service, in France and Germany at a regional and local level although in Germany the main regulation occurs through ministerial guidelines at state (as opposed to federal) level. In other words, the PPSs are lent considerable powers by law, but how these are used is always defined more closely by guidelines to ensure uniform application in line with defined public interest and or policy considerations.

Table 17. Private Prosecution

Frequency of use (as a proportion of all cases)	EW N.d.a.	FR N.d.a.	DE	NL (Not possible)	PL N.d.a.	SE N.d.a.
Never						
Rarely < 1 %	X					X[a]
Regularly 1–10 %			X			
Frequently > 10 %		X[b]				

[a] Reference is made to the answers concerning the right of the victim to take over the prosecution in court.
[b] There is no statistical information. Legal aid is available to bring these actions (magistrates complain that they are used too frequently so the conditional disposal is an attempt to consider the victim more strongly).

4.2 Discretionary Prosecutorial Powers

This study has identified two types of discretionary power being given to the prosecution services across Europe: 1) the drop (public interest) which enables the PPS to halt a prosecution for public interest reasons with no further action ensuing and 2) the conditional disposal, which means that the PPS halts a prosecution attaching a condition to the case being closed.

4.2.1 The Drop (Public Interest)

The drop (public interest) is available in all of the countries studied except Poland (in Sweden the requirement is that a prosecution of certain offences may only take place in so far as there is public interest in a prosecution, where this is not the case, the police or prosecution service will refrain from recording the case. Thus no information is available on these kinds of drops). Table 18 shows the conditions for its use. The presumption is that the suspect is guilty and this presumption will, of course, be noted in internal files and so will remain visible should the suspect become the subject of criminal proceedings in the future. Where this is the case, it will be less likely that this future case is dropped with no further action taken. The use of such drops is restricted to cases of a less serious nature, in which the PPS will presumably expect this decision to be acceptable to all concerned. Because the presumption of guilt remains, the lack of ability to appeal against such decisions (as is found, e.g. in Germany) should be regarded critically. The fact is: a slur remains and should the person be subject to investigation again, the "no smoke without fire" attitude will be to his/her disadvantage. Naturally one can argue about the practical relevance of such problems, also about whether a drop which is categorised as on evidential grounds is so much less prejudicial than one on public interest grounds. Nevertheless a presumption of guilt is attached to a person, based upon legally trained, prosecutorial judgement and this is recorded. If one suspects that prosecutors are using such drops without strict adherence to the legal parameters (see for example Kilchling's suspicion that PPs prefer this form to an evidentially based drop because victims can attempt to force a charge being brought after the latter (Kilchling, 2000)), one should recognise a creeping change in the system. It means that PPs are invoking a slight slur, in very minor cases, with a significant risk that innocent persons will also be affected, for the sake of efficiency. This represents a change of priorities for all systems of a fundamental legal nature. Any involvement in the criminal process invokes a slur, but such legally founded presumptions, recorded in non-public files should not be shrugged off altogether. It is not without reason that the Dutch PPS is reported as consciously taking cases to court in order to wholly exonerate the suspect.

Table 18. Conditions for a Drop (Public Interest)

		EW		FR	DE	NL	PL N.a.	SE[a] N.d.a.
		Public interest	Caution					
Recorded in	Criminal register					X[b]		
	PPS register	X		X[c]	X	X		
	Police register	X	X					
In later investigations access for	Court					X		
	PPS	X		X[c]	X	X		
	Police	X			X	X		
	Potential employer							
Suspect must actively agree			X					
Suspect has right to reject								
Victim must actively agree								
Court approval necessary					[d]			

[a] PPS drop is not registered.
[b] CJS access only. Can distinguish whether drop on legal/factual grounds or public interest because entry is for a different paragraph.
[c] There is only an electronic file, which is accessible locally.
[d] By law, in exceptional cases, no approval is necessary if the case is of a "Vergehen" for which the minimum punishment is not heightened and the consequences of the act are minor (§ 153 I 2 StPO). In practice, this is the normal case.

Table 19. A Drop (Public Interest) is usually Used for

	EW		FR	DE	NL	PL	SE
	Public interest[a]	Caution	N.d.a.		N.d.a.	N.d.a.	N.d.a.
Petty theft		X		X[b]			
Cannabis possession - personal use		X		X[c]			
Traffic offences							
Less serious violent offences		X					
Minor property offences				X[b]			
1st time offender		X		X[d]			
Recidivist							
Suspect with addiction							
Female suspects							
Suspects with psychiatric problems							

[a] No figures, but in cases, where the suspect is terminally ill, old (esp. female), ill with certain problems such as Alzheimer's, etc.

[b] Basically a drop (no public interest) in accordance with § 153 StPO is available for all the offences listed. The PPS will always have to decide whether a prosecution is appropriate. This is the case as soon as there is public interest in a prosecution. For property related and assets related offences a drop (no public interest) should be used: Where the value of the damage done or of the matter concerned does not exceed, e.g. 50,- DM/25,- € (approx. – this value boundary is subject to considerable variation from state to state) and the damage, in so far as any was caused, has been made good.

[c] In this case, a drop (public interest) occurs in accordance not with the general rules but with special a drug offence related regulation (§ 31a BtMG) – related to possession for personal use.

[d] A drop (no public interest) in accordance with § 153 StPO is first and foremost to be considered for first time offenders. When particular circumstances apply it is not excluded for repeat offenders.

The extent to which efficiency is a criterion the PPS is overtly required to consider varies. The Swedish law lays it out as a criterion, others regard efficiency alone as an illegitimate consideration although it is difficult to avoid the impression that it must play a role, at least at the back of a PP's mind. All systems do allow its consideration where a suspect is subject to more than one charge. Where a PP recognises that the charge being brought or the punishment likely to ensue is irrelevant or insignificant in comparison to other charges being brought or sanctions sought, s/he is expected to drop the charges, request that the court do so or bring the charges together in joinder proceedings. In this regard, all the PPSs examined are charged with ensuring court time, in regard to any one suspect, is used efficiently.

A public interest drop is available in Germany for all less serious offences and tends to be used for petty theft, cannabis possession and minor property offences. Interestingly this is the same pattern that can be seen in relation to the use of cautioning in England & Wales (see table 19).

Table 20. The Form in Which the Decision to Drop is Made:

	EW		FR	DE	NL	PL	SE
	Public interest	Caution			N.a.		N.a.[a]
Box ticked – standard form	X	X	X[b]				
In writing – standardised form						X[c]	
Written description/ explanation				X		X[d]	
Written explanation + file + statement from defence							
In connection with a brief court hearing							

[a] The drop is made by a decision not to record the offence.
[b] Differentiated so legal and public interest drop difference evident.
[c] Simple note that case dropped in file for all offences subject to an investigation.
[d] Full explanation must be made for offences subject to an inquiry.

As can be seen from table 20, this decision is recorded cursorily in England & Wales and France. It appears that intense scrutiny is not expected nor regarded as necessary. In Germany this is, however, subject to court approval in all but the most minor of cases, so a check of sorts exists, although in practice it is rare that prosecution decisions are not accepted. The Polish form, as one would expect, allows greater scrutiny to enable the judicial scrutiny required.

4.2.2 Conditional Disposals

The study regards the PPS as making a conditional disposal when the PP halts proceedings, but attaches certain conditions to this halting. This is a power available in all the jurisdictions studied except Poland (it was withdrawn from the PPS in 1997 – in so far Poland, at the legal level at least, is bucking the trend towards more prosecutorial power, a phenomenon regarded as highly problematic there after the experiences under communist regimes, and is returning to the principle of mandatory prosecution). In England and Wales it should further be noted, it is a power formally held by the police (cautioning, cautioning plus etc.). Factually it can be regarded as increasingly in joint hands with the PPS as the two agencies are working more and more closely together. As the PPS now has statutory responsibility for charging (since autumn 2005), their influence on this decision will have grown even stronger (a PP can now inform a police officer that s/he regards a charge as inappropriate, recommending that a caution/caution plus should be used instead). A political discussion is underway as to whether the PPS should be given diversionary powers of their own. The prosecution service in Sweden is also exceptional in that it does not only impose a condition, but, in fact, independently convicts a person and imposes a true sanction. In other words, the PPS there has even stronger decision making powers than those discussed here for which reason they are dealt with in the next section.

Table 21 shows the forms of conditional disposal available in the jurisdictions studied, what pre-conditions are required and what consequences follow.

In theory at least, the halting of proceedings is conditional upon the suspect accepting certain conditions and complying with these; i.e. if s/he does not fulfill them, the case will be brought to court. In some cases victim and/or court agreement is also required. Where the condition is complied with, the state right to prosecute for the offence committed is spent. There is a presumption of guilt, which the person acknowledges by fulfilling the condition, and herewith goes some way to repairing the damage done to society or at least removing any public interest in a "full" prosecution. There is no formal admission of guilt and no conviction. The person is *presumed* to be but not *found guilty*, he or she complies with a kind of sanction voluntarily, but no sanction in the true sense is imposed. There is a trade-off of sorts; almost guilty and almost punished – justice, almost to traditional standards, but without a court. The worst consequences for the offender are avoided (the "sanction" is usually less severe, there is no public hearing and no condemnation or slur invoked publicly) and the state saves court time and precious resources. a legal consequence is imposed, not by a judge however and thus ne bis in idem questions arise (what of the person caught smuggling narcotics in a border region facing charges in one state having fulfilled the conditions of a conditional disposal in the other?). Is this decision binding for other jurisdictions (which may actively have decided against the use of such mechanisms)? Beyond these problems, this is a very efficient solution. It is regarded as more desirable than a public interest drop because the presumed offender is required to make some amends. A justice of sorts is achieved, the criminal justice system is seen to react but not overly harshly. As we shall see these disposals are only legally available and factually used for certain offences and types of offender.

Table 21 also shows, however, that a stigma of sorts remains should the person subjected to the disposal come to the attention of the criminal justice system again. S/he is presumed to have been guilty (and has indeed performed actions based upon a willingness to accept this presumption of guilt). The law prescribes that the suspect should not be treated as a recidivist, but the system is unlikely to treat him or her as a first-time offender (which at the same time is not desired politically). There is a sanction and a record of sorts.

Naturally the PPS cannot impose this type of case ending entirely according to the individual PP's will. Other parties are clearly involved. However, it is apparent that the PPS will be key in deciding whether such a solution can be strived for (naturally bound by guidelines and legal parameters set) and its suggestions will be complied with in most cases.

Table 21. Regulation of Conditional Disposals*

		EW	FR				DE	NL		PL	SE[a]
		N. a.	"Alternatives"			Comp. Pénale[b]	§ 153 a	Transactie	Cond. Disposal		
			Rappel a loi	Injonc-tion	Méd. pénale						
Requires admission of guilt					X[c]					X	X
Recorded in	Criminal register					X[d]		X	X	X	X
	Court register							X	X		
	PPS register		X	X	X	X	X	X	X		
	Police register										
In later investigations access for	Court					X[e]		X	X	X	X
	PPS		X	X	X	X	X	X	X	X	X
	Police						X	X	X	X	X
	Potential employer					X[f]				X	
Suspect must actively agree					X[g]	X[h]	X[i]	X			
Suspect has right to reject			X	X	X	X			X	X	X[j]
Victim must actively agree			X[k]		X						
Victim has right to appeal								X	X		X
Court approval necessary						X[l]	X[m]				

* footnote in annex 8

Table 22. A Conditional Disposal is usually Used for/usually Leads to*

	EW N.a.	FR				DE	NL		PL N.d.a.	SE
		Rappel a loi	Injonction	Méd. pénale	Comp. pénale[a]		Transactie	Cond. disposal N.d.a.		
Petty theft		X[b]			X[c]		X[d]			X
Cannabis possession - personal use			X[e]		X[a]		X[b]			X
Traffic offences			X[f]		X[a]	X[g]	X[b]			X
Less serious violent offences				X[h]	X[a]	X[g]	X[b]			
Minor property offences					X[a]	X[g]	X[b]			X
1st time offender		X	X	X[i]		X[j]				X
Recidivist				X[k]	[l]					
Suspect with addiction										
Female suspects										
Suspects with psychiatric problems										
Fine/payment to					X[m]	X	X			
Confiscation/seizure							X			
Mediation				X		X				
Retribution		X				[n]	X			
Community service					X[o]	[p]	X			
Addiction treatment		X								
Psychiatric treatment										

* footnote in annex 9

The types of condition imposed can be seen in table 22. This displays the PPS as having a range of options in deciding how best to deal with offenders (see also table 29 below). On the continent, this emerges as the mechanism used to deal with offenders who are regarded as requiring something other than classical punishment (e.g. treatment, a warning, an opportunity to learn whilst making good their offence). The most frequently imposed condition is a payment to the state or a charitable organisation – this requirement to make a payment is regarded as entirely different to a fine imposed as a sanction; at least legally. It would be wrong, however, to conclude that the Polish, British or Swedish PPS are not involved in the mechanisms for achieving such goals for suspects in their respective countries. These systems are different; often requiring the PPS to make the decision as to which reaction should follow, but PPs are required to make an application for a court order for e.g., mediation, community service, addiction treatment, etc. Effectively the service's roles are likely to be similar and, as such, so are the thought processes an individual prosecutor has when deciding how to handle cases. In France, Germany and the Netherlands it is clear, however, that the PPS is regarded as capable of making such decisions alone at least in less serious cases. This says a great deal about the PPS' status in those jurisdictions. The PPS are increasingly regarded as the right institution to decide on tailor-made, quasi-punishment and treatment of offenders. The result is a criminal justice institution initiating decisive intervention in the lives of suspected offenders, with an ability to do so detached from any hard and fast question of guilt. The state's intervention in its (presumably) erring subject's rights is happening faster and more simply than was previously considered acceptable. This is justified with the voluntary nature of the situation for the presumed offender. For many, above all first time offenders and those accused of less serious offences, the PPS is the decisive instance in orchestrating this intervention.

The next few years will be decisive in establishing whether this is a role also to be assumed by the English and Welsh PPS, most likely in co-operation with the police, as the decision is made as to whether the CPS should be given such diversionary powers or not. How much or how little power the Polish PPS wields factually is yet to be seen.

Table 22 shows clearly that these kinds of disposals are used for all kinds of less serious offences, re-enforcing the impression that this is a flexible, decisive criminal justice tool being used to deal with less serious offences and those suspected of having committed them.

Table 23 shows how such decisions are made. Usually they are not such to allow detailed scrutiny. Thus it is clear that PPS decisions have a very high status and challenges are not generally expected.

Table 23. Form in Which the Decision to Drop/Dispose is Made:

	EW	FR				DE	NL		PL	SE
		Rappel a loi	Injonc-tion	Méd. pénale	Comp. pénale[a]		Transactie	Cond. disp.		
By ticking a box – standardised form		X[b]	X	X			X	X		
In writing – standardised form		X[c]	X	X					X	X
By written description/explanation						X				
By written explanation, file + statement from defence					X					
Possibly with brief hearing					X[d]					X

[a] Stage, med. treatment, Tâche d'intérêt public.
[b] Final decision.
[c] Request to the "délégué du procureur".
[d] If president of Tribunal (or accused until 2004) requests it.

5 Alternative Court Procedures

Table 24. Alternative Proceedings Available

		EW	FR	DE	NL	PL	SE
Penal order			X	X		X	X
Trial after guilty plea		X[a]	X[b]			X	[c]
Accel-erated pro-ceed-ings	Simplification in pre-trial stage		X[d]	X	X[e]		
	Simplification during interlocu-tory proceedings			X			
	Simplification during trial	X[f]	X[g]				
Judge joining trials in court			X		X		

[a] Trial is shorter, or little evidence is needed; used before Magistrates' Court: 75 % in 2004; used before Crown Court: 65 % in 2004.
[b] The CRPC is meant here. It is not equal with the English trial after guilty plea.
[c] There is no special procedure and no procedural rule, but if the defendant confesses, the hearing factually is simpler because less witnesses must be heard.
[d] No EM, stage though pre-trial detention is possible.
[e] AU proceedings, written charge done by standard computer printout.
[f] For a large number of summary offences after guilty plea (fast-tracked cases).
[g] Shorter hearing in practice.

Table 24 shows the forms of alternative procedures involving the courts available in the jurisdictions studied.

Alternative court procedures refer to those which are decided by a court after proceedings which involve short cuts and timesaving mechanisms when compared to a full, "normal" trial. These were examined closely in the course of the study and judged to be an effective PPS decision because of the influence borne by the PPS in deciding what evidence is presented to the court and the rarity with which courts refuse to follow the PPS's suggestions.

5.1 Penal Order Proceedings

The most important procedural form of this type is what we refer to as a penal order. It is to be found in France (Ordonnance Penale), Germany (Strafbefehl), Poland (Nakaz karny) and Sweden (Strafförelaggande) and is categorised by this study as providing for a PPS imposed sanction. The person subjected to it is considered guilty, given a punishment and a criminal record ensues. Considering the changes made to the Polish system, which actively aim at strengthening the court and weakening the PPS position, one might have expected penal order proceedings to represent a true court decision, but the study results show that the general European trend is followed. Time pressure causes the courts to accept PPS assessment of the case.

The Swedish penal order is very straight forward in that it is, in fact, also formally a PPS decision. The person subject to it is declared guilty and a punishment imposed. The PPS assumes a court role and imposes a sanction. We have grouped the French, German and Polish forms in this same group because, though formally a court decision, we effectively see a PPS enforced sanction, rubber-stamped by a court, in the vast majority of cases. In these proceedings the PPS (or in the case of the French Contraventions 1–4th class, the police) submit written evidence in standardised form, requesting that the court impose a specific sanction. The court can either accept this application or reject it, therewith submitting the case for a full trial. This happens so rarely and the PPS position is so strong, that this study evaluates such proceedings as the PPS effectively pre-forming court decisions.

The suspect retains the right to protest against such decisions; s/he is required to lodge a protest within a fairly limited time-frame (between 8 days and 1 month), in which case a full trial ensues. Only in the Swedish case must the suspect's agreement be actively sought. The question as to in how far the person subjected to such proceedings fully understands what s/he is agreeing to, or failing to protest against, remains to be examined.

Table 25. Regulation of Penal Orders[*]

		EW N.a.	FR[a]	DE	NL N.a.	PL	SE
Recorded in	Criminal register		X	X		X	X
	PPS register		X				
	Police register						
In later investigations access for	Court		X	X		X	X
	PPS		X	X		X	X
	Police			X		X	X
	Potential employer			b		b	c
Suspect must actively agree							X[d]
Suspect has right to reject			X[e]	X[f]		X	
Victim must actively agree			g				
Court approval necessary**			X***	X[h]***		X	

* Leading to a conviction.

** Formally a court decision factually is merely approval of a PPS decision. For this reason considered at PPS level.

*** NB court can only accept or reject PPS suggestion in its entirety.

[a] Ordonnance pénale.

[b] The provision of a police record is frequently a pre-condition for employment. A person may apply for a certificate containing the relevant information from the Federal Central Register (in accordance with § 30 BZRG). The certificates for private (§ 30 I BZRG) and official functions (§§ 30 V, 31 BZRG) are different. "Private certificates" only contain a limited excerpt of potential entries (selection in accordance to the type of sanction, its level, time limits and first-time sanctions). The certificate for official purposes goes beyond this (§§ 32 III, IV BZRG).

[c] The employer doesn't have access to the criminal register, but he can ask the applicant for an excerpt of the register.

[d] Suspect must actively agree. If suspect refuses his consent the case will go to court.

[e] Suspect's consent is tacit. If the suspect asks for a public trial, the case will go to court.

[f] Suspect's agreement is not necessary before, but he has the possibility to object to the penal order after it has been issued. Then the case will go to court.

[g] Cannot be used for offences involving a victim.

[h] Formally the penal order is a court decision, in practice it is a PPS decision, because the court refuses its consent only in 3–5 %.

Table 26. Penal Order is Used for/usually Leads to

	EW N.a.	FR[a]	DE	NL N.a.	PL N.d.a.	SE
Petty theft						X
Cannabis possession - personal use						X
Traffic offences		X[b]	X[c]			X
Less serious violent offences			X			X
Minor property offences			X			X
Recidivist		X[d]	X[e]			X[f]
Suspect with addiction						
Suspects with psychiatric problems						
Imprisonment						
Prison sentence suspended						X[g]
Fine/payment to		X[h]	X			X
Mediation						
Retribution						
Community Service						
Addiction Treatment						
Psychiatric Treatment						
Suspension of driving licence						

[a] "Ordonannce pénale" is meant. This is just a legal statement.

[b] Penal order on PPS stage seems to be appropriate for traffic offences. In cases of minor property offences/less serious violent offences a penal order by police is possible.

[c] An application for a penal order is only not granted when main proceedings seem necessary to enable the complete understanding of all circumstances relevant to the legal consequence or for reasons of general or individual crime prevention. Therefore this procedure is available for all offences. The guidelines do not exclude its use for certain offence groups either. It is to be assumed that the penal order procedure is usually used for traffic, minor property and less serious violent offences.

[d] It is also possible for recidivist suspects, but the main sanction must be a fine.

[e] Penal order proceedings are not restricted to particular offender groups either. It may well be used for recidivist, is very unlikely to be used for offenders with addiction or psychiatrics problems.

[f] The penal order can be used for recidivist, if – despite of the recidivism – the sentence still can be fines.

[g] Conditional sentence.

[h] Other sanctions may be imposed together with a fine but not as a main sanction.

As can be seen in the questionnaires and country reports, such proceedings can only be used for certain offences and in order to impose a limited range of sanctions. Theoretically at least, however, short custodial sentences fall within this range. Table 26 shows actual practice using penal order proceedings more restrictively. Except in Sweden, the penal order is usually used for traffic offences and in order to impose fines. Its use is not excluded in relation to recidivists, its use is more likely against 1st time offenders, however. In Sweden its use is more varied. If one recalls that the Swedish PP cannot fall back on the range of conditional disposals available in the other countries this variation may seem natural.

5.2 Accelerated Procedures

Alongside the penal order there are further forms which allow other procedural short cuts. In the countries in which the penal order is available, their use is limited so they are of lesser importance – e.g. Beschleunigtes Verfahren in Germany. They remain as PPS driven vehicles in which the court's decision is pre-formed and they may be used more frequently in the future. Table 27 displays under what circumstances they may be used and that more severe sanctions, including significant custodial sentences, are possible.

As table 27 shows, however, the level of court scrutiny expected is considerable. This is possibly the decisive reason as to why such proceedings are not particularly frequent in many cases. It may well be that the PPS sees little to be gained from using such, rather than the "normal" trial mechanisms.

The English & Welsh form of "bulk-proceedings" requires special attention. In these the PPS or the relevant prosecutorial agency (the TV licensing authority, etc.) submits a list of names of people to be convicted for certain offences (e.g. of having a TV without having paid the license fee) whom the court will find guilty. In this way, thousands of offenders are processed during one afternoon session and found guilty upon PPS (or equivalent) request. It is difficult to imagine a procedural form in which a court decision is pre-formed more strongly.

Table 28 illustrates the procedural short cuts these proceedings provide. No real common trend can be seen.

Table 27. Conditions for the Use of Accelerated Proceedings

	EW[a]	FR		DE	NL	PL	SE N.a.[b]
		CRPC[c]	Comp. immed.[d]				
Defendant has confessed	X	X[e]		[f]		X	
Case is simple & clear	X	X[e]	X	X[g]	X[h]	X	
Fine only possible penalty	X						
Penalty max.		12 M.i.*	12 M.i.	12 M.i.[i]	12 M.i.	12 M.i.	
For a restricted catalogue of offences	X[e]	[j]	[l]	[k]	X[l]		
When defendant agrees		X[m]				X	
Court actively has to approve use of proceedings (will consider whether pre-conditions fulfilled)	X	X	[n]	X		X	

* M.i. = month imprisonment

a It is usual in practice but not required by law.
b There aren't quicker procedural paths at court stage.
c Since 2004.
d Abbreviation for composition immediate.
e It is required by law.
f But it is usual in practice.
g It is usual in practice but also required by law.
h Only these ones, which fall under the competence of the police/juvenile judge. The cases have to be simple especially in regard to the evidence and the enforcement of the law.
i It is required by law.
j Maximum penalty incurred = 5 years imprisonment, some specific offences are excluded, also minors.
k There are catalogues of offences defined in guidelines.
l Offences against order and crimes.
m Has to agree with the procedure and the penalty.
n Court has not to approve actively but should consider particular the legality of the assent.

Table 28. PPS Role in Accelerated Proceedings

	EW	FR		DE	NL N.a.	PL	SE N.a.
		CRPC[a]	Comp. immed.				
Written evidence only - PPS prepares case	X[b]	[c]	X	[d]			
Effectively pre-forms court decision	X	N.a.				X	
Suggests a sentence which court can only accept or reject proceedings entirely		X		[d]		X	
Written charge							
Writes charge in standardised form		X	X[e]				
Lodges charge orally				X			

[a] Comparation sur reconnaissance de culpabilité, existing since 2004.
[b] There is always an oral hearing.
[c] There is (only) an offender hearing, not a usual hearing.
[d] Accelerated proceedings do not vary from "normal" proceedings relating to these points. Nevertheless they allow proceedings to be carried out more swiftly as e.g. no written charge is required and the main hearing is carried out immediately or after a very brief period of time. Additionally the proceedings themselves involve certain simplifications, e.g. simplified presentation of evidence.
[e] Mainly written evidence.

5.3 Conclusions

Many offenders who are formally dealt with by court decision are in fact subject to a sanction decided upon by the PPS after a PP has reviewed the facts of a case and come to the conclusion that the offender is guilty. This will not be the case in more serious cases, but numerically the proportion is very high. The PP is not merely the judge before the judge in such cases; s/he is effectively the judge, leading the judicial hand in signing an order to punish. This may not be wrong; in the vast majority of cases one can assume that a factually guilty person is receiving a suitable sanction, as efficiently as possible. Judges do reject a small proportion of cases and there is no reason to assume that they are not ensuring the general parameters of such proceedings are correct. Where they feel the need for more information before making a decision, they can demand it; where a suspect feels unfairly treated, s/he can insist upon a full trial. Nevertheless two statements remain true: The court and PPS function is fundamentally changed. It is the PP who is expected to form an opinion as to guilt and who will decide what a suitable punishment will be. Judges, working under time pressure, have a serious disincentive to question this PPS judgement.

If one considers that many suspects may not understand the consequences of inaction, together with the relatively short period of time in which they can lodge a protest, the one-sided situation in which the decision over guilt or innocence is made (behind closed doors by a prosecutor) and the cursory control provided by the courts, the danger of an unsound conviction is undoubtedly higher.

Table 29 summarises the options this study found the PPS in the jurisdictions studied to have in terms of the consequences that can follow a PP decision not to prosecute using the "normal" path.

Table 29. Overview of PPS Options in Dealing with Suspected Offenders*

	EW	FR		DE	NL	PL		SE
Drop (prosecution halted)								
Legal/factual	X[a]	X		X	X	X		X
Public interest	X X[c]	X		X	X			b
For procedural economy/ efficiency reasons	X[d]	X		X	X[d]			X
Disposal with condition on voluntary basis (does not lead to a conviction)	X[e]							
Fine/payment to		X		X	X			
Mediation		X		X		X[f]		
Retribution		X		X	X[g]			
Community service		X		X	X[g]			
Treatment for addiction		X			X			
Psychological treatment		X			X			
Other		X[h]						
PPS sanction (leads to a conviction)	N.a.	X[i] ■	X[j] ▲	X[k]	N.a.[l]	X[m]	X[n]	X[o]
Imprisonment						X[p]		
Prison sentence suspended				X[q]				X[r]
Fine/payment to		X	X	X		X	X	X[s]
Mediation								
Retribution						X		
Community service			X					
Treatment for addiction						X		
Psychological treatment								
Other		X[t]	X[u]	X[v]		X[w]	X[x]	
Alternative	X[y]							X[z]

■ Ordonnance pénale ▲ Composition pénale

* footnotes in annex 10

5.4 A New Trend: Prosecutorial Adjudication

Traditionally a distinguishing feature of common law systems, a trial after a guilty plea is also a simplified procedure in that no further evidence of the offence is required to be brought before court. The charge remains uncontested and there is no question of guilt. This form of proceedings is used frequently in England and Wales[10] where the defendant agrees and leads to a trial being based upon written evidence only, prepared by the PPS.

As will be seen below, this form of proceedings is providing the basis or inspiration for new procedural forms on the continent and, when given to powerful prosecution services, for a new prosecutorial role. Table 30 provides an overview of the proceedings being discussed.

Table 30. PPS Negotiated Case-Settlement Procedures Available

	EW	FR	DE	NL	PL	SE
Pre-trial	X[a]	X[b]	[c]	---	X[d]	---
Also during trial	X[e]	---	[f]	---	X[g]	---

[a] Charge bargaining: A guilty plea is made to a charge with lesser scope. A public trial ensues.
[b] CRPC: negotiation between offender and PPS without court.
[c] No legal provision but negotiations between the PPS and the defence are usual in order to decide which case ending is imposed (e.g. conditional disposal, penal order, etc.).
[d] Judgement without trial: PPS and defence agree on a punishment in order to avoid a main hearing; a court decision ensues, however. This only applies to a less serious crime, which can be punished by a maximum of 10 years imprisonment.
[e] A guilty plea leads to a lighter sentence.
[f] No legal provision. Nevertheless agreements within the main proceedings are not unusual and higher court precedent accepts this practice within certain bounds.
[g] Voluntary submission to punishment. The accused makes an application for a specified sanction, without the court gathering evidence. It must be a less serious crime.

Because the proceedings in question in France and Poland are very new, little can be said about them beyond the description of their legal parameters provided in the country reports. This study was unable to incorporate any reports from French practice, whilst in Poland the only certain conclusion is that such proceedings are being used with dramatically increasing frequency.

They represent an evolved version of prosecutorial discretion which this study evaluates as a new prosecutorial function; "case-settlement negotiation." As similar proceedings are currently being discussed politically in Germany and being planned in the Netherlands (with the difference in the latter case that no court involvement is foreseen there – the suggestion sits somewhere between these proce-

[10] In 2004 63 % of cases before Magistrates and 61 % of cases before Crown Courts were brought in this form.

dures and the more traditional use of discretion), it seems fair to speak of a new European trend.

The procedures are particular because they strengthen the consensual elements arguably already present in conditional disposals; for which the PPS proposes a solution and it can only be used where the defendant agrees. Here the PPS, or as in Poland, even the defendant in one variant, will enter the court stage with a suggestion for the charge to be brought and the punishment to be imposed after this has been the subject of negotiation between the PPS and the defence. The court will check the basic parameters and approve the deal negotiated. How much scrutiny courts can and will factually exercise remains to be seen. A conviction and sanction, including longer custodial sentences, ensues. Usually no appeal is possible. These proceedings are intended to deal with moderately serious and more serious cases, which might warrant up to 10 years of imprisonment. They are a pragmatic solution and an open declaration that the PPS and, indeed court, role is fundamentally altered in this sphere.

The benefits hoped for are obvious, quicker trials and more efficient dealing with even difficult cases, in which the suspect profits from a willingness to spare the state the complexities of a full trial. Punishment ensues, but more efficiently. The issues to be considered more negatively are that this trend drastically furthers the range of offences for which the court role and thus public scrutiny is likely to be marginalised, if not almost entirely excluded. Justice is increasingly being done behind closed doors. The better the defendant's financial and legal resources are, the more he or she will be in a position to influence the outcome of such proceedings. This is not a new problem, but one more than likely to gain weight in such proceedings.

The legal provisions for such case-settlements are often that they may be used provided "the aims of the proceedings are still fulfilled" (as the Polish Procedural Code requires but many provisions have similar requirements). This begs the question as to what the aims of criminal proceedings truly are. Such proceedings aim at a compromise, a lower punishment than truly deserved (why else would a defendant agree to it?) and efficiency, without the shame or burden of a public trial. A bit of punishment, achieved by a bit of a trial, by means of a deal of the kind always abhorred by civilian systems.

A defence lawyer is required. Thus one may hope that the suspect position is secured. It seems unlikely that resourceful defendants will not profit relatively, whilst less resourceful ones are pressed into less advantageous deals. Only highly principled PPs or robust courts would prevent this.

The nature of the PPS, the judiciary and the criminal trial are fundamentally changed. The full, public trial and indeed the right to appeal against a court decision (again making the importance of a good defence lawyer paramount) are declared to be unnecessary in the cases for which the PPS has decided this to be the appropriate procedural form and succeeded in gaining defence agreement to this. One might speculate that we may even see certain offence types become less stigmatised, if this kind of non-public procedure tends to be used for them.

In any case, the introduction of such proceedings is a further step towards providing a tiered-criminal justice response. A further procedural alternative is made available for a certain range of offences. Some serious crime will be dealt with using these proceedings. Other will go to court "normally." Depending upon how this mechanism is used, convicted offenders for one and the same offence may to see themselves subject to very different procedures and possibly sanctions. This may be regarded as desirable, but the danger for equality before the law is self-evident.

Above all, these procedures bear witness to the faith placed in the PPS. They complement and confirm the European trend towards the PPS becoming the key institution in making decisions as to which procedural form should be used in order to achieve a certain CJS response, to which offences.

6 Court Remaining Central Decision-maker

Naturally, each system still retains a legally "normal" procedural form. That which is regarded as a full, public trial, from which the procedures just described deviate by allowing short cuts. These also vary in the systems studied and an understanding of such variation may be vital to understanding the system as a whole and thus also the other procedural means which flank this "ideal picture".

The fact that trials in the Netherlands rely to a great extent upon written submissions and rarely last longer than a few hours (very complex serious cases may take 2 days), may go some way to explaining why we are not seeing alternative (time-saving) proceedings involving courts there. The fact that Swedish judges deal with both civil and criminal matters explains why civil claims are made more often during criminal proceedings there.

This study was naturally unable to chart all of the differences one might regard as relevant and had to be restricted to examining the PPS role in interaction with the court. Our findings are shown below.

Table 31. PPS Role during a Full Trial

		EW	FR	DE	NL	PL	SE
Decides which charge to bring before court		X[a]	X[b]	X[c]	X[d]	X	X[e]
Decides what to charge – with EM where one is involved			X[f]				
Decides what to charge – together with the police		X[a]	X[b]				
Decides what evidence to disclose (pre-trial) to defendant		X[g]		X	[h]		X[i]
Decides what evidence to bring to court		X		[j]	X[k]	X	X
Decides which witnesses to call		X	X	[l]	X[m]	X	X
Presents prosecution case in court	orally	X[n]	X	X	X	X	X
	in writing	X[n]	[o]	X	X	X	X
Assists court in finding the truth			X[p]	X	X	X	X[q]
Makes a sentencing suggestion			X[r]	X[s]	X[t]	X	X
Presents evidence - also for defendant				X[u]	X	X	X[v]
Plea bargaining		X		X[w]			
Decides which mode of trial to use		[x]					
Suggest an alternative settlement during trial							
Appeal against verdict			X	X	X	X	X
Appeal against sentence		X	X	X	X	X	X

[a] Depends on the case, whether the police or the PPS decides what to charge. They can also decide together. The court can change this decision.

[b] The police and the prosecutor decide together whether the decision should be made during the "real-time treatment", the prosecutor decides alone for other direct summons. The court can change a charge and does this regularly.

[c] The PPS is bound by the principle of legality and thus obliged to press charges where there is sufficient evidence. The court is, however, not bound by the PPS applications and is entirely free in the evaluation of evidence and legal evaluation of an act. Nevertheless the PPS makes the decision which offence to define as the subject of proceedings. However, the court may well find a suspect guilty of a different offence to that charged by the PPS (e. g. manslaughter instead of murder).

[d] Court can change this.

Table 31 displays the PPS role before court as a comprehensive one in deciding upon a charge, bringing evidence, (England & Wales providing the anticipated exception) bearing a responsibility to assist the court in finding out the truth, strengthened (except in France) by the duty to bring all relevant, even exonerating, evidence and to help guide the court towards a correct sentence.

---

[e] The court can change a charge (i.e. the legal definition of an act) and does this regularly.

[f] When the EM is involved, the PPS decides to charge first and then the EM decides to retain the whole accusation or to leave it partially (or totally but then there will be no trial), so it is not necessarily an agreement.

[g] Usually defined by law, but CPS clearly has an important role within this legal requirement. PACE regulates pre-trial disclosure.

[h] Defendant has access to all relevant information.

[i] PPS is obliged to disclose to defence all evidence, which will be brought before the court.

[j] The court makes the final decision as to which evidence should be brought before it. As is the case for other participants, the PPS has the right to make applications.

[k] Defence lawyer and judge also.

[l] The PPS may name witnesses; the court makes the final decision whether or not to hear them.

[m] The defence (and the judge) may also call witnesses.

[n] Depends on case. Some petty cases are dealt with in writing only, especially if a guilty plea has been entered.

[o] The written file is of great importance but comes from the police (direct summons) or from the police and examining magistrate (judicial investigation).

[p] The court may adjourn the decision in order to get more information and PPS must act consequently (calling for witnesses or victims in court, criminal record). But if the court finds that more investigation is needed, the transfer to an examining magistrate is possible (quite rare).

[q] This obligation is not provided expressis verbis by law. However, in the preliminary investigation, the PPS is obliged to collect both exonerating and aggravating evidence. This principle of objectivity is considered to be valid during the whole procedure.

[r] Asking for a sentence is the main PPS role during court hearing for normal courts.

[s] The court can change this suggestion.

[t] The claim of the PP is usually higher than the final decision but the final sentence can be higher than the claim of the PP.

[u] The law requires the PPS to find and present all evidence, including evidence exonerating the accused. Further research is required to discover in how far the PPS is able to fulfil this role in practice.

[v] This is a consequence of the principle of objectivity.

[w] Deals are also made in Germany at prosecutorial level. There is no legislative basis although a draft has now been brought before Parliament. The criteria listed by the Bundesgerichtshof are accordingly to form the basis of future norms. These relate to deals made at court level.

[x] There are guidelines set by the Lord Chief Justice for magistrates to decide whether cases should be tried in the crown court when the offence in "triable either way" and where the defendant does nor indicate a guilty plea. CPS should recommend Crown Court trial when they are satisfied that the guidelines require them to do so. The court can change this decision.

This final duty varies from a very strong one to a mere request across the jurisdictions studied.

Nevertheless, it is augmented by a right to appeal against a sentence it regards as incorrect in all countries. The PPS is expected to provide a check for the courts in this respect.

7 Statistical Analysis of the Use of Powers

As has been shown above, the PPS role in all the jurisdictions studied is an extremely varied one. In almost all of these the PPS has potential mechanisms to deal with suspected offenders in a variety of different procedures leading to no CJS reaction, a warning, "quasi-"punishment or a conviction, with more or less court involvement. This section shows the factual extent of these practices more clearly. Table 32 provides an overview of the options available in each system.

Table 32. Summary of PPS Powers Available

	EW	FR	DE	NL	PL	SE
Simple drop (insufficient evidence, technical reasons)	X	X	X	X	X	X
Drop (public interest)	X	X	X	X		X
Drop for procedural economy/efficiency reasons	X	X	X	X		X
Conditional disposal		X	X	X	X	
Penal order		X	X		X	X
Other simplified/ accelerated proceedings	X[a]	X[b]	X[c]		X[d]	
Bring charges for full „normal" trial	X	X	X	X	X	X

[a] Bulk proceedings.
[b] CRPC.
[c] Beschleunigtes Verfahren.
[d] Voluntary submission to penalty/Application for conviction without trial.

Figure 3 shows the proportion of cases dealt with in various ways by the PPS in 2002. It is notable that only in England & Wales and the Netherlands is a large proportion of cases brought to court – here it must be borne in mind that these two jurisdictions have comparatively simple court proceedings (almost entirely written in the Netherlands and a large proportion in guilty plea or bulk proceedings in E&W), so the need to provide relief is not felt quite so keenly as in other systems. The Polish situation is perhaps reflective of the political desire to strengthen the court's role.

The relatively high rates of simple drops in some jurisdictions are explained by cases involving unknown offenders being passed on to the PPS.

In France and Germany it is clear that the majority of CJS reactions no longer ensue as the result of a court decision. If a court decision results it is often one (by penal order) effectively pre-determined by the PPS.

In the Netherlands the PPS is decisive in around 30% of cases, the court retains its importance, but the relative strength of the PPS and the high value placed upon its file during trial should not be over-looked. It is arguably more rather than less a key institution there. In Poland the PPS seems to have little influence as is intended by recent reforms. In how far it is influential in guiding court decisions remains to be seen. Its former strength and the chronic over-loading of the Polish system speak for the European trend towards a stronger PPS taking hold there too, upon the evidence we have, however, it appears to be bucking it. The Swedish model displays the features of a model which has remained fairly traditional, although one must not forget that a very large number of cases have already been sanctioned by the police and those subject to a penal order are adjudicated exclusively by the PPS. The court is dominant in the area for which it is assigned responsibility, but that is more limited than in other jurisdictions, with the police and PPS being given areas of independent competence not to be found in other jurisdictions.

The British picture is, not surprisingly, indicative of a fairly weak prosecution service. Again, one must naturally bear in mind that around 15 % of cases are ended at police level and that this now occurs with increasing PPS influence. Furthermore many of the results achieved by conditional disposal in other jurisdictions (such as mediation, addiction treatment etc.) are done by court order and a conditional dismissal often applied for by the PPS in England & Wales. Thus, these figures cannot be interpreted as absolute proof of a weak PPS, there is reason to believe that the trend of growing importance seen in other jurisdictions applies equally here. Nevertheless the British PPS doubtlessly starts from a fairly weak position. Determining its exact role requires further and more detailed observation of the situation emerging.

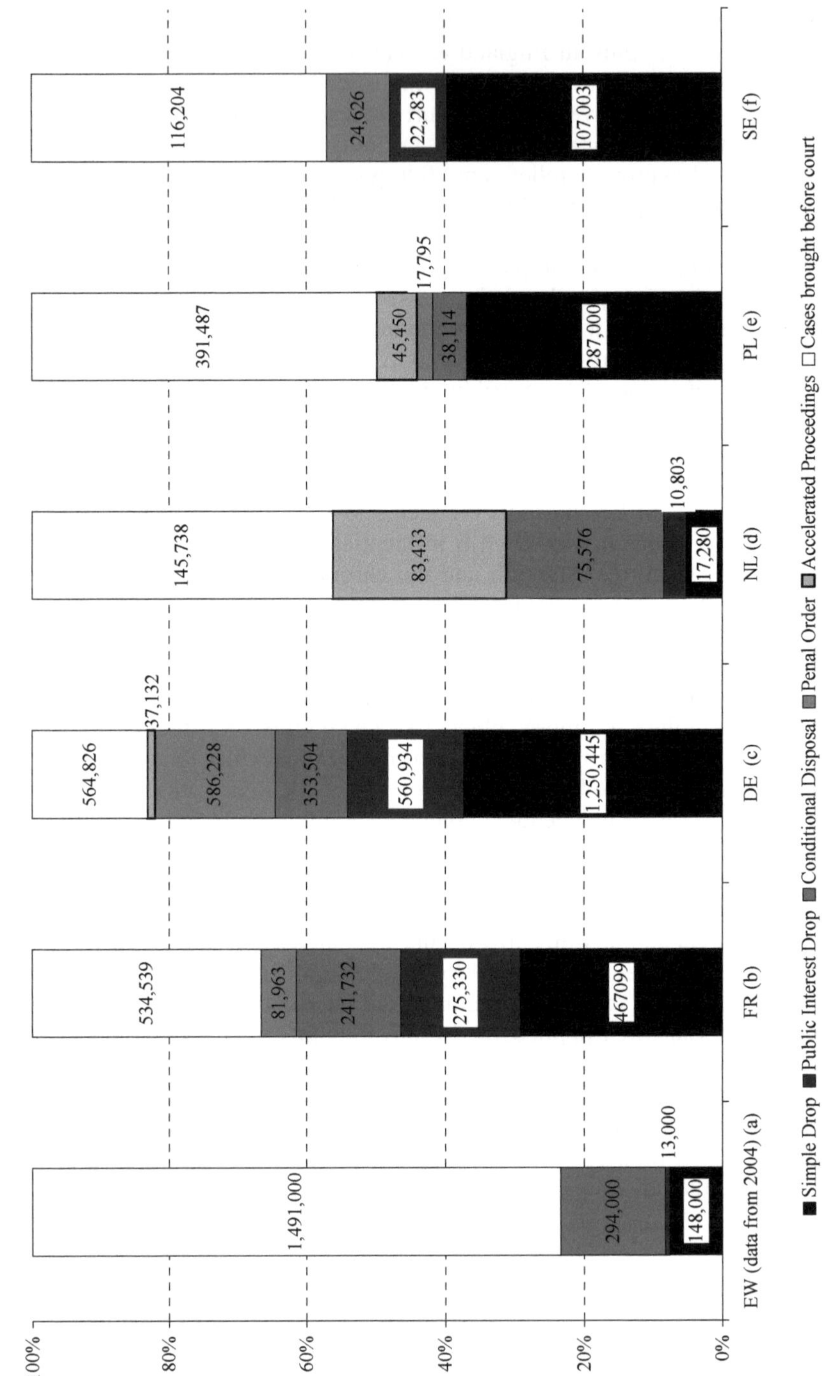

Fig. 3. PPS Case-ending Decisions (2002)

Source: EW: Global Numbers Questionnaire Annex ; FR: Questionnaire VII. Table 10; DE: Prosecution Statistics 2002, Tab. 2.2, published by the Federal Statistical Office Wiesbaden; NL: Questionnaire Table VII.10; PL: The Prosecution Service Function within the Polish Criminal Justice System; SE: Official Statistics.

[a] Including data for juveniles
Simple drop (n= 148,000): evidence test
public interest drop (n= 13,000)
Conditional disposal (n= 294,000): *Cautions* (including *Final Warnings* and *Reprimands*
Cases brought before court (n= 1,491,000): all cases that are brought to court for a full trial by the PPS (Indictable, TEW, Summary Offences).

[b] Simple drop (n=467099)
Public interest drop (n= 275,330)
Conditional disposal (n=241732)
Penal order (n=81,963): *Ordonnance Penal* by PPS (for 5th contraventions only)
Cases brought before court (n= 534,539): only by PPS, no contraventions 1-4 class and therefore no OMP-decision included.

[c] Including data for juveniles
The number of proceedings dealt with by the Public Prosecution Service at the Regional Courts and dealt with by the Amtsanwaltschaften (assistant prosecutor offices) are included.
Simple drop (n= 1,250,445): including insufficient evidence and no criminal responsibility found; unknown offenders are not included in the statistics
Public interest drop (n= 560,934): Section 153 paragraph 1 StPO, Section 31a paragraph 1 BtMG, Section 45 paragraph 1J GG
Conditional disposal (n= 353,504): Section 153a paragraph 1 StPO, Section 45 paragraph 2,3 JGG
Penal order (n=586,228): *Strafbefehl*
Accelerated proceedings: *Beschleunigtes Verfahren* (n= 37,132) NB this procedure is accelerated in the pre-trial phase.
Cases brought before court (n=564,826).

[d] Simple drop (n= 17280): including drop because of insufficient evidence (n= 9,899) and for technical reasons (*technisch sepot*) (n= 7,381)
Public interest drop (n= 10,803): policy drop (*opportuniteitssepot*)
Conditional disposal (n= 75,576): including *voorwaardelijk sepot* (n= 2798) and *transactie* (n=72,778)
Accelerated proceedings (n= 83,433): *AU-practice/vlugrecht (CCP 370a/1)* NB this procedure is accelerated in the pre-trial phase.
Cases brought before court (n= 145, 738).

[e] Simple drop (n= 287,000)
Conditional disposal (n= 38,114)
Special forms (n= 45,450): including *Judgement without Trial (art. 335 CPC)* (n= 9,194), *Voluntary Submission to Punishment (art.387 CPC)* (n= 36,256)
Penal order (n= 17,795): *Nakaz Karny, art. 500 onwards CPC*
Cases brought before court (n= 391,487).

[f] Cases brought before court (n= 116,204)
Penal order (n= 24,626): *Strafförelaggande* by PPS
Public interest drop (n= 22,283): *Waiver of Prosecution and 23, 4a CCP*
Simple Drop (107,003): drop not initiated, drop for other reasons, drop because offence is not proved, drop because no prosecution in court, drop because of other decisions.

With the exception of Poland[11] and possibly to a lesser degree for Sweden and only considering recent developments in England & Wales, the picture this study paints of European jurisdictions is of PPS strength in deciding how to deal with and, indeed, to end cases either in its own right, in co-operation with the police or by pre-determining court decisions. It is one of growing power.

Figure 4, which shows the cases taken to court including penal order proceedings (which are functionally a PPS decision, formally a court conviction – only in Sweden are they independent police/PPS decision). The proportion of different procedural forms used demonstrates clearly that the courts are by no means able to claim a monopoly on convicting judgements; the Netherlands proving the exception. A large proportion of convictions across Europe must be regarded as effective PPS judgements.[12] For England & Wales this diagram includes bulk proceedings[13] and thus clearly displays that court decisions there are also frequently predetermined by other agencies.

More detailed information as to how discretion is actually used is available for the Netherlands and Sweden, for England & Wales the data provided are not comparable and therefore shown separately.

Figure 5 shows the statistics for the Netherlands and Sweden together to allow direct comparison.

[11] for which it is arguably too early to draw any conclusions. The situation cannot be described as anything other than highly dynamic, especially relating to practice. The dramatic increases in the number of negotiated-settlements being used is, for example, indicative of PPS strength.

[12] the question remains in how far this might even be the case in the Netherlands.

[13] in which a list of hundreds or even thousands of suspects is handed to the court and all convicted for the same offence, e.g. TV licence fraud, during one court sitting.

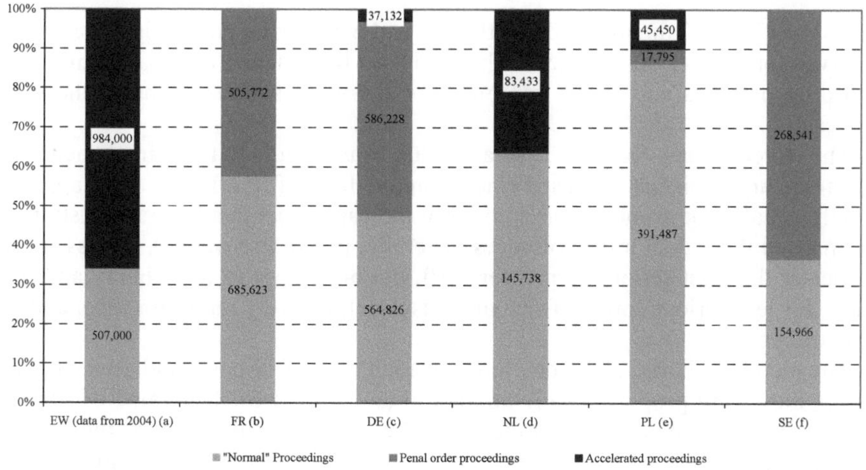

Fig. 4. Convictions by Procedural Type reflecting Prosector-Court Relationship (2002)

Source: EW: Global Numbers Questionnaire Annex; FR: Questionnaire Table V.1 und VII.10; DE: Prosecution Statistics, tab. 2.2, publ. by the Federal Statistical Office Wiesbaden; NL: Questionnaire Table VII.10; PL: The Prosecution Service Function within the Polish Criminal Justice System; SE: Official Statistics.

[a] Normal criminal proceedings before Crown and Magistrates Court (n= 507,000): all cases that are brought to court for a full trial by the PPS (*Indictable, TEW, Summary Offences*)
Accelerated Proceedings (n= 984,000): *Bulk-proceedings.*

[b] Normal criminal proceedings (n= 685,623): including all contraventions (1-5 class), delits, crime that are brought to court by PPS (n= 534,539) or OMP (n= 151.084).
Penal order: *Ordonnance pénale* (OMP: n= 423,809; PPS: n= 81,503), *Composition pénale*
(n= 6,755).

[c] The number of proceedings dealt with by the Public Prosecution Service at the Regional Courts and those dealt with by the Amtsanwaltschaften (assistant prosecutor offices) are counted.
"Normal" criminal proceedings: cases brought before Local Courts (Amtsgerichte) and Regional Courts (*Landgerichte)* (n= 564,826)
Penal order (n= 586,228): *Strafbefehl*
Accelerated proceedings (n= 37,132): *Beschleunigtes Verfahren* NB this procedure is accelerated in the pre-trial phase.

[d] "Normal" criminal proceedings (n= 145,738): all cases that are brought to court for a full trial by PPS.
Accelerated proceedings (n= 83,433): *AU-practice/Vlugrecht (CCP 370a/1)* NB this procedure is accelerated in the pre-trial phase.

In Sweden in 2002 the use of discretionary and penal order powers is quite clearly reserved for less serious offences. They are used for traffic offences, assault, theft, and drug offences and much less often for the more serious forms of these offences.

The Dutch figures for both 1994 and 2002 bear witness to the same conclusion. Discretionary decisions are used (increasingly) for traffic offences (and approximately equally for drunk driving, possibly indicative that this is no more strongly stigmatised there than traffic offences generally, unlike in Sweden), for assault, in particular the least serious forms, for theft, but much less so for robbery and burglary, for less serious forms of sexual harassment, but very rarely for rape, and for drug offences.

The picture is borne out if one looks at each type of disposal and sees what offences they were proportionately applied to (see Figure 6). The value of such an analysis must be regarded as limited because, as one would suspect, the proportions allotted to the various offence types also correspond to their statistical frequency. Thus, e.g. theft, drug and traffic offences are strongly represented. However, firstly, this indicates that these forms of disposal are indeed used for efficiency purposes, that is why they are used for dealing with such "mass crimes" and, secondly, this in no way contradicts the likelihood that these alternative case-endings are used to deal with less serious offences.

Due to issues of availability and comparability, the data gathered by the study can only give a limited indication of prosecutorial practice but it is clearly indicative of PPS strength and of principled use of PPS and police discretionary powers (the latter guided by the PPS) to deal with less serious offence types. Prosecutorial discretion is a tool for dealing with mass crimes.

Figure 7 shows the statistics for England and Wales. Both in 1994 and 2002 the use of cautioning, as opposed to submitting a case for court judgement, is relatively high there for violence, theft and handling, criminal damage and drug offences. The theft category is clearly higher than for burglary, fraud and robbery. All of these categories, which are known to contain high proportions of less serious forms are well above the rate for "other" offences, indicating higher cautioning use, as one would expect, for less serious offences.

---

[e] "Normal" criminal proceedings (n=391,487): all cases that are brought to court for a full trial.
Penal order (n=17,795)
Accelerated proceedings (n= 45,450): including *Judgement without Trial* (n= 9,194) and *Voluntary Submission to Punishment* (n= 36,256).

[f] "Normal" criminal proceedings (n= 154,966): all cases that are brought to court for a full trial by PPS.
Penal order: including *Strafförelaggande* (PPS) (n= 40,112) and *Brotförelaggande* (Police) (n= 228, 429). NB these two procedural forms do not involve a court at all but are implemented by the respective pre-trial agency. This study, however, categorises them as equivalent proceedings because they lead to a record and are considered an establishment of guilt.

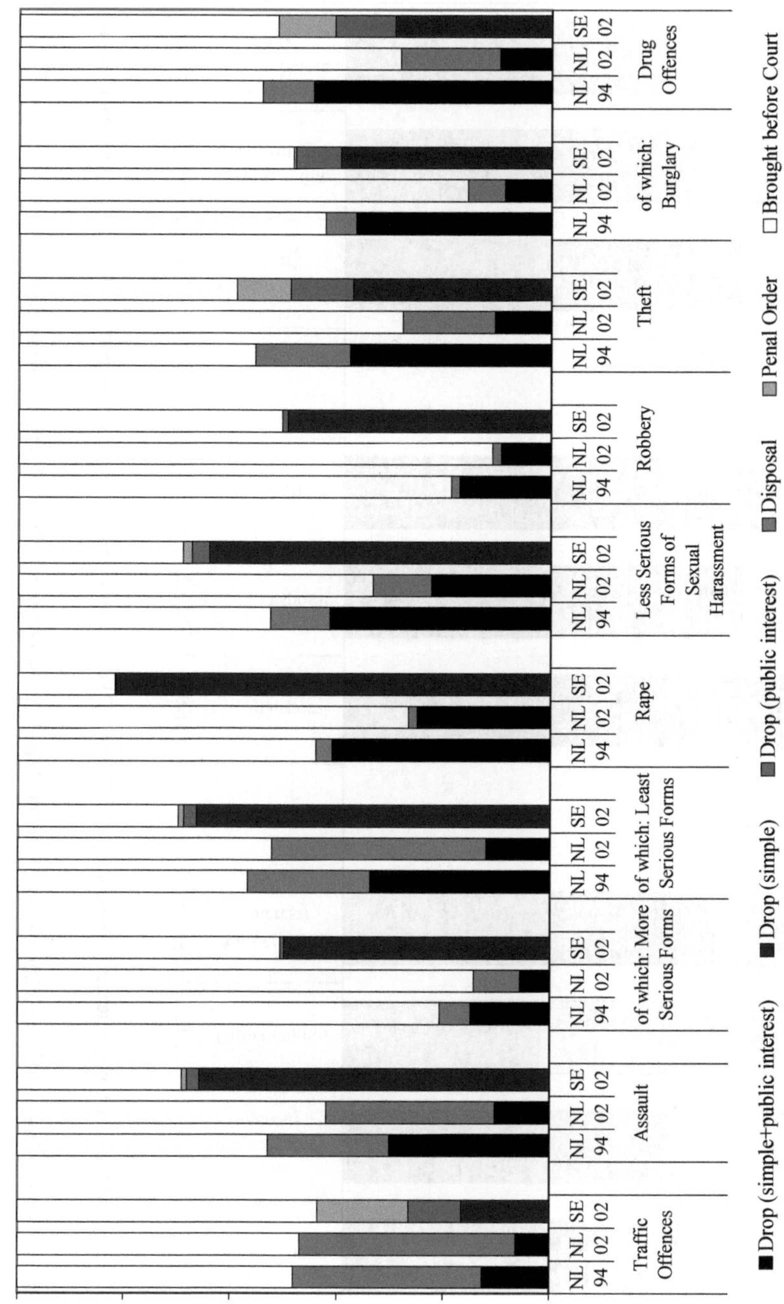

Fig. 5. Case-Ending Decisions Development – The Netherlands and Sweden. See annex table in annex 4

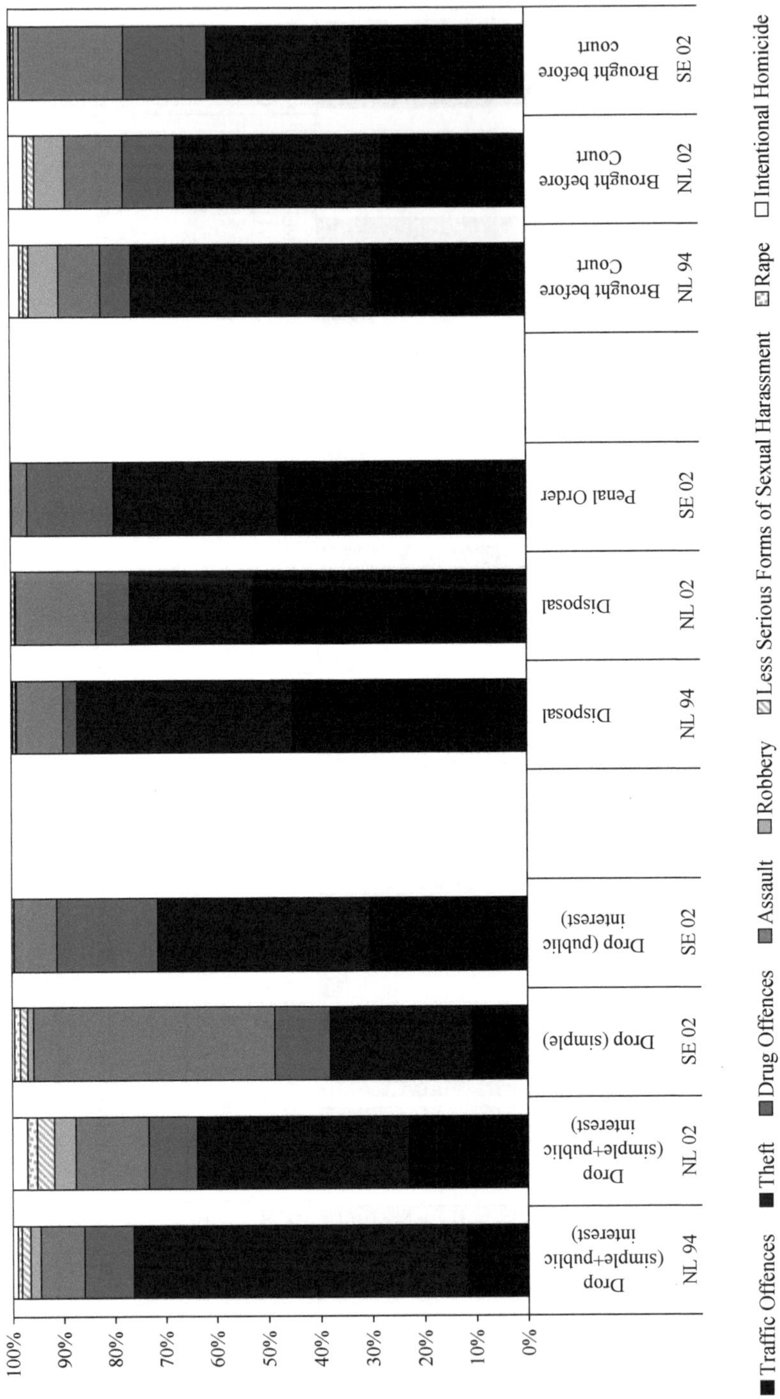

Fig. 6. Case-Ending Decisions - Offence Related in the Netherlands and Sweden (data relating to this figure in annex 4)

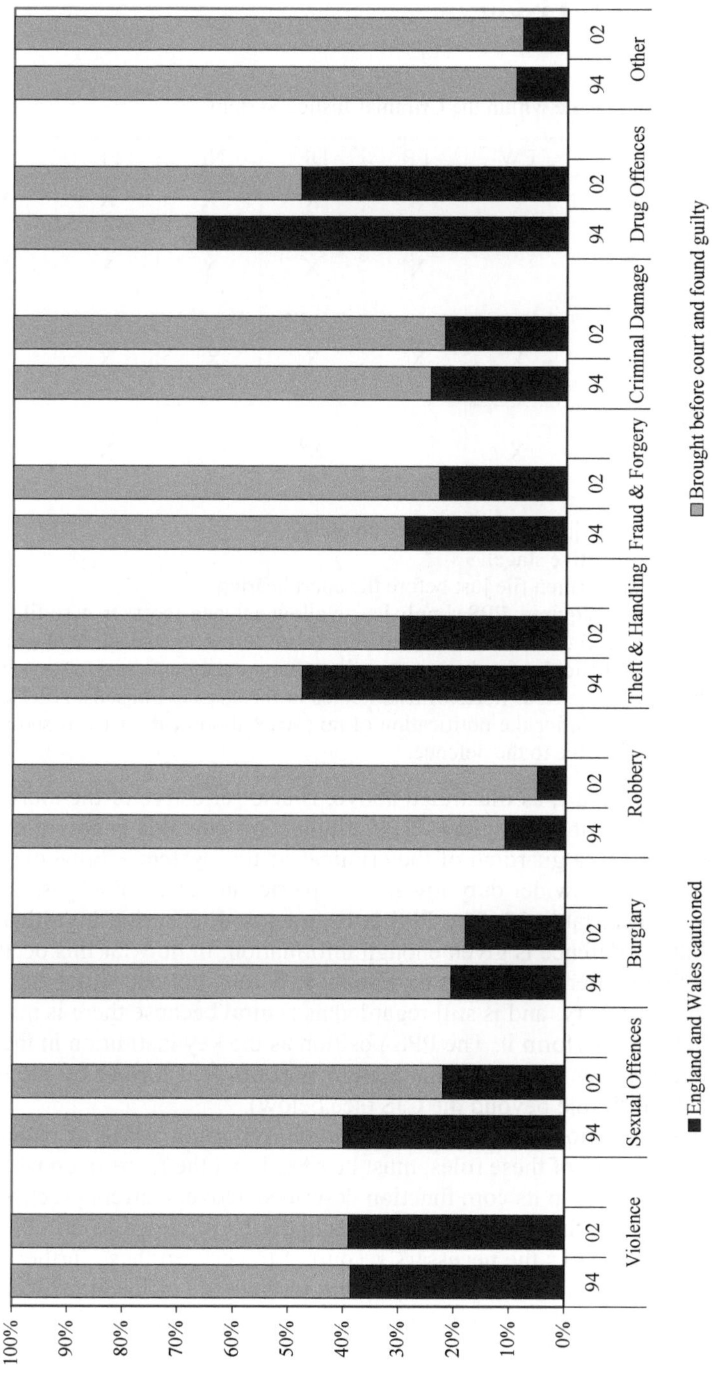

Fig. 7. Suspects Cautioned by Offence Type as a Proportion of those Convicted in Court & Cautioned in England & Wales

8 The General PPS Role

Table 33. PPS' General Role within the Criminal Justice System

	EW	FR	DE	NL	PL	SE
PPS is an objective body		X	X	X	X	X
PPS obliged to ensure all aspects of a case are investigated		X[a]	X	X	X	X
PPS obliged to ensure court receives all relevant information	X	X[a]	X	X[b]	X	X
PPS obliged to provide accused/defence with all relevant information	X	[c]	X[d]	X[e]	X	X

[a] In all cases, in which no juge d'instruction is involved.
[b] Not during the investigative stage.
[c] Defence has access to written file just before the court hearing.
[d] No active cooperation required. PPS simply has to allow defence access to case file.
[e] The defence has the right to have all information (also during investigative stage), provided that there's no difficulty for the investigation. Some documents may always be examined by the defence (such as notes of testimonies of the suspect himself). After the pti (or if no pti took place, after the notification of no prosecution or the writ of summons) all documents are available to the defence.

The PPS role before court, as illustrated above, is also reflective of the more general profile ascribed to it within the CJS. In civilian systems this is one of a more neutral instance and as a guardian of the criminal justice system as a whole. This is displayed in the PPS' wider duty towards all parties in the criminal justice system as can be seen in table 33. The PPS is charged with ensuring investigations are fair and that the defence is given enough information. In how far this occurs in practice is another matter. This is the traditional PPS role, but one which has been retained, at least in theory, and is still regarded as central because there is no other institution which can perform it. The PPS position as the key institution in the system is only enforced by this role. This picture is confirmed further by the study findings as to the PPS role beyond the CJS (see below).

The legitimate question how a single institution, reporting a lack of resources, can possibly perform all of these roles, must be raised. All the more so considering the strongly altering role in its core function described above. Current practice certainly justifies concern that the PPS cannot factually be regarded as an objective body and doubtlessly lacks the necessary resources to perform these further roles. A great deal of procedural corners are being cut to facilitate efficient prosecution. This is not easily compatible with or supportive of an objective role. Our findings bear witness to inquisitorial systems increasingly adopting adversarial procedural aspects.

The Defence An adoption of adversarial elements is equally to be seen in relation to the strengthening of the defence's position. The current position can be seen in table 34.

Table 34. Defendant/Defence Rights (in Law) during the Pre-trial Stage

Has Right to	EW	FR	DE	NL	PL	SE
be present at interviews	X[a] ▲ ■		X[b] ■	X[c] ■	X	X[d] ▲ ■
interrogate witnesses				[e]		X[f] ▲ ■
see the written file or other means to get case information		[g] ▲	X[h] ■	X[i] ▲■	X	X[j] ▲ ■
apply to the court for release of evidence	X[k] ▲ ■	[l]		X ▲ ■		
try to direct the investigation/what evidence is collected		X[m] ■	[n]	X[o] ▲ ■		X[p] ▲ ■

▲ own right ■ right of the defence

NB the English and Welsh, Dutch and Swedish system do not differentiate as far as the defendant and the defence are concerned

[a] The suspect can call in a defence lawyer from the start, who can, and indeed has a right to, be present when ever the suspect is interviewed.

[b] The defence has a limited right to be present when the suspect is being interrogated by the PPS, not, however, where witnesses or experts are being heard.

[c] The suspect doesn't have the right to be present. The suspect's lawyer may be present during the interrogation of witnesses.

[d] The suspect has the right to present when a person is interrogated on the suspect's application. He (or his attorney) also has the right to present by other interrogations, if the head of investigation allows it.

[e] Interrogation of witnesses in time of the investigation phase occurs only on voluntary basis. The suspect doesn't have the right to be present in witnesses' interrogation; though s/he has the right to inspect the documents (supposed there is no objection for the investigation).

[f] The suspect has the right if he is present, to put questions to the interrogated person in the manner decided by the head of investigation. He also has the right to express his opinion as regards the choice of an expert witness.

[g] It depends on the kind of inquiry. During the "preliminary inquiry" or for "flagrant délit" the defence do not have access to the written file (it is possible for a direct summons only before court hearing) or any other means to gain access to case information. During a judicial inquiry (examining magistrate), the suspect has access to the written file. A person charged by the EM has access to the written file, but when the police are investigating under the authority of the EM this right does not arise immediately.

This trend should doubtlessly be welcomed in terms of ensuring that the PPS does not become overly powerful. The long-standing desire for a source of legally trained control of the investigatory stage by a more neutral agency should, however, not be forgotten entirely and is not addressed by this trend. This is a role traditionally performed by the PPS in civilian systems and it will be interesting to see how systems expect this function to be performed. The investigatory stage is a field in which changes to this function will quickly become apparent.

---

[h] The defence has a basic right to view the file during the entire course of proceedings. Access can, however, be denied in particular where the investigation is not yet complete and their aim would be endangered. The most frequent jurisprudential view is that no right to complain applies. The accused has no right to view the file. The defence has an unlimited right to view the file relating to protocols of the suspect being interrogated or judicial investigatory measures to which the presence of the defence is allowed or should have been allowed. Access must also be given to written opinions provided by expert witnesses. This applies at all procedural stages, where this access should be denied §§ 23 ff EGGVG provides a legal recourse.

[i] The defence has the right to have all information, provided that there is no difficulty for the investigation.

[j] Access to the written file is possible with consent of the head of investigation, and - after that the investigation has finished - they have the right to examine the whole file without limitations.

[k] The defence can apply to the court for release of material of examination. The court will also hear from the police and make judgement accordingly.

[l] Again it depends on the kind of inquiry. The right to apply to the court for release of examination material exist only during judicial inquiries (by the examining magistrate). The defence has this right during the court hearing.

[m] This means exists during all stages of inquiry.

[n] § 163a II StPO lends the accused the right to request that certain exonerating evidence be admitted. But s/he does not have the right to force the desired gathering of evidence. Only in the main proceedings stage is the accused lent a stronger right to make applications for evidence to be heard by means of which s/he can introduce certain evidence to the proceedings. The defence has an inherent right to make applications, independent from that of the accused.

[o] The suspect may request a pre-trial investigation (the offence has to be that serious pre-trial detention can be ordered). If the pre-trial investigation is started, the suspect has the right to assign witnesses or facts to be investigated, in writing (or orally during the interrogation). The EM may refuse this, to which the suspect, for his part, can file a protest.

[p] The suspect has right to propose collection of evidence.

The current trend is towards more police independence in relation to less serious crimes.[14] Dissatisfaction with this situation has, however, repeatedly led to reform in the Netherlands, can be interpreted by the introduction of "real-time" treatment in France, inter-agency guidelines in Sweden and even the presence of PPS personnel in police stations in England & Wales. Ultimately the aim of the investigatory stage remains to provide sufficient and admissible evidence for later stages of the criminal justice process. Previously the PPS was expected to ensure this occurred. It is no longer able to do so in many jurisdictions and certain signs of discontent with this situation can be observed. There are indications that the right balance of responsibilities is still being sought in this field and it will be interesting to see which balance between the demands of practice and (traditional but still valid) legal requirements is struck.

9 The Nature of the PPS

The study also collected some information about the PPS' position and the services' organisational structure. This is summarised in this section.

Table 35 shows what kind of an institution the PPS is; one having to strike a balance between political independence and an ability to enforce uniform policy within the criminal justice system. Except in France this is achieved by written national or regional guidelines and a strong internal hierarchy.

The French system is perhaps exceptional in that individual prosecutors have a stronger status – they are also members of the judiciary – and are bound in what they write and do, but also have a right to speak freely before court (in other words they can be required to bring a case to court but cannot be prevented from telling the court that they believe the charges are unfounded[15]). Furthermore regional influence appears to be greater there (although in terms of policy, state rather than central guidelines are decisive). The French variation may, however, merely be reflective of the relationship between politics and the prosecution service being regarded more critically there.

It is not, however, only in France that the evolving PPS role is being treated very consciously. There is no denying that it is changing and remains dynamic across Europe and is subject to discussion in all jurisdictions studied bar Sweden.[16]

[14] see above and Elsner 2006.

[15] In how far they will do so, influenced, e.g. by career considerations, is another matter

[16] All of the systems studied here are subject to on-going reforms of a significant nature in relation to prosecutorial responsibilities or practice is just beginning to apply the latest legal reforms, for this reason this study has been extended and expanded to become a 10-country project sponsored by the AGIS programme of the European Commission.

Table 35. PPS' Status and Accountability

	EW	FR	DE	NL	PL	SE
PPS has a formal legal basis	X	X	X	X	X	X
PPS is an independent institution with very independent individual PPS	X[a]					
PPS is an politically independent institution with strong internal hierarchical binding	X[b]		X	X	X	X
PPS is a strongly tied institution externally and internally	X[b]	X[c]	[d]	[e]		
PPS is bound by ministerial instruction		X	X	X	X	
PPS is bound by written national guidelines	X		X	X	X	X
PPS is bound by regional political guidelines		X	X		X	
PPS is answerable to external complaints institution	X[f]				[g]	

[a] Independent of political direction.

[b] The PPS is an institution somewhere between these two options. It is too early to say where it will end up. It is quite a weak institution within the CJS, but it could develop its powers over the next 10–20 years. The ministry cannot issue general instructions (guidelines) to the PPS.

[c] Because the Minister of Justice is the head of service.

[d] Theoretically true, less so in practice although Ministries of Justice do provide a significant amount of guidelines to guide practice in general.

[e] Theoretically Minister of Justice can give orders at case level.

[f] The PPS is controlled by an Independent Inspectorate, which has the power to inspect the PPS. It cannot give case specific orders but a report criticising PPS decisions carries considerable political weight.

[g] Answerable to Ombudsman and Parliamentary Commission of Justice and Human Rights.

Table 36, which shows the hierarchical position of individual PPs within the service, bears out the information provided above of a service fairly independent in relation to the outside world, but with a more stringent internal binding. This is of course vital if equivalent treatment of approximately equivalent offences and offenders is to be ensured. Structurally this is provided for. The extent to which further provision is made for such concerns, in particular through guidelines, is subject to considerable variation although, as the factual use of measures evaluated above shows, there are clear patterns to be found, compatible with the stated aims of the systems.

Table 36. Individual PP Can be Given Orders by

	EW[a]	FR	DE	NL	PL	SE
Government						
Ministry of Justice or equivalent		X[b]		X[c]	X	
Federal State Ministry ("Länder")			X[d]			
Organisational head of service	X	X[e]		X	X	
Regional PP management	X	X[e]	X[d]	X		X[f]
Superior PP	X	X[d]	X[d]	X[d]	X	X[f]

[a] A PP can be given orders, general and case-specific, by any superior.
[b] Can order further investigation, can order PP to prosecute, can instruct what to charge.
[c] Can order further investigation, can order PP to prosecute, can instruct what to charge, can order PP to drop case, can order what condition to impose (but does not happen in practice).
[d] Can order further investigation, can order PP to prosecute, can instruct what to charge, can order PP to drop case, can order what condition to impose.
[e] Can order further investigation, can order PP to prosecute, can instruct what to charge.
[f] Can order further investigation, can order PP to prosecute.

Table 37. PPS' Wider Role

PPS also active as/in	EW	FR	DE	NL	PL	SE
National Crime Policy	X	X		X		X[a]
Local crime policy	X	X		X	X	X
Crime prevention	X	X		X	X	
Victims' interests	X	X	X	X	X	X
Victims' compensation claim				X ■	X■ ▲	X■
Compensate victim where offender unknown	[b]	X				
Ordering execution of sentence		X	X	X		[c]
Ensuring fines paid				X		[b]
Ensuring prison sentence served		X	X	X		
Can prosecute administrative offences			X	X	X	
Civil cases if this is in the public interest		X		X	X	
Recovery of assets through civil courts	X				X	

■ before a criminal court ▲ before a civil court.

[a] The PPS is of course active in national crime policy, it is one of the main tasks of the PPS. The PPS is regarded as doing this by its work, i.e. there is no further form by which it affects policy.
[b] This is done by the CICA – Criminal Injuries Compensation Authority and does not depend on the offender being unknown.
[c] PPS has controlling function to ensure others are doing their job.

Table 37 provides an overview of the tasks assigned to the PPSs in the study jurisdictions displaying clearly that there is still great variation as to what is expected from the PPS. The Dutch PPS has a very wide task profile, but it is interesting to note that all services have a role beyond the boundaries of criminal prosecutions. Although it must be noted that several are performed by special agencies. These are organisationally within the PPS but have separate staff. Therefore such tasks do not affect the personnel dealing with criminal proceedings. The status of some services as the guardian of public interest even in civil cases, i.e. well beyond the realms of criminal justice, is currently being explored by the Council of Europe's Meeting of Prosecutor-Generals. Seeing the kind of status these institutions have in their legal systems as a whole may well be a useful indicator for understanding why some services are entrusted with lesser or greater powers than others. There are grounds to speculate, however, that PPSs are tending to concentrate on their core business – namely the criminal justice system.

10 Criminal Justice Responses to Juveniles

Table 38. Age of Criminal Responsibility

	EW	FR	DE	NL	PL	SE
Age of criminal responsibility	10	7[a]	14	12	17[b]	15
Full adult responsibility at age	18	18	18/21	16/21[c]	17/21	18/21
Group in between?		[d]	X[e]	X[f]	X[g]	X[h]

[a] Minors under 13 cannot receive penalty (only educational measures).
[b] In cases of some serious crimes it is 15 years.
[c] In principle < 18 = juvenile, > 18 = adult. In exceptional cases the judge can decide to treat a 16–18 year old as an adult (in practice usually treated as juvenile) and an 18–21 year old as a juvenile (in practice usually treated as adult) This decision is made by the judge and not by the PPS.
[d] ≤ 13 no penalty, only educational measure. 13– ≤ 16 max penalty ½, priority to educational measure. No pre-trial detention for "délits". 16– ≤ 18 max. penalty reduced but full penalty possible for serious cases.
[e] According to legislation, 18–20 year olds (so called "Heranwachsende") are basically to be treated in accordance to adult criminal law and only according to juvenile criminal law where the pre-conditions laid down in § 105 I JGG are met, i.e. where the perpetrator was on the level of a juvenile as far as his/her moral or mental development was concerned or the act was a case of a youthful mistake. In practice this group tends to be treated in accordance with juvenile criminal law (circa 64 % in 2002).
[f] 16–17 years old can be dealt with according to adult criminal law. In practice this group is usually treated as juveniles. 18, 19, 20 years old can be dealt with according to juvenile criminal law. In practice this group is usually treated as adults. The judge decides whether to apply juvenile criminal law or not.
[g] There is a group – named young criminals – between 17–21.
[h] 18–20 years old are treated mostly as adults, but with a few exceptions.

Table 39. Juvenile Offenders are:

	EW	FR	DE	NL	PL	SE
Considered criminal	X	X	X	X	X	X
Dealt with by the CJS	X	X	X	X	X	X
Subject to different proceedings	X	X	X		X	X
Dealt with by a different investigative authority					X	
Dealt with by PPS	X	X[a]	X	X		X
Dealt with by special division criminal court	X	X[b]	X[c]	X[d]		
Dealt with by non-criminal court	X				X	
Subject to milder consequences/sanctions	X	X		X		X
Subject to different reactions	X	X[e]	X	X	X	X[f]
Accelerated/Simplified proceedings are available	X	X	X[g]	X		[h]
Subject to decisions for which other institutions are also responsible	X[i]					

[a] PPS section in charge of minors.
[b] This is a totally separate criminal court the Tribunal d'enfants, which is, however, also a civil court making decisions on whom, e.g. goes into care. A judicial investigation by the juge d'enfants, whose court this is, is mandatory, i.e. investigating and sanctioning judge is the same person. It is possible that only "family" consequences are drawn. Appeal instance is the Vice-President, also a juge d'enfants.
[c] The juvenile courts preside over offences committed by juveniles. These are not independent judicial bodies, but special departments of the local and upper regional courts. The "Heranwachsende" are also brought before the juvenile court independent of whether juvenile or adult substantive criminal law is applied.
[d] The juvenile courts preside over offences committed by juveniles. These are not independent judicial bodies but special departments of the local and upper regional courts.
[e] Not only milder sanctions are possible, also educational measures.
[f] There are some reactions that can be used only against juveniles.
[g] Although the accelerated proceedings defined under adult criminal law are excluded, simplified juvenile proceedings, a special form of accelerated proceedings for juveniles, may be used.
[h] There is no special kind of proceedings, but the PPS is obliged to handle the cases against juveniles speedily.
[i] Youth offending teams.

In order to understand the treatment of juveniles some basic information is required. Which age groups are subject to such treatment can be seen in table 38. What being subject to juvenile criminal law means is summarised in table 39.

Bar the Netherlands, the countries studied subject juveniles to different proceedings but they are dealt with using "normal" criminal justice institutions (in some cases, however, by special staff and special divisions. In Poland the family, i.e. a civil court has jurisdiction). They will be subject to different and/or milder forms of punishment.

Table 40 shows clearly that the PPS is the key institution in deciding whether to divert juvenile cases from the traditional criminal justice path. Only in Poland is the court responsible for this, not surprisingly as the PPS role in juvenile proceedings is merely to transfer any cases it receives to the competent family court, which also leads the investigation. The statistics show diversionary measures being used more often than for adult suspects. This is the legally desired expression of a stronger will to educate juvenile offenders.

Table 40. Diversionary Powers for Juvenile Cases

	EW	FR	DE	NL	PL	SE
Police	X					X[a]
Conditionally				X		
PPS	X	X	X	X		X
Conditionally		X	X			X
Court only					X	

[a] As far as the police disposal is concerned, this is the possibility to "refrain from reporting the case" according to the Police Act (Par. 8). It is possible, if the offence is a really petty one/trivial. A remark concerning "public interest" decisions by both the police and PPS: there is no possibility to drop the case because of a lack of public interest in prosecution. The "public interest" plays a role from another point of view: the PPS should not drop or dispose of the case if there is public (and sometimes private (victims)) interest in prosecution. That is, the public interest is not a reason to drop the case, but it might be a reason not to drop (dispose of) the case.

Table 41 shows clearly, however, that a record will be kept of such measures so that the awareness of what has been done before will mark the treatment a juvenile receives from the CJS. Again this means that a slur remains without the juvenile having been found formally guilty. Naturally, particularly where the subject profits so strongly from informal responses, the need that the state is in a position to judge when a “full” response is required, is understandable and indeed criminologically desirable.

Table 41. Records kept for Juveniles of

	EW	FR[a]	DE	NL	PL	SE
Police drop (public interest)	▲ X *			▲[b]	N.a.	▲ ■ [c]
Police conditional disposal	▲ X *			▲[b]	▲	
PPS drop (public interest)		▲ ■	▲ ■	▲ *	N.a.	▲ ■
PPS conditional disposal		▲ ■	▲ ■	▲ *		▲ X *
Conviction by criminal court (for juveniles)	▲ X *	▲ X ■	▲ X[d] ■	▲ X *	▲ X[e]	▲ X *
Court decision other than conviction (in criminal court for juveniles)		▲	▲	▲ X *	▲ X ■	
Other court	▲[f] *				▲ X	

▲ = entry into register
X = "normal" criminal record
■ = limited access
• = unlimited access (n.a.)
* = access as for normal criminal record

[a] PPS files are local only whilst juge d'enfants decision usually goes to the national register. However, it is possible to decide not to include information in the record.
[b] It is a local record.
[c] Police can "refrain from reporting" in which case there will only be a note in police files.
[d] Only if sentenced to youth imprisonment.
[e] Only for art. 10 PC.
[f] When juveniles are tried together with adults, in non-juvenile courts.

11 Summary

This study drew together and compared informational and empirical data from England and Wales, France, Germany, the Netherlands, Poland and Sweden concerning the police, prosecution and court stages as well as several aspects of the respective criminal justice systems in order to determine the function performed by the prosecutions services within these systems. The core prosecutorial function was defined within this study as being to evaluate cases upon their evidential merit in order to decide whether or not they should be brought to court. Above all, the picture painted of prosecution services across Europe by this study, the central findings of which are presented in international comparison in this report, is a dynamic one. All the systems studied, arguably bar Sweden – where recent reform has been structural rather than as to the actual role played by the prosecution service -, are undergoing clear change and subject to reform to a greater or lesser degree.

Whilst there are doubtless a multitude of differences, particularly on the legislative level, much justification is to be found for a statement that the prosecution function is growing and becoming increasingly similar across Europe. Although the common/civil law divide and other fundamental differences between systems are still tangible, the direction of development is such that one feels the beginnings of a type of "European" practice emerging slowly with an evolved and evolving prosecution function apparent. The impression is of criminal justice systems working at full or beyond their capacities and consequently a great deal of adjustment and adaptation being undertaken, in particular, at prosecution service level.

Criminal Justice System Jurisdiction (see 2.2.) This study set out to determine the function performed by the prosecution services in their respective systems. The first defining moment of the prosecutorial role is the question of criminal justice system jurisdiction, i.e. res materiae as a whole. This is a matter of great variation across Europe; as is the degree to which systems are (not) prepared to decriminalise certain offences in order to relieve increasing caseload pressure on their systems. This study indicates decriminalisation as providing a great deal of relief to criminal justice systems but little evidence that this will be the method chosen to do so in the future. The tentatively drawn common trend is towards further criminalisation, if there is one with England and Wales and France having created further public order offences and Poland bringing the Wykrocenia back into the criminal justice sphere. It is necessary to note, however, that no criminal justice system deals with all the forms of behaviour for which a state reaction is foreseen. There is no European consensus as to where the jurisdictional line is to be drawn, i.e. what the role of the criminal justice system is nor as to that of the prosecution service within it. Furthermore one cannot oversee that any formal trend towards criminalisation must be seen in context of the factual situation of institutions unable to deal with their caseloads via a full criminal procedure and thus turning to practices or using discretionary powers to find alternative solutions. Factually one can certainly argue that de-penalising policies are taking hold. One should note, however, that conditional disposal possibilities are increasingly being made available due to dissatisfaction with the high rate of drops. In other words, total de-penalisation, meaning that offences meet no response at all, is regarded as unacceptable.

Prosecution Service involvement in the Investigative Stage (see 3) As far as prosecution service interaction with the police is concerned, a common trend can be observed. Where PPS involvement in and indeed leadership of the investigative stage was traditionally foreseen (e.g. Germany, the Netherlands), it has been reduced. In these countries, the PPS role is one of active involvement only in more serious and complicated cases; it retains a decisive role in deciding where more intense investigatory mechanisms may be used. Beyond that, the prosecution services studied exercise more general, guiding control of the majority of moderately serious and less serious cases. Where police independence was the norm (England & Wales), there is a strong move towards prosecution service involvement via less formal mechanisms; consultation and co-operative decision-making, the level of which intensifies with the complexity of the case in particular. Thus one can speak of practical convergence with similarities emerging as to when and how the PPS and police work together during investigations.

Police Case-ending Powers (see 3.2) The extent to which the police have powers to end-cases, whether on legal or discretionary grounds, is also a matter of variation across jurisdictions but there is a clear trend towards the police gaining power and practical influence upon prosecution service decisions as to which cases should be ended pre-trial on discretionary grounds. There seems to be a growing consensus between the police and the prosecution services as to how many and which kind of resources should be dedicated to which types of cases and to what end. This applies, in particular, to where it is considered appropriate that a case remain solely in police hands and further criminal justice system resources be spared. The police have independent powers to drop cases on public interest grounds in: England and Wales and Sweden and factually do so in France and the Netherlands for minor cases, to dispose of cases (meaning that a condition can be attached) in: England and Wales, the Netherlands and Sweden (where this in fact amounts to a power to sanction), and to recommend a drop or disposal to the PPS in: Poland and, under very limited circumstances, in Germany. This study found indications that this consensus is running along similar lines across Europe. Where the police have independent powers to end cases or are gaining them, this is restricted to less serious cases and subject to more or less tightly defined prosecution service control. Where precisely the line between prosecution and police service competence is being drawn is not yet clear in most of the jurisdictions studied. One can further argue that this line is being blurred as co-operation increases. Further research will be necessary in the future to track this development.

Prosecutorial Case-ending Powers (see 4 and 7) Prosecutorial options in deciding how to end and process cases, i.e. how actually to deal with offenders, is one of the most strongly evolving fields across the jurisdictions studied. Except in Poland, where such powers have recently been made entirely subject to court approval, all the prosecution services studied have independent powers to end cases for reasons beyond evidential sufficiency, i.e. have overt *independent discretionary power*. How far this goes legally varies significantly. Even where court approval of such cases is necessary (as is frequently the case e.g. in the German model), it is apparent that the prosecution service has the decisive influence as to how pre-trial, case-ending solutions should be reached.

The prosecution service has discretionary powers to end cases on grounds other than evidential insufficiency in all the countries studied bar Poland, where this can only be done via application to a court. Information about how such powers are used is limited but where it was available their use was for minor offences such as petty theft and cannabis possession above all for 1st time-offenders. Furthermore all prosecution services except Poland have powers to attach conditions to halting a case and make what this study refers to as a conditional disposal. In England & Wales, however, these are police powers, now used in consultation with the prosecution. Conditional disposals are used to deal with a wider range of petty and less serious offences; a payment to a state or charitable institution is the most common condition imposed but a variety of conditions is available. Their use is not limited to first-time offenders, but it is more frequent for this category of offenders.

Prosecutorial influence upon Procedural Form (see 5 and 7) Prosecution service power also goes beyond this; all of the prosecution services studied have powers to exercise decisive influence upon how convictions are made in at least moderately serious cases, because they all have options to choose *alternative procedural forms* in which they at least if not formally, effectively pre-determine court decisions in the vast majority of cases. These procedural forms involve, in particular, evidential simplifications which lead to the evidence presented by the prosecution service having greater weight. Beyond that, courts usually have the choice whether to accept the prosecution service's proposal or to reject it entirely and order a full trial. These powers and alternative routes are available for less serious offences (e.g. in Germany: the penal order for imposing punishments of up to 1 year of imprisonment). They are used e.g. for traffic or less serious violent offences, also for recidivists, almost exclusively to impose a fine. They display the prosecution service exercising great influence over a conviction.

Evolving Prosecutorial Power (see 5.4) Such powers are evolving further, however. A true *adjudicatory role* is emerging in a number of the jurisdictions studied with the Swedish prosecution service having and the Dutch on set to gain true sanctioning (convicting) powers of its own; whilst the French and Polish prosecution services have powers to negotiate a (convicting) settlement with the accused. The latter is confirmed briefly in a court hearing but the power to negotiate and make key decision rests with the prosecution service, which, with this procedure, gains such influence even for more serious cases because such proceedings can also be used for these (e.g. in Poland for offences punishable by up to 10 years imprisonment. The introduction of such adjudicative powers is currently subject to political discussion in Germany. What options the British prosecution service is given entirely independent of the police remains to be seen. It is well placed to be taking on a stronger role and is certainly gaining strength. The use of guilty plea proceedings there goes some way to making such powers superfluous however.

Such powers have only recently been introduced in study countries, so little statistical information is available about how they are used.

Court Remaining Central Decision-maker (see 6 and 7) In those cases in which the court remains the central decision-maker, i.e. those brought to a full trial (and in all of the jurisdictions studied bar England and Wales this is around or even significantly less than 50% of cases), prosecution services across Europe play a significant role subject to some variation. Their role involves decisions as to charging and what evidence is brought, over which they have greater or lesser control. Their appeal powers also facilitate their, much less visible, position as a guardian instance in relation to court decisions made.

Prosecution Services in a wider Context (see 8 and 9) The tasks which the prosecution is charged with within the respective criminal justice systems varies significantly with some services playing a wider role as guardians of the public interest in a wider sense. They tend to be fairly independent institutions as a whole with more stringent mechanisms binding individual prosecutors internally.

Juveniles (see 10) Juveniles are dealt with by the prosecution services in all the countries studied except Poland. They are treated as criminal offenders but subject to different reactions than adults. All but the Polish prosecution service have the option to use discretionary measures in juvenile proceedings and in England and Wales, the Netherlands and Sweden, the police also have some powers of this kind. Such measures are used more frequently for juveniles than for adults.

12 Final Evaluation and Outlook

The jurisdictions studied all have a prosecution service (a statement which would not have been true 20 years ago) and these have common features with a clearly identifiable trend towards a similar practical role in many respects: it is to lead serious investigation and control more loosely moderately and less serious investigations, to decide which cases are deserving of a reaction less formal than a court trial and what form this reaction should take, as well as which offenders deserve to have a court judgement made against them (naturally also considering the likelihood that the evidence they have will be sufficient to achieve this). Where a court judgement is regarded as appropriate the prosecution service further has significant scope in deciding whether this should occur after a full trial or by using a simplified procedural alternative over which they exercise greater influence. A full criminal trial is exceptional rather than the rule in France, Germany and Sweden and only slightly outweighs the use of other solutions in Poland and the Netherlands. The prosecution services' roles and status are, however, very varied in other aspects, in particular in their interaction with the courts during full criminal proceedings. The trend clearly identified by this study is, however, a strongly increasing prosecution service role in deciding whether and via which modalities the criminal justice system should deal with all but the most serious suspected offenders (for whom this decision is left to the court, naturally still in dialogue with the prosecution service). Another perceivable trend is the tendency to look at other systems and to adopt practices tried and tested in other jurisdictions.[17] Thus the emergence of increasingly similar practices is to be expected. It is precisely for this reason that intensive research into and close evaluation of this area is neces-

[17] Preliminary results of this study have been drawn upon for discussions as to legislative and guideline changes in England & Wales, Germany and the Netherlands.

sary. The dynamic situation must be tracked and analysed as to its desirability. This is vital if the solutions adopted by criminal justice systems are to remain principled and not wholly determined by efficiency criteria. This study has shown clearly that efficient solutions are associated with procedural corner cutting, in which the defendant's right and opportunity to be heard are reduced.

There are a number of issues which require closer attention in relation to such changes and which must be addressed here, even if it is not possible to do so fully. The changes described are (at least part of) a major development and have, in part profound, consequences for criminal justices systems and criminal law as a whole. They represent fundamental changes for the systems studied. Whilst considering these trends in light of this broader perspective, it should be borne in mind that such changes are being introduced because criminal justice systems are overloaded to the point where cases are not being dealt with in a timely manner or the proportion of cases simply being dropped, i.e. receiving no criminal justice reaction at all, is considered to have reached an unacceptable level. Both are very real problems which left alone may well lead to a number of undesirable practices emerging spontaneously and which have human rights ramifications of their own.

The development traced by this study is one moving away from the ideal that a suspected offender should be brought before a court, if appropriate found guilty after a full, public trial and sentenced accordingly, to one in which such treatment is reserved only for the most serious cases. It is one in which pre-trial institutions, originally created for quite different purposes, are given powers to administer (a) punishment (of sorts) or to determine the procedures and treatment suspected offenders, of various levels of seriousness, face. The most obvious consequence of this scenario is the blurring of boundaries between criminal justice system institutions and their tasks and between the types of state reactions available (criminal sanctions, administrative reactions etc.) for a breach of the criminal law. The clearly structured ultima ratio, criminal law becomes a more complex system with a variety of potential paths; a jungle of procedural alternatives and potentially softer and harder reactions resulting from a number of discretionary decisions. This may arguably be seen as a good thing allowing criminal justice workers closer to the case to introduce desirable alternatives such as mediation and treatment as solutions for cases where it is deemed appropriate to do so. On the other hand, the procedures by which such decisions are made become less transparent and the danger of different reactions to similar cases increases the more the solution depends upon individual decisions not subject to public scrutiny.

Person suspected of breaching the law will find themselves facing a variety of different procedures and differently qualified reactions. If systems introduce such options as a response to over-loading in other words as a means to make the system more efficient, the danger that less desirable results follow is high. The question is in how far discretionary decisions will not be made along more pragmatic lines determined more strongly by how many cases the prosecution service needs to deal with, rather than any more objective criteria reflecting the principles based upon which the system has measured the justified severity of punishment up to that point. First of all, a tiered justice system is created in which suspected perpetrators are dealt with more or less intensely, more or less publicly, leading to a more or less severe reaction or sanction. This system may be regarded as objectionable in itself. Clearer issues concerning equality before the law arise if this development is considered in combination with the question as to where the lines are drawn between the manner in which different (categories of) perpetrators are treated (i.e. using a quasi- or real sanction and by which form of procedure) . This is especially the case where such lines are drawn by guidelines issued by several institutions within the same jurisdiction (see e.g. the differences present in the Federal Republic of Germany). If one considers further that these mechanisms are associated with lesser protection of suspect's rights – in order to provide real relief for the system – lesser standards of evidence scrutiny in particular, the issue becomes even more sensitive. In view of the fact that a suspect may not have the right to object to his or her treatment or associate risks with doing so, one must regard the risk of a wrongful (quasi-) punishment as increased. In other words, this tiered justice system is not only one which treats offenders differently but which may treat wrongly suspected individuals in the same way. This increased risk for a small minority is accepted as the price for ensuring a reaction ensues against a larger number of offenders, who are in turn stigmatised to a lesser degree (the argument being that the stigma is not so great and the quasi-punishment not so severe as to require the same level of certainty as for a conviction). The vast majority, those who are factually guilty, profit from less severe treatment. Where an innocent person is affected (and decides not to contest the state reaction imposed[18]), he or she is not really convicted. This represents a clear breach of several principles and cannot really be welcomed by those striving for clearly construed criminal justice systems. The fact that such breaches occur, above all, in relation to less serious cases and thus less serious "sanctions", do not lessen their breaching character. This is a clear development towards a system managing offenders, criminality and the criminal justice system workload, treating suspected offenders less as individuals facing ultimate state interference and more as categories of persons who require certain treatment. Individual characteristics, even such as guilt or innocence and indeed the impact that such contact with the criminal justice system may (indeed should) have on an average citizen, are pushed aside in favour of an efficient system. The question as to the purpose of the criminal justice system must be posed anew. Seen through a prosecutor's eyes, this development may well make sense, he or she is given mechanisms to deal with routine cases, routinely. How a suspect subject to this treatment, especially for whom it is not routine, perceives it, is a different matter. Criminal justice was designed to be an ultima ratio, should it be allowed to become routine?

[18] Where anything more than a pure assumption of guilt noted in a file is imposed or possibly a warning, i.e. a quasi-punishment, follows the suspected person must, of course, factually make a payment, perform an action etc. - an argument which is frequently presented to underline the unlikeliness of this constellation. Two factors must be considered, however: a) the possibility that an innocent person chooses to accept this informal consequence rather than face a public trial and risk more severe punishment; and b) the possibility that a person himself may consider guilty and thus accept this punishment, although legally, they are not guilty because they have a valid, e.g. excusing, defence.

The clear lines strived for by criminal justice systems in defining offences and the punishment suitable, the transparency of proceedings, the stigma imposed and equality before the law are eroded and a bit of justice achieved more efficiently in exchange for the acceptance of a bit of punishment. The suspected offender is regarded as profiting and thus given less opportunity to object. Otherwise this solution would not be efficient. The criminal justice system is given a new goal: dealing with offenders efficiently. The question is whether this is compatible with the moral and social goals strived for.

The legitimate counter-question is of course whether these are being provided for where a system is failing altogether or cases are being sorted out by some other means. Prosecutorial discretion being used under clear guidelines at least bears potential to provide for well-regulated practice, for legally qualified, objective treatment and for a reaction by the criminal justice system. Stronger defence rights can be provided for to protect the innocent (the question in how far this is not counterproductive to the reform aims and the question of resources remains). Where further resources are not made available, how else is a criminal justice system to cope?

The problems discussed above become keener when considered in the currently emerging context; where the judicial function is being eroded and alternative procedural forms being used to provide for convictions and true punishment against which no (or very limited) appeal mechanisms are available. In such cases discretionary decisions (either as to which procedural form to use or as to the settlement negotiated) are leading to true, more serious sanctions. Questions as to treatment of various defendants, their ability to understand what is happening and whether those with better resources will not profit disproportionately, spring to mind. Where such mechanisms are being used for more serious cases and the public excluded, the loss of accountability of the criminal justice system becomes particularly acute. Again the question as to how lines are drawn within the criminal justice system is raised, in this case even more urgently. The prosecutorial decision as to which procedure to follow may have strong ramifications for the sentence imposed. If practice is not very clearly regulated (and there has been little sign of this as yet) fundamental issues of fairness are raised (and the question as to who will scrutinise this practice remains unanswered). A further issue is the question as to whether offenders sentenced by such alternative procedures will not be stigmatised less and indeed, where they tend to be used to deal with certain offences, whether these will in turn not come to be regarded as less serious. Particularly considering that such mechanisms are likely to be used for more complicated cases such as economic crime thus strengthening traditional lines between white-collar and other crime, lends such questions greater urgency. Interestingly many of the legal provisions introducing such procedural options allow their use only "where the aim of proceedings" is still fulfilled. Their introduction begs the question what the aim of criminal proceedings should be. The development of prosecution service powers currently taking place raises fundamental issues as to the purpose of criminal justice systems and how they are expected to interact with society. Issues which should be considered, before the pressures of practice alone define the prosecution service, and with it the police and court, function anew.[19]

This study shows beyond doubt that the prosecution service role has changed and is evolving further. Prosecution services across Europe are not only acting as judges before the judge, but are replacing the judge in all but the most serious cases. This development is underway and must be tracked further. There can be no doubt that it has serious consequences for the function role and impact of the criminal justice system as a whole and that the effect it has upon the principles which it is supposed to serve must be reviewed critically. Further research into the focal areas of this study is necessary and should be augmented by 1) a detailed examination as to the lower jurisdictional boundary of the criminal justice system as a whole (what types of behaviour are criminal justice systems expected to deal with and which are dealt with in other ways), 2) by a closer examination of the workings of police and prosecution service inter-play, as well as 3) of the extent of court scrutiny of prosecution service decisions to which courts must give their formal approval. As criminal justice systems are subject to rapid change and the lines between its agencies becoming blurred, a stock-taking as to the exact role being played by each institution and an evaluation of the positive and negative effects of such change is essential.

[19] For a further and more detailed analysis of human rights implication see: Wade, 2005.

13 References

Aebi M et al (2005) European Sourcebook of Crime and Criminal Justice Statistics (3rd edn). WODC, The Hague

Aubusson de Cavarlay B (2006) The Prosecution Service Function within the French Criminal Justice System. Springer, Berlin Heidelberg New York, pp 185–205 this volume

Blom M, Smit P (2006) The Prosecution Service Function within the Dutch Criminal Justice System. Springer, Berlin Heidelberg New York, pp 237–256 this volume

Bulenda T, Gruszczynska B, Kremplewski A, Sobota P (2006) The Prosecution Service Function within the Polish Criminal Justice System. Springer, Berlin Heidelberg New York, pp 257–284 this volume

Elsner B (in print) Reformüberlegungen zur Erweiterung polizeilicher Kompetenzen im strafrechtlichen Ermittlungsverfahren, eine deutsch-niederländisch rechtsvergleichende Analyse in rechtlicher und rechtstatsächlicher Hinsicht. Dissertation submitted to the University of Göttingen

Elsner B, Peters J (2006) The Prosecution Service Function within the German Criminal Justice System. Springer, Berlin Heidelberg New York, pp 207–236 this volume

Jehle JM (2000) Prosecution in Europe: Varying Structures, Convergent Trends. The European Journal on Criminal Policy and Research 8: 27–42

Jehle JM (2006) The Function of Public Prosecution within the Criminal Justice System – Aim, Approach and Outcome of a European Comparative Study. Springer, Berlin Heidelberg New York, pp 3–25 this volume

Kilchling M (2000) The Role of the Public Prosecutor in Germany. In: Vander Beken T, Kilchling M (eds) The Role of the Public Prosecutor in the European Criminal Justice Systems. VWK, Brussels, pp 73–93

Lewis C (2006) The Prosecution Service Function within the English Criminal Justice System. Springer, Berlin Heidelberg New York, pp 151–184 this volume

Sanders A, Young R (2000) Criminal Justice (2nd edn). Butterworths, London

Tak P (2003) The Dutch Criminal Justice System: organization and operation (2nd edn). Boom, Meppel

Tak P (2004) Introduction. In: Tak P (ed) Tasks and Powers of the Prosecution Services in the EU Member States. Wolf Legal Publishers, Nijmegen, pp 1–15.

Wade M (2005) The Changing Role of European Prosecution. Criminology in Europe 2, (*http://www.esc-eurocrim.org/newsletter/July05ESCnewsletter.pdf - 22.05.2006*)

Zila J (2006) The Prosecution Service Function within the Swedish Criminal Justice System. Springer, Berlin Heidelberg New York, pp 285–311 this volume

14 Annex

Annex 1

Table Annex 1. Case Categorisation by Court Jurisdiction

	EW	FR	DE	NL	PL	SE
Serious cases	Crown Court[a]	Le Cour d' Assises[b]	Landgericht[c]	Rechtbank full bench of three judges[d]	Regional Court[e]	District Court
Less serious cases	Magistrates Court[f]	Tribunal Correctionnel (delits)[g]	Amtsgericht[h]	Lower Court Kantonrechter single cantonal judge of a district court[i] Politierechter[j]	District Court[k]	District Court[l]

[a] Indictable offences/also possible for triable either way offences (depends on the situation and the type of offence.
[b] Crimes.
[c] Cases with a legal provision of a prison-sentence of more than 4 years.
[d] For all crimes, especially more serious crimes.
[e] More serious offences.
[f] Summary offences/also possible for triable either way offences (depends on the situation and the type of offence).
[g] Contraventions 1–5 are carried before the Tribunal de Police. Those are not mentioned in the table because they can't be seen as less serious offences in this comparison.
[h] Cases with a provided sentence of up to 4 years of imprisonment.
[i] For all infractions and some less serious crimes.
[j] All offences with a provided sentence of up to one year of imprisonment go to the Politierechter.
[k] Less serious cases as well as all petty offences, heard by Mag. Division of District Courts.
[l] There is no distinction between the treatment of cases depending of their seriousness.

Annex 2

Table Annex 2. Regulation of PPS/Police Interplay during Investigative Stage

Regulated by:	EW	FR	DE	NL	PL	SE
Law		X	X[a]	X	X[b]	X
(National) Ministerial Guidelines		X	X[c]			
National Guidelines negotiated between police & PPS	X[d]					X[e]
PPS – operational head of service only			X[f]	X[g]	X[h]	X
PPS regionally			X[i]			X[j]
National police only						X[k]
Regional/local police only						
Oral local agreement		X[l]				
Informal tradition/working practice		X				

[a] German procedural code and RiStBV (= guidelines that are legally binding, issued by all federal states together, valid for all federal states).

[b] Art 304 § 3 CCP: The police shall immediately inform PPS about a discovered offence and hand over any collected material.

[c] Guidelines issued by ministries of each federal state.

[d] Kind of written local and national agreements between police, (local) PPS and any other legal authority about how they should work together in specific cases, for example investigation and prosecution of immigration offences between police, immigration service and CPS, they cooperate in cases of child abuse cases, work-related death, proceeds of Crime Act. The guidelines are national ones. Of course, the incidences of different offences do vary regionally: e.g. immigration offences tend to be at ports and airports.

[e] The Guidelines are issued by the Office of the Prosecutor General, in consultation with the National Police Board. Here the division of competence is regulated by the CJP and the Guidelines of the Prosecutor General (adopted in consultation with the National Police Board). The legal regulation is very vague and the guidelines are not binding. The Office of the Prosecutor General has issued a certain number of guidelines concerning special types of offences (for example, so called "hate crimes" and offences against the prohibition of discrimination), which also contain instructions regarding the way to properly organize investigation(s), what kinds of facts should be presented in court, and what kind of sentence should be proposed in court There are also corresponding guidelines with instructions for the police (issued by the National Police Board). Those regulations are relatively wide-ranging with what means that there is enough space left for local regulations as well.

[f] Generalstaatsanwalt.

[g] Board of Prosecutors General.

[h] Public Prosecutor (attorney) General issues such guidelines for particular proceedings in specific cases.

[i] Leitender Oberstaatsanwalt.

[j] Through The Guidelines on the Division of Competence between the PPS and the police, it has lay down that the more detailed division of competence should be made by means of local agreements between the police units and the prosecution offices. The agreements should take into account the particular situation of the given locality, qualifications of the prosecutors and the police staff, their experience, etc.

[k] There are corresponding guidelines for the police with instructions what kind of measures are appropriate in a typical investigation into certain types of offences issued by the National Police Board.

[l] As a local and oral agreement.

Annex 3

Table Annex 3. Regulation of PPS Case Take-over

Regulated by:	EW[a]	FR	DE[b]	NL	PL	SE
Law		X	X[c]	X	X[d]	X
(National) ministerial guidelines		X[e]	X	X		
National guidelines negotiated between police & PPS	X					X[f]
Regional/local guidelines negotiated between police & PPS	X[g]	X[h]				X
PPS - operational head of service only			X	X[i]		
PPS regionally						
National police only						
Regional/local police alone						
Oral local agreement	X	X[j]	X[k]		X[l]	X
Informal tradition/working practice	X	X	X[l]	X		X

[a] It depends on circumstances.

[b] Formally, the police are obliged to hand over at the beginning of an investigation. Factually, in accordance to rules laid down in guidelines, they do not.

[c] German procedural code and RiStBV (= guidelines that are legally binding, issued by all federal states together, valid for all federal states).

[d] In general, the obligation to hand over after a certain number of days, CCP art. 15 § 1.

[e] Circulars exist but they can't be seen as regulating rules because the PPS often ignores them and decides in cooperation with the police office on regional or local level.

[f] Prosecutor General in cooperation with National Police Board. Guidelines contain a list of offences that are left totally in police hands of police and under their full responsibility.

[g] These guidelines deal with PPS – police inter-action at local level all together.

[h] In practice there are often guidelines negotiated between PPS and police that do not necessarily correspond to the ministerial ones.
[i] Board of Prosecutors General issue national guidelines.
[j] Guidelines develop out of working practice between PP and police on the phone (real time Treatment).
[k] No available information, only guess.
[l] Case specific.

Annex 4

Table Annex 4. Case-Ending Decisions (data relating to Fig. 5 and 7)

	Traffic offences			Theft			of which: burglary		
	NL 94	NL 02	SE 02	NL 94	NL 02	SE 02	NL 94	NL 02	SE 02
Drop (simple+public interest)	5063	2921		28014	5178		3628	568	
Drop (simple)			11332			29371			6689
Drop (public interest)			6776			9160			1421
Disposal	14183	18806		13130	8555		562	457	
Penal order			11729	32987	35553	32301	5695	5503	8717
Brought before court	20761	24581	38606			7956			68

	Drug offences		
	NL 94	NL 02	SE 02
Drop (simple+public interest)	4167	1232	
Drop (simple)			11477
Drop (public interest)			4412
Disposal	891	2377	
Penal order	4266	9117	18996
Brought before court			4154

	Assault			Of which: more serious forms			Of which: least serious forms		
	NL 94	NL 02	SE 02	NL 94	NL 02	SE 02	NL 94	NL 02	SE 02
Drop (simple+public interest)	3707	1800		354	262		3353	1538	
Drop (simple)			50411			1409			49002
Drop (public interest)			1831			21			1810
Disposal	2796	5549		138	412		2261	5137	
Penal order			746			0			746
Brought before court	5784	10156	23691	1883	4044	1391	4275	6112	22300

	Robbery			Rape			Less serious forms of sexual harassment		
	NL 94	NL 02	SE 02	NL 94	NL 02	SE 02	NL 94	NL 02	SE 02
Drop (simple+public interest)	849	550		341	227		694	426	
Drop (simple)			1091			1242			1461
Drop (public interest)			23			1			74
Disposal	79	94		25	15		186	209	
Penal order	4020	5241	1096	465	666	278	793	1265	706
Brought before court			0			0			39

	Intentional homicide		
	NL 94	NL 02	SE 02
Drop (simple+public interest)	419	366	
Drop (simple)			507
Drop (public interest)			2
Disposal	62	26	
Penal order	1406	2494	321
Brought before court			0

Annex 5 Comments on Table 6

[a] The police have complete discretion about when to inform PPS about a case, but they tend to follow the guidelines set down by CPS. The police also inform the CPS when it is asked to carry out some non-prosecution functions.

[b] When suspect is arrested for being under suspicion of having committed a delit (situation of flagrant delit).

[c] Police officers work out a report about the discovered case and send it directly to the PPS. He has to send it first to the assistant PP (hulpofficier van justitie) every time he has not sworn in, the assistant PP will then take a look at the report and send it to PPS in his name.

[d] Depends especially on complexity of legal aspects (the seriousness of case is only a further reason for immediate information but not, as in the other countries, the decisive category), according to the guidelines: < 2 years of imprisonment In Sweden the independency of Police in terms of investigation does not depend on the seriousness of a case but on the complexity of investigation which is usually expected in those cases.

[e] Except for "flagrant delits".

[f] In all cases which are not of a simple nature.

[g] Except where guidelines state PPS responsible, in these cases they are already informed.

[h] Flagrants delit and contraventions 5 classe.

[i] Police can take some preparatory actions.

[j] In Poland the police immediately have to report the case to PPS. By law there is no possibility for the PPS to leave certain cases entirely in police hands in general except in cases laid down in art. 311 § 3 and § 5 CCP: Here PPS can enable the police to conduct (a part of) an investigation or to take certain measures by themselves. Normally this will happen in less serious cases. PPS will always be involved from the very beginning in case of crimes (homicide) or misdemeanours in which the suspect is a member of an investigating agency.

[k] Where s/he is to be placed in police custody.

[l] The PPS has to be informed at least when suspect is found because then the PPS has to inform the suspect of the charges against him.

[m] In cases where PPS is definitely in charge of preliminary investigation.

[n] If the police wish to hold on to the offender for longer than the statutory requirement, they must ask the PPS to make an application to a magistrate.

[o] Except for flagrant delits – when wanted to search premises – needed EM permission until March 2003, so PP had to be informed and transfer case to EM.

[p] Result of working tradition.

[q] E.g. in cases of search of houses, the suspect has to be informed about PPS` decision and given permission for such an action within 7 days.

[r] In case of applicable coercive measures, the intervention of a court is required or "special examination of prosecution" is provided.

Annex 6 Comments on Table 8

[a] No legal provisions, depends on the case. In the Netherlands the file is not handed on but only the suspect and all information laid down in a report. The file remains at police station so that at the end the where will be two files at both levels.

[b] If the investigation has been instituted by the police and the case is not of a simple nature, the police shall hand over the case to the PPS as soon as a person is suspected for

good reasons of committing the offence. The PPS shall also take over the investigation in other cases, if there are special reasons for doing so.

[c] Cases starting "in flagranti" and with use of police custody and offender handed over to the prosecutor for immediate hearing.

[d] Shortly after preliminary investigation.

[e] And in police custody.

[f] If the investigation has been instituted by the police and the case is not of a simple nature, the police shall hand over the case to the PPS as soon as a person is suspected for good reasons of committing the offence. The PPS shall also take over the investigation in other cases, if there are special reasons for doing so, i.e. in cases with an intensive media interest. That means that PPS can take over an investigation even if the case is of simple nature.

[g] Could be if the court needs to give a judgement on some procedural aspect: i.e. keeping the accused in custody for more than a day, and the PPS needs to make the application for the police.

[h] If the police conduct an "in flagranti" investigation, which is limited to 8 days, but they want to remain in this mode after 8 days (in order to retain the extra powers they have), this must be approved by a juge d'instruction, so the PPS must become involved in order to make this request.

[i] Cases, in which the investigation cannot go on as a "preliminary investigation" or as a "flagrant délit", and the intervention of the EM is needed.

[j] Detention > 6/12 hours, search of premises, if this is extensive (Pros.-Gen. Guidelines state: police may decide independently where a search is not extensive, if it is very extensive, court permission is required).

[k] In this context, less serious cases are contraventions 5. classe.

[l] If the police itself continue the investigation, which will happen, in cases of a simple nature, the case will be handed over after the investigation has been completed. There is no special legal provision for this, but as only the PPS may bring the case to court, there is no alternative. Furthermore a handing over at this stage is also possible if the case is not of simple nature and PPS head the investigation but asked police conducting the investigation instead.

[m] Case will remain as file, either active or passive. It can be revived if it comes up to new evidence, or new technology to help the investigation.

Annex 7 Comments on Table 9

[a] EM: in general; PPS: in fields of organised crime (since 2004).

[b] In cases, where the suspect is caught red-handed or where the legal threat is 4 years or more. A post-facto of the EM is required. The EM can always initiate a search of premises.

[c] Police indep.: if the search is not too extensive; PPS: If the search is extensive; EM: if search is very extensive.

[d] Only to make application to court.

[e] Every time there is a real suspicion and the suspect is stopped or arrested the police are authorized to confiscate goods the suspect carries with him and which are capable for confiscation (CCP 95 I) needed.

[f] Only for confiscation.

[g] The procedural measures, seizure of, e.g. documents or other things which are necessary for investigation, may be ordered by the head of the investigation, that is, a police officer

or the PPS. Decisions as to the forfeiture of dangerous objects (weapon etc.) may be taken by the police but the final decision is made by the court.

[h] Assets frozen may be imposed by court only.

[i] Police can use/initiate DNA-tests independently when comparing with material traces.

[j] PPS or EM is necessary to compare suspects´ DNA with the national DNA-File (serious offences, mainly sexual offences but not only).

[k] During gvo.

[l] Legal threat has to be 4 years or more.

[m] PPS must be informed as soon as offender is put in custody.

[n] Assistant PP: police officer with tasks of PP. Police can stop the suspect for identification and hold him at police station for a maximum of 6 hours (ophouden voor onderzoek).

[o] As far as the period of seizure is concerned there are no figures mentioned in the law. According to § 8 Chap. 24 CJP the suspect shall be immediately interrogated by PPS or Police and PPS immediately has to be informed about the seizure. PPS needed if person is not only stopped and searched but shall be interrogated because there seems to be a reason for pre-trial detention. For this the Court has to be informed to make a decision about pre-trial detention within 4 days.

[p] Where the police discover a suspect red-handed or in cases of a legal threat of 4 years and more, it can keep the suspect at police station up to 3 days (inverzekeringstelling). This can be approved by (assistant-) PP.

[q] From 24–48 in general; 72 hours for drug traffic and org. crime.

[r] Possible to detain a person up to three days, then court decision is required.

[s] Especially in case of football hooligans; usually police and PPS will apply to this.

[t] Usually PPS and police will apply.

[u] Since 2001, before it had to be given by juge d'instruction.

[v] Max 10 days: EM (bewaring), thereafter full court is needed for "gevangenhouding" or "gevangenneming", which both result of the EM permit of pre-trial-detention. The court then can keep the suspect in trial for a maximum of 90 days.

[w] An application to the court for a detention order shall be made without delay and not later than 12 o'clock on the third day after the arrest order."

Annex 8 Comments on Table 21

[a] A "disposal with condition" doesn't exist in Swedish law. However, what does exist, is the waiver of prosecution according to Chap. 20 § 7 CJP. It is clear a disposal, but not joined with any conditions. On the other hand, the waiver may be withdrawn if a PP finds it "appropriate" later.

[b] Stage, med. treatment, Tâche d'intérêt public.

[c] Mediation, retribution etc. requires an admission of guilt. A rappel a loi does not.

[d] This is merely a form of simplification. Judgement after ordonnance penale is a conviction and taken into account in relation to recidivism. As of 2003 the composition penale is recorded. There is no possibility to appeal; the law states that it should not be used for recidivist offenders. In practice, however, it will be used even for recidivists where the desired punishment lies below the maximum, which can be applied for using a composition penale. It is still merely a further form of conditional disposal.

[e] This is merely a form of simplification. Judgement after ordonnance penale is a conviction and taken into account in relation to recidivism.

[f] Public employers, specific professions.

[g] The law requires agreement only to mediation, however guidelines indicate that where a disposal requires suspect involvement, both an admission of guilt and consent are required.

[h] If refuses, PP in principle should prosecute but in practice may as well decide for an unconditional drop.

[i] The suspect plays an active role because s/he is required to fulfil a condition. Where s/he refuses his consent the case will go to court.

[j] But only if a PP applies the disposal during the trial.

[k] Victim must agree to mediation.

[l] Is subject to judicial approval – PPS sends file with the request of a validation. The judge can call a hearing.

[m] The court must actively agree. It imposes the condition.

Annex 9 Comments on Table 22

[a] Legal statements only.

[b] Reparation often used.

[c] Limited by the law to a list of offences: assault without aggravating factors leading to more than 3 years imprisonment, desertion of family and offences against parental authority, simple theft, some frauds, criminal damage, contempt of public officer (mainly police officers and agents), drunk driving, drug use → no pattern known as jet.

[d] Theoretically possible against all of these offences because can be used for any offence punishable by < 6 years imprisonment.

[e] Drug use in general is a classic case for such "alternative" treatment by PPS. Where there was no other offence associated with this offence the classic reaction was a requirement to undergo medical treatment.

[f] Also used for certain traffic offences, where can require suspect to sort out situation.

[g] Basically a disposal in accordance with § 153a StPO is available for all the offences listed. However, it is likely that it is used most frequently for the offences as indicated above.

[h] Classic case for mediation.

[i] First time suspects are the norm for everything except mediation. Mediation can be used for recidivists where it is regarded as likely that this will solve the conflict.

[j] A disposal in accordance with § 153a StPO is first and foremost to be considered for first time offenders. When particular circumstances apply it is not excluded for repeat offenders.

[k] First time suspects are the norm for everything except mediation. Mediation can be used for recidivists where it is regarded as likely that this will solve the conflict.

[l] There is no general rule. It can be used for recidivists, or at least for offenders who have previously been subject to disposals (condition drop, mediation, etc.). But since prison is not possible, multi-recidivists are not treated here.

[m] Legally possible – no pattern known as yet.

[n] Although retribution is an appropriate condition in accordance to guidelines, it is not used in practice.

[o] See Fn m). Suspension of driving licence is also possible.

[p] Community service is available, but rarely used.

Annex 10 Comments on Table 29

[a] Stopping the case until more evidence found. The PPS cannot dispose, but it can suggest to the police that cautions are given or that reparation orders are requested from the court.
[b] There is no public interest drop regulated in the Swedish procedural law, but the regulation is a part of substantive criminal law. There are a number of descriptions of offences in the Penal code saying that the particular offence shall be prosecuted only if there is a substantial public interest in prosecution. However, even if not directly expressed, the lack of public interest is ratio of some of the provisions on drop of investigation.
[c] Police caution, generally with CPS agreement.
[d] Drops joining cases, which the judge can take into consideration. The case is dropped and the court merely informed of these offences.
[e] Available as police power only.
[f] As of July 2003, Art. 23a CCP, where victim and suspect agree, PPS can apply for court approval to send a case to another institution for mediation (the court also has this option), thereafter the case will be dropped.
[g] HALT Buro.
[h] Driving licence.
[i] Ordonnance pénale.
[j] Composition pénale.
[k] Strafbefehl.
[l] Will be in 2007.
[m] Simplified proceeding.
[n] Penal order.
[o] Strafförelaggande.
[p] < 60 months imprisonment.
[q] Up to a year if the accused has a defence lawyer.
[r] NB. Conditional sentence, not suspended in usual sense.
[s] This PPS sanction requires suspect agreement.
[t] Also confiscation, suspension of driving licence.
[u] Suspension/confiscation of driving licence, social, medical or professional training ("stage").
[v] In particular driving ban and withdrawal of the permission to drive.
[w] Driving ban.
[x] Performing between 20 and 40 hours community service per month (Art. 35 § 1 KK). If the convict is employed the court can alternatively confiscate 10 to 25% of his/her earnings or donate this to a charitable cause (Art. 35 § 2 KK). Furthermore, during execution of sentence the convict may not change his/her permanent place of residence without court permission. S/He is obliged to perform the work ordered and to provide information as to progress made (Art. 34 § 2 KK).
[y] PPS/Police joint decision on certain disposals.
[z] Waiver [§ 20 § 7] leads to a record.

Dealing with Various Offence Types in Different Criminal Justice Systems – Case Examples

Bruno Aubusson de Cavarley, Martine Blom, Teodor Bulenda, Beatrix Elsner, Beata Grusczynska, Jörg-Martin Jehle, Andrzej Kremplewski, Christopher Lewis, Julia Peters, Paul Smit, Piotr Sobota, Marianne Wade, Josef Zila

A full picture of the national criminal justice systems and their workings is presented in the country reports in this volume as well as in the study questionnaires. However, the sheer volume of information makes it difficult not to lose sight of what these differences or common features mean in practice. In order to present the systems studied comparatively in a less abstract way and to show the study results more tangibly, a few case examples were developed and the partners asked to describe the most likely handling the cases would receive through their criminal justice systems. The examples were chosen to facilitate a demonstration of some basic differences within and between the systems and to illustrate the different procedural forms discussed in the study.

Case 1 *An offender is caught driving 30 km/hour above the speed limit. It is his first offence.*

If in *England & Wales* an offender is caught driving 30 km/hour above the speed limit and if it is his first offence, the police will first inform the owner of the car. He has to respond within 28 days with the name of the driver. A fixed penalty of £60 (€ 87.48) plus three penalty points on the driving licence will be the sanction. The driver can fight the case in court, but the penalty on conviction will be greater. If the driver already has 9 points on his licence then the 3 points will cause him to be prosecuted under the 'clocking-up' system because he will then have 12 points and hence he will be banned from driving for a year.

In *France*, this kind of road traffic offence is a 4th class contravention offence. This incurs a maximum fine of € 750 payable according to the set fine proceeding; the reduced set fine may apply (€ 90). The fine has to be paid within a specific time limit.[1] If this time limit is overstepped the set fine rises to € 135. In case of wilful non-payment within 30 days, the file is transmitted to the OMP, who demands a set fine with surcharge (€ 375), which is collected by the Treasury De-

[1] If the ticket is given directly by the officer reporting the offence, the fine has to be paid within 3 days, within 7 days if the ticket is mailed.

partment. This petty offence automatically takes 3 points off the driving license (out of 12). When all 12 points are lost, the license is cancelled and the person must wait six months to pass the licensing examination to get a new license, and undergo a medical examination.

In *Germany* the offender has committed a traffic offence against order, which is investigated and prosecuted by the police. The offence can be punished by an administrative fine. This provision does not specify the maximum level and so this can be a maximum of € 1,000 for deliberate, € 500 for negligent behaviour. In order to ensure equality before the law, catalogues of administrative fines have been issued (this is, indeed, required for mass offences) in particular road traffic offences. According to the applicable guidelines (*Bußgeldkatalogverordnung*), having exceeded the speed limit by 30 km/hour, the offender will face an administrative fine of between € 60 (outside of settlements) and 90 (within settlements). The offence against order will be registered in the central traffic register. It will be deleted after 2 years.

In *the Netherlands* this kind of offence is a 'Mulder-law' offence. If the speed was more than 30 km/hour above the speed limit and on secondary roads, it would have been an offence in the B category (*kantonzaken*). Since 'Mulder-law' offences are not registered in criminal records it does not matter that it is a first offence. Also, penalty points on the driver's license are not given[2]. The driver (if known) or else the registered owner of the car will receive, usually within a few weeks, from the CJIB a pre-printed giro card inviting payment of the fine, which is in this situation € 115 (motorway) or € 125 (other roads). If it was at a place were road workers were at work, the fine will be € 170. These are fixed penalties, deviations do not occur.

In *Poland* it is a petty offence. Most frequently it is revealed by the police officers using speed measurement instruments. In that case the perpetrator is stopped at the place of event and informed about his/her having committed an offence – found by the police. Most probably the police's reaction will consist in imposing a fine ticket of € 25–50 upon the perpetrator. The driver may refuse to accept the ticket. In that case the police prepare a request for punishment – addressed to the competent Magistrates' Court. Having considered the case the Magistrates' Court may decide on penalty within PLN 20.00–3,000,00 (€ 4.86–729.12) or reprimand.

If the offence registered by automatic speed-recording instruments (photo-radar), the owner of the vehicle will be informed. He may either accept the fine imposed in default (in the amount as above) or point out an offender in fact to the competent agency.

The offence commitment will be entered in the register of drivers. Also the number of penalty scores adequate to the petty offence committed (in this particular case: 4) will be recorded in the register. If a driver "gains" 20 penalty scores within a year of the date of granting a driving licence, his licence will be with-

[2] In the Netherlands there is no penalty point system for driver's licenses. However, since 2002, drivers can lose their licence if they commit three serious traffic offences (such as causing accidents, excessive speeding, etc.) within the first 5 years after they received their first driver's license (*Bron: www.verkeershandhaving.nl*).

drawn. 24 scores acquired by another driver will cause addressing such a driver for control checking up his/her qualification ranged to all the categories of the driving license obtained[3].

In *Sweden* the offender has committed an offence according to the Traffic Regulation (*Trafikförordning).* The offence is on the list of the offences – issued by the Prosecutor General in consultation with National Police Board – that can be prosecuted by means of *summary fines order* by a police officer. In this case, if the offender confesses to the offence, the police officer gives him a decision and he has to pay a sum, approximately 1,500 SEK (€ 160.76). If he doesn't agree, the case will be handed over to the PPS, who may either issue a *penal order* or bring the case to the court. It depends on the offender's attitude. The sanction will not be changed, regardless of the litigation costs. The decision will be recorded in the criminal register.

Case 2 *Petty theft – An adult steals a sweatshirt worth 20 Euros from a shop. This is a first offence.*

In *England & Wales* the offence usually is discovered by a store assistant or detective. Many stores will prosecute: some will have their own sanction, eg. by photographing the offender and/or banning him from the store in the future. Others will report the offender to the police. A first offender will not be prosecuted, but will be cautioned, which is a formal warning from a policeman. If the offender is caught again for a similar offence, then he is likely to be prosecuted.
If the offender is caught *in flagrante*, then the goods being stolen are likely to have been recovered. If the offender is caught by a CCTV film being recognised and the goods are not recovered, then a condition of a caution may be that the police tell the offender that he must pay the cost of the goods stolen to the store.

In *France* shoplifting for small sums is not prosecuted if it is the first offence known to the police or the PPS. However, the situation varies considerably from one court to another: It depends on the methods used to track repeated shoplifting, on the cut-offs used to define the type of response, on the relations between the store's security guards, the police services and the PPS. In the situation most frequently encountered, the security guards stop the offender, who must immediately return the stolen goods to the owner (or in some stores pay for the stolen goods). Next, prior agreements between the security guards, the police and the PPS determine those cases in which the police are called in to arrest the offender. For most courts, the sum of € 20 is in the category in which the case is simply recorded (usually on a simplified form sent in by the store) on the police or PPS files. In some courts, a *rappel à la loi* may be decided, in the form of a letter sent to the offender.

In *Germany* this offence is a misdemeanour punishable by fine or a custodial sentence of up to 5 years. The PPS (in practice the police) will initiate the necessary investigative measures. In cases of simple theft, most Länder allow the use of

---

[3] Ordinance of 20 December 2002 of Minister of Internal Affairs and Administration on procedures related to the drivers infringing the road traffic regulations, JoL No 236 item 1998 as amended.

simplified investigative proceedings. This usually makes use of a pre-formulated standard form. The police will investigate the case independently and inform the PPS once it has closed the investigation. Where there is sufficient suspicion, it will decide whether to bring the case to court or to end the case out of court.

Being a first-time offender, speaks for guilt of a minor nature in almost all cases.[4] The presence of public interest often results primarily from the value of the damage caused/ value of property involved. This varies from Land to Land; in Hessen it lies at € 5, in Schleswig-Holstein at € 50. In Hessen, therefore, a discretionary drop would be out of the question, a conditional disposal possible. In Schleswig-Holstein this criteria would not necessitate the exclusion of a discretionary drop. In as far as one is defined, the maximum value limit for a conditional disposal is very high and so one can assume that a shop-lifting case with a value of € 20 would be met with a conditional disposal for a first-time offender (in as far as not with a discretionary drop).

In *the Netherlands* this will usually be detected by the shop owner or his personnel. Most shop owners will inform the police and if possible they will detain the offender (they may do this, but are not allowed to use excessive force). They may not prosecute or impose sanctions or measures themselves. It is a simple theft, a category C offence (*rechtbankzaak*). And it is the only offence in this category for which a police-*transactie* is possible. For a first-time offender this will indeed be the most probable outcome. The *transactie* will be € 125 (or € 210 if the stolen good is worth more than € 50). If the offender refuses the *transactie* (or does not pay) a writ of summons for a court hearing (the single police judge will handle this) will follow. Most probably a community service or a slightly higher fine than the original *transactie* will then be the verdict and the offence will be added to the criminal record.

In *Poland* theft of things with a value not exceeding € 60 is a petty offence. Disclosure of such a theft usually takes place at the moment of commitment or of the attempt of taking the stolen good away from the shop. In that case, the shop guards or workers may call the police and detain the thief until the police arrive. But they are not obliged to inform the police if they find it sufficient that the offender gives the stolen thing back or pays for it. In case of police participation, the police officer finally addresses a request for punishment to the competent Magistrates' Court. The court may decide on 5–30-day arrest, one-month restricted freedom (hardly applicable) or a fine of PLN 20.00–5,000,00 (€ 4.86–1,215.20), which is most frequently applicable especially in relation to the first-time offenders. In the case under consideration, a fine is most probable to be applied, however, the amount is unpredictable on the grounds of data in hand, as the value is subject to a number of circumstances.

In *Sweden* the offence will be qualified as a petty theft (*snatteri* with a prescribed sanction up to 6 months imprisonment or day-fines). The offence will be reported to the police or the PPS (more likely to the police). The police initiates

[4] It is usually the considerations mentioned in § 46 II StGB which are used as indicators for the extent of guilt. These include the suspects past and therefore also offending record.

investigation, takes the necessary measures (interrogation of the suspect, victim and other witnesses, if any) and the case will be handed over to the PPS. The PPS, in this case, most probably issues a penal order and sends it to the suspect. The sanction will probably be 30 day-fines. If the suspect doesn't agree to the penal order, the case will be brought to court. Otherwise, the case will be finished by penal order and the decision will be recorded in the criminal register.

Case 2 var. a *Petty theft – A 15 years old steals a sweatshirt worth 20 Euros from a shop. This is a first offence.*

In *England & Wales* the procedure for a young person is the same as for an adult. A 15-year old would receive a similar sanction, but it would be called a reprimand.

In *France* the proceeding would be the same. In some courts the police are called in for relatively small sums (this is the principle of the systematic response) and the juvenile is turned over to his parents.

In *Germany* a 15 years old is a juvenile, so the relevant criminal law is regulated in the JGG. The authorities treat juveniles somewhat differently to adults. The investigation will focus, in particular, on the social context and personality and this will influence what path the proceedings take. The police (in this case, in particular the officer responsible for juveniles) are required to review the case in order to establish in how far a drop or disposal might be appropriate. This decision will be made in line with the guidelines developed. Like all guidelines for diversionary measures, these present diversion-favourable and unfavourable criteria. In case of a first-time offender and a limited value of the stolen good, a drop/disposal is probable if the findings relating to his personality and social context are positive. Whether a drop or disposal will be used, depends upon the specific Land's guidelines and provisions, which will also determine in how far the police, the PPS or other institutions are involved. In most cases the police are almost solely responsible for carrying out investigative proceedings and will fundamentally influence and participate in diversionary proceedings.

In *the Netherlands* a police-*transactie* is not possible (it is only for adult offenders). Instead a HALT measure will be offered by the police, but only if the offender admits the offence and agrees with the HALT measure. Typically, the HALT measure will consist of a few hours work, if possible (if the shop owner agrees) at the shop were he did the shoplifting.

In *Poland* a 15 years old is not treated by criminal law. Hence, if the shop personnel report an offence to the police such a case will be passed to a competent family court. In the event that the offender's identity cannot be established or there are justified grounds for fear that it may be hidden, the police may detain such a juvenile and place him/her in the police shelter. The juvenile's parents or custodians are informed of the event.

A family court judge will order an inquiry at domicile to be conducted by a professional probation officer. The inquiry will contain particulars as to the juvenile's situation and behaviour in family, at school and possibly in organizations a child is a member of. If it turns out that this is the first punishable act the child has committed and the minor shows no other features of demoralization, the most probable reaction of the family court will consist of an admonition administered to the juvenile. If such a juvenile happens to have violated the law before, the court may apply other educational measures like submitting the minor to the probation officer's custody.

In *Sweden* the procedure will be the same up to the moment at which the PPS takes over the case. However, the police (or the PPS) will contact the social authorities and the parents. Most probably, the prosecutor will invite the offender to his/her office (maybe together with the parents) and waves the prosecution. Another outcome (penal order) is not impossible, but unlikely. In that case, the sanction would be much more lenient than for an adult. The waver of prosecution will be recorded in the criminal register.

Case 2 var. b *Petty theft – An adult steals a sweatshirt worth 20 Euros from a shop. He is a persistent offender.*

In *England and Wales* now more serious sanctions would follow. The offender is likely to face some form of probation, or even a short prison sentence. For a young person, more emphasis is given to some sort of restorative justice, through a referral order. This refers offender from the youth court to a youth offending panel to try to negotiate a contract between the offender and the victim or the local society.

When a given degree of repetition is ascertained, in *France* the offender is arrested by the police and a proceeding is initiated under the authority of the PPS, which indicates what follow-up should be given. Depending on the offender's characteristics (such as occupation and residence), this may be an alternative measure such as *composition pénale*, or prosecution before a *tribunal correctionnel*, the offender being summoned at the end of a police proceeding, or if the author is homeless and is a well-known recidivist, there may be a summary trial. The sanction pronounced will also depend to a large degree on any previous convictions found in the offender's criminal record. If there are only convictions for acts of the same nature, generally punished the first time by a fine or a simple suspended prison sentence, the need to increase the sanction leads to pronouncement of suspension of the sentence with probation, or a community service order. Simple theft is punishable by a maximum prison term of 3 years and twice that in case of repetition. However, there would have to be a series of quite serious aggravating circumstances for shoplifting of an object worth € 20 to lead to an unsuspended prison sentence.

In *Germany* basically the procedure can be exactly the same as in the answer above. The law does not exclude the PPS using diversionary proceedings against repeat offenders. But the precondition "no public interest in further prosecution" is not fulfilled if there is a danger of re-offending. Therefore most Länder guidelines refer to recidivism within a certain period as key-criteria in relation to drops/disposals.[5] It is possible to make this type of case-ending decision even for a person who has become recidivist more than twice (either previous convictions or diversionary measures imposed against him/her), but repeat offending will go

5 It is a particularly important criterion in relation to juveniles and drug-related diversion (§ 45 onwards JGG and 31a BtMG).

against using them in most Länder. Thus it is likely that the case will be brought to court, the PPS either applying for a penal order or bringing public charges (normally or using accelerated proceedings). A judgement is likely.

In *the Netherlands* for persistent offenders (adult as well as juvenile) a writ of summons for a court hearing will be the normal decision of the prosecutor. The sentence requested will probably be a € 150 fine (for the adult offender) or 24 hours community service (for the juvenile).

In *Poland* the course of proceedings will be similar to that related to an adult, first-time offender. Arrest is more likely in this case.

In *Sweden*, most probably, the procedure will be the same as in case of an first-time-offender. The sanction imposed will be severer. However, under certain circumstances, the act could be qualified as theft. It wouldn't exclude issuing of penal order.

Case 3 *Bodily harm – Two adults who are strangers to that date, become involved in an argument in a pub. A hits B with a glass bottle causing a wound to B's face that requires stitching in a hospital. B is unable to work for 3 days.*

In *England and Wales* this would depend on the past behaviour of both parties, whether the attack was unprovoked and whether there was any racist involvement or aggravation. It is possible that the police would caution one or both people, but more likely that the case would be prosecuted in court. The exact injury is not particularly relevant or set out in statute, but the court may use the extent of the injury to award any compensation from the attacker to the victim. The court may also award any penalty up to a short period of imprisonment, particularly if the offender has previous convictions for violence. In such cases, there is often a lack of witnesses for the police to obtain evidence and the CPS would have to take this into account when considering whether to prosecute.

However, if there is no previous history, the court may then bind over the offender to keep the peace. In some cases, where both have some *mens rea* in the incident, the court could bound both parties over, especially if there seems likelihood of a further fight. Orders could be made banning one or both parties from the pub, although it is likely that the publican himself will have placed such an order on one or both of them. If the offender was thought to be on drugs, then he can be ordered to be drug tested and a condition of any sanction made that he goes on a drug treatment course. This will depend on the availability of such treatment in his local area.

In *France* for this act to be qualified as a misdemeanour, the aggravating circumstance of use of a weapon would have to be taken into consideration. This charge may very well be accepted, especially if B lodges a complaint and expresses the intention to demand compensation. However, the moderate seriousness of the case will lead the PPS to examine the possibility of a disposal. Since the two individuals are not acquainted, *composition pénale* will be preferred to mediation. However, in many PPS, the standard response will be a summons to a hearing by the *tribunal correctionnel*, with the victim being advised of the date to enable him to attend the hearing and join the case on civil grounds. The usual sanction, if this is a first conviction, is a short, suspended prison sentence, possibly accompanied by a fine. Some judges prefer paroling, with the explicit condition that the victim be given compensation. The judge will probably also try to find out whether the offender's violent behaviour is due to a problem of alcohol abuse. If he is convinced that this is the case, he will link the suspended imprisonment on parole to the obligation to attend a specialized medical consultation in view of treatment as needed.

In case of repetition, and especially if the offender is poorly integrated socially, summary trial will be the normal track, leading to an unsuspended prison term of several months.

In *Germany* A's actions amount to dangerous bodily harm. This is punishable by a custodial sentence of 6 months to 10 years, in less serious cases 3 months to 5 years. A less serious case cannot be assumed here because B was unable to work for 3 days. Unlike the shop-lifting case, this one cannot be the subject of simplified investigative proceedings but in terms of potential reactions, this misdemeanour leaves the PPS with the same options as above.

Almost all Länder guidelines exclude the use of a drop. As far as a conditional disposal is concerned, the picture varies, but in most cases, its use would seem unlikely. Only if one defines 3 days absence from work as a mild consequence, one can conditionally dispose according to some Länder guidelines. Usually perpetrator-victim mediation would then be the condition attached. The PPS is, however, most likely to bring public charges.

In *the Netherlands* this is seen as the simplest form of assault. It is a crime (category C offence) described in article 300/1 of the CC. The maximum penalty for this article is a prison sentence of 2 years. More serious forms of assault can occur (and can have penalties of up to 15 years) if the consequences are more serious (lasting injuries) or if the assault was intentional and / or premeditated.

If there are no other special circumstances (e.g. a previous history of violent offences) a *transactie* is the most probable outcome. However, the *transactie* will not be a sum of money (because a weapon was used and there was an injury) but 70 hours of community service.

In *Poland* A's conduct exemplified above would most probably exhaust the attributes of offence under Article 157 § 2 of the Criminal Code (causing impairment of a bodily organ functioning that lasts not longer than 7 days). It should be stressed here that – according to the fixed practice – the time of incapacity for work must hardly be equal to that of "impairment of a bodily organ functioning or disturbance of health". Hence in order to find out the kind of wounds suffered by B in the case under consideration there should be appointed a court medical consultant.

The offence under Article 156 § 2 of CC is prosecuted upon private indictment (a wronged person may file an indictment himself to the court; a prosecutor may decide on prosecution *ex officio* only when a public interest is found).

The following scenario seems to be the most probable; B informs the police of the occurrence which is followed by the police's institution of inquiry and addressing the injured person to the court medical consultant for examination. In the court consultant's opinion it is ascertained that the wounds suffered by B result in impairment of bodily organ functioning or disturbance of health for the time not exceeding 7 days. The police send the files to the prosecutor who discontinues the proceedings having found no public interest in continuation of prosecution *ex officio*. At the same time the injured party is informed of his right to file an indictment according to the private complaint procedure. In the event that such an indictment is filed A may be sentenced to fine, freedom restriction or imprisonment of up to 2 years. Sentencing depends on the accused person's personal conditions; however, a sentence of imprisonment without a conditional stay of execution seems unlikely. Then, if the injured files a respective request the court will decree a duty to redress damage caused in whole or in part. Also possible will be a sanction imposing a payment to the injured due to his impairment of a bodily organ function / health disturbance, as well as due to the injury sustained. In addition, the court adjudicates a sanction of payment to the public purse – related to health protection. In the proceedings of cases under private indictment a reconciliation of the parties may occur (possibly preceded by mediation). Along with reconciliation, the parties may also settle the matter (including claims connected with the indictment) amicably. In this case the court will not decide about guilt and punishment.

In *Sweden* the act of A will probably be qualified as assault (*misshandel*) according to Chap. 3, Sec. 5 Penal Code (the sanction is imprisonment of up to 2 years).

After that the offence has been reported to the police and the preliminary investigation will be initiated. The leader of investigation will most probably be the police. When the investigation has been finished, the case is handed over to the PPS. Issuing of a penal order is not possible. The case will be brought to the court. Depending on the circumstances of the offence, a prison-sentence is not excluded. However, a conditional sentence combined with community service or probation is more likely.

Case 3 var. a *Bodily harm – Two juveniles who are strangers to that date, become involved in an argument in a pub. A hits B with a glass bottle causing a wound to B's face that requires stitching in a hospital. B is unable to work for 3 days.*

In *England and Wales* a juvenile, under 18, of course, should not be in a pub and might be prosecuted for drinking under age, in addition to anything else. However, the procedure is likely to be the same, with the addition that the court is able to attempt some restorative justice procedure, if the CPS and the judge think that to be relevant. The main aim of the police and the CPS would be to prevent future offending. This means that, with a young person, more attempt will be made to 'treat' the person in preference to punishing him, e.g. by some form of drug or alcohol or anger management courses if they are relevant and exist in his area. Also some form of mediation is likely to be tried, and the offender made to offer some recompense to the victim: this can happen formally through the court, or informally through a reparation process with the youth offending panel.

If the youth is under age 16 or is aged 16 to 18 and has no previous history of problems with the police, in *France* the facts will probably be viewed as sufficiently serious to require summoning before the juvenile court judge, who will decide whether educational monitoring is required, following an investigation of the child's personality and family environment. The solution chosen by the judge will be guided essentially by the offender's personality and educational needs. For a 16 to 18 year-old youth (and especially one approaching age 18) who had moreover already been in contact with the juvenile justice system, a hearing before the juvenile court and pronouncement of a sentence are conceivable. However, if the juvenile is a multi-recidivist of the same age who has already been subjected to a number of educational measures, an incident of this type may lead the judge to prescribe pre-trial detention for no more than two months, which will be followed by a short, unsuspended prison sentence.

In *Germany* the investigative stage would be as described in the juvenile case above. Because § 45 II JGG is also applicable to crimes, the majority of Länder guidelines place even a serious misdemeanour like dangerous bodily harm within its area of application. The difference between practice relating to adults and juveniles becomes particularly clear here: theoretically, diversion is possible for both. However, for adults it is an offence at the upper end of the spectrum for which diversionary measures can be used at all and so the tendency would go against it. For juveniles, it is well within the range, and so their use is much more likely. The use of perpetrator-victim mediation is also particularly likely here, in this case as an educational measure. The use of penal order proceedings is not possible, at most simplified proceedings can be used (§ 76 JGG) or the PPS will bring proceedings to the juvenile criminal court.

In *the Netherlands* in case of a juvenile offender a writ of summons for a court hearing will be the most probable outcome. With a sentence requested of 24 hours community service.

In *Poland* the procedure applied and reaction of the prosecution and justice agencies will be similar to that when a juvenile perpetrator commits a theft in a shop – as above. However it is possible, though hardly probable, to apply a correcting measure in the form of placing the offender in a juvenile delinquent centre if "there is every indication of the juvenile's high degree demoralization and the circumstances and character of the offence justify it, especially when other educational measures proved to have been inefficient or there is no prognosis for resocialisation of the juvenile" (Article 10 of the above said Act of 26 October 1982 on procedure in juvenile cases) hence in the situations when there are other – than body injury – circumstances in proof of the juvenile's demoralization. One of such circumstances consists in alcohol drinking in a pub.

In *Sweden* the qualification of the offence and the proceedings are the same as sub e), but the leader of investigation should be a prosecutor. The social authorities shall be contacted and the personal situation of the offender investigated more thoroughly. Prosecution in court will be instituted. A prison-sentence is excluded. The conditional sentence combined with community service is possible. However, depending on the circumstances, the most probable sanction in this case will be the committal to special care by social services.

Case 4 *Two persons are caught ram-raiding (breaking into a shop by driving a vehicle through the shop window in order to steal as much as possible) a clothing store. When their houses are searched, evidence is found that they are members of a gang which regularly ram-raids shops in various city centres.*

In *England and Wales* this would be a serious (indictable) offence that would be tried at the Crown Court, after initial hearing at a Magistrates' Court, even for young offenders. The charge would involve violence as well as theft and would probably thus involve some form of robbery charge, subject to severe penalties such as 6 years or more in prison. However, past behaviour of the offenders would be relevant, as well as the amount of previous offending. If this were the first offence for which they were prosecuted, then the sentence would not be a severe one, although some years in prison would be expected, especially if some injury resulted from their ram-raiding.

The CPS and the police would work together on the investigation to see what sort of charge best fitted the whole evidence, not only for this crime, but for previous offending. The offenders would be encouraged to admit to previous offending which would then be 'taken into account' when they were charged with the current offence. The offence would be tried before a judge and a jury who would be local citizens and aware of the public disquiet that had come about from the various ram-raiding events, and would be more likely to give a verdict of guilty. The judge would gear his sentence towards improving public confidence locally and thus would tend to be higher than if only one offence had been committed.

In *France* the charge here would be theft with three aggravating circumstances (offending in a group, entering, deterioration), punishable by up to ten years imprisonment. This indictment may entail prosecution by summary trial, with the length of the prison term depending on the previous legal history of the accused. Consideration of the existence of an organized gang would turn the charges into a felony incurring a prison sentence not exceeding fifteen years. The *cour d'assises* would not necessarily pronounce a more severe sentence than a *tribunal correctionnel*. Furthermore, prosecution of the case before a *cour d'assises* would require a prior judicial inquiry entrusted to an examining magistrate. The PPS will not chose that track unless the police had put the case in the hands of a national criminal investigations service which already had a sufficient basis for extending the suit to other members of the organized gang. If the suit only involves the two offenders caught in the act (or immediately after committing the offence) on the basis of immediate findings (on-the-spot inventory, house search), the PPS will probably prefer summary trial, knowing that it will obtain a prison term of 5 to 10 years (and even more for recidivists).

Thanks to the recent law on organized crime, the PPS is able, since October 2004, to continue the flagrant violation investigation for a longer period of time, with long periods of police custody and means similar to those of a full-fledged inquiry supervised by an examining magistrate. The police investigation would therefore be able to continue without having to start a judicial inquiry. Referral to an examining magistrate still remains compulsory if the offence is to be prosecuted as a theft committed by an organized gang.

In *Germany* this is a case of serious, professional gang theft (§ 244 StGB). It is a crime punishable by a custodial sentence of between 1 and 10 years. Due to the seriousness of the crime, unlike the previous cases, the PPS will be informed of the crime as soon as the police learn of it and will be involved in the investigation from the very beginning. This will in no way proceed according to simplified or standardised procedure, but as the individual case requires. After comprehensive investigation the PPS will bring charges before a court in as far as evidential sufficiency is achieved. Procedural simplifications are not possible. The case will probably be tried by a grand criminal panel or at least by *Schöffengericht*.

In *the Netherlands* this can be seen as a qualified theft (crime, category C offence) as described in article 311 of the CC, possibly in combination with being a member of a criminal organisation (art 140 CC). Most certainly this offence will be brought before the court. While the maximum penalty for qualified theft is 6 years, usually when you have qualified theft in combination with damage caused and repeat offending the sentence requested will be either 210 hours community service or 105 days imprisonment. However, in this specific case, where the offenders are members of a gang and the damage caused will be considerable, the sentences requested will probably be a lot higher. Also, both offenders will be held in pre-trial detention.

In *Poland* the above described offence would be most probably qualified as a burglary (Article 279 § 1 CC). If it is proved they belong to a gang that has committed a number of offences of the same kind in a short period of time, the perpetrators would be presented with charges referring to all the disclosed acts of burglary committed within the frames of the gang's activities (Article 279 § 1 in concurrence with Article 258 § 1 CC and in conjunction with Article 91 § 1 CC).

It is very probable that a prosecutor would file a request for preliminary detention of the offenders at court. That request is very likely to be approved by the court. Preliminary proceedings would be conducted by the police in the form of investigation. Formulated indictment might make the court sentence from one to fifteen-year[6] imprisonment, as well as, a fine. It is hard to say if penalty depends on the offenders' personal characteristics or attitudes, as well as the damages they have caused.

Nevertheless, imprisonment is most likely to be sentenced without conditional stay of execution thereof. The things recovered would be returned to the owners. The wronged may claim for compensation due to the damages suffered in the course of court proceedings by bringing their civil law action to the court or requesting damage redress. In the event such compensation fails to be sentenced at all or to be sentenced in the amount far from covering the damages suffered, the wronged may pursue their entitlement in this respect via civil law procedure.

In *Sweden* the offence should be qualified as *gross theft* (Chap. 8 Sec. 4 Penal Code) and *gross infliction of damage* (Chap. 12 Sec. 3 Penal Code). The sanctions prescribed for these offences are imprisonment 6 months – 6 years and up to 4

[6] Provision of Article 279 § 1 CC stipulates threat of imprisonment from 1 to 10 years. However, the upper limit of threat of imprisonment would be increased by half under Article 91 § 1 CC).

years respectively. The fact that the suspects are members of a gang could be considered an aggravating circumstance for sentencing, not as an offence itself.

Whether the investigation is to be led by the police or the PPS is not quite clear. Both are possible. In this case, however, pre-trial detention will probably be imposed, which means that the leader of investigation must be a prosecutor. The case will be brought to court. The only sanction in question is imprisonment. It is not possible to estimate how long the prison-term might be without knowing more circumstances. Probably between 1–3 years.

Case 5 *Murder – A breaks into B's home in order to take revenge for B's affair with A's wife. A kills B through a blow to the head. He feigns a burglary in order to cover his tracks.*

In *England and Wales* A would be charged with murder at a Crown Court, and, if found guilty, would be given a mandatory life sentence. The CPS would have the option of charging A with manslaughter if there was evidence that A had not intended to commit murder, or if B had used undue force to attack A, but the likelihood is that, with the motive clear the charge would be murder. The fact that the motive was based on revenge for 'stealing ones wife' is not a particular defence against a charge of murder or a justification for the CPS to reduce the charge.

The fact that a burglary was committed is again not particularly relevant. A is not likely to be charged with burglary, or if he was the case may not be proceeded with, and the burglary left on file in case he is found not guilty of the murder charge. The case would be heard before a jury and judge: the jury's role is to assess guilt or innocence: the judge has no role in the sentence in this case, as it is a mandatory one. However, he has to set a minimum length of sentence that the defendant has to serve before release.

In *France* the death of the victim leaves no choice as to the prosecution track. The charge will be intentional manslaughter (”*meurtre*”, 30 years imprisonment) or premeditated murder (*”assassinat”*, life sentence) if the premeditation indicated by the description of the facts is proved. Feigning a burglary will not change the charges, but will play a role as establishing the intentional, or even premeditated character of the homicide. If the investigation (or the *cour d'assises* hearing) ascertains that A simply caused B's death without the intention of doing so, this will still be a felony (15 years imprisonment). The *cour d'assises* composed of three judges and a jury of 9 members drawn by lots will have to decide whether the offender is guilty and set the sentence. If the offender is found guilty of murder, a security period must be set, during which the sentence cannot be suspended nor can conditional release be granted (18 years if he is sentenced to life, which is not compulsory, or if not, half of the sentence, with some possible modulations). A will most probably be placed in pre-trial detention at the beginning of the judicial inquiry. Since this inquiry will take a long time even though the facts are not very complex, A will perhaps benefit from pre-trial release if he can provide sufficient guarantees against absconding (a home and a job).

In *Germany* this is a case of murder with lowly motive (§ 211 StGB) and herewith a crime punishable by a life sentence. The investigative and court procedure will not vary significantly from the ram-raiding case. Possibly the PPS' involvement in the investigation will be even more pronounced. There are no alternative procedural forms available. Potential charges for trespass, burglary, etc. could be dropped as irrelevant in comparison to the sanction expected for the murder charge in acc. with § 154 I StPO. The case will be heard by a Schwurgericht or Grand Criminal Panel.

In *the Netherlands,* homicides (i.e. manslaughter and murder) are dealt with in articles 287–295 of the CC. The main articles are article 287 (intentional, but not premeditated) with a maximum penalty of 15 years and article 289 (intentional and premeditated) with a maximum penalty of 20 years or life imprisonment[7].

In the case described here the burglary will probably be irrelevant. The sentence will depend heavily on the fact if the murder is premeditated or not. Experience shows that premeditation is in general hard to prove.

In this case, even if premeditation is proved, a life sentence is not probable. Usually life sentences are given for murders with more than one victim.

In *Poland* A's act is most likely to be qualified as the homicide crime defined in Article 148 § 1 CC. Preparatory proceedings would be conducted in the form of investigation instituted by a prosecutor and entrusted to the police in whole or in part. A would be arrested preliminarily and submitted to psychiatric examination. Such examination is always conducted by two court consultants. If there is a medical opinion of a specialist needed, A may be submitted to psychiatric examination and observation in an appropriate hospital. The purpose of those examinations is to establish whether he was sane at the time of committing the homicide and whether he is capable of participating in criminal proceedings. He would also be given a counsel for the defence *ex officio* (provided he has no defence counsel by choice). The case would be heard by the competent regional court in a panel of two judges and three lay persons assisting the judges.

The regulation under Article 148 § 1 CC provides for a possible judgement of imprisonment from 8 to 15 years, 25-year imprisonment or a life sentence. It is hard to say, without details as to the perpetrator's personality, which of the above might be sentenced. Nevertheless covering his tracks would be treated as the circumstance aggravating the penalty. Independent of the penalty, upon application by the harmed (closest person to the deceased), the court would adjudicate redressing the loss in whole or in part or a sanction imposing a payment to right a wrong.

In *Sweden* the offence is murder according to the Chap. 3 Sec. 1 Penal Code. The sanction for the offence is 10 years or life imprisonment.

The leader of investigation in this case will be a prosecutor. A will be detained. It is not possible to estimate the sentence, whether 10 years or life imprisonment.

---

[7] In the Netherlands life imprisonment means exactly that: imprisonment for life. An early release is only possible when a pardon is granted by the Crown. Until now only two offenders were given a pardon (one of which was terminally ill and died a few days after his release). Because most life sentences are fairly recent there is no experience yet if, and after how many years, a pardon will usually be granted.

Case 1. A is caught driving 30 km/hour above the speed limit. It is his first offence

	EW	FR	DE	NL	PL	SE
Type of offence	Minor criminal offence	Minor criminal offence (*Contr. 4.*)	Offence against order (*Ordnungswidrigkeit*)	Minor criminal offence (*Mulder law*)	Minor criminal offences (*Wykroczenia*)	Minor criminal offence
Type of procedure	Simplified (automated) proceeding: police have special units to track speeding cars via police cameras and issue fixed penalties. Offender is mostly caught by camera.	Admin. (automated) procedure: police is investigative/ prosecutorial agency. Offender is mostly caught by camera. Procedural alternative: police takes case to court.	Admin. (automated) procedure: police is investigative/ prosecutorial agency. Offender is mostly caught by camera.	Admin. (automated) procedure: police is investigative/ prosecutorial agency. Offender is mostly caught by camera.	Admin. (automated) procedure: police is investigative/ prosecutorial agency. Offender is mostly caught by camera Procedural alternative: police take case to mag. court.	Simplified proceeding: police is investigative/ prosecutorial agency.
Type of reaction	Fixed admin. fine and 3 penalty points on the driving licence.	Fixed admin. fine and 3 penalty points on the driving licence.	Fixed admin. fine and penalty points on the driving licence.	Fixed admin. fine.	Fixed (admin.) fine.	Fixed summary fine by police and record in the criminal register.

Case 2. An adult steals a sweatshirt worth 20 Euros from a shop. This is a first offence

	EW	FR	DE	NL	PL	SE
Type of offence	Less serious criminal offence (*Summary offence*)	Less serious criminal offence (*Delit*)	Less serious criminal offence (*Vergehen*)	Less serious criminal offence (*Misdrivjen*)	Less serious criminal offences (*Wykroczenia*)	Less serious criminal offence
Type of procedure	Some stores will prosecute themselves; they have their own sanction. Alternatively the case is reported to Police that will caution.	1st-time offender is usually not prosecuted: shop owner can force offender to return the stolen good and/or pay for it. Alternatively police can be called and then initiate prosecution.	Police investigate independently, PPS then decides how to proceed. Alternative proceedings possible: which one depends on individual case and guidelines.	Shop owner report the case to police that will then initiate investigation and decide in how far a *politietransactie* is appropriate. If not possible: writ of summons is issued and handed over to PPS.	Investigation is carried out by police independently. Case is then brought to mag. court by police.	Police leads the whole investigation. Then case is handed over to PPS. PPS probably issues a penal order. If no suspect's agreement: case will go to court.
Type of reaction	Fixed fine imposed by shop owner or caution (formal warning) by police officer.	Fixed fine imposed by shop owner. *Rappel a la loi* is possible.	Case will probably be dropped (public interest) or disposed off.	Police transaction	Court may impose a fine or a 5–30 day arrest.	Probably 30 day-fines.

Case 2 var. a. Petty theft – A 15 years old steals a sweatshirt worth 20 Euros from a shop. This is a first offence.

	EW	FR	DE	NL	PL	SE
Type of offence	Less serious criminal offence (*Summary offence*)	Less serious criminal offence (*Delit*)	Less serious criminal offence (*Vergehen*)	Less serious criminal offence (*Misdrivjen*)	Less serious criminal offence (*Wykroczenia*)	Less serious criminal offence
Type of procedure	Some stores will prosecute themselves; they have their own sanction. Alternatively the case is reported to the police who will caution.	1st-time offender is usually not prosecuted: shop owner can force offender to return the stolen good and/or pay for it. Alternatively police can be called and then initiate prosecution.	Police investigate independently, PPS then decides how to proceed. Alternative proceedings possible; which one depends on individual case and guidelines.	Police initiate investigation and decide in how far a *Halt*-reaction is appropriate. If not possible: writ of summons is issued and handed over to PPS.	Investigation is carried out by police independently. Case is then brought to mag. court by police.	Police leads whole investigation Before case is handed over to PPS. PPS probably issues a penal order. If no suspect's agreement: Case will go to court.
Type of reaction	Fixed fine imposed by shop owner; reprimand by police officer.	Fixed fine imposed by shop owner; *Rappel a la loi* is possible.	Probably dropped (public interest) or at least disposed off (with condition).	Probably HALT-measure will be offered by police officer. Then offender will be sent to a HALT-Office.	1st-time offender: Admonition by court. Recidivist: educational measure by court.	Waiver of prosecution and the offence recorded in the criminal register.

Case **2 var. b.** Petty theft – An adult steals a sweatshirt worth 20 Euros from a shop. He is a persistent offender.

	EW	FR	DE	NL	PL	SE
Type of offence	Less serious criminal offence (*Summary offence*)	Less serious criminal offence (*Delit*)	Less serious criminal offence (*Vergehen*)	Less serious criminal offence (*Misdrivjen*)	Less serious criminal offence (*Wykroczenia*)	Less serious criminal offence
Type of procedure	Some stores will prosecute themselves; they have their own sanction. Alternatively, case is reported to police who will initiate an investigation. Court process is possible.	Investigation will be carried out by police under PPS′ instructions. Alternative proceedings possible as: *Composition penale* or main hearing before *tribunal correctionnel.*	Police investigate independently. PPS then decides how to proceed. If alternative proceedings possible depends on the content of the different Länder guidelines; drop or disposal seems unlikely.	Police will then initiate investigation and decide in how far a (police-) transaction is appropriate (i.e. no recidivism within 5 years). Otherwise writ of summons is issued and handed over to PPS.	Investigation is carried out by police independently. Case is then brought to mag. court by police.	Police leads the whole investigation. Then case is handed over to PPS that will probably issue a penal order. If suspect doesn't agree: case will go to court.
Type of reaction	Fixed fine by shop owner or court sanction (short prison sentence).	Short prison sentence likely, with the order of suspension and probation.	Probably PPS will bring public charges.	(Police-) transaction or PPS brings charges.	Most likely court may order an arrest (5–30 days). Also fine is possible.	Most likely sanction will be more severe than in case of a 1st-time offender.

Case 3. Two adults (A&B) who are strangers to that date, become involved in an argument in a pub. A hits B with a glass bottle causing a wound to B´s face. This requires stitching in a hospital. B is unable to work for 3 days.

	EW	FR	DE	NL	PL	SE
Type of offence	Less serious criminal offence (*Summary offence*)	Less serious criminal offence (aggravating circumstances) (*Delit*)	Less serious criminal offence (*Vergehen*)	Less serious criminal offence (*Misdrijven*)	Less serious criminal offence	Less serious criminal offence
Type of procedure	Investigation by police. A caution might be still possible. Alternatively case is investigated by police then brought before court.	Investigation will be carried out by police under PPS´ instructions. Alternative proceedings possible as: *Disposal; Composition penale.* Most likely main hearing before *tribunal correctionnel.*	Police investigate independently. PPS then decides how to proceed. If alternative proceedings possible depends on the content of the different Länder guidelines.	Police will carry out investigation under PPS´ instructions. Out of court proceedings possible (depends on the consequences of the offence and offender personality).	Police will initiate investigation under PPS´ instructions. If public interest exists, prosecution proceeds. If not: private complaint procedure possible.	Police leads the whole investigation. Then case is handed over to PPS who will bring the case before court.
Type of reaction	Short prison-sentence possible accompanied by victim's compensation.	Short prison-sentence, primarily accompanied by victim's compensation.	Full court trial is most likely. Alternative proc. seem unlikely.	Transaction most probable (community service).	Public trial: court sanction, primarily in form of victim's compensation. Private pros.: reconciliation.	Most likely conditional sentence combined with com. service or probation.

Case 3 var. a. Bodily harm – Two juveniles who are strangers to that date become involved in an argument in a pub. A hits B with a glass bottle causing a wound to B´s face that requires stitching in a hospital. B is unable to work for 3 days.

	EW	FR	DE	NL	PL	SE
Type of offence	Less serious criminal offence (*Summary offence*)	Less serious criminal offence (aggravating circumstances) (*Delit*)	Less serious criminal offence (*Vergehen*)	Less serious criminal offence (*Misdrijven*)	Less serious criminal offence	Less serious criminal offence
Type of procedure	Whole criminal procedure is the same as for adults: Court is able to attempt some restorative justice procedure.	Investigation by police and PPS. Summoning before the Juvenile Court. Judge decides about edu. monitoring. Court hearing conceivable, if offender has already been in contact with criminal system.	Investigation by police more or less independently. Alternative proceedings most probable if offenders personality is within the range (simplified proceeding, § 76 JGG/ diversion, § 45 JGG).	Investigation by police under PPS instructions Writ of summons for a court hearing.	Investigation by police. Case brought to family court which will investigate offender's social surroundings and personality.	Proceedings are the same as in case of an adult perpetrator, although leader of investigation will be a PP. Perpetrators´ personality more in focus. Prosecution before a court will be instituted.
Type of reaction	Informal reaction through a reparation process (youth offending panel or by court). Special treatment (drug/anger/alcohol management courses) or mediation.	1st-time offender: edu. measures Recidivist: sentence Multi-recidivist: 2 month pre-trial detention/short, unsuspended prison sentence.	Diversionary measure is most likely (§ 45 II JGG), perpetrator-victim-mediation is particularly likely here.	Sentence of 24 hours community service.	1st-time offender: admonition by court. Recidivist: edu. measure by court; Juvenile delinquent centre for highly problematic juveniles.	No prison-sentence Conditional sentence combined with community service possible (probably leads to a committal to special care by social service).

Case 4. Two persons are caught ram-raiding (breaking into a shop by driving a vehicle through the shop window in order to steal as much as possible) a clothing store. When their houses are searched, evidence is found that they are members of a gang which regularly ram-raids shops in various city centres.

	EW	FR	DE	NL	PL	SE
Type of offence	Serious (indictable) offence	Serious criminal offence (aggravating circumstances) (*Crime*)	Serious criminal offence (*Verbrechen*)	Serious criminal offence (*Misdrijven*)	Serious criminal offence	Serious criminal offence
Type of procedure	CPS and Police work together on investigation Brought before crown court after initial hearing before mag. court No simplified procedure.	Summary trial if PPS after nationwide investigation (Police under PPS′ advice) is sure that only the two offenders are involved and not other members of a gang as well.	PPS leads the investigation from the very beginning; Case will be brought before court. No simplified procedure.	Investigation headed by PPS. Charge brought before court, main hearing probable) No simplified procedure.	Investigation by police. Case is probably brought to court.	Leader and conductor of investigation is PPS. Case is probably brought before court.
Type of reaction	Subject to a (severe) prison sentence of several years.	Offence punishable by up to 10 years of imprisonment. Considerations of an organized gang would lead to a prison sentence not exceeding 15 years.	Custodial sentence between 1–10 years.	Max. 6 years prison sentence. If damaged caused/ repeat offending the most probable sentence will be either 210 hours community service/ 105 days imprisonment minimum.	1–15 years of imprisonment or even a fine possible.	Only prison sentence of max. 6 years (most likely 1–3 years) will be a possible reaction. If offenders are members of a gang, this leads to aggravating circumstance relevant for sentencing.

Case 5. Murder- A breaks into B`s home in order to take revenge for B`s affair with A`s wife. A kills B through a blow to the head. He feigns a burglary in order to cover his tracks

	EW	FR	DE	NL	PL	SE
Type of offence	Serious criminal offence	Serious criminal offence (aggravating circumstances) (*Crime*)	Serious criminal offence (*Verbrechen*)	Serious criminal offence (*Misdrijven*)	Serious criminal offence	Serious criminal offence
Type of procedure	CPS and police work together on investigation. Case brought before court, consisting of a jury and judge (who has no role in sentencing but has to set a minimum sentence length).	Investigation by PPS. Court hearing (judge and a jury of 9 members).	PPS leads the investigation from the very beginning; Case will be brought before court. No alternative proceedings.	Normal investigation headed by PPS. Charge brought before court (main hearing).	PPS is leader of the investigation. Normal court hearing with psychiatric examination.	Leader of investigation is PPS. Case will be brought before court (normal court hearing).
Type of reaction	Subject to a mandatory life prison-sentence (min. 15/20 years).	Subject to a mandatory life sentence or 30 years of imprisonment; security period must be set in case of murder (ensures that the sentence can't be suspended within a certain period).	Subject to a mandatory life prison-sentence (at minimum 15 years).	Subject to a long life sentence. Mandatory life prison-sentence is possible, but most likely this will only be given for murders with more than one victim.	Long prison sentence 8-25 years, up to life.	Imprisonment of 10 years or for life.

Part II

The Prosecution Service Function within the Criminal Justice System

Country Reports

The Prosecution Service Function within the English Criminal Justice System

Chris Lewis

1 General

The United Kingdom is made up of three jurisdictions and each has a very different public prosecution service. This chapter covers the public prosecution service in England & Wales: a brief description of the Scottish system is at Appendix: the Northern Ireland system is not covered here[1]. The England and Wales public prosecution service is called the Crown Prosecution Service (CPS) and is very different from the two other UK services and from prosecution services in Europe. The main differences are:

- The CPS was set up in 1986. It has none of the history or the power of other European prosecution systems. Its powers and relationships with other justice agencies are still evolving.
- The police remain the stronger body in investigating offences and to some extent in sanctioning offenders.
- There is no Ministry of Justice, as such. The various agencies of the criminal justice system come under three different ministries and much cooperation is informal rather than statutory.
- There is no Penal Code as such: criminal law is made up of statute law passed by parliament and common law and practices which pay authority to precedents and practices that have become accepted over the years.
- There are many non-CPS prosecuting authorities in England & Wales that deal mainly, although not exclusively, with less serious and regulatory offences.
- The England & Wales system contains much more discretion about processing cases than many other jurisdictions.
- There is no system of examining magistrates in England & Wales.

---

[1] The Northern Ireland Public Prosecution Service is very new and was launched on 13 June 2005. A brief description of the system can be found at *www.cjsni.gov.uk/index.cfm/area/information/page/ppservice*.

- England & Wales has an adversarial system of justice: i.e. lawyers do not so much aim to get at the truth behind an event, but to prove a case to acceptable standards.

Given its short history, the CPS has spent much of its life in pressing for the correct structure and resources to do the job it was set up for. Having achieved this, the CPS is now beginning to modify its relationships with other CJ agencies, especially the police. Up to now, it has not been very much influenced by other prosecution systems within the EU. However, over the last two or three years there are signs that the future may see important changes in the CPS role, with more CPS influence on investigation and on sanctions.

Such changes would come about as part of the UK government's desire to bring the criminal justice system as a whole up to date. This was summed up in September 2005 when the British Prime Minister talked about 21st century problems being met by 19th century structures. Such changes will be likely to come about as a result of the government's desires to see more offenders brought to justice, more cases diverted from the courts, and a more efficient Criminal Justice System.

The justification for these policies has come about through the continuing high crime rate and a falling rate of clear-ups by the police. Figure 1 shows the trends in survey crime, recorded crime, courts business and prison population since 1980.

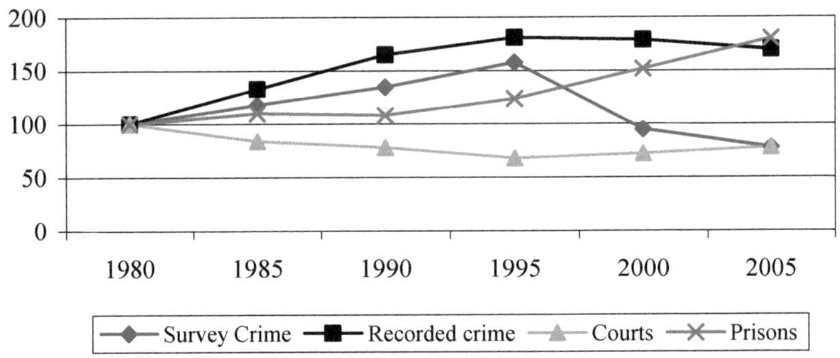

Fig. 1. Trends in Crime, Courts, Business and Prison Population: England & Wales[2]

The chart shows that:

- recorded crime[3] remains high, although there have been some recent drops and Survey crime[4] is now below its 1980 level,

[2] The trends in this chart have been estimated from published material. They are accurate to show broad trends in crime, courts and prison numbers but should not be used for any other purposes.

[3] Crime as recorded by the police. There have been many changes in the definitions over this period, especially since 1995. For the most recent material on recorded crime in England & Wales see Nicholas, Povey, Walker & Kershaw, *Crime in England and Wales 2004/5*, downloadable from *www.homeoffice.gov.uk/rds*.

- court numbers[5] have fallen compared to the change in recorded crime,
- despite all this Prison numbers[6] have soared, reflecting more severe sentencing.

Although all justice agencies agree that a significant amount of diversion from the courts is essential, criminal justice agencies differ in their understanding of the correct way of doing this. With no history of a powerful PPS, politicians tend to look first to 'more traditionally British' methods of diversion, usually involving formal or informal use of police powers, such as an increase in the use of fixed penalty notices. The CPS itself would favour developing prosecutorial fines, cautions and warning letters, provided resources and legislation were available to develop these. They feel recent Scottish experience[7] supports their view.

Developments since 1995 to bring more criminals to justice have increased court proceedings rather than diverted from them. Moreover, they have lead to a continuing increase in the prison population, which at 28 October 2005 had reached 77,749. This was 145 per 100,000 population of England and Wales, higher than any Western European Country save Luxembourg.[8]

1.1 The Role of the CPS

The CPS is a public service for England & Wales headed by the Director of Public Prosecutions. It is answerable to Parliament through a government minister, the Attorney General. It is a national organisation of 42 geographical areas headed by a Chief Crown Prosecutor. Each area has substantial autonomy acting within a national framework, particularly a Code of Conduct for Prosecutors and various guidelines about the procedures to follow for particular types of offence. The police are responsible for the investigation of crime but the CPS can request further investigation, if they assess that current evidence is insufficient. This relationship has been and continues to evolve: e.g. the Director of Public Prosecutions announced in November 2005[9] that the CPS wished to start interviewing victims of crime, particularly rape cases, in order to achieve more effective prosecution of such cases.

Up to 2002 the police decided on any charge against an offender. In October 2002, *Lord Justice Auld's Review of the Criminal Courts* (Auld 2002) recommended the CPS should be given greater legal powers to determine the decision to charge in all but minor cases. Successful pilot schemes were run in 2003 and fol-

---

[4] Crime as measured by the British Crime Survey, see Nicholas et al, op cit.

[5] Indictable or either way offences tried in Court. See *www.homeoffice.gov.uk/rds*.

[6] Average number of prisoners in custody throughout the year. See *www.hmprisonservice.gov.uk*.

[7] See description in Appendix.

[8] Figures from the World Prison Population List, Sixth Edition 2005 Roy Walmsley, published by Kings College, London, UK see *http://www.kcl.ac.uk/depsta/rel/icps/world-prison-population-list-2005.pdf*.

[9] See report in *The Guardian*, 11 November 2005. The piloting of such arrangements will start in 4 areas of the North of England in January 2006.

lowing the Criminal Justice Act 2003, the CPS is now in the process of moving to 'statutory' charging. This means that the CPS will determine the charge in all but the most routine cases. By October 2004, around 60 % of CPS cases were dealt with under statutory charging schemes and it is planned that all areas will move to statutory charging by March 2007.[10]

Apart from this move to charging, the CPS does not have any powers to itself issue fines, cautions, warning letters, or do anything else directly and needs to work through the police or the courts in issuing sanctions. The idea of more direct intervention by the prosecutor is one that is favoured by the CPS to some extent. However, recent public discussion has concentrated on giving the police more powers for summary justice in the form of more speedy sanctions.

1.2 The Role of the Courts

There are three main courts:

- the Youth Court deals with young people up to the age of 17,
- the Magistrates' Court deals with most criminal cases and is the court that makes an initial decision on bail in all cases,
- the Crown Court deals with the most serious cases e.g. murder, rape, etc. and some less serious cases where the accused claims a right to trial by jury. It also deals with appeals and referrals for sentencing from the Magistrates' Court.

Higher Courts deal with appeals from Crown Court. The highest court at present is the House of Lords. A Supreme Court will be set up, independent of Parliament, within the next 10 years.

A summary of the Role and responsibilities of the CPS and how these have evolved over the last 20 years can be found on their web site at *www.cps.gov.uk* and of the way the CPS interacts with the rest of the criminal justice system at *www.cjsonline.gov.uk*. These web sites are kept up to date on developments in policy and practice and should be consulted for more recent developments.

Other commentators have considered different aspects of the CPS: see Sanders (Sanders 2004) for a chapter comparing the English system with other European systems and Sanders & Young (Sanders & Young 1999, but in the process of being updated) for a large-scale account of how the CPS interacts with the rest of the English justice system.

[10] Under The Statutory Charging Scheme local arrangements are complemented by the implementation of an out of hours service, CPS Direct. CPS Direct, staffed by experienced prosecutors, operates from 5pm to 9am Monday to Friday and all day at weekends and public holidays enabling the CPS to offer round the clock coverage.

1.3 Offence Classifications

Indictable offences are those that must be tried at the higher court, the Crown Court. These are very serious offences such as murder and rape. Offences that are 'triable-either way' can be tried at either the Crown Court or the Magistrates' Court. These are not as serious as indictable offences and cover such offences as theft and criminal damage. Summary offences are offences that are not serious. These can be tried at Magistrates' Courts. Details of these can be found in the appendices of Criminal Statistics, England & Wales, (Home Office 2004): Appendix 4 of that volume shows the following main classifications:

Indictable

Indictable offences must be dealt with at the Crown Court. These are typically: Violence against the person and sexual offences (mostly indictable), robbery (all indictable), burglary (some indictable).

Triable Either Way

These can be dealt with at the Magistrates' Court, although cases can then be sent to the higher court for sentencing. Typically these are: Theft and handling stolen goods; fraud and forgery; criminal Damage; drug offences.

Summary Offences

These are typically dealt with at the Magistrates' Court, typically by guilty plea and often by a bulk procedure. Common Assault, Explosives laws, Game Laws, Highway laws, Liquor laws, Labour laws, Naval, Military and Air Force laws, Local regulations, Prostitution, Revenue Laws, Vagrancy offences, Miscellaneous offences, including regulatory offences.

However, as we shall see below, the police can also deal with these offences through various sanctions. In fact, the vast majority of these summary offences are petty motoring offences that come nowhere near court, but are dealt with by a fixed penalty scheme, by the police or other local bodies. Also, since 2003 the police can deal with a small number of non-motoring offences such as those connected with public disorder (Drunkenness, Prostitution, Petty Theft) by means of a fixed penalty notice for disorder.

2 PPS Structure

The CPS is a national prosecuting body created by the Prosecution of Offences Act 1985, which has been operating in England & Wales only since October 1986. Despite being a young organisation, it has undergone many fundamental reorganisations in its first 20 years. The most recent of these, the Glidewell report

(Glidewell 1998), restructured the CPS from April 1999, into 42 areas, each under the control of a Chief Crown Prosecutor, co-terminus with other CJ areas[11], and each with a fair degree of autonomy. Glidewell also recommended that CPS staff be located in police stations so that they could give advice much earlier in the process between investigation and court case[12]. The benefits of this include better communication, reduced duplication and reduced time spent completing tasks. Specifically, the number of cases decided on first hearing has increased and the number of discontinuances fallen. Also there have been increased opportunities for the CPS to be consulted by the police about case investigation, evidence gathering, interview planning and disclosure management. In the English system none of these are controlled by statute as in some other jurisdictions, so a flexible approach is possible.

The success of early pilots of the Glidewell suggestions has meant that they are now being rolled out throughout the country. However, as each area is autonomous, it is not clear whether every area will benefit to the same degree.

In parallel with CPS changes, the Courts system is also being changed, from 1 April 2005, so that the lower and higher courts will have a unified administration, and be run within the 42 criminal areas. Changes to the higher courts and the selection of judges are also being planned over a longer timescale. All this will lead to greater efficiency of justice through closely working of all justice agencies. The actual working together of the CPS and the courts will continue to evolve within the more flexible English system.

By 2003 the CPS had become a moderately sized government department with approximately 7,100 staff, of whom 2,365 were lawyers and 4,779 caseworkers or administrative staff.

Lawyers must be solicitors admitted in England & Wales, with a full current practising certificate, or a barrister called to the English Bar who has completed pupillage. A few lawyers are recruited and trained internally. Professional training after qualification is provided locally and externally through courses accredited by the Law Society or the Civil Service College. Once working, each prosecutor can discuss cases with his colleagues and his seniors and will be managed with regular job interviews and assessments.

Caseworkers need not be lawyers and they are allowed to review and present cases in Magistrates' Courts, involving a limited range of cases with straightforward guilty pleas (e.g. Shoplifting, Possession of Cannabis, non-contentious motoring offences, often presented in bulk with essentially an abbreviated hearing). Caseworkers need to pass a testing training course, validated by an external body, before they can undertake this work.

CPS areas vary greatly in size and workload: London oversees 13 branches: others have only one branch. In each area, the Chief Crown Prosecutor sits on ma-

[11] A more recent development (HMIC, 2005) has proposed that the current 42 police force areas be merged into a smaller number of larger areas. Were such a change to happen, some local changes to CPS areas would be likely.

[12] It is interesting to note that, despite the greater powers of the Scottish PPS (shown in Appendix), very few Scottish prosecutors actually sit in police stations.

nagement groups such as the local Criminal Justice Board, along with the Chief Constable, the Head of Probation, the Head of the Courts Service, the Head of the Youth Justice Board, and local manager of the Prison Service. Within each area, there is a strict hierarchy, with each prosecutor being supervised directly and in a chain of command that stretches to the local Chief Crown Prosecutor.

Following current English management, job descriptions and performance indicators are set for each prosecutor and his progress and future career can be dependent on the judgements of his seniors as to how well he has fulfilled the guidelines set down locally and nationally and the local workload targets. The CPS has not been in existence for long enough to judge the extent to which lawyers will stay in its employ. However, pay can be much higher for lawyers, who work privately, especially in commercial law. At the moment the CPS, and indeed criminal law as a whole, has a reputation amongst some as being a poor career for an ambitious lawyer.

Partly because of lower salaries, the CPS has never been able to carry out its full workload without resorting to hiring prosecutors from private practice to appear in court on behalf of the CPS. These are known as 'agents'. About 27 % of Magistrates' Court sessions were covered by agents in 2004–5, a proportion that is gradually falling. The extent to which agents work to national and local guidelines, or could be sanctioned if they did not, is not known. However, much of the CPS work where guidelines are relevant is pre-court, where agents are not used.

2.1 Control of PPS Case-ending

There are many national guidelines under which the CPS works. These set uniformity in what prosecutors do throughout the country. The most important of these is the *Code for Crown Prosecutors* (See *www.cps.gov.uk* for copies of the code in many of the languages used in England). The Code is designed to help the CPS in seeing that justice is done. Its enforcement encourages prosecutors to be fair and objective and not to be affected by improper or undue pressure from any source. Under the code they may provide advice to the police on lines of inquiry, evidential requirements and assistance in any pre-charge procedures. They should bring to a conclusion cases that cannot be strengthened by further investigation.

Prosecutors must ensure all relevant evidence is put before the court and shared with the defence beforehand as laid down in the Code. They must follow the articles of the European Convention on Human Rights. Before a case goes to court, it must be put through the *Full Code Test.* This has two parts:

Evidence Test

Prosecutors must be satisfied that there is enough evidence to provide a 'realistic prospect of conviction' against each defendant on each charge. They must consider what the defence case might be and how that is likely to affect the prosecution case. They must consider e.g. the reliability of the evidence, the chances of a witness changing his evidence and the chances a judge might exclude the evidence for legal reasons.

Public Interest Test

This stems from obiter dicta[13] of a long dead English Attorney General: 'It has never been the rule in this country… I hope never will be…. That suspected criminal offences must automatically be the subject of prosecution' (Hansard, vol. 483, col. 681, 29 January 1951).

The Code sets out public interest factors in favour and against prosecution examples are:

For Prosecution: a conviction would lead to a significant sentence, confiscation or other order, a weapon was used or threat made, the victim was a public servant or vulnerable in some other way, the victim was a child, the offence was motivated by any form of discrimination, the defendant was in a position of trust or a ringleader in the crime or had previous 'form' that the offence was planned or that prosecution would enhance public confidence.

Against Prosecution: If there would be a nominal penalty on conviction, if the defendant has already been sentenced, e.g. for a similar crime, if there was a genuine mistake by the defendant, if there has already been a long delay, if the victim suffered little harm or would suffer more harm from having to give evidence, if the defendant is very ill or elderly or has put right the loss or harm that was caused. Finally, there will be no prosecution if details may thus be made public that could harm sources of information, national security, etc.

The Code sets out grounds the prosecutor must apply when considering whether to agree to bail, to ask the police to offer a caution or conditional caution, or some form of alternative such as restorative procedures, particularly for those under 18, to suggest in which type of court the case should be heard and to agree to various forms of plea bargaining.

The Code also confines the prosecutor's role in sentencing to drawing the courts attention to legislation relevant to the case and to warning them if the defence makes a misleading case when pleading mitigation. There are several other codes and guidelines agreed between various criminal justice agencies that the CPS must follow when dealing with types of case such as child abuse, domestic violence or immigration cases[14].

An example of a more detailed CPS code is that listing policy for prosecuting cases of domestic violence[15]: this reflects modern social concerns that 'all people

---

[13] *Obiter dicta* are judges' statements from a court case which are quoted as a precedent. Such views, stated in public, become accepted by all other judges and magistrates and have the force of law.

[14] Full details of all CPS Codes can be found on *www.cps.gov.uk.*

[15] *Policy for prosecuting Cases of Domestic violence*: CPS 2005, explains the way the CPS deals with cases involving domestic violence: a summary booklet, *Domestic Violence – how prosecution decisions are reached* – is widely available to be handed out, in many

have the right to feel safe and be safe in their personal relationships'. This document goes into considerable detail about the likely behaviours that occur in such situations and shows how the perpetrator is likely to be charged with a particular offence.[16]

The CPS is also in the forefront of the justice agencies in England & Wales in fulfilling the responsibilities under the Race Relations (Amendment) Act 2000 in carrying out assessments of its policy and practice to see that they conform to fair treatment of offenders of different genders and races.[17] In particular a recent report details how the results of the charging process differ by gender and for different ethnic classifications (Lewis 2005).

2.2 PPS Jurisdiction and further Fields of Activity

There is a large number of types of activities conducted by the CPS that have little to do with prosecution, especially at Magistrates' Courts.

The CPS has no special role in carrying out investigations, although recent developments in charging will lead the CPS in practice to more often ask the police to re-commence some investigations if the CPS feels evidence is insufficient. However, following the Regulation of Investigatory Powers Act 2000 (RIPA) the CPS has a significant role in the interpretation of the way in which investigations should proceed and evidence so gathered should be presented in court. It does this by providing guidance in easily available form, so that magistrates, judges, the police and the general public knows the rules under which evidence is gathered and used.

Thus, CPS sets and publishes guidance on the way evidence should be presented in court: e.g. on the visual identification of suspects, on how confessions should be obtained, on breaches of Police Codes of practice, on general abuse of process, on the use of scientific and high-tech evidence, on transcripts of evidence, on how prisoners letters and telephone calls can be used, on self-incrimination, when proceedings should be in camera, how witnesses should be anonymous, on the law of self-defence, and so on. These guidelines (see CPS 2005a) ensure that all judges and magistrates work to the same rules and these are publicly available.

The CPS also has a significant role in the conduct of cases that involve the international community: e.g. with regard to diplomatic immunity, visiting forces, extradition, evidence and information from abroad, letters of request and the position vis-à-vis European Courts. Very importantly, in the era of terrorism, the CPS issues and sets guidance in Disclosure and Covert Law enforcement (CPS 2005b).

languages, at police stations and community centres and includes many anonymous helplines for specific types of violence.

[16] E.g. Throwing plates could lead to a charge of common assault: tying someone up to false imprisonment: dowry abuse to blackmail or harassment: offensive telephone calls or texts to a malicious communications charge.

[17] See *CPS Race Equality scheme 2005–2008*, available on CPS web site, which includes an analysis of those employed by the CPS accoridng to their minority ethnic classification.

This covers when certain sensitive material should be disclosed to third parties, covert surveillance, including how the use of covert techniques have had to be reassessed in the light of Articles 6 and 8 of the European Convention on Human Rights, the use of telephone tapping.

In the near future the CPS will play a crucial role in providing high quality independent prosecution services to the new Serious Organised Crime Agency (SOCA)[18]. The CPS has worked with the Revenue & Customs Prosecution Office (RCPO), the Home Office and other law enforcement and intelligence agencies to develop the prosecution arrangements SOCA. CPS arrangements for prosecuting serious and organised crime have been modified in the light of terrorist events and the new SOCA structure. As a result CPS Casework Directorate has become three new divisions dealing with organised crime, counter-terrorism and specialized crime.From October 2005 a cadre of expert prosecutors will be established to provide a dedicated prosecution service to SOCA ready for it becoming fully operational in April 2006.

The CPS has no role in asking the judge to impose a specific sentence, but it does have a specific role in some aspects ancillary to sentencing such as being able to draw the courts' attention to its powers to award compensation and publishes guidelines on how compensation should be awarded (CPS 2005c.).

The CPS also gives guidance on the treatment of victims and witnesses, on diversity and fairness, on appeals, on Advocates' fees, on how agencies should cooperate on specific offences, restrictions on reporting cases, and on racially and religiously motivated crime (See CPS Web Site). Such activities take up, perhaps, little more than 5 % of the time of an average prosecutor.

There are many thousands of mainly summary and mainly regulatory cases that are brought to court by alternative prosecuting agencies that are covered in Section 6 below. These do not involve the CPS at all, whereas in many other jurisdictions, if such infractions were brought to court, they would need to be dealt with by the public prosecution service.

3 Cases Brought to Court

3.1 Normal Cases at a Magistrates' Court

Recent changes in CPS practice are reflected in the statistics in this section. Table 1. shows cases dealt with by the CPS in 2004–5 and two preceding years. The number of cases where the CPS provided pre-charge advice to the police rose by 126.3 % during 2004–5, reflecting the impact of prosecutors assuming responsibility for the decision to charge in all but minor cases. Over the period 2004–5 all areas have been providing pre-charge advice, some via the statutory scheme, and

[18] Set up under the Serious Organised Crime and Police Act, 2005 to prevent and detect serious organised crime, and to contribute to the reduction of such crime in other ways and to the mitigation of its consequences. See *http://www.opsi.gov.uk/acts/acts2005/20050015.htm*.

some by operating a shadow non-statutory scheme. The number of cases prosecuted fell by 80.4 % in 2004–5. Several factors affect this figure, including arrests, the impact of the early involvement of prosecutors, offences cleared up by the police and offenders cautioned by the police. CPS has managed to get through many more cases in the last two years, due to the changes in giving pre-charge decisions and in taking over charging. 64 % of the cases dealt with by the CPS in the Magistrates' Courts were summary and the rest indictable or triable either way.

Table 1. Magistrates' Court Cases Processed by the CPS

	2002–3	2003–4	2004–5
Pre-charge decisions	64,456	194,928	441,194
Prosecuted by CPS	1,274,854	1,274,615	1,168,078
Other proceedings	8,853	17,225	7,028
Total	1,348,163	1,486,768	1,619,300

Table 2. Outcomes of CPS Cases at Magistrates' Courts

	2002–3	2003–4	2004–5
Discontinuances	197,680	175,779	146,268
Warrants, etc	80,477	72,078	53,408
Discharges	1,006	2,225	3,444
Dismissals – no case to answer	1,745	3,053	3,681
Dismissals after trial	15,452	15,997	17,839
Proofs in absence	126,518	152,757	169,681
Guilty Pleas	811,583	800,525	716,082
Convictions after trial	40,391	52,201	57,645
Total[19]	1,274,852	1,274,615	1,168,078

[19] *Discontinuances:* Circumstances often leave the CPS no choice but to discontinue: eg when witnesses fail to attend court or change their evidence; when defendants wait until the day of the trial before producing documents proving their innocence (such as a driving licence); or when the police are unable to fill gaps in the evidence. Discontinuance can occur at any time up until the start of trial, or the defendant pleads guilty. The figures include both cases discontinued in advance of the hearing and those withdrawn at court. Also included are cases in which the defendant was bound over to keep the peace.
Warrants etc are when the prosecution cannot proceed because the defendant has failed to appear at court and a Bench Warrant has been issued for his or her arrest; or the defendant has died; or where proceedings are adjourned indefinitely. These cases are not discontinued. The majority could not proceed because the police could not find a defendant: if the defendant is subsequently traced, then the prosecution may continue.
Discharges are committal proceedings in which the defendant is discharged. The number of discharges may be misleading. The new Compass Case Management System has only recently begun to capture these cases to be reported as a discrete outcome. The numbers are expected to stabilise and then gradually decrease.
Dismissals no case to answer: are cases in which the defendant pleads not guilty and

Table 2 shows that the *outcomes* of trials at Magistrates' Courts are also changing.[20] Discontinuances have continued to fall since 2001–2: convictions rose from 76.8 % of all outcomes in 2002–3 to 80.8 % in 2004–5: unsuccessful outcomes fell from 23.2 % in 2002–3, to 19.2 % in 2004–5: all positive outcomes of the new charging process. Nearly 98 % of cases proceeding to a hearing (trial or guilty plea) resulted in a conviction. Also 20,000 cases were committed for sentencing to the Crown Court as magistrates felt their sentencing powers are insufficiently severe.

The CPS also has a role in whether the Magistrates' Court allows bail, for serious cases. They have the right to appeal to the Crown Court against a decision of magistrates to grant bail in cases that carry a maximum sentence of 5 years or more. Once the court has ordered a particular outcome, the CPS does not become involved with the case again, except on appeal. There is no prosecution role in ensuring that a sentence is carried out effectively. 12,000 appeals from the Magistrates' Court were taken at higher courts in 2004–5. The CPS appears at the Crown Court to speak against these appeals. Although theoretically possible, there is no effective role for the CPS in appealing Magistrates' Court decisions itself.

3.2 Source of Cases for the Crown Court

Table 3. Source of Cases for the Crown Court

	2002–3	2003–4	2004–5
Magistrates' direction[21]	40,274	41,997	49,355
Defendant's direction[22]	15,051	13,037	5,045
Indictable only	39,221	40,200	36,490
Total	94,546	95,234	90,890

There has been a gradual change over the last 10 years in the rules for how cases can go to the Crown Court. There is now less flexibility for the defendant to elect for this and there were only 5 % of such cases in 2004–5. This has led to a steep rise in the proportion of the more serious 'indictable' cases , which now rep-

prosecution evidence is heard, but proceedings are dismissed by the magistrates without hearing the defence case.
Dismissals after trial: are cases in which the defendant pleads not guilty and proceedings are dismissed by the magistrates after hearing the defence case – a not guilty verdict.
Proofs in absence: mostly minor motoring matters which are heard by the court in the absence of the defendant.
Guilty pleas: where the defendant pleads guilty.

[20] Where a defendant pleads guilty to some charges in a set of proceedings, and not guilty to others, the above figures include both the guilty plea and the outcome of the subsequent contested hearing.

[21] Magistrates' directions are triable either way proceedings which the magistrates' thought were serious enough to call for trial in the Crown Court.

[22] Defendants' elections are either way proceedings in which the defendant chose Crown Court trial.

resent over 40 % of the total compared with 18 % in 1991–92, leading to more efficient processing of the more serious cases.

3.3 Normal Cases at the Crown Court

For more serious cases, CPS prepares cases before the court proceedings, presents the case at the Crown Court, and acts against appeals from Magistrates' Courts decisions. In 2004–5 CPS was involved in 126,000 Crown Court cases: of these 75 % were committed by magistrates' for trial: 16 % were committed for sentence and 9 % were appeals from Magistrates' Courts.

Table 4. CPS Cases at the Crown Court

	2002–3	2003–4	2004–5
Prosecuted	96,233	97,375	94,737
Appeals from lower court	11,504	11,418	11,960
Committals for sentence	19,659	20,191	19,672
Total cases	127,399	128,984	126,369

Table 5. Outcomes of CPS Cases at Crown Court

	2002–3	2003–4	2004–5
Judge ordered acquittals	14,671	14,538	13,430
Warrants	1,766	2,171	1,635
Judge directed acquittals	1,500	1,538	1,883
Acquittals	6,573	6,652	5,976
Guilty Pleas	58,624	59,537	58,222
Convictions after trial	13,099	13,119	13,591
Total[23]	96,233	97,375	94,737

[23] *Judge ordered acquittals:* where problems are identified after a case is sent to the Crown Court. The prosecution offers no evidence, and the judge orders a formal acquittal. These include cases where the defendant has serious medical problems; has already been dealt with for other offences; or witnesses are missing. Cases sent under s51 Crime and Disorder Act 1998 and subsequently discontinued are also included s are cases where charges do not proceed to a trial, and the defendant is bound over to keep the peace.
Warrants etc: when the prosecution cannot proceed because the defendant fails to attend court and a Bench Warrant has been issued for his/her arrest; the defendant has died; or is found unfit to plead. If the police trace a missing defendant, proceedings can continue.
Judge directed acquittals are cases where, at the close of the prosecution case against the defendant, a successful submission of 'no case' or 'unsafe' is made. The judge directs an acquittal rather than allow the case to go to a jury.
Acquittals after trial are when the defendant pleads not guilty and, following a trial, is

There was little change in the levels and patterns, convictions were around three-quarters of all outcomes, unsuccessful outcomes around a quarter. 90 % of cases proceeding to a hearing (trial or guilty plea), resulted in a conviction.

For very serious cases, the Attorney General, can appeal against the sentence given by the Crown Court on the grounds that it is insufficient. This is done in only a handful of cases a year when the government of the day feels that a judge has been too lenient.

3.4 Simplified Court Proceedings

Many minor and straightforward cases tend to get to (Magistrates') court without much involvement of the CPS. CPS may, if the case is more complex, give advice before charge, or appear if the defendant pleads not guilty, but often such cases are bundled together in large numbers and taken by magistrates at a special sitting, at which a CPS caseworker, who is usually not a lawyer, is present. This happens particularly in large cities such as London.

Examples are the high volume of petty motoring offences that have not been dealt with by a fixed penalty. There has been a gradual growth in the types of cases that are dealt with by means of a fixed penalty over the last 20 years, so that many millions of motorists who speed or park illegally now pay a fixed penalty to, often a non-criminal justice, enforcement body. However, as many as 862,000 defendants were proceeded against at Magistrates' Courts in 2002 for summary motoring offences and, although separate figures are not available, most of these cases are thought to have been dealt with in the shortened procedure. We assume that two-thirds of such cases are dealt with by a special form of procedure in the estimates we used in section 11 below.

When we discuss alternative prosecution agencies below, we shall see that many of these also use the simplified court procedures. The CPS takes no part in presenting such cases before the court. Such cases will be presented by the staff of the alternative prosecuting agencies and practices will vary considerably.

These simplified court proceedings are not formal: no guidelines exist: thus some courts may do them slightly differently from others: the estimates in Section 11. below are for the purposes of this chapter and are not official figures. However, the government has taken more interest in the large number of such low level offences which are taking up court time and has recently announced its intention to deal with selected low-level offences in alternative ways to ensure the best use is made of Magistrates' Court time.[24] Such formal changes will not take place until at least 2007, but are likely to include the following moves to speed administration of justice

---

acquitted by the jury.

Guilty pleas are where the defendant pleads guilty.

[24] Announced in Chapter 3 of *Supporting Magistrates' Courts to provide justice,* Cm. 6681, November 2005, *www.official-documents.co.uk/document/cm66/6681/6681.pdf.*

- New ways of handling the administrative and judicial processes in TV licence cases without automatic recourse to a full Magistrates' Court hearing. These cases amount to 12 % of all Magistrates' Court business by volume, although only 0.3 % by time.
- Establishing an administrative process with the Driver and Vehicle Licensing Agency that will enable uncontested high volume, low level motoring offences to be dealt with outside the courts. Summary motoring offences are a half of Magistrates' Court business.
- Extending the use of dedicated courts to handle road traffic offences. This will build on the experience of the London Traffic Courts, where the number of court sessions has been cut by 80 %.

3.5 Recent Developments in Charging

By 2005, CPS had taken charging over from the police in over two thirds of cases. An indication of the difference that this made can be found by comparing the results in areas where CPS had taken over charging compared to the areas where the charging remained with the police.

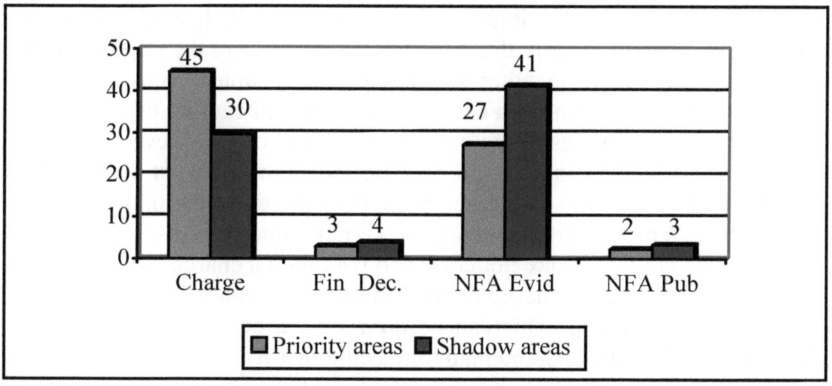

Fig. 2. Result of Charging Process for Males: Percentages Finalized by Priority Areas and Shadow Areas

Figures 2 and 3 compare the results of the charging process, in the priority areas (where CPS now charge) against shadow areas (where the police still charge) for the period September 2004 to February 2005. For both, males and females, a much higher proportion of cases now face a charge and no further action on evidence grounds is taken in a much lower proportion of cases.

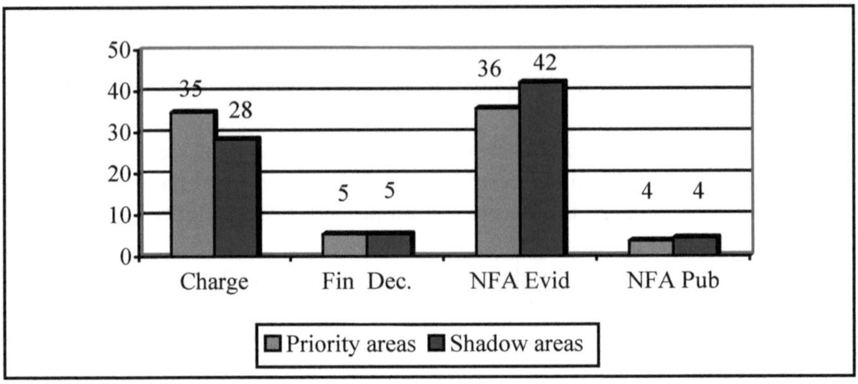

Fig. 3. Result of Charging Process for Females: Percentages Finalised by Priority Areas and Shadow Areas

4 Cases Dealt with by the Prosecution Service

The CPS has no authority to impose any sanctions itself. It works through other agencies of the system, mainly the courts or the police, and the imposition of such sanctions is covered in the other sections of this chapter. Thus, it decides on whether the police should offer a caution, a conditional caution or a charge and in choosing the charge implies to the court a judgement on how severe the CPS judges the crime. However, there is no specific indication of what penalty the CPS expects from the court. In some cases, the CPS will advise the police that a caution should be offered to the defendant, on certain conditions as to his behaviour, and that, if such conditions are not complied with then a charge will be preferred.

If the CPS feels that no charge or caution should be made, then the case can be dropped with no sanction. This can be done on various grounds, set out in the Code for Crown Prosecutors, the main one being that it is not in the public interest to prosecute. No routine statistics are available on how often this is done, although some estimates have been made later in this chapter.

The CPS has a role when the defendant pleads guilty or when he or she is found guilty following a trial. In such cases the CPS presents to the court the facts about the appropriate charges. However, this is done in a neutral manner.

Many sentences contain conditions, for example, reporting to a probation officer or attending offender programmes or drug centres. If these sentences are breached the case is usually brought back to court by the probation officer and the CPS has no role in breaches.

5 Cases Dealt with by the Police

The police have complete discretion to drop a case, to issue a sanction, called a caution, sometimes with conditions, for a few types of offence to issue a fixed penalty notice or penalty notice for disorder or to agree with the CPS a charge that will cause the defendant to be prosecuted in court. Police statistics in this area are much more detailed than those for the CPS and are summarised below. More detail, e.g. by age of offence, can be found on the Home Office web site (*www.homeoffice.gov.uk/rds*) However, for some sanctions that have only come into operation more recently, such as conditional cautions and penalty notices for disorder, statistics are not yet available, and only estimates have been made.

In 2004/5 it was estimated that households in England & Wales experienced 10.8 million property crimes or crimes against the person[25]. Police were informed of and recorded nearly 5.6 million of these and detected 1.4 million of them. Around 56 % of those detected were prosecuted at court, 16 % were cautioned, in 8 % of cases no further action was taken as the offender was already being prosecuted for a similar offence, usually theft or burglary, and in 20 % of cases other action was taken. This ranged from some form of restorative action to a complete lack of any action because the offender disappeared abroad, or to some other part of the country.

A *Caution* has, for over 30 years, been administered by the police to an offender who admits his offence. In 2004/5 256,000 offenders were cautioned by the police, including around 30,000 juvenile offenders given final warnings and over 50,000 given reprimands.[26] This represents a 'saving' to the work of the courts, and are in many ways analogous to systems in place in other countries to deal with minor offences in a more administrative way.

The giving of cautions varies greatly by the type of offence. Nearly a half of drug offenders are cautioned and nearly 40 % of violent offenders, mainly young men in fight. 30 % of thieves are cautioned, mainly shoplifters, who would be likely to be given a conditional discharge if they were taken to court. Around a quarter of those committing sexual offences, fraud or criminal damage were cautioned, mainly because the likelihood of significant penalties being imposed by the court was small, due to the relatively minor nature of the offence committed.

The history of cautioning is indicative of the 'English' approach. For over 20 years police administered a caution, with no legal authority at all, simply because they wished to avoid overburdening the courts with petty cases. They were able to do this because of their very large discretion about what cases they have to take to court. Cautions were only made statutory in the 1990s, because politicians felt the

[25] The figures in this paragraph can be found on p. 11 onwards of *Sentencing Statistics: England & Wales, 2004*, Home Office Statistical Bulletin 15/2005, London, 2005 or *www.homeoffice.gov.uk/rds/pdfs05/hosb1505.pdf.*

[26] Cautioning figures can be found in Chapter 2 of *Criminal Statistics, England & Wales, 2003,* Cm 6361, HMSO, London or *www.homeoffice.gov.uk/rds* and equivalent publications for succeeding years.

police were cautioning offenders who ought to have been given some more effective punishment.

A *Fixed Penalty Notice (FPN)* is a generic term for a range of fines given under many acts and issued by different agencies, dominated by the police, for road traffic offences and local authorities, for parking vehicles in illegal places. FPNs are by far the largest in number of any sanction and have existed for many years, e.g. there were 3.6 million FPNs issued by the police for road traffic infringements in 2003, 27 % up in 2002, and most of these were for speeding, many as a result of automatic detection by police cameras. Such offences can be challenged in court, but this rarely happens, as the fine tends to be greater if the case is fought.

Since 2003, a range of new sanctions have been brought in for the police as part of a new process for dealing with crime (The fact that it is the police that have been given these powers is an indication of way criminal justice develops in England & Wales. In many other jurisdictions it would have been more natural for the PPS to be brought into this development.).

Broadly speaking, the aim is to bring more offenders to justice without overloading the courts. Thus, a significant part of these new measures involve diversion from the courts into some other form of sanction. Some of these measures were first brought only in parts of the country and then extended more widely.

Penalty Notices for Disorder (PNDs) or 'on the spot penalties' were introduced by the Criminal Justice and Police Act 2001 as part of the government's strategy to tackle low-level, anti-social and nuisance offending. The legislation allows police to issue penalty notices to offenders for a range of minor disorder offences such as 'causing harassment, alarm or distress' and 'disorderly behavior while drunk' occurring often late at night in town centres and associated with the night time economy. The penalty is a fine of £80, or £50 for lesser offences. Their introduction is aimed at providing the police with a quick and effective tool for dealing with these minor offences, which reduces the workloads of both the police and the courts. Since 2002 their use has been extended to a larger range of offences.[27] PNDs are being used in places of cautions by the police.

63,600 PNDs were issued in the year 2004/5, 94 % to adults.[28] 28,790 PNDs were issued for 'causing harassment, alarm or distress' and 26,609 for 'drunk and disorderly', making up 87 % of all PNDs issued. 85 % of PNDs were issued to males and 15 % to females. Just over a half, 52 %, of these were paid in full without any court action and 44 % were registered as a fine in courts, the fine amount-

---

[27] Since the introduction of the PND scheme in the Criminal Justice and Police Act 2001 further offences have been added. The offence under section 5 of the Public Order Act 1986 of words or behaviour likely to cause harassment, alarm or distress was added in July 2002. Three firework offences were added from 11 October 2004. A further seven offences including retail theft (under £200), criminal damage (under £500), four alcohol offences targeting underage drinking and littering were added from November 2004. Purchase of alcohol under 18 and selling alcohol to a drunken person were added from April 2005. The Government has announced that it is considering adding to the offences that can attract a FPN.

[28] Detailed statistics on Penalty Notices for Disorder can be found in Home Office RDS Online publication 35/2005. see *www.homeoffice.gov.uk/rds*.

ing to 50 % more than the PND. It is expected that the use of PNDs will increase substantially in the future.[29]

Conditional Cautions are statutory disposals for adults. They are approved by the CPS and administered by the police who approve the proposed conditions, which are required to be rehabilitative and/or reparative and can include payment of compensation or other aspects of restorative justice. They are used for those offenders to drug addiction, and for offences concerned with alcohol and prostitution. No statistics are available as they have been piloted in only a small number of police areas. However, it is likely that their use in 2005 will not exceed 2,000.

Anti-Social Behavioural Strategy: This provides a staged approach to anti-social behaviour which focuses on early and effective intervention and involves the community. There are many tools, most of which are civil orders rather than criminal ones, including injunctions, evictions, dispersal orders, closure of crack houses, acceptable behavioural contracts (ABCs) and anti-social behavioural orders (ASBOs.) There are also preventing orders for parents of those involved. Breaching one of these civil orders can lead to punishment in a criminal court. Most of these orders are applied for by the police/local authority and the CPS is not often involved. There is an expectation that the use of such orders will grow and new legislation is expected in 2006.

Drug-related interventions are made in police custody suites, by drug workers independent of the police who assess and refer those arrested to treatment for drug misuse problems. The Drug Intervention Programme (DIP) exists at all steps in the CJ process and is a batch of measures to direct adult drug-misusing offenders out of crime and into treatment/support. It is also possible for Bail to be restricted if drug assessment or treatment is refused by an offender. Again the CPS tends not to become involved at this stage and no statistics are yet available.

6 Cases Dealt with by Alternative Procedural Forms

There is no concept of administrative crime in England & Wales. We have seen how police powers against petty criminals and drug-addicts have been used to reduce court burdens. However, many other crimes are dealt with in non-criminal ways that approach the administrative concepts of jurisdictions such as Germany and The Netherlands. The English system comes about from parliament giving authority to different organisations outside the CJS to deal with its customers in different ways. Detailed statistics are not available on how such agencies work, and several of them now exercise their authority through private companies who tend to report on financial rather than judicial matters. The main organisations are given below:

[29] The Anti-Social Behaviour Act 2003 provided for the PND scheme to be extended to 16 and 17 year olds and a power for the Secretary of State to extend the scheme to 10–15 year olds. PNDs were extended to 16 and 17 year olds from 20 January 2004 and pilots for PNDs for 10–15 year olds are now being held in six police force areas.

- Environmental crimes are dealt with by the environmental agency. They do not prosecute each offence, but tend to be selective to act as a deterrent.
- Those who do not pay their TV licence are dealt with by a separate agency, recently privatised.
- Those who defraud on their social security can be prosecuted by the enforcement agencies of the Department of Social Security.
- Those who do not pay their driving licence can be prosecuted by the Driving agency.
- Most travel companies issue fixed penalty fines on those travelling without paying.
- Most local authorities issue fixed penalties on those parking illegally or not paying a congestion charge.
- Most police have special units to track speeding vehicles via police cameras and issue fixed penalties.
- Local shopkeepers and merchants are subject to the authority of local trading standards officials.

These organisations deal with a large number of 'crimes' committed by people in England & Wales and it has been estimated that around 300,000 people are sanctioned in this way through alternative prosecution agencies, usually receiving a fine from the court. However, such agencies vary greatly in the way they proceed. Some will choose to do a deal with the offender, often amounting to a summary fine, imposed without any court action.

This way of working, especially for those offering fixed penalties, rely on the fact that people would prefer to, say, pay a £60 fine for speeding, rather than be prosecuted and pay £90 plus court costs. This is a very practical way of doing things, but because it has been set up piecemeal, there is no consistency in the way that different incidents, comparable in a social context, are dealt with. Thus, some commentators have claimed that the present system is illogical and leads to inconsistencies of justice (Sanders & Young, 1999). To illustrate this, let us take the example of a person caught obtaining, say £100, in an illegal way.

- If he does this by stealing goods from a shop, he can be reported to the police and prosecuted in court, especially if he has done this frequently. Many shops always prosecute as a deterrent. He can have a penalty notice for disorder, a fine or even end up in prison.
- If he does this by not paying a licence: e.g. to watch TV, or drive a car, the agency concerned will invariably prosecute, maybe after a warning. A fine of at least £100 is levied in addition to the licence fee. Some people refuse to pay and end up in prison. Even if he simply fails to report that his car is unlicensed because it is scrapped, he can be given a fixed penalty of £80.
- If he does not pay National Insurance as a self-employed consultant, the Tax office will charge him an extra £100 fixed penalty, with no police, CPS or court involved.

- If he travels without paying by train from London to Manchester, he will be given a fixed penalty of £20, in addition to the full fare, with no police, CPS or court involvement.
- If he defrauds the social security by claiming unemployment pay when working, he is likely to be prosecuted in court and fined heavily, or, if a serial offender, he could go to prison.
- If he overcharges customers in his shop, the local trading standards authority may prosecute him in court, but few cases tend to be brought.

At a counter to all this, a person defrauding others of many millions may be able to avoid prosecution completely, because of the complexity of his financial transactions and the difficulty and cost of bringing such as case to court. The Serious Fraud Office, which acts as both investigator and prosecutor, has its own code to follow when deciding which cases to prosecute, and the likelihood of a successful prosecution.

7 PPS Function in Investigative Proceedings

The CPS has a very limited function in investigative procedures. Under their Code of Practice:

Crown Prosecutors should provide guidance and advice to investigators throughout the investigative and prosecution process. This may include lines of inquiry, evidential requirements and assistance in any pre-charge procedures. Crown Prosecutors will be proactive in identifying and, where possible, rectifying evidential deficiencies and in bringing to an early conclusion those cases that cannot be strengthened by further investigations.

In the early days of the CPS this was done in a more formal way, through notes on case files that were passed to and from the police. The original idea was to separate the CPS and the police as much as possible. More recent experience, including pilot studies, has led to a growing process whereby CPS and police are co-located in the same office and investigative ideas are discussed informally. No statistics are available on cases where CPS feels police evidence is incomplete.

The CPS has no resources to carry out any investigation itself and must work through the police. The need for new evidence is judged as to whether the case will succeed in court, not on any wider public interest, such as the need for the truth of a particular case to be pursued. However, if the CPS sees a particular pattern of cases emerging, it may well suggest general investigative lines of enquiry: for example, a series of recent cases on multiple 'cot deaths' of infants led to the sentencing of some mothers, in what later were judged as miscarriages of justice. This was partly because of evidence given in court, and the CPS subsequently changed its way of looking at the evidence in such cases.

In a normal case the Police will act upon the suggestion of the CPS to look for more evidence, by conducting interviews, collecting forensic evidence, blanket

DNA testing of an area, or whatever is recommended, taking into account the cost of the investigation.

Other prosecuting authorities have no restriction on investigation. Nearly all organisations mentioned in section 6 above are primarily investigative authorities, who have the option to proceed to prosecution in court, but do not always do so, depending on the difficulty of obtaining evidence and the legal and practical possibility of 'doing a deal' with the offender in a cost-effective way. In particular, the Serious Fraud Office (SFO) is a public prosecution service that, as its name implies, investigates and prosecutes cases of serious and complex fraud.

The SFO is a much smaller organisation than the CPS, with only 244 staff. It is organised nationally, with 4 investigation and prosecution divisions, each division containing a number of multi-disciplinary case teams comprising lawyers, financial investigators and support of staff. In 2002 the SFO ended their financial year with 71 active cases, representing an aggregate value of alleged frauds (i.e. sums at risk) of around £1.9b. Cases are referred to them from many sources, especially the police, the Department of Trade and Industry and the Financial Services Authority. In 2002 they prosecuted 39 defendants of whom 20 were found guilty. Confiscation orders amounting to £2.9m were awarded, a very small proportion of the total amounts at risk. As these cases have to be heard by a jury, the SFO has to consider the balance of the likelihood of a jury convicting against the cost of bringing such a case to court, which can be considerable, in both money and time terms. Often serious cases can cost £1m or more in all to being to court and this would only be done if the sums at risk were really worth doing so.

The SFO can issue orders to other organisations and its own staff to investigate particular aspects of a case. This was done in 668 cases in 2002, and a further 261 such orders were given to foreign organisations to assist with enquiries. These orders are usually to third parties to release information that is otherwise subject to their code of confidentiality.

The CPS does not 'control' the investigations of the police, but will reconsider the evidence when the file is eventually presented to them and may again return it. The CPS has to judge whether the court will allow all the evidence gathered and whether the jury is likely to convict, having heard the evidence. When the evidence is presented in court by the CPS it is subject to the general rules of evidence of the court. For example, the judge may refuse to allow 'hearsay' evidence, evidence that has been obtained through a trick or an 'agent provocateur' or evidence about past defendant or witness behaviour if he or she thinks this is not relevant to the case.

8 Particular Issues

There are variations to the rules and procedures noted above for particular types of defendant or for particular types of case. It is not possible to go into full detail here, but full references are given. Much has changed over the last few years and more changes are in progress of development. Such changes are noted in Section 9.

8.1 Special Arrangements for Victims

Victims in England & Wales have no rights as such but a good deal of money is put into services for them, and their position is probably at least as good as in most European countries. The broad characteristics for many years have been the following:

- A Victim's Charter has been developed to ensure victims of crime understand what kind of service they should expect to receive (see *www.homeoffice.gov.uk/justice/victioms/charter/index.html*).
- A victim can make a Victim Personal Statement to tell the authorities of any support they might need and how the crime has affected them. This can be used by the CPS and the courts, e.g. in granting bail.
- There is a Criminal Injuries Compensation Scheme to provide payments to blameless victims of crimes of violence and those injured trying to catch criminals. There is no need for the offender to be caught.
- Courts may award compensation against the offender to be paid to the victim. Such orders do not necessary provide full recompense, but can bring an element of mediation to all proceedings.
- The Probation Service has a role to tell victims of serious sexual or violent crime abut the release of offenders after serving their sentence in custody.
- Criminal Justice professionals are trained in the needs of victims.
- Various restorative justice schemes are in operation. For young people these are integral to the court process and referral orders can be made, as is covered in the section on young people below. For adults, most restorative justice schemes are pilot studies in certain areas of the country.
- A private Victims Support scheme exists in all areas to provide a service to victims and witnesses and work closely with criminal justice agencies.
- Special arrangements exist for vulnerable or young victims when they give evidence in court. Protection can also be given to witnesses who might be intimidated before trial. These arrangements are being improved following a recent act (see section 9).

8.2 Special Arrangements for Juveniles

CPS is committed to many special arrangements for young people. Some of these provisions come from the ECHR, some from statute law and some from the Code for Crown Prosecutors. There are also special pre-court disposals used by the police and the youth offending teams before the case gets considered by the CPS, e.g. anti-social behavioural orders, reprimands, final warnings, and, in a small number of cases, police fixed penalties. These are intended to prevent re-offending and the fact that a further offence has been committed indicates that they have not worked. Thus, by the time the CPS sees the file, several previous attempts have been tried. If the CPS feels more attempts to divert are needed he can suggest this.

When the CPS considers the case for court, it must:

- work closely with all other agencies (Youth and Crown Courts, Youth Offending team managers, police, CPS, the defence and victim support coordinates),
- work to keep the targets for delay (Youth cases must be dealt with quickly),
- ensure that special arrangements are followed for certain types of offence, e.g. Sexual relations between young people, Offences committed in residential care, School bullying Motoring offences, Sexual and child abuse by young offenders,
- ensure the court considers the possibility of referral orders, which are encouraged for proceedings against young offenders. Referral orders are a primary sentencing disposal for 10–17 year olds pleading guilty and convicted for the first time by the courts. The offender has to work with a youth offending panel to agree a reparation contract with the victim or the wider community, which he has to complete successfully for his conviction to be spent.

There is a stronger tendency to use diversion for juveniles. Of the 185,000 disposals involving young people in 2003–4, there were 6,500 sent to custody, but 27,000 referral orders, where the court agreed that mediation should be tried, 9,700 compensation orders and 3,800 reparation orders. There is a lot more detail on the Youth Justice Board web site (*www.youth-justice-board.gov.uk.*).

8.3 Special Arrangements for Women

There are seven times as many male offenders as female ones. Thus, the main rules, although they do not discriminate by sex, tend to be dominated by the need to deal with male offenders. However, there have been many recent improvements in the way women are treated. These tend to be around the position of the women as victim of a violent or sexual offence. These are reflected in a new series of guidelines issued by the CPS.

- *Sexual Offences At 2004:* A new law came into force on 1 May 2004, bringing the law on sexual offences up to date for the first time for more than a century. This introduced special protection for both young girls and boys against sexual acts, sexual exploitation or abuse within the family. It also introduced new offences of abuse against both women and men who have a learning disability or mental disorder. Specific offences of grooming young girls towards sexual activity are now in force. A much wider definition of Rape now exists, and new offences of sexual trafficking of women and the commercial sexual exploitation of children have been introduced. CPS guidelines have also been introduced discouraging on public interest grounds the prosecution of consensual sexual activity between children under 16 (See *www.cps.gov.uk/news/pressreleases/archive/119_04.html.*).

- *Female Genital Mutilation Act 2003:* CPS now has a duty to prosecute cases of female genital mutilation.
- *Domestic Violence Crime and Victims Act 2004:* CPS has also issued new guidance on the way they will treat domestic violence cases. 1 in 6 violent crimes are of domestic violence, mainly against women, and the new act is the biggest overhaul of law in this area for more than 30 years. This new guidance is one of the first to acknowledge that from now on the CPS will have the responsibility for deciding to charge a suspect and encourages the CPS to think imaginatively about the charge, for example, charging with witness intimidation when the defendant pressures their partner to drop a case, false imprisonment when a victim is prevented from leaving their home or sexual charges in a forced marriage. The guidelines also give the CPS more power to direct the police investigation: e.g. by asking for recordings of emergency calls, photos of the scene and injuries, medical statements and forensic evidence, also to suggest tougher bail conditions for the defendant such as keeping away from the victims' home, work, school, etc. The CPS and the police have also set up special caseworkers and special courts for domestic violence cases, and make more use of expert witnesses (See *www.cps.gov.uk/news/pressreleases/111_05.html*).
- *Prosecution within Marriage:* It is now common practice for CPS to consider prosecution for sexual offences within marriage, if these are non-consensual.
- *Prosecution of offences connected with Prostitution:* CPS guidelines now concentrate on the prosecution of offences to keep prostitutes off the street, prevent people leading or forcing others into prostitution, stop people who organise and make a living from their earnings and stopping children becoming involved. Thus, prostitutes who avoid such considerations tend to be left alone by the CPS, as long as they go about their work in a peaceful way.
- *Homophobic Crime:* The CPS will now crack down and prosecute incidents that are 'perceived to be homophobic or transphobic by the victim or anyone else'.

8.4 Special Arrangements for the Mentally Disordered

The CPS also has arrangements for dealing with the mentally disordered offenders. If there is significant evidence to establish that a defendant or suspect has a significant mental illness, a prosecution may not be appropriate. A prosecutor will need to take into account medical evidence from appropriate sources. Proceeding may be terminated in cases of mental disorder. There are also separate arrangements for offenders to be detained in a hospital under the Mental Health Act and other guidelines require that certain avenues of diversion for mentally disordered offenders such as cautioning and/or admission to hospital or support in the community should be considered before deciding that prosecution is necessary. In broad terms it is regarded as preferable for a mentally disordered offender to receive care and treatment from the health and social services rather than from the penal system (see *www.cps.gov.uk/legal/section3/chapter_a.html*).

8.5 Special Arrangements for Foreigners

Broadly speaking the CPS treats foreigners as it would treat anyone else.

- The law is applied to them, using the same courts and procedures. It is assumed that a foreigner must be aware of the way the law may differ from those in his own country.
- Special arrangements are made for the proceedings to be translated for the foreigner.
- If there is a need for evidence to be collected from abroad, then the CPS could suggest that the police do this. There is a particular need to find out whether a defendant has a past history of the offence for which he is charged.
- The court has the possibility of deporting the offender once he has served his sentence.
- A small number of laws on immigration or terrorism are different for foreigners.
- Special arrangements can be made for evidence from abroad to be given by video link.
- The arrangements for foreigners suspected of terrorist offences are being revised following the July 2005 bombings. These are the subject of considerable Parliamentary debate, especially the introduction of new offences, the deportation of 'undesirables' and the proposed detention of suspects without trial for long periods. A new law is expected in 2006.

8.6 Special Arrangements for Minorities

Under the Race Relations (Amendment) Act 2000, CPS has to prepare, publish and deliver a Race Equality Scheme (RES) to make sure policies, service delivery and employment systems tackle unlawful racism by eliminating racial discrimination, promoting equality of opportunity, and promoting good race relations between different groups. The CPS RES aims to:

- monitor CPS policies for any negative or adverse impact on promoting race equality,
- consult on the impact of CPS policies on the promotion of race equality,
- assess and review the impact of CPS policy,
- publish the results of such consultations and assessments,
- train staff in connection with CPS race policy,
- look particularly at their employment policies.

Areas that impact most on minority communities are:

- Racially and religiously aggravated crime – CPS has put a good deal of training, consultation, research and routine statistical analysis has been carried out,
- Deaths in custody – CPS is developing policies in this area,

- Direct communication with victims – CPS has sensitive policies and monitors their effect,
- Identifying cases with vulnerable victims – over 1,100 CPS staff have been trained,
- Terrorism – there is a particular concern that terrorism legislation might impact adversely on minority communities. CPS is developing policies in this area,
- Public confidence in the CPS – it is particularly important that minority communities are confident of fair and appropriate treatment by the CPS. CPS aims to boost this confidence,
- The need for better statistics on how the CPS deals with minority groups is being addressed (see *www.cps.gov.uk/news/nationalnews/01jul2003.html*).

9 Current Changes

9.1 Co-operation between Police and CPS

The Glidewell Report (Glidewell 1998) made the general recommendation for 'closer and more effective cooperation between the agencies at local level, in response to local needs and conditions'.

The Auld report (Auld 2001) made the recommendation that 'The CPS should take over from the police responsibility for charging and for disclosure of evidence (to reduce delay and to ensure more accurate charging at the beginning of the process)'.

These two recommendations have dominated the way that the CPS has developed over the last few years and is likely to move in the future with regard to the charging process. Up to 2002, CPS got involved with charging by making the recommendation on the file when it was sent to them. This led to delays and a large number of cases being discontinued at court, because of inappropriate charges. Since then a series of pilot studies and a move towards co-location of some CPS staff at local police stations has led to the CPS gradually taking over charging.

Pilot schemes were conducted in Kent, Avon and Somerset, Essex, West Yorkshire & North Wales over a 6 month period during 2002 and found to be very encouraging. As a result of these – during 2003 – CPS, in partnership with the Association of Chief Police Officers (ACPO), developed charging arrangements to enable each area to develop, trial, and roll out its approach to meeting the principles of statutory charging. By December 2003, charging arrangements were in place in at least one site across all 42 areas.

The statutory charging scheme begins to operate as the Director of Public Prosecutions (DPP) issues 'statutory' guidance to the area. A Commencement Order under the CJA 2003 was issued on 29 January 2004, allowing the DPP to issue his guidance when areas are ready to progress to the statutory scheme. Under the Statutory Charging Scheme local arrangements are complemented by the implementation of an out of hours service, CPS Direct. CPS Direct, staffed by experienced

Prosecutors, operates from 5pm to 9am Monday to Friday and all day at weekends and public holidays enabling the CPS to offer round the clock coverage.

Statutory charging was first implemented in 14 priority areas covering 60 % of CPS business by November 2004. It will be introduced in the rest of the country by March 2007 and Hampshire was the first non-priority areas to move to the statutory charging scheme on 18 April 2005.

9.2 Review of the Code for Crown Prosecutors

The Code is the most important single document under which the CPS works, and needs to be under continuous review to take into account of the most recent changes in procedures. The next review is expected to update the Code to include recent developments in the charging process.

9.3 Victims and Witnesses

The position on victims will develop in 2005 and a consultation is taking place on a new Victims Code. This code is drawn up following the Domestic Violence Crime and Victims Act 2004. It sets out the services that victims can receive from each criminal justice organisation. In a typical English way the code does not impose a legal duty on criminal justice organisations to comply with it, but failure to follow it could be referred to in legal proceedings. The Victims Code is based upon the Victim's Charter described above.

The Victims Code sets out the duties of each organisation, including the CPS. Many of these are joint duties with the police, e.g. as part of the joint police/CPS witness care units. The basic duty is to keep the victim of a crime more completely informed of progress of his/her case. There is a particular duty to provide more information to victims expected to appear in court, especially they are vulnerable in some way, or under 18. Outcomes of such cases must also be given to victims, including whether the case is taken to appeal.

The particular duties of the CPS will be to:

- inform the victim if no prosecution is to be brought or some charges are dropped, and if the case is very serious, a meeting between the victim and the prosecutor must be offered,
- take into account victims statement when presenting their evidence in court,
- have special procedures for vulnerable witnesses,
- ensure that the CPS and the witness meet before the court hearing,
- explain delays,
- pay reasonable expenses.

Many other duties are provided by the victims' service Victims Support, including Witness Services for all types of court. The police and the courts have other duties under the code.

10 Summary of the 2005 position of the CPS

The English prosecution system is a unique one in European terms and is still developing. Its strength is that the flexibility of the English system, based on guidelines and common law, allows developments of the justice system in a way that is more flexible and likely to be happen more quickly than more formal jurisdictions where changes in the penal code need many years to work through. The relative youthfulness of the CPS also means that there is an expectation that its powers are still developing and will continue to develop, perhaps for the next 20 years, as they have for the first 20.

The speed by which the CPS develops will be constrained by the following political imperatives:

- The current government approach to criminal justice rests on a promise to the public to bring more offenders to justice and make the resources available to do so. This tends to clash with the idea of diverting more offenders from the justice system or from the courts.
- There is a difference of opinion among justice agencies as to the best way of diverting offenders from the courts. The more traditional English way of doing this would be to trust in the flexibility of the police rather than in relying on the CPS.
- There is a problem of resources in that priority is being given to public sector improvements in health and education rather than justice.
- Even within the justice system, the police and the prisons are more likely, under English priorities to get more resources than the CPS.
- Whether changes in CPS practice can be achieved within existing legislation: eg in interviewing witnesses, or whether new legislation would be necessary: eg in allowing the CPS to impose sanctions itself.

The CPS does now has a national structure appropriate to the 21st century, with central guidelines as well as local accountability to the public, staff, victims and witnesses. Although it is a young organisation, all other criminal justice organisations have undergone significant change over the last 20 years: some, such as the Courts system do not change until 2005, and the police are expected to move to a different structure, with the setting up of the Serious and Organised Crime Agency on a national basis from 2007 and the proposed merging of some smaller police forces. In many ways the CPS is better positioned to develop as a national Service than other agencies.

This flexibility means the way CPS deals with particular victims and witnesses such as women, those who are vulnerable, young people, minority communities, foreigners and those who are mentally disordered, can be developed quickly to reflect the views of society, the changing law, both at national and European level and changing populations within England & Wales.

The negative side of the English PPS is that its powers are still relatively constrained. Although charging has moved to the CPS, and there is more scope for making suggestions about investigation, there is no real power in the relationship with the police over investigation, there is no real power in the relationship with the court, over the sentence given: there is no real power in the relationship with the corrections services about the way sentences are carried out. The relationship with the courts is complicated by the fact that most sentencers remain 'amateurs' in European jurisdictional terms: at the lower court magistrates are mainly lay members of the public; at the Crown Court, judges are mainly older men and women who have spent most of their life as successful lawyers, often not in criminal law, rather than being career judges.

Also there is no real authority structure within the government: because of the lack of a Ministry of Justice all sorts of informal and non-statutory mechanisms have to be put in place to try to keep the development of CPS policies in line with the development of criminal justice policies as a whole. Thus, at the national level, there is currently a non-statutory Office for Criminal Justice Reform that reports to three ministers. At local level there are 42 Criminal Justice Boards that are not statutory bodies but which have a role in directing criminal justice policies in a local area.

Finally, CPS staff are regarded as not being very high up the ladder of the hierarchy of legal employment, partly because they are public servants and hence not as well paid as private lawyers: also because the CPS is still a relatively new service. Until this changes, the CPS is likely to remain a little of a Cinderella amongst English criminal justice agencies.

The English system for victims & witnesses seems quite a positive one as it both provides resources and gives legal backing and guidelines for all agencies as to how to treat victims. Under the new Code victims will have rights for the first time. A strength of the code is how it includes the responsibilities of all criminal justice and voluntary agencies within the same code.

Under present arrangements the CPS does not interview victims and cannot judge as to how their evidence would be accepted in court. Such arrangements are likely to change in the future if a series of pilots is successful.[30]

The CPS is also likely to become involved in more cases where a defendant has been acquitted in the past but where new evidence has become available. Until 2003 there was a double jeopardy rule whereby a person found not guilty could not be retried for the same crime. However, following new legislation, the Director of Public Prosecutions announced in November 2005 that the first prosecution under the new law would take place in 2006 of a man found not guilty of murder in 1991.

---

[30] The Director of Public Prosecutions announced in November 2005 that there would be a series of pilots in which the CPS would interview victims of sexual assaults. This would be in an attempt to ensure more effective prosecutions and boost the conviction rate for Rape, which had fallen from 28 % in 1998 to 21 % in 2002.

11 Statistical summary[31]

The following estimates of the breakdown of the annual number of 1.959.000 cases have been based on published material for 2003 unless otherwise stated. The proportions give broad comparisons with other countries in this study.

• *Conditional disposals*	307,000
• Cautions (Adult)	150,000
• Final warnings (juveniles)	31,000
• Reprimands (juveniles)	61,000
• Conditional cautions[32]	2,000
• Penalty notices for disorder[33]	63,000
• *Cases brought before the court with a special form of proceedings*[34]	984,000
• *Cases brought before the court in the normal way* (The complement of the above)	507,000
• *Cases dropped in the public_interest*[35]	13,000
• *Cases dropped on evidence grounds*[36]	148,000

[31] The figures in Section 11 should only be used for comparative purposes within this study.

[32] These have only been used in certain police force areas and 2,000 is a likely upper limit for 2004. The Government Carter report in 2002 estimated that they could reach 20,000 in due course, once they were used throughout the country.

[33] The use of PNDs is expected to grow quickly. See Home Office online report 35/05 *www.homeoffice.gov.uk/rds.*

[34] This is the 66 % of summary offence that are known to be prosecuted in large numbers, either by alternative prosecution agencies or with non-legal CPS staff presenting cases in bulk. Such proceedings are usually shortened by magistrates, although the defendant is allowed a full trial, 90 % or more plead guilty and do not attend court.

[35] Estimates made from the case management statistics quoted in the CPS Equality Impact assessment, (Lewis 2005).

[36] See footnote 30.

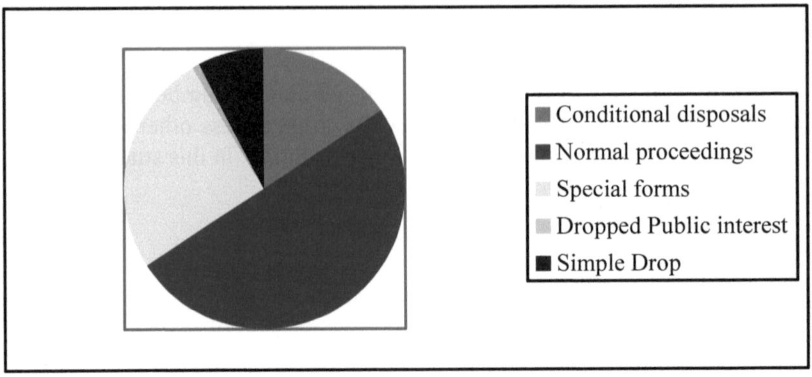

Fig. 4. Statistical Summary of Cases

12 Appendix: The Prosecution System in Scotland

Scotland has a population of 5 million and a completely different criminal justice system from England and Wales. For the majority of crimes, The Procurator Fiscal presents the case for the prosecution in the Sheriff or District Courts. The Procurator Fiscal Service is a department of the Scottish Executive, led by the Lord Advocate and the Solicitor General for Scotland, who are the legal advisors to the Executive and may participate in the proceedings of the Scottish Executive[37]. The Lord Advocate's position dates back to the 15th century and procurator fiscals were first appointed in the early part of the 19th century. Thus, procedures for prosecuting criminal cases in Scotland have a long history of independence.

The most serious cases are prosecuted in the High Court by the Lord Advocate or his team of Advocates Depute: their decision to prosecute is taken as a result of the Procurator Fiscal's recommendations and a report prepared by the police. Most other crimes are prosecuted by the local procurator fiscal. He makes preliminary investigations into criminal cases, takes written statements from witnesses, and is responsible for the investigation and prosecution of crime. This includes the power to direct the police in their investigation, but, except for very serious crimes, the police complete their investigations before involving the Fiscal. Once someone has been charged with an offence, the case must be brought to trial within 110 days or the accused will be freed.

The law in Scotland does not say that a crime must be prosecuted and the procurator fiscals have considerable discretion over what action to take. If they consider it appropriate, they can offer a confidential warning that precludes future

[37] The Scottish Executive is the recently set up Parliament for Scotland that has powers over certain aspects of domestic policy in Scotland, including civil and criminal justice. See *www.scottishexecutive.gov.uk*.

prosecution, or can make conditional offers of fixed penalty fines for minor offences which, if paid, avoid the case going to court. In some cases, the Fiscal can refer the accused to a social worker or a psychiatrist for support and treatment rather than punishment with the aim of treating the cause of the problem to prevent the accused re-offending. There is a network of 48 fiscal offices, one for each Sheriff's Court district.

The service publishes a prosecution code[38] that has some similarities to the Code for Chief Crown Prosecutors in England & Wales. It gives details of Criteria for decisions, Evidential considerations, Public interest considerations, Options for the prosecutor, Procedures for reviewing cases, publishing reasons for decisions, and ancillary matters. The options for the prosecutor in Scotland are much wider than in England and Wales and more similar to some other jurisdictions in Europe. They include: Prosecution in court, No proceedings taken, No proceedings taken 'meantime': ie unless and until any further evidence has been produced, Procurator Fiscal Warnings, Fiscal fines (Statutory conditional offers of fixed penalty), Conditional offers of road traffic offences fixed penalties, Diversion from prosecution, Referral to Scottish Children's reporter (usually for a social work 'solution'.

The Scottish Executive is considering changes to the role of the procurator fiscal, following the report of the Scottish Summary Law Review Committee in 2003 (The McInnes Committee) and published its views in March 2005[39]. The main conclusions published by the Executive in March 2005 were that Fixed penalty notices should be used throughout Scotland, The level of prosecutor fines should be raised, Fiscal compensation orders should be introduced up to £5,000, where quantifiable loss has been established, Fiscal fines and FCOs should be able to quoted in subsequent court appearances for up to 2 years only, Further consultation was needed before the fiscal could be allowed to issue community fiscal fines: ie making the accused carry out some useful work in his local community, The new procedures should be subject to firm guidelines and their use should be carefully monitored.

References

This chapter has not been able to cover all aspects of the work of the CPS and other authorities in England & Wales. More detail, more up-to-date information, and a description of how the process is evolving, can usually be found in the references below. Many of these are constantly changing web sites of the organisations described in this chapter.

Auld C (2002) Review of the Criminal Courts. CPS, London

CPS (2005a) Evidential considerations. Downloaded from *www.cps.gov.uk/legal/section13/index.html* on 29 August 2005.

---

[38] This can be found at *www.crownoffice.gov.uk/publications/ProsecutionCode.doc.*

[39] This can be found at *www.scottishexecutive.gov.uk/publications/2005/March.*

CPS (2005b) Disclosure and Covert Law Enforcement. Downloaded from *www.cps.gov.uk/legal/section20/index.html* on 29 August 2005.
CPS (2005c) Sentence and ancillary orders applications. Downloaded from *www.cps.gov.uk/legal/section15/index.html* on 29 August 2005.
Glidwell I (1998) Review of the Crown Prosecution System. Home Office, London
Home Office (2004) Criminal Statistics, England and Wales, 2003. Downloaded from *www.homeoffice.gov.uk/rds/commandpubs1.html* on 29 August 2005.
Lewis C Equality and Diversity Impact Assessment of CPS Statutory Charging; England and Wales: September 2004–February 2005. CPS Web Site, 2005
Sanders A (2004) Prosecutions in England and Wales. In: Tak P (ed) Tasks and Powers of the Prosecution Services in EU Member States, Nijmegen.
Sanders A, Young R (2000) Criminal Justice, 2nd edn. Butterworth, London

Criminal Injuries Compensation Scheme: Details of the organisation of this and levels of compensation are given in *www.cica.gov.uk.*

Crown Prosecution Service: Details of the organisation and legal framework, as well as annual reports can be found on *www.cps.gov.uk.* The Code of Practice for Crown Prosecutors can be found on *www.cps.gov.uk/victims_witnesses/code.ht.* The way that the CPS fits into the rest of the criminal justice system can be found on *www.cjsonline.org.*

Young People: Details of the special arrangements the CPS has for dealing with young people can be found on the web site *www.cps.gov.uk/legal/section4/chapter_b.html.* Information about how young people are dealt with by the CJS as a whole, including pre-court diversion, are given on the web site of the Youth Justice Board, *www.youth-justice-board.gov.uk.*

Serious Fraud Office: Details of the organisation and legal framework, as well as annual reports and all the cases covered, sentences and confiscation orders given are to be found on *www.sfo.gov.uk,* for example the 2003–4 annual report can be found at *www.sfo.gov.uk/publictions/2003_2004/seection02.asp#04.*

Victims: As mentioned above, the position on this is changing and a new victims code has just been issued for consultation. Details can be found on *www.cjsonline.org/the_cjs/what_new/news-3121.htm.*

Witnesses: The CPS has issued an on-line guide to its services to Witnesses, called the Witness Virtual Walkthrough accessible through the website: see *www.cjsonline.gov.uk/witness/walkthrough/index.html.*

Home Office: Details of changes to the law and the way all agencies of the criminal justice system interact with each other are to be found on the Home Office web site *www.homeoffice.gov.uk.*

The Prosecution Service Function within the French Criminal Justice System

Bruno Aubusson de Cavarlay

1 General

The French criminal justice system is grounded in institutions that were created during the revolutionary period and the Napoleonic Empire. The 1808 code of criminal investigation set up the main structure, with three court levels (*cour d'assises*, *tribunal correctionnel* and *tribunal de police*) corresponding to three degrees of seriousness of offences (*crimes*, *délits* and *contraventions* – that is, felonies, misdemeanours and petty offences). The public prosecution service (*le parquet*) was given the main role in selecting and dispatching cases and an examining magistrate was created, whose intervention (judicial inquiry) is compulsory for felonies and optional for misdemeanours, and who is the only person who can maintain an offender in pre-trial detention. The only major addition in the 19th century was the summary proceeding for flagrant violations (1863) which avoids judicial inquiry while maintaining the possibility of immediate incarceration, ordered, in this case, by the PPS prior to a very rapid court hearing. From then on, for a long time, the only changes had to do with judicial practice, with a rising rate of drops and continuous reinforcement of direct prosecution to the detriment of judicial inquiry, with a gradual decline in the number of proceedings taken to *cours d'assises*. The soaring inflation of suits in the 1970s finally brought about legislation reinforcing the provisions for simplified and rapid proceedings (including *ordonnances pénales* and direct referral, the latter soon being turned into summary trial, thus enlarging the field of application of flagrant violation proceedings, but with the need for a judge to decide imprisonment). In the mid-80s, in spite of these solutions, the number of drops was still growing, and courts continued to be clogged up with cases, leading to longer waits before handling and producing sharp criticism of the justice system. There then began a period of experimenting with disposals, known as alternative proceedings, which produced a rapid succession of legislative reforms starting in 1993. It is difficult to foresee the point at which a balance will be achieved, since further changes are still being introduced. The French situation will be described using 2002 as a reference year, and with the addition of indications, when needed, as to arrangements still in the developmental or even in the introductory phase.

2 Cases Brought to the Courts

2.1 In General

In 2002, about 542,000 cases were sent to the criminal courts by the PPS, along the normal tracks. In terms of seriousness, these are a heterogeneous assortment of felonies punishable by a prison term of ten years to life, misdemeanours punishable by up to ten years in prison or a fine of over 1,500 € or 5th class petty offences punished by a fine of 560 € to 1,500 €, and the types of proceedings are variable as well.

For instance, about 37,000 cases were transmitted to examining magistrates – a compulsory phase for felonies only, which represent about one fifth of these cases. At the end of the judicial inquiry about 29,000 cases were sent for a trial, while another 8,000 (a low estimation) were dropped (on legally founded bases).

Another 56,000-odd cases prosecuted by the PPS in "normal" fashion were handed over to a juvenile court judge, who is competent to deal with offenders under age 18, although some cases – in particular, felonies committed by underage offenders – must go before an examining magistrate.

However, the vast majority of the "normal" prosecutions is provided by cases brought directly to a court for adults, representing some 384,000 direct prosecutions by a *tribunal correctionnel* (for misdemeanours) and 65,000 direct prosecutions before a *tribunal de police* (for 5th class petty offences). As agreed, the *ordonnances pénales* referred to the latter courts (about 82,000 in 2002) are not included here.

These figures show PPS output. It is very hard to give a detailed account of cases judged, using the same counting statistical units. Rather, we suggest counting the number of individuals prosecuted (one person prosecuted in several cases being counted as many times).

In 2002, for about 534,000 cases transmitted, the number of individuals who appeared before a court for a "normal" hearing was about 533,000 for adults (including 3,000 for *cours d'assises*, 453,000 for *tribunaux correctionnels* and 77,000 for 5th class *tribunaux de police*) and about 80,000 for juveniles who appeared before a specialized jurisdiction (a *cour d'assises* for juveniles, a juvenile court or a judge for juveniles). This makes a total of 603,000 individuals judged after a hearing (those prosecuted in several cases are counted several times).

The sundry nature of this series must be emphasized. The 3,000 indicted individuals appearing before *cours d'assises* all appeared before an examining magistrate, and the judicial inquiry took an average of 23 months, to which we must add an average delay of about one year for the hearing to be scheduled. A growing portion of suits for felonies are rape cases (about one half in 2002). Some of the defendants judged by a *tribunal correctionnel* had gone through the same long proceeding (about 33,500, for approximately 20,000 cases), but others are prosecuted on the very fast summary trial track (about 38,000 cases, the number of offenders is not known). On this track a person may be tried within two days of his arrest by the police when the case has been handed over to the PPS. Most cases involve aggravated theft, personal violence or drug dealing. For these two extreme opposites in terms of length of process, but both involving the most serious offences, pre-trial detention is frequent and the judgment is collegial (in *cours d'assises*, by a popular jury, in *tribunaux correctionnels* by three judges). However, the majority of proceedings (for misdemeanours or petty offences) involve cases in which the PPS decides to prosecute following a police investigation, by summoning the offender for a hearing. The prevailing model for these suits is real-time (or direct) treatment, with the decision often made at the end of the police custody, with the cases then usually examined by a single judge. A great many of these directly treated cases involve road traffic offences (probably about one third) as well as less serious personal and property offences for which the PPS does not ask for an unsuspended prison sentence. Since it is the PPS that decides what prosecution track will be used, its choice has major consequences as to the ultimate sentence.

When handing the case over to the examining magistrate, the PPS states the facts prosecuted and their legal qualification in its introductory brief (a written document) and the examining magistrate must confine the investigation (for the prosecution and for the defence) to these facts. If any new facts are uncovered, the PPS must state whether they are to be added to the file. At the end of the judicial inquiry, the examining magistrate again consults the PPS on the charges to be retained. The PPS issues its final brief and the examining magistrate closes the inquiry either by an *ordonnance de non-lieu* dropping the case or by an *ordonnance de renvoi* referring it to the competent court (*assises* for serious offences, *tribunal correctionnel* for misdemeanours or *tribunal de police* for petty offences). The PPS can appeal all of the examining magistrates' *ordonnances*, and especially those that close the inquiry. In case of direct prosecution, the PPS alone decides what the charges will be and represents the state at the trial, sometimes taking action jointly with an administrative agency in some specialized spheres (cases involving taxes, customs or the public domain, etc.).

The role of the PPS varies with the type of court. In *cours d'assises* in particular, where the findings of the judicial inquiry must be summed up orally, the PPS (as well as the counsel for the defence) calls in witnesses, the investigating police officers who participated in the investigation and experts. The same is true for complex cases examined by a *tribunal correctionnel*, especially in economic and financial offences. Conversely, for a "standard" *correctionnel* trial, the written proceedings are usually the sole basis for the trial, along with the judge's questioning of the defendant. Victims are heard when they are present at the trial, and the PPS or the court may insist on hearing them and have the case postponed so that the victim may be summoned.

When the defendant has been questioned and the case examined at the hearing, the PPS takes the floor to tell the court what it demands. It does not simply demand a conviction (or acquittal when the hearing brings new elements to light, justifying that the case be dropped), it also calls for a specific sentence. Where the sentence handed down may vary within a large spectrum (there is no minimum sentence and the maximum is far higher than the average for pronounced sentences) and inasmuch as French judges do not apply any guidelines, the final sentence is primarily influenced by what is demanded by the PPS, as well as by legal factors (choice of the indictment) and procedural factors (type of prosecution, pre-trial detention).

The PPS can appeal any verdict by the *cour d'assises* or decision by a *tribunal correctionnel* or a *tribunal de police* or some portion of those verdicts and decisions. According to the French criminal code, the consequences of an appeal by the PPS or by the convicted person are not symmetrical. The fate of an offender cannot be worsened exclusively on account of his own appeal. An appeal by the PPS, however, gives the appeals court the same latitude as the lower court. The rather systematic use of the incident appeal mechanism (an additional delay granted to the PPS when the offender appeals) helps limit appeals. Figures on this are quite imprecise. In 2002 the proportion of offenders affected by an appeal decision ranged from 5 to 7 % depending on the sources on which the estimation is based.

The normal prosecutorial track is legally open to private parties taking action on civil grounds as well. Unfortunately no figures are available as to the number of proceedings engaged exclusively on that basis, either coming before an examining magistrate or by direct summons to appear at the trial. Most judicial statistics are the product of computerized files on case-handling: they therefore include cases for which the PPS chose not to take action itself. Aside from the managerial aspect, this inclusion is understandable inasmuch as the PPS must make its demand even in cases prosecuted on the request of a private party on civil grounds. Suits of that kind dwindled in the 1970s to the point where it seemed useless to count them separately. Nowadays, practitioners feel that the trend has been reversed, and complaints taken to an examining magistrate with private parties taking action on civil grounds and direct summonses to appear by private parties sometimes represent a considerable portion of the court workload, now that victims are more systematically informed of their rights and of the availability of legal aid. This trend may apply mainly to suits in which both the penal and the civil track are open. While the various legislative reforms have not fundamentally changed the rights of civil parties to independent access to criminal courts, nonetheless the gradual introduction of disposal arrangements has significantly modified the responses to the demands of victims.

2.2 The First Four Classes of Petty Offences

The tribunal de police judges the first four classes of petty offences. In those cases, as opposed to 5th class petty offences, the public prosecutor generally delegates his authority to a police commissioner who represents the PPS (henceforth, OMP). In practice, the entire prosecutorial function is in the hands of a department attached to the police but which is able to orient cases in a large range of directions (prosecution at the hearing, *ordonnance pénale*, set fine with surcharge, case dropped).

In 2002, about 151,000 cases were prosecuted by an OMP and dealt with by summoning before a court for a normal hearing (with a single judge). The distribution for types of offence is not known. There are probably a great many traffic offences, but other kinds of breaches of specialized legislations (labor, health and environmental laws) may also be involved, as well as some breaches of the criminal code (petty violence, insults, slight deterioration, rowdiness, etc), some of which may involve a victim. The latter may join the case on civil grounds and request compensation at the hearing. When a case comes for a hearing, the OMP plays the same role as the PPS for more serious offences. In particular, he demands a sentence, which is usually a fine. The courts may also simply pronounce one of the complementary sentences prescribed for a specific petty offence (suspension of driving license, restriction of rights, etc). When the sentence is only a fine, it is not recorded on the criminal record.

In some instances the case is examined at a hearing at the request of the accused, when the latter challenges the fine handed down by the proceeding, be it administrative (set fine or set fine with surcharge) or judicial (*ordonnance pénale*). The proportion of petty offences in the first four classes judged at a hearing is not known.

3 Disposals and Diversion

On the whole, it is clear that the limited faculty to prosecute on the normal track (to take a case to court) has facilitated the development of alternative penal responses at the PPS level. For the most part, when the PPS does not take a case to court, and provided there is no suit by a private party on civil grounds, the case ends, formally, by being dropped. This out-of-court decision does not preclude reopening of the dossier until the statute of limitations for the facts is reached. The PPS can revise its decision if new factual elements arise or if the offender commits other similar acts.

According to this traditional, formal presentation, nearly 88 % of cases handled by the PPS in 2002 were dropped. But for one thing, this extremely high percentage is due to the huge number of dropped cases with an unknown offender (66 % of cases). So, since 1998, to improve assessment of the actual perimeter of the decision on whether to prosecute, (the principle of the expediency of prosecution) statisticians first subtract "non-prosecutable" cases (that is, offender unknown, offence not patent, statute of limitations, insufficient evidence) from the total, so as to evaluate the proportion of dropped cases which really do depend on the PPS. In 2002, 73 % of cases were tallied as non-prosecutable. Furthermore, an increasingly large proportion of cases not prosecuted by the normal track were dealt with by the PPS by various disposal procedures (including *composition pénale*, penal mediation and reparation, conditional dropping, *rappel à la loi* – a warning, so to speak, which will be discussed below). Lastly, the current presentation of official

PPS statistics shows a "rate of penal response"; that is, the total number of prosecutions and disposals in proportion to prosecutable cases. In 2002 the rate was 68 %. The term "dropped" (32 % of prosecutable cases) is reserved here for cases that could have been prosecuted and were not dealt with penalty. Slightly over one third of these (37 %, or 11 % of prosecutable cases) are dropped because the damage or disorder caused by the offence was very slight. This gives a better idea of the extent of the application of the expediency principle the principle of the expediency of prosecution: it is now up to the PPS to first try to deliver a solution avoiding appearance at court, in some cases.

Recent reforms in the code of criminal procedure have given legal status to what the official statistical presentation had been doing since 1998 in its presentation of PPS decisions. Article 40-1 now says: "When he considers that the facts brought to his knowledge in application of the clauses of article 40 constitute an offence committed by a person whose identity and place of residence are known and for whom there is no legal obstacle to the implementation of a state action, the territorially competent Public Prosecutor decides whether it is fitting to: 1) either prosecute the case; or 2) implement an alternative proceeding (a disposal) as prescribed in articles 41-1 and 41-2, or 3) drop the proceedings when justified by the particular circumstances surrounding the acts committed."

This division of PPS decisions into three categories (the advocates of this reform systematically used the term "third track" for disposals) does not correspond to the division applied here, since it does not mention the degree of involvement of the judge on the one hand and of the accused on the other hand. In the forthcoming presentation, *ordonnances pénales* and *compositions pénales* are placed in the same category inasmuch as both are proceedings formally involving a judge, and disposals other than *composition pénale* are categorised according to their content and the involvement of both the PPS and the offender in the measure decided.

3.1 Sanctions Following Simplified Proceeding Involving a Judge

With the Implicit Consent of the Accused: the Ordonnance Pénale

This form of simplified proceeding is the oldest arrangement in existence in France, resulting in a penal sanction viewed as a conviction but obtained without a hearing. Between 1972 and 2002 this proceeding is allowed for all petty offences, including 5th class ones. Originally, it was introduced for the rapid, simplified punishment of the least serious offences by fines. The PPS formulates a written recommendation to the judge, using a standard form. Once the judge has signed it, it is sent to the accused. Theoretically the judge may also acquit the person or modify the amount of the fine, but in practice the recommendations of the PPS are systematically accepted. The offender may object to the decision, in which case he is given a public hearing. When there is no objection he is implicitly viewed as consenting to the PPS decision and the *ordonnance pénale* is enforced like an ordinary sentence. If it involves a 5th class petty offence, then, it is written onto the criminal record.

Since 1999 fines may be replaced by any complementary measure prescribed by the law for a given offence. This is particularly true for suspension of driving licenses for road traffic offences. It is a fact that *ordonnances pénales* are mostly used for this type of offence (but no figures are available on this point).

In 2002, there were more *ordonnances pénales* for 5th class petty offences than cases judged (82,000 as against 65,000), but all in all they only represent a relatively small portion of penal responses (about 9 %). In France, this proceeding is viewed as a conventional criminal prosecution rather than a kind of disposal, probably because it has been in existence for so long. In the previous paragraph (normal prosecution before a court of law) they were not counted, to respect the classification used in this comparative study.

In 2003, in application of the 9/09/2002 Act, this proceeding was extended to moderately serious traffic offences, for which stronger repression was instated at the same time. For that year, the offences sanctioned by an *ordonnance pénale* amounted to only about 14,000, representing approximately one out of ten convictions. However, this arrangement, along with *composition pénale*, may rapidly become consequential now that some petty traffic offences have been transformed into misdemeanours.

With the Explicit Consent of the Offender: Composition Pénale

Composition pénale was first mentioned in the code of criminal procedure in 1999 and enforced starting in 2001. It was explicitly conceived as a disposal arrangement rather than a simplified trial. In 2002 about 6,700 cases ended with *composition pénale*.

This arrangement stipulates that the PPS may recommend a sanction which, if accepted, would avoid prosecution provided the offence is moderately serious and the sentence incurred does not exceed five years in prison or a fine only. To begin with the list was to be restrictive, including violence with no aggravating circumstances, simple theft, receiving of stolen goods, deterioration of property, substance abuse, drunken driving and desertion of home, all of which are punished by no more than 3 years imprisonment. The proceeding, which is not applicable to juveniles, requires that the offender must explicitly admit to guilt. The PPS then formulates a written proposal mentioning the indictment and the nature and quantum of the measures proposed. The person involved can request the assistance of a lawyer and has ten days to respond. If he agrees, the *composition pénale* proposal must be validated by the president of the competent court, be it the *tribunal correctionnel* for misdemeanours or the *tribunal de police* for a petty offence. The judge may demand that the offender, and possibly the victim, be heard. Hearings are not compulsory, even if one of the parties requests one. The idea, then, is that of a written decision by the judge, in the form of an *ordonnance*: it may be refusal or consent, but not a modification of the sanction proposed by the PPS and accepted by the offender.

Sanctions include fines (initially no more than half of the maximum incurred but that limit was eliminated by the 9/03/2004 Act), confiscation, immobilization of the vehicle for no more than 6 months, suspension of the drivers' license for no more than 4 months, unpaid work for no more than 60 hours and miscellaneous other measures involving prohibitions or obligations. When the proceeding fails the PPS must prosecute along the normal track. However, if the *composition pénale* is accepted, enforcement of the sanction or measure puts an end to the public prosecution, meaning that the case cannot be said to be dropped, according to the legal definition. Although this is not a conviction, either, theoretically, the 9/09/2002 Act modified the original regime of *composition pénale* by prescribing that it be written onto the criminal record.

The extension of the field of application of *composition pénale* and the diversification of the sanctions involved were accompanied by the elimination of the initial restriction as to the requisites for its implementation. The PPS can now suggest *composition pénale* to the offender through the mediation of a judiciary police officer, including during the period of police custody (but the offender may still call in a lawyer, and still has ten days to respond). However this reform also retained the original "normal" framework for the implementation of disposals, which is to say, "*maisons de justice*" and duly authorized individuals ("*délégués du Procureur*", representative of the PPS henceforth) with a specific mandate from the public prosecutor to recommend *composition pénale* and monitor its enforcement.

In 2003 the number of cases ended in this way doubled (about 15,000) and the number of proposals (under way) was much higher (about 29,000). There are relatively few instances in which the judge refused to validate the outcome (about 600 in 2003). Evaluation research on the subject points to a broad range of practices, both in the degree of recourse to *composition pénale* depending on the court, and in the practicalities. In some cases the proceeding ends up being quite similar to the *ordonnance pénale* (with the difference that the sanctioned person must explicitly agree to it beforehand) and it is used to obtain the enforcement (and not simply the pronouncement) of a conventional sanction such as a fine in the framework of a simplified proceeding. In other cases it is more in the spirit of disposal without the intervention of a judge, combining measures tending more toward reparation or rehabilitation and a modicum of monitoring through a *maison de justice*. *Composition pénale* then tends to be more like other disposal measures.

3.2 Measures Proposed by the PPS without the Intervention of a Judge (Conditional disposals)

Historically, the first measure clearly conceived as a disposal measure and introducing a scheme for conditional dropping may be traced back to the December 31, 1970 Act creating the offence of drug use. The measure was an order to undergo treatment, issued by the PPS only but implemented in collaboration with the health services. If the person subjected to that order complies with the minimum medical requirements, the PPS does not institute prosecution for what is still, to this day (2005) a misdemeanour punishable by a one-year prison term. The idea of conditional dropping then gained ground, outside of any explicit legal frame. Given the increase in some petty offences (offences relative to legal requisites for driving a vehicle, shoplifting and so on), decisions to drop prosecution were tied to various conditions imposed on the offender, such as getting his papers in order or giving compensation to the victim. The need for a legal framework began to be felt with the first experiments in mediation: not only to define what measures could be taken, but also to officialize the intervention of the new actors involved in the implementation of those measures. The first bill to modify the code of criminal proceedings along these lines was passed on 4/01/1993: it instated penal mediation. The 23/06/1999 Act contains a more exhaustive, more systematic presentation of the range of possibilities open to the PPS without its having to resort to a court. These measures may be divided into two broad categories according to the type of involvement they imply both on the part of the offender and of the people in charge of enforcing the measures.

Low Degree of Offender Involvement: Conditional Dropping, Rappel à la Loi

These measures are of the type initially viewed as a kind of conditional dropping. A modicum of requirements may be set by the PPS for dropping, including giving the victim compensation, setting an illegal situation straight, showing that one is trying to improve one's social or occupational situation. These measures are not directly dealt with by judicial institutions and some simply imply that the police services notify the offender of the order, on behalf of the PPS. This category represents some 47,000 dropped cases in 2002.

In 1999 the *rappel à la loi* was introduced. As its name suggests, this "call to order", has no immediate consequences if the offender does not repeat the offensive act. Theoretically, this measure should be administered quite formally, with the offender being summoned to the *maison de justice* by the representative of the PPS. In practice, there is no proof that the protocol was really enforced in the 145,000 cases dropped following a *rappel à la loi*. The official instructions for its enforcement stipulate that the *rappel à la loi* may be implemented by a judiciary police officer, which represents a modern version, in a criminal justice framework, of the extremely ancient practice of admonition by a police officer, requested by the PPS and delivered in a much more informal framework. There is nothing trivial about this remark, since for a large part, the increase in what are now viewed officially as "disposal measures" represents a form of alternative to pure and simple dropping of the case. In fact, the enforcement instructions clearly recall that what counts is that thanks to these schemes a response is given to every kind of offending, however petty.

All in all, cases ended following a *rappel à la loi*, effective regularization or compensation as prescribed by the PPS, or referral to a non-penal care scheme represent some 192,000 cases, or about 14 % of prosecutable cases and 21 % of what may be viewed as a "penal response". In the nomenclature of grounds for dropping there is also a heading "other prosecutions or sanctions of a non-penal nature", the content of which is not otherwise specified. It probably covers all those cases in which the uncovering of an offence led either to a reaction not tied to referral to the PPS (such as a disciplinary sanction, dismissal, breaking of a contract with a financial penalty) or to a judicial proceeding on civil grounds brought by a plaintiff (a divorce suit following domestic violence, for example). In all, this group represents another 55,000-odd cases counted as a "penal response", the content of which is probably minor in terms of follow-up by the PPS, and which probably represent more a threat of possible prosecution for the offender if he or she fails to settle the affair by non-penal means.

Significant Involvement of the Offender and of the Public Prosecution Service: Mediation and Reparation

These measures deserve more explicitly to be called "disposal". In addition to the injunction to receive treatment, mentioned above, they include penal mediation for adults and reparation for juveniles. The idea behind these two measures is similar: it is to get the offender to engage in a process also involving the victim, toward whom he or she must meet some specific conditions set in agreement with the person in charge of enforcing the measure. For these measures, a person or an accredited non-profit organization must be designated by the public prosecutor or one of his deputies, and the encounters involved normally take place outside the courthouse, in a *maison de justice* or in the organization's facilities. This partakes both of what is known as "restorative" justice (restoring normal social ties is more important than the enforcement of a sanction) and of what is called "local" justice as opposed to more institutional justice meted out in places often remote from citizens.

In 2002, about 34,000 cases were ended by mediation and some 5,000 following reparation, a measure specifically aimed at juveniles. The general text does not explicitly exclude juveniles from penal mediation (and in fact statistics show about 3,000 mediations for cases involving at least one juvenile) whereas the text prescribing the proceeding applicable to juveniles (the "1945 *ordonnance*") states that reparation (which does not formally imply an attempt to reach an agreement with the victim) may also be ordered by the juvenile court judge and involve the same type of follow-up for the juvenile by an organization specialized in this type of measure.

The mediation process is defined by an official order and may vary from one court to another. The law only stipulates the minimal conditions of enforcement: the parties, and therefore the offender, must agree to it (this agreement is not explicitly mentioned for the measures discussed in the paragraph about conditional dropping), the designation of the mediator by the PPS, the summoning of the parties, the attempt to come to an agreement materialized by a written document which is returned to the public prosecutor and which may be used by the victim to bring a civil suit for recovery if necessary. The nature of the offences for which mediation should be preferred may also vary from one court to another. However, as a rule, emphasis seems to be placed on offences connected with repeated, prolonged conflicts for which a conventional form of proceedings and punishment are viewed as aggravating factors rather than as a way of restoring less conflicting relations. According to national statistics on mediations handled by non-profit organizations, the largest group is represented by insult and injury (47 %, including 13 % for violence within the family) followed by conflicts connected with a divorce (child custody, alimony, 14 % in all), thefts represent about 8 % and deterioration 11 %, whereas the rest comes under the heading "other offences". Note that according to this source, only a little over one half of mediations (55 %) is stated to be successful. On the basis of available information it is difficult to say whether the unsuccessful mediations (45 % of the measures handled) then led to prosecution or to drops. It is probable; however, that the total figure given above (34,000 cases closed following mediation) is far lower than the total number of measures implemented. Non-profit organizations alone dealt with 41,000 in 2002, not to mention the cases turned over to accredited individuals.

The number of cases closed without prosecution following mediation has risen constantly since 1998 (date at which this heading began to be counted). However, the increment (+ 31 % between 1998 and 2003) is far below the increase in *rappels à la loi* and admonitions (+ 173 %), whereas the number of prosecutable cases rose by 14 %. This is understandable, since mediation requires more human resources than a simple *rappel à la loi* or an admonition (28 % of mediations turned over to organizations last at least three months), especially when the latter is administered by the police at the request of the PPS.

3.3 Drops (Strict Definition)

This only includes what are called cases dropped for expediency. We do not count cases in which the PPS simply records the case, noting that the offender is not identified (3.4 million cases in 2002), or considers that the dossier does not bear evidence to the existence of a criminal offence (118,000 cases), only contains an insufficiently clear offence or insufficient charges (184,000 cases), or cannot be prosecuted on other, purely legal grounds (78,000 cases). This series of some 3.7 million cases is called "non-prosecutable cases". According to official statistical classifications, in 2002, about 429,000 of the 1.35 million prosecutable cases were dropped on grounds pertaining to the expediency of prosecution. However, the details of these grounds show a much lower figure if a more restrictive definition is adopted.

Firstly, about 121,000 cases are dropped because attempts to find the offender were fruitless. This may be because the offender is known but has absconded, or because there was sufficient evidence pointing to an offender who was not found, in the end. Next we have about 6,000 cases for which the offender is claimed to be mentally deficient. These grounds – penal irresponsibility – may put an end to prosecution when the case is submitted to an examining magistrate. By extension, the PPS applies this principle, covered by the expediency of prosecution, for the least serious cases, without even convening an expert for a psychiatric examination. These two headings are actually quite similar to those in which a case is declared non-prosecutable.

Dropping for expediency also involves cases in which the situation was regularized or the victim given compensation immediately, therefore without any intervention of the PPS: this represents some 67,000 cases in 2002. Note that this figure is much higher than the one for regularization and compensation obtained in compliance with a PPS request. Although the difference between the two situations may in fact not be that clear-cut, it seems that the simple fact of a complaint to the police or report by the police probably led to settlement without any formal PPS action: in these cases, the mere threat of action sufficed.

Next we have cases in which the victim's position in the dossier causes the case to be dropped. French criminal law contains very few instances in which the victim's complaint is required for prosecution (these include breaches of private life, slander and injurious remarks in the press). In practice, on the other hand, the PPS accepts desisting of the plaintiff, absence of the plaintiff (who does not respond to summonses after having lodged a complaint), partial responsibility of the victim in the offence suffered (especially with respect to unintentional injury) as grounds for not prosecuting. These three grounds, taken together, represent about 81,000 dropped cases in 2002.

There then remains the largest heading of all, with about 154,000 cases for which the grounds for dropping is the slight damage or disorder caused by the offence. In 2002, they represent 36 % of prosecutable cases dropped with no other intervention of the PPS and about 11 % of all prosecutable cases. Between 1998 and 2003, whereas the number of prosecutable cases increased by 14 %, the total number of drops classed as dropped by expediency declined by 7 % and the number of drops on the grounds that the damage or disorder caused by the offence was slight declined by 40 %. This trend corresponds to an objective openly formulated in the government's criminal justice policy orientations and relayed by the PPS hierarchy.

Petty Offences in the First Four Classes

The prosecutorial functions of the OMP do not include as broad a range of possibilities as for the PPS. In 2002, aside from the normal track described in part I, there is the *ordonnance pénale*, which takes the form described in paragraph a.1 (about 416,000 decisions in 2002), the set fine with surcharge (see part 6.) and dropping (2.4 million in 2002). The grounds for dropping are the same as for the PPS. However, there are no statistics on their distribution. The majority probably have to do with disagreement over the reported offence submitted to the OMP (for traffic offences in particular), acceptance of the person's arguments or insufficient information not allowing the offender to be found.

Marginally, drops may involve cases of petty violence, public insults or slight deterioration of property. This is what is designated, in France, by the broad term of incivilities. The use of this term indicates that the criminal nature of the behaviour involved is not always obvious, even if much of it can be classed as petty offences in the first four classes. The 9/09/2002 Act instated a new jurisdiction, the local judge, a non-professional judge competent, in particular, for those petty offences and for civil litigation of lesser importance. These jurisdictions, reminiscent of the justices of the peace, can receive cases referred by the PPS, the OMP and private parties. Since the principle of this jurisdiction was introduced without much preparation, its implementation has turned out to be very slow, and, in fact, laborious. In 2003, about 21,000 cases were heard by local judges who meted out slightly over 15,000 judgments for petty offences in the first four classes. These same judges are also called on to rule on recommendations for *ordonnances pénales* (24,000 rulings in 2003) and in the future they will be able to ratify *compositions pénales* as well. For the time being, this seems to represent a transfer of the activity of the tribunal de police (with a professional judge) to the local judge. A similar transfer is being considered for fifth class petty offences.

4 Organisation of the PPS

In France, the PPS is clearly organized hierarchically, and its structure coincides with that of the courts of law. Whereas the Minister of Justice is at the top of this hierarchy, it is up to the general public prosecutors, representing the public ministry at the appeal courts, to run their particular PPS. The general public prosecutors (there are 34) are appointed by the council of ministers, but like all prosecutors and their deputies, they are magistrates. The public prosecutor heads the PPS for each *tribunal correctionnel* (there are 180) and the number of deputies assisting him or her obviously varies with the size of the court (the average is six). PPS judges are assisted by court clerks, with a national average of two court clerks for one judge. In the course of their career, judges may work alternatively for the PPS and for the bench.

The orientation of the PPS aims mainly at implementing "criminal justice policy". The latter contains the broad guidelines expressed in official instructions at the national level and in guideline notes at the local level. These discuss the means of law enforcement – and especially, in recent years, an interpretation of the newly passed texts, given the major, recurrent legislative changes – along with the concrete organizational means of dealing with cases. This also takes the form of models for written forms, computerized managerial tools, the distribution of human and material means, the allotment of budgetary resources to be used to pay private individuals or non-profit organizations (especially necessary for the extension of disposal measures). In criminal justice affairs, general public prosecutors and ordinary public prosecutors play a decisive role in all aspects having to do with law enforcement, in the broadest sense of the term, of which they are in charge. At the local level, the practical application of criminal justice policy takes the form of organizational choices: the distribution of spheres of competence among sections and deputies, the organization of round-the-clock shifts for handling judicial problems and the establishment, with institutional partners and first of all with the police, of protocols for handling cases.

However, the code of criminal proceedings also gives the Minister of Justice and the general prosecutors the capacity to intervene more specifically in the course taken by a given case. This capacity has been a source of controversy. In the 1990s the possibility of eliminating it was considered. In 1993 an addition to the code specified that instructions transmitted by the hierarchy for a given case must be put in writing and included in the dossier. A legislative reform bill was then drawn up, "severing" the hierarchical tie and giving PPS magistrates a position similar to that of judges (magistrates of the bench) while maintaining the possibility for the government to determine the overall orientation of criminal justice policy, but it was dropped, finally. Then came a period during which the Ministers of Justice claimed to have refrained from giving any particular instructions, after which the hierarchical organization thereon was reinstated in 2002. Concretely, this means that for the most sensitive cases the members of the PPS request the opinion of their hierarchical superior, sometimes going up as high as the ministry of Justice. The latter has the power both to impose prosecution and to determine what the public prosecutor is to request of the court, but theoretically, according to the code of proceedings, not to order that a case be dropped.

This reversion to the situation underlying the centralized organization of the PPS in France since the early 19th century is partially motivated by the desire to achieve homogeneous practices among public prosecutors and their deputies. In a way, this acknowledges the fact that these practices are quite variable, despite the principle according to which the PPS is "one and indivisible". The individual dimension of these variations is certainly not negligible, but it is less important, since the PPS magistrates are far more involved than magistrates from the bench in the collective organization of their work throughout the criminal justice process. On the other hand, the diversity of local situations, tied to the context, history and the impetus given by officials over time, is sufficiently evident, and the assertion that criminal justice policy is one and the same everywhere remains quite theoretical. This diversity is probably increased by the fact that for some recent schemes, courts are in a state of constant experimentation, owing to the repeated legislative changes and to the fact that the successive laws accumulating solutions which are relatively similar, at least in respect to their goals (*ordonnance pénale*, *composition pénale*, hearing following prior admission of guilt) leads local actors to make their own choices, preferring one solution to another.

5 Cases Dealt with by the Police

According to French law, judicial police officers at all levels are never allowed to decide independently of the track to be followed by a criminal offence once it is reported. We have shown above how the handling of petty offences in the first four classes implies that police services, authorized by the public prosecutor, are given prosecutorial functions in accordance with the range of judicial responses allowed. Actually, the vast majority of these petty offences is dealt with administratively, according to the set fine proceeding described below. They are not given judicial treatment unless the offender takes issue with the offence.

However, this formal presentation is inadequate. Empirical studies agree that there is a form of selection of cases referred to the PPS by the police. Some cases go no farther than the police docket, which is now being computerized, and which contains a day-to-day listing of those interventions and demands which do not immediately lead to the writing of a police report (in the Gendarmerie it is called the registration notebook). This register mostly contains information on facts that do not constitute offences, but for some entries it is really a sort of preliminary to a police report of an offence, for which there may not be any follow-up.

It is impossible to measure the number of those cases. They may be petty offences uncovered on the initiative of the police (use of cannabis for instance) or else, and apparently more frequently, cases in which the victim decides not to lodge a complaint after having gone to the police. Family conflicts are most often mentioned (domestic violence, desertion, etc.). The PPS can obtain a copy of this recording on the police docket in the framework of another suit. The informant (usually the victim) can also obtain a copy through the intercession of the PPS. In the absence of any official count, it should be noted that some differences between estimations by victimization surveys and police statistics may be due to the hiatus between facts which victims claim to have reported to the police and those counted by the police as having been the object of a police report transmitted to the PPS. The extent of the gap probably depends on the circumstances surrounding the offence (seriousness, attempts) and on whether or not the lodging of a formal complaint is compulsory. For example, the victim of a burglary attempt may call in the police at the time, and then neglect to go to the police station to file a complaint.

These various instances actually amount to a selection, at the police level, of cases referred to the PPS, but one which does not imply that the police exert some occult authority bordering on the illicit. In fact, the PPS may hand down overall instructions indicating which cases may be settled in this way. But a general trend is observed, then, tending to set up simplified inquiry proceedings enabling the PPS to take these facts into consideration in case of subsequent judicial proceedings for a similar offence. For shoplifting, for instance, the PPS usually sets a sum for damage beyond which the facts should be referred, to be dealt with penalty. In the absence of specific circumstances, a theft representing a smaller sum will be transmitted to the PPS via a simplified notification form. However, in some places the old practice of using the police docket to record cases of shoplifting representing a sum lower than the minimum defined by the PPS still continues.

6 Borders between Penal and Administrative Treatment

The criminal justice system does not have exclusive power to sanction deviation from the legal norm: some administrations may do so as well. Furthermore, for petty criminal offences, the normal track may be essentially administrative, even if judicial recourse is available. Both of these types of borders between penal and administrative treatment exist in France.

Quantitatively, the larger group involves the treatment of the first four classes of petty offences by the set fine proceeding. There are regulations defining the amount of the set fine, to be paid directly to the officer who records the offence, to the officer's administration or directly to the Treasury Department. This is the general rule, which always leaves leeway for the offender to take issue with the fine by referring to the OMP of the *tribunal de police*. There is strong incitement not to do so however, especially for traffic offences, since the fine imposed by the administrative proceeding is about 35 % lower than the rate applied by the court when it deals with the same case. Conversely, late payment of the fine is punished by a surcharge (multiplication by about 2.7), with recovery of the sum entrusted to the Treasury Department on the basis of a ticket issued by the OMP. Aside from traffic offences, the offences dealt with in this way include those involving public transportation (no ticket, disturbing public order) and those pertaining to the countryside or the environment. The diversity of the administrative agencies and public services resorting to set fines is such that the overall number of such fines cannot be counted. The only statistics available are for late payment: in 2002, there were 12.4 million set fines with surcharge recorded by the OMP and 10.2 million enforceable collection orders transmitted to the Treasury Department.

In some spheres, the administration has significantly greater powers to sanction. Income taxes and customs prevail here, quantitatively. The sanctions are mostly financial, but may also be accompanied by seizure of property. In these fields, the PPS is not advised unless the administrative service has also recorded a criminal offence (such as fraud, false declaration, impeding an investigation), and in that case the administrative agency involved may join in with the PPS in bringing suit.

Control of immigration is a very peculiar area requiring separate discussion. A foreigner residing illegally in France commits a misdemeanour punishable by no more than one year in prison. As a rule, every offence recorded must be referred to the PPS. But at the same time, the administrative authority has another form of proceedings at its disposal for illegal foreigners, namely escort to the border, which may entail their placement in administrative custody. The latter requires submission to the public prosecutor for an opinion and to the ordinary criminal court for a possible extension of custody beyond 48 hours (for 10 days at most). The order to escort the person to the border can only be challenged before an administrative court, with the possibility of an emergency proceeding. A distinct administrative proceeding, expulsion, also exists for foreigners whose presence is claimed to represent a serious threat to public order. These administrative proceedings may be further intertwined with criminal proceedings inasmuch as foreigners who reside illegally or commit other offences in France, if convicted, are susceptible of being barred from entering French territory, the implementation of which sentence also implies administrative monitoring. These administrative treatments (escort to the border, expulsion, barring from the French territory) are handed over to the police, with possible recourse for the individuals involved, and constraint mechanisms involving both the administrative judge and the judiciary judge. In 2002 the number of foreigners charged with illegal residence offences by the police was about 62,000; the number of convictions for this offence was about 9,300; the number of convictions involving barring from the territory was about 8,600.

For the same year, there were about 42,000 orders to escort to the border (7,600 of which were enforced).

7 The Role of the PPS in the Investigation Phase

The code of criminal proceedings asserts two broad principles: the public prosecutor oversees the judicial police officers (article 19) who are in charge of recording offences, collecting evidence and finding offenders (article 14); these officers have the obligation to inform the public prosecutor immediately of any offences of which they are aware (article 40). In practice, the importance of these two principles depends on the legal framework within which the investigation takes place, be it a preliminary investigation, a flagrant violation or referral to an examining magistrate.

A preliminary investigation may be initiated at the request of the PPS or automatically. In this framework the investigational powers of the police are not very great. In particular, searches, house searches and seizure of exhibits cannot be done without the consent of the person involved. The PPS must be informed of the outcome of the preliminary investigation within six months of its onset or as soon as a suspect is identified. The judiciary police officer can put the suspect in police custody for 24 hours (for ordinary cases), renewable once, and must inform the public prosecutor immediately. The latter then indicates what course he wishes the case to take at the end of that period.

When the offender is discovered at the same time as the offence the normal procedural framework for the police is a flagrant violation investigation (for either a felony or a misdemeanour). The police then have greater powers (it can make searches, seizures, and do scientific and technical evidence-collecting work, etc) but it has much less time to do so. At the end of one week (the usual case) the PPS must choose another framework within which the investigation may be extended or else decide to prosecute. Police custody is possible from the start of the investigation and the PPS must be informed of it immediately.

When a judicial inquiry is started after referral to the examining magistrate, the police is under the authority of the latter. It is the magistrate who defines the content of the investigations he wishes to have conducted. This process is compulsory for some investigation techniques in the ordinary regime (phone tapping for instance) or when, at the end of the delay for a flagrant violation investigation, the police needs to continue to implement investigational means involving a restriction of individual liberties. While the magistrate gives specific instructions in letters rogatory, he may also use rather vague formulations ("do everything that may help to reveal the truth"), leaving a considerable margin open to the judicial police services within which to maneuver. The PPS may also decide to start a judicial inquiry so as to be able to request the pre-trial detention of suspects. The legislative reforms designed to increasingly control, if not to reduce, recourse to pre-trial detention have hardly produced any drop in the relative frequency of this measure, which continues to be applied to about four out of ten suspects. The June 15, 2000

Act went a step further by setting up a liberty and custody judge, separate from the examining magistrate, and handing over to him the power to place a suspect in pre-trial detention at the request of the PPS or the examining magistrate.

There are no statistics which enable us to categorise investigations on the basis of their judicial framework. It is obvious however that recourse to an examining magistrate represents a minority, and is declining. Only 7 % of cases prosecuted by the PPS in 2002 along a normal track (to the exclusion of *ordonnances pénales*) involved referral to an examining magistrate. The proportion was 9 % in 1992. This decline is particularly evident since the mid 1980s, although it actually started much earlier. Conversely, there is a rise in summary trials, which are preceded by flagrant violation investigations. In police statistics, the only indication available on the investigational means used is the number of individuals placed in police custody. In 2002, it was about 381,000, representing 42 % of suspects. This proportion is certainly higher for adults, and has increased, overall, since 2002, reaching 45 % in 2004, probably because of a rise in flagrant violation investigations.

Criminal justice policy guidelines recommend increasingly insistently that referral to an examining magistrate be reserved for the most serious offences or for cases in which the investigation is complex. Recent legislative reforms, and especially the March 9, 2004 Act, have given legislative backing to this orientation by strengthening the powers of the police and the PPS when a preliminary or flagrant violation investigation is used. It extends the latter (up to 8 additional days with PPS authorization when a prison term of five years or more is incurred), lengthens police custody for offences relating to organized crime, extends possibilities for requisitions, and especially those involving personal information in computer files, permits searches within preliminary investigations with the consent of the liberty and custody judge.

These changes theoretically reinforce the control of the PPS over the course of investigations, especially when the police are investigating one or several suspects. In practice, for the most ordinary cases, this control is mainly exerted through direct contact between the deputy prosecutor on duty and the judicial police officer. During the very short period of police custody, and in accordance with the explanations received during a first referral, the deputy prosecutor may orient the content of the investigation under way and may grant (or not) the powers requested by the police (extension of police custody, requisitions) after which he indicates the track chosen. The fact that the case is dealt with in a brief period of time requires, and enables, a more condensed exchange of information between the police (acts under way and visualized, achievements) and the PPS (orientation considered). In this context, their relations may in practice lead to the establishment of routines of a sort, enabling the police to have advance knowledge of the PPS' requirements as to how to deal with a particular kind of offence, while the PPS is able to confine itself to checking on the police investigation afterwards. The preliminary investigation usually rests on written exchanges with less monitoring of the advancement of the investigation and its foreseeable outcome by the PPS. When the PPS has chosen to transmit the case to an examining magistrate the latter is responsible for monitoring the progress of the investigation (and does not simply give his consent for the use of some specific investigational means). The only resource open to the PPS (the general public prosecutor in this case) is to influence the allotment of human resources to the examining magistrate and the degree of priority assigned to investigations, which will always be protracted—an average of one and a half years in 2002—and will involve specialized police services.

8 Special Proceedings

The broad principles of criminal proceedings are applicable to juveniles with some restrictions mentioned in a specific text (the 1945 *Ordonnance*), which calls for the intervention of specialized courts competent for judging offenders who were under age 18 when the offence was committed. The measures and sentences applicable to juveniles are of a particular nature: the judge must prefer educational measures, and the maximum sentences incurred are shorter. In fact, most of the measures and sanctions enforced are educational measures. Prosecutorial proceedings are also of a particular nature: the examining magistrate phase is compulsory, even if it is usually entrusted to the juvenile court judge. Delays may now be imposed on the judge for appearance in court, but the shortest proceedings (summary trial) and simplified ones (*ordonnance pénale*) are not applicable. However, the PPS retains its role, which has even tended to be reinforced over the last decade. In the largest courts, there are sections of the PPS specialized in dealing with cases involving juveniles, and they work with the educational agencies in charge of conducting rapid socio-educational investigations for the juvenile court. These are compulsory whenever the PPS hands a juvenile over to the court and considers summoning the person shortly or issuing a committal order.

The principle of a systematic penal response to the least serious kinds of delinquency was put into action sooner for juveniles, producing a considerable increase in the number of cases prosecuted by referral to a juvenile court judge. However, the most important change during this period has been the development of measures decided by the PPS. These are proceedings which it controls all by itself since juveniles still cannot be given disposals involving the consent of a court. The figures given in part one includes juveniles, but differentiation is possible. In 2002, whereas about 59,000 cases involving at least one juvenile were prosecuted along a conventional track (essentially referral to a juvenile court judge), about 50,000 were ended by disposal, including close to 35,000 following a *rappel à la loi* and 8,000 following a measure involving reparation or mediation. Some of these measures are implemented by representatives of the public prosecutor or through non-profit organizations. About 30,000 cases involving at least one juvenile were dropped in 2002, including slightly fewer than 17,000 for slight damage or disorder; the proportion, with respect to all prosecutable cases, is therefore the same as for the entire series (about 11 %).

9 Evolutions and Trends

The long-term decline in the percentage of cases submitted to examining magistrates is continuing. That has not prevented the number of cases taken to *cours d'assises* from rising, owing to the increased repression of sexual assault. The length of the process for this long track is not decreasing, since the growing complexity of cases more than compensates for the drop in absolute numbers. At the same time, there is a rise in rapid proceedings leading to unsuspended prison sentences, with persistent criticism of the quality of the handling of cases, both at the police investigation level and during the hearing phase. In spite of this criticism, the possibility of resorting to this rapid track was further extended in 2004. It is true that at the same time the sentence enforcement phase received increased attention. It gained a full-fledged judiciary status in 2000, with the instatement of a judge of sentence enforcement (*juge de l'application des peines*). But this simply corroborates the lesser weight of the court, which has less and less power over the initial decision to imprison and on the final decision to release prisoners, at least for sentences involving personal restraint.

For a bit over ten years now, the development of disposal schemes is claimed to be the pivotal element in criminal justice policy. This should help to provide a more systematic penal response for police suspects, while reserving the normal prosecution track for cases sufficiently serious to justify the intervention of a judge. However, it must be admitted that only the former goal has been achieved so far, and the schemes set up since 1993 (*rappel à la loi*, conditional drops, mediation) are above all alternatives to pure and simple dropping. The second goal does not seem to have been achieved, and the criminal courts are still overworked in spite of the development of an accumulation of schemes that give the PPS increasing possibilities for having a measure or a sentence meted out without going through a normal hearing.

In fact, it is perhaps this accumulation of schemes and the heterogeneity of local practices generated by it that is most detrimental to these reforms. The scheme that has the greatest future is probably the *ordonnance pénale* for misdemeanours, with an unknown, nonetheless, as to how the sentences meted out this way will be enforced. In particular, it is probable that French judges lost interest in fines because of the difficulty in getting them paid, which in turn led to the devaluing of the simplified proceedings used to do so. Whence, conversely, the more positive assessment both of *composition pénale*, which ties the end of prosecution to the enforcement of the measure pronounced (possibly a fine) and more generally of schemes in which cases may be monitored over time before a final decision is made. But it is particularly surprising, then, to discover that the same mechanisms (conditional adjournment of sentencing possibly resulting in exemption from a sanction) did not enjoy the same success when set up earlier at the court level.

Whereas the reinforcement of the role of the PPS is undeniable, we should not underestimate the growing weight of victims in the decisions taken, not to speak of the probable development of civil suits to get around PPS decisions to drop cases. When a victim is involved in the proceedings, all the new schemes define the way his or her interests are to be defended or even reinforced. For prosecuted cases, growing attention is being paid to the victim's expectations as well, and actually takes the form of considerably harsher sanctions when the victim has suffered physical assault, and especially sexual abuse. However, from the victim's viewpoint, the penal response is still quite incomplete. In particular, with the focalization of criminal justice policy on responses to prosecutable cases, the vast majority of cases with no known offender is left exclusively in the hands of the police services, although these are theoretically under the authority of the public prosecutors. This omission may be the cause of the growing gap between public opinion, which remains convinced that repression is not sufficiently severe, and judges who wonder how far they will have to go to satisfy the demands of victims, and express justifiable reserves on this count.

The fact remains, then, that the French criminal justice system still suffers enormously from the lack of coherent mechanisms for allotting resources and means so as to respond to offending in accordance with the severity of the offence, using appropriately severe measures and sanctions. This inconsistency is particularly salient for offences on two different levels of seriousness. For the most serious offences, we find, with practically no transition, criminal prosecution offering the most serious legal guarantees but taking three years, and summary trial taking three days. For moderately serious offences, a same case may entail a long, resource-consuming process (such as mediation) or an extremely short process (*ordonnance pénale*, recognition of guilt) with guidelines for the sanctions incurred. Moreover, this incoherence is further reinforced by the lack of a clear principle as to the process leading to a decision declaring the person guilty and as to the rights of the defence during this process (in particular when the decision is practically taken during the period of police custody). One consequence of this is probably a persistent inequality among citizens in their access to a proceeding providing the most complete legal guarantees, in other words, to one of the forms of handling which are obviously a rare, perhaps excessively rare resource. There is ongoing suspicion In France a two-speed justice system is developing. Whereas the penal architecture set up in France served as a model for many continental European countries in the early 19th century, the fact is that the country's criminal justice system is presently unable to achieve a new balance between the various schemes it is trying to borrow from its neighbours without making sure they form the necessary whole required.

The Prosecution Service Function within the German Criminal Justice System

Beatrix Elsner, Julia Peters

1 General

German criminal procedure is fundamentally marked by the principle of legality and traditionally by the principle of mandatory prosecution, with the role of punishment reserved for the courts.

In relation to the investigation of crimes, the police are to be regarded as a subservient institution, carrying out the prosecution service's (PPS) will. They are required to pass all cases, even where an offender is not found, and information on to the PPS, whose traditional duty it is to review a case as to whether there is sufficient evidence to bring it to court. This is the ideal model of the criminal justice system still basically in place legislatively. But in the last decades remarkable deviations from this ideal type have developed in relation to a significant proportion of criminal cases.

As far as the structure of offences is concerned, certain types of offences, previously considered criminal were de-criminalised in the 1970's and became offences against order dealt with administratively. A large number of forms of behaviour regarded as socially unacceptable, fall into this category. There are two types of criminal offences: less serious crimes (Vergehen) and crimes (Verbrechen). Crimes are punishable by a minimum of one years imprisonment, less serious crimes by less.

2 PPS Structure

2.1 The PPS

External Structures

Section 147 GVG (Act on Court Constitution) provides that the PPS in Germany is a hierarchically structured institution. "The following have the right to supervise and to lead: 1. the Federal Minister of Justice in Relation to the Federal Prosecutor

General and the Federal Prosecutors; 2. the judicial administration of the Länder (Federal States) in relation to all prosecutorial staff of the Land (Federal State) concerned; 3. the highest ranking prosecutor at the upper regional courts and the regional courts in relation to all the prosecutors in their jurisdiction." In accordance with Section 146 GVG, prosecutors are required to follow the professional directions issued by their superiors. In this, the Justice Minister's right to direct is different from that of a superior prosecutor. As the Justice Minister is not a prosecutor, his right to direct is regarded as external, that of a superior as internal. Directions can be of a general nature or they can relate to individual cases; in both cases, they may refer to legal or factual aspects. The right to direct is limited by the principle of legality. A PP decision not to prosecute can be the subject of criminal proceedings in its own right (see Section 258a StGB [Criminal Code]).

The question as to which state power – the executive or the judicative – the prosecution service should be associated with, is a matter of debate. Judicial evaluation has regarded the prosecution service as an equivalent to the courts; a power of legal interpretation and as a necessary organ of the criminal justice system responsible, together with the courts, for the provision of justice (BGHSt 24, 170, 171; BVerfGE 9, 223, 228). As of 2001, however, the Federal Constitutional Court regards the prosecution as a part of the Executive – despite its role in the justice system (BVerfGE 103, 142, 156).

Internal Structures

The individual Federal States have so-called "Anordnungen" (directives) for the organisation and workings of the PPS which regulate the institutional structure and the areas of responsibility of PPS employees working in a jurisdiction (Anordnungen über Organisation und Dienstbetrieb der Staatsanwaltschaft [OrgStA]). The OrgStA are based on the Conclusions of a Justice Ministers Conference and are therefore as good as uniform.

The individual PPS offices are usually structured as follows: There is a series of units (general and specialised) which are administered by a single prosecutor. Three units constitute a department led by an "Oberstaatsanwalt" (senior prosecutor) as the Departmental head. In the larger PPS offices a number of departments form a main department, led by a main departmental head. The prosecutor managing a divisional branch of a prosecution office is usually also a departmental head.

Above the departmental heads one finds the head of office who is referred to as the "Leitender Oberstaatsanwalt" (leading senior prosecutor). S/he is supported by civil servants of low to intermediary rank as well as the heads of department or units, who perform administrative tasks alongside their other duties, such as the allocation of hearings, co-operation with the press, personnel matters or training.

Beyond that legal assistants, civil servants administering the site, secretarial and security workers are to be found in every PPS office.

The incoming work is distributed in accordance to a work distribution plan produced by the head of office annually. In producing the work plan the so-called „Pensenschlüssel" is used in practice. This is in fact a model to calculate the personnel needs for judges, prosecutors, assistant prosecutors and para-legal staff.

Key figures are used to convert the case-load into personnel requirements. The values are determined by calculating how many typical cases of that sort an "average" decision-maker can deal with in the course of a year, if s/he only dealt with procedures of that sort.

2.2 The "Amtsanwaltschaft"

One of the special features of German criminal procedure is the existence of "Amtsanwaltschaften" (assistant prosecutor offices). Their work and tasks structurally resemble closely those of the prosecutors. As an institution they are usually fused with the PPS, only rarely do local courts have an Amtsanwaltschaft of their own. Unlike prosecutors, these para-legals do not have to be qualified to hold judicial office (see Section 122 DRiG [German Law of Magistracy]). They are mostly civil servants of intermediary level ("gehobener Dienst") or even lawyers in training ("Referendare"); Section 142 paragraph 3 GVG.

In accordance with Section 142 paragraph 2 and 145 paragraph 2 GVG an Amtsanwalt can act where the local court has jurisdiction. The OrgStA provides for further limitation. It states that an Amtsanwalt may only be given work for which a single criminal judge will have jurisdiction (compare Section 25 GVG). This excludes Schöffengerichte (one professional, two lay judges) cases entirely from the Amtsanwalts' field of responsibility. Even where a single judge's jurisdiction is given, the OrgStA restrict transferral to the Amtsanwalt to certain offences. If one considers the cases which can be transferred to the Amtsanwalt by offence type, it becomes clear that the Amtsanwaltschaften are responsible for dealing with a significant proportion of crime (about 40 % of all proceedings[1]). One should, however, assume that Amtsanwälte end cases by bringing them to court (even) less often than prosecutors (7.4 % in 2003). Due to the nature of the offences which can potentially be transferred, the majority of cases will presumably be dealt with by diversionary measures based on the principle of opportunity (19.9 % without condition in 2003; 7.4 % with condition in 2003) or by means of a penal order application (18.9 % in 2003).

3 Case-ending Decisions

3.1. The PPS Role during "Normal" Proceedings

First of all, this section is concerned with normal criminal proceedings. *Normal* criminal proceedings are those by which *every* criminal offence, no matter what its nature or severity, can be dealt with by. This is the case where the PPS[2] brings charges after concluding its investigations, the court opens main proceedings after

[1] In 2003 1,614,450 were dealt with by the Amtsanwaltschaft, 2,551,203 were dealt with by the Staatsanwaltschaft (without Bavaria).

[2] PPS now includes always the Prosecution Service and the "Amtsanwaltschaft".

an intermediary stage and these are ended by a judgement during the main hearing stage. There is a fundamental right to appeal against court judgements of this kind.

Cases Brought before Court

The PPS' task is to decide, after conducting investigative proceedings, whether to press public charges based on adequate suspicion (so called "hinreichender Tatverdacht") or whether to drop the proceedings due to inadequate suspicion in accordance with Section 170 StPO (German Criminal Procedure Code). In 2003 the PPS dropped 26.7 % of proceedings due to inadequate suspicion. This is the single most common type of case-closing decision. However, the PPS is not free in making this decision; the fundamentally valid principle of legality binds it to bring charges where adequate suspicion is found.

In bringing public charges the PPS defines the procedural act – the factual behaviour which, in its view, requires punishment. The main hearing and judgement which follow are restricted to this as the procedural subject. In other words, further offences, other factual occurrences, cannot easily be taken into consideration during the proceedings. This is only possible by means of a supplementary charge application in accordance to Section 266 StPO. The court can, however, change the charge brought, if its legal evaluation of the procedural act is different.

Table 1 (see main proceedings) shows the proportion of cases brought to court (leading to a main hearing) in relation to the number of case-ending decisions made by the PPS altogether. One should remember that the prosecution statistics count the number of proceedings. Therefore it is possible that more than one offence is dealt with in one case or that proceedings deal with more than one suspect. The total figures also include

- proceedings passed on to another Public Prosecution Office[3],
- the offences against order which are passed on to administrative authorities[4],
- proceedings in connection with another matter[5],
- the recommendation that private proceedings should be brought[6],

but not proceedings in which no offender was identified[7]. Furthermore, there is no differentiation of cases against juveniles or involving adult offenders.

As can be seen, the PPS brings cases to court – leading to a main hearing – in only about 12 % of cases. This proportion does not include the so called penal order which formally is a court punishment but functionally a PPS-sanction (see penal order proceedings) and accelerated proceedings (see accelerated proceedings). If one subtracts the 27 % of cases in which the PPS drops the case because of inadequate suspicion, i.e. evidential insufficiency, this still leaves a total of 61 % in

[3] In 2003 there were 196,152 proceedings passed on to another Prosecution Office.
[4] In 2003 the PPS passed 218,244 proceedings on to administrative authorities in accordance with Sections 41 paragraph 2 and 43 OWiG (Act on Offences against Order).
[5] In 2003 there were 249,001 proceedings connected with another matter.
[6] In 2003 the PPS advises 163,537 proceedings to private prosecution.
[7] In 2003 there were 3,561,471 cases reported in which the offender was not known.

which the PPS does not bring charges in spite of knowing who the offender is and having sufficient evidence.[8]

Main Proceedings

Once the PPS has brought charges, the court has control over proceedings. It decides during intermediary proceedings (Sections 199-211 StPO) whether to proceed to main proceedings. If it decides to do so, preparation for the main hearing begins (Sections 213-225a StPO), in order to provide for as efficient progress as possible. The law presents the main hearing as the core piece of German criminal procedure. Current practice, however, witnesses its decreasing importance.

Statistical Evaluation of the Main Hearing It should be pointed out that the figures in table 1 are drawn from different statistical sources with diverging parameters so that a satisfactory comparison may seem unattainable. Because, however, the statistics are based upon the same counting unit and we have chosen three different years, the percentages calculated are not without worth if one bears the basic problem in mind.

Table 1 shows that the majority of proceedings end other than by a judgement given at the end of full main proceedings. The proportion of actual first instance judgements seems to be even lower in relation to PPS case-ending decisions than the 12 % indicated. Only in about 7 % there is a court judgement after a full trial although the PPS brought a charge. In relation to the proportion of charges made, this means that a big amount of cases end other than by a court judgement. This can not be explained by the PPS itself reversing its decision to bring charges.[9] It results far more from the fact that the court also has alternative means to end cases. Such alternative means can be seen in a court refusal to open main proceedings in accordance with Section 203 StPO, in a court drop, in a court disposal or in a penal order after opening the main hearing. These decisions are quite rare however. The most frequent occurrence is that the proceedings are merged with others. Such joinders will, however, frequently lead to a court making a judgement. In so far the impression gained from table 1 must be seen in this perspective. Furthermore table 1 does not include the first instance judgements which resulted on the courts' initiative despite the PPS not having brought charges but having sought an alternative case-ending. Those cases in which the PPS initially applied for a penal order but in which a full judgement was made (n=69,878 in 2003) should be paid special attention in this case.

All in all, one can conclude that the proportion of cases ended with a full "normal" trial is very low.

---

[8] This proportion does not change if one compares the type of case-ending decision made with the number of people subjected to investigative proceedings.

[9] The PPS reverses its charge very rarely; the opportunity to do so is only given before the court opens the main proceeding.

Table 1. PPS Case-ending Decisions[a] and First Instance Judgements

	1993[b]		1998[c]		2003[d]	
	Absolute number	%	Absolute number	%	Absolute number	%
(a) Total PPS case-ending decisions	3,355,259	100.0	4,583,228	100.0	4,766,070	100.0
(b) Of which: cases[e] brought before court	451,289	13.5	538,807	11.8	573,345	12.0
(c) First-instance judgements[f]	252,636	7.5 of (a)[g]	308,202	6.7 of (a)[g]	330,488	6.9 of (a)[g]

Source: Prosecution Statistics, Tab. 2.2 und Court Statistics, Tab. 2.2, 4.2, publ. by the Federal Statistical Office Wiesbaden

[a] Only proceedings dealt with by the PPS at the regional courts and dealt with by the Amtsanwaltschaften (assistant prosecutor offices); excluding those (n=15 in 2003) dealt with by the PPS at the upper regional courts.

[b] Previous Federal territory including East-Berlin.

[c] Results of (a) and (b) for Hamburg and Schleswig-Holstein are for 1997.

[d] Results of (a) and (b) for Schleswig-Holstein are for 1997.

[e] Without penal order proceedings and accelerated proceedings.

[f] 1st instance courts are local, regional and upper regional courts. Nearly all first instance judgements are passed at local courts (97 %). These are only considered in so far as they resulted after public charges were brought by the PPS. Only local court statistics differentiate in this way, therefore judgements by regional courts include those made after trials were initiated in other ways. The latter, however, form a barely significant proportion of cases. Judgements by the upper regional courts are not included (n=11 in 2003).

[g] The data for this calculation stem from different data sources. So, the proportion given is not an exact value.

PPS Rights during the Main Hearing The court has the exclusive competence to make decisions during the main hearing. The PPS merely has various rights during the oral hearing which enable it to influence the course of the proceedings.

Bringing Evidence: It is the courts' role to gather evidence. Above all the fundamental principles of oral evidence and immediacy are central in this context. Only the trial material presented and explained orally may form the basis for the judgement (to be concluded in particular from § 261 and § 264 StPO). Furthermore the court must itself perceive what is presented and must draw facts from the source itself (as indicated by § 244 paragraph 2 StPO), i.e. no surrogates may be used. These fundamental principles are, however, subject to many exceptions and limitations. Just like the defence and the accused, the PPS can only use applications to bring evidence in order to influence what evidence is gathered by the court. In making such applications, due to its obligation to remain objective (Section 160 paragraph 2 StPO, Nr. 127 RiStBV [Guidelines for Criminal and Fine Proceedings]), the PPS is also required to file ones which are in the defendant's favour. In practice this is a rare occurrence.

The court must allow a PPS application to bring evidence unless reasons to reject exist in accordance with Section 244 and Section 245 StPO. An application to bring evidence is to be rejected where the bringing of such evidence is inadmissible (Section 244 paragraph 3 line 1 StPO). Beyond that, an application may only be refused on the following grounds:

- the obviousness of the evidence to be brought
- the matter to be proved is irrelevant for the decision or it is proved
- the complete unsuitability or non-availability of the evidence
- the application is intended to slow down the proceedings
- the fact to be proved is presumed to be true

There are specific grounds for refusal in relation to expert witnesses and evidence to be presented as well as a narrow catalogue in relation to pieces of evidence already brought. The court must issue a formal court decision when refusing an application to bring evidence (Section 244 paragraph 6 StPO).

The court is not bound by the PPS' evaluation of evidence but decides in accordance to its free conviction gained during the hearing (Section 216 StPO).

The Right to Question: The PPS' right to apply to bring evidence is closely related to its right to question the accused, witnesses and expert witnesses in accordance with Section 240 paragraph 2 StPO. However, the presiding judge has the right to lead the hearing (Section 238 StPO), thus s/he can first use his/her right to interrogate and the PPS will only question in as far as it regards this interrogation as insufficient.

Pleading: According to Section 258 paragraph 1 StPO the PPS has the right to make a closing statement after all evidence has been brought. Although this is a legislative right, a prosecutor is obliged to make use of it by internal regulations (nrs. 138/9 RiStBV). S/he must evaluate the result of the hearing factually and legally in summary, argue the grounds for a specific severity of sentence and make certain applications.

Appeal

The PPS has the right to appeal against court decisions both in favour of and against the interests of the accused (Section 296 StPO).

An appeal on the facts of the case is possible against the decisions of the local court (single criminal judges and "Schöffengericht") in accordance with Section 312 StPO. The small criminal chamber of the Regional Court is the appeal instance (Section 74 paragraph 3 GVG). The court makes a formal decision as to whether to allow or reject the appeal. If it is allowed, a main hearing must be prepared again (Section 323 StPO). In the main hearing evidence is gathered anew and the PPS has a right to make applications to bring evidence, to question and to make a closing statement as in the first instance.

Table 2. Appeals (on Fact) to the Regional Courts[a]

	1993[b]		1998		2003	
	Absolute number	%	Absolute number	%	Absolute number	%
(a) Proceedings in which an appeal is possible	335,500	100.0	409,001	100.0	419,688	100.0
(b) Appeals before the regional courts[c]	46,661	13.9 of (a)[d]	57,284	14.0 of (a)[d]	56,159	13.4 of (a)[d]
(c) Of which: appeals brought by the PPS (total)	6,187	13.3	8,612	15.0	10,168	18.1
Of which: in the defendant's interest	97	1.6	126	1.5	159	1.6
Of which: not in the defendant's interest	6,090	98.4	8,486	98.5	10,009	98.4
(d) Of which: appeals brought by others[e]	43,429	93.1	53,029	92.6	51,558	91.8

Source: Court Statistics, Tab. 2.2, 5.1, publ. by the Federal Statistical Office Wiesbaden

[a] Figures also include proceedings against juveniles. The restricted possibilities to appeal in cases involving juveniles (Section 55 JGG [Act on Juvenile Courts]) must be taken into consideration.

[b] Without Mecklenburg-Vorpommern and Saxony.

[c] The higher number of appeals lodged in comparison to the total number of appeal trials is to be explained by both the PPS and the defence lodging appeals against certain judgements.

[d] The appeals made in one year are not necessarily equivalent to the proceedings in which an appeal is possible in that year. So, the proportion given is not an exact value.

[e] The defendant, adhesiory prosecutor, private prosecutor, guardian/legal representative. The vast majority of this category is brought by the defendant (2003: 51,182=99.3%).

Sections 333–358 StPO concern the rules about an appeal on points of law: Instead of such an appeal (on the facts of the case), it is also possible to lodge an appeal with the Upper Regional Court on points of law regarding the ruling made in the first instance by the criminal judge or the "Schöffengericht". Appeals on points of law can also be lodged against the appellate judgement by the Small Criminal Chamber at the Regional Court. If the court of first instance is the Grand Criminal Chambers at a Regional Court or the Schwurgericht, an appeal can be made on points of law to the Federal Court of Justice (in exceptional cases to the Upper Regional Court). If the court of first instance is the Upper Regional Court, appeal on points of law can only be made to the Federal Court of Justice. In all cases, an appeal on points of law can only be based on the argument that the judgement is based on a violation of the law.

The main hearing must not be repeated for appeals on points of law because evidence is not gathered anew. The PPS pleadings and applications are heard in accordance with Section 351 paragraph 2 line 1 StPO.

Table 3. Appeals (on Points of Law) before the Upper Regional Courts[a]

	1993[b]		1998		2003	
	Absolute number	%	Absolute number	%	Absolute number	%
(a) Proceedings in which an appeal is possible[c]	360,225	100.0	438,861	100.0	447,730	100.0
(b) Appeals before the upper regional courts[d]	4,831	1.3 of (a)[e]	6,054	1.4 of (a)[e]	5,402	1.2 of (a)[e]
(c) Of which: appeals brought by the PPS (total)	179	3.7	208	3.4	233	4.3
Of which: in the defendant's interest	4	2.2	5	2.4	18	7.7
Of which: not in the defendant's interest	175	97.8	203	97.6	215	92.3
(d) Of which: appeals brought by others[f]	4,660	96.5	5,873	97.0	5,196	96.2

Source: Court Statistics, Tab. 2.2, 5.2, 8.1, publ. by the Federal Statistical Office Wiesbaden

[a] Figures also include proceedings against juveniles. The limited appeal possibilities of juvenile criminal law (Section 55 JGG) should, however, be borne in mind.
[b] Without Mecklenburg-Vorpommern and Saxony.
[c] This includes all the appeal judgements of the regional courts as well as all local court judgements. The first-instance cases brought before the regional courts, for which the upper regional courts have jurisdiction in accordance with Section 121 paragraph 1 nr. 1c GVG cannot be included. Thus the number of cases in which an appeal is possible given here is somewhat lower than in reality.
[d] The higher number of appeals lodged in comparison to the total number of appeal trials is to be explained by both the PPS and the defence lodging appeals against certain judgements.
[e] The appeals made in one year are not necessarily equivalent to the proceedings in which an appeal is possible in that year. So, the proportion given is not an exact value.
[f] The defendant, adhesiory prosecutor, private prosecutor, guardian/legal representative. The vast majority of this category is brought by the defendant (2003: 5,165 = 99.4%).

Tables 2 and 3 show that appeals, of whatever kind, are not usually lodged by the PPS. Especially a rise in the number of appeals on fact submitted by the PPS is to be noted. As one would expect, the PPS lodges appeals almost exclusively against the interests of the defendant. This low proportion of appeals may be explained by the PPS being satisfied with court decisions, one cannot, however, exclude the possibility that the connected workload is too high and the PPS therefore restricts its use of the right to appeal to particularly serious cases.

3.2 The PPS Role in Simplified Proceedings

The low number of proceedings dealt with by means of charges being brought and a main hearing following raises the question as to how the vast majority of cases are dealt with. The Criminal Procedure Code provides a number of possibilities.

Accelerated Proceedings

Sections 417–420 StPO provide for accelerated proceedings. They also see the PPS bringing charges and a main hearing takes place. There are, however, significant differences to normal proceedings.

Most importantly the main hearing takes place immediately or very quickly, i.e. intermediary proceedings are dispensed with (see Section 418 paragraph 1 StPO). Beyond that, written charges must not necessarily be brought but the charge can be lodged orally at the start of the main hearing (Section 418 paragraph 3 StPO). The defendant need also not be formally summoned in so far as s/he voluntarily submits to the main hearing (Section 418 paragraph 2 StPO). Evidence is gathered in a simplified manner: the interrogation of witnesses, expert witnesses or accessories can be substituted for the reading of protocols and the narrow requirements of Section 256 StPO do not apply for declarations made by government institutions. Section 420 paragraph 4 StPO provides that the judge decides as to the extent of evidence to be gathered, Section 244 paragraph 2 StPO not withstanding.

The use of accelerated proceedings with its simplifications, which are simultaneously limitations of the fundamental procedural principles, is not always possible. They may not be used against juveniles (Section 79 paragraph 2 JGG) but are also tied to certain conditions against adults. The PPS must first make an application that they be used, i.e. only the PPS can initiate such proceedings and introduce the simplifications and limitations. An application of this kind is only allowed where a single judge or the "Schöffengericht" has jurisdiction and the matter is suited to immediate hearing because: either the factual situation or the evidence to be brought is so simple (Section 417 StPO). In other words the facts of the case must be easily understandable for all concerned, there should not be a multitude of offences to be dealt with and there should be no reason to examine the accused's past in any great detail. There is no requirement that a confession has been made, but evidential suitability for immediate hearing will presumably usually mean just that. The court checks that these conditions are fulfilled and will only allow the application upon a positive finding. It is not possible to sentence to a custodial sentence of more than one year or a rehabilitative or incapacitating measure other than the withdrawal of the permission to drive (Section 419 paragraph 1 line 2 and 3 StPO).

In 1993[10] the PPS made an application in accordance with Section 417 StPO only in 0.5 % in relation to all PPS case-ending decisions, in 1998 in 0.9 % and in

[10] At that time: Application for immediate main hearing.

2003 in 0.8 %.[11] So, over the years a slight rise can be noted. This may be explained by the Act to Fight Serious Crime, which came into force on the 01/12/1994. Its goal was to increase the use of this type of proceedings in order to relieve the courts and prosecution services. All in all accelerated proceedings are used very rarely. However, where the PPS makes such an application, the court accepts it in over 90 % of cases. Only very rarely does the PPS itself withdraw its application (n=805 in 2003).[12]

Penal Order Proceedings

Penal order proceedings provide a further type of procedural simplification (regulated by Sections 407–412 StPO). The difference to normal proceedings is that although public charges are brought, the consequences of this are determined in the course of written proceedings, with no main hearing taking place. Their use is permissible for less serious crimes (Vergehen) for which a single judge or "Schöffengericht" has jurisdiction. The PPS must regard a main hearing as unnecessary and make a written application. In its application the PPS requests a specific punishment (in particular fines and suspended custodial sentences of up to 1 year are the punishments permitted; Section 407 paragraph 2 StPO), which the court can merely accept or reject. The defendant only has the possibility of objecting to the penal order within 2 weeks of it being issued. Where this is admissible, a main hearing will be scheduled.

If an objection is not lodged in time against it a penal order is equivalent to a judgement with legal force. Issuing a penal order has the same effect as a judgement following a main hearing. An entry into the central federal register (Bundeszentralregister) ensues. In consequence a note being made in the certificate of good character (Führungszeugnis) if more than 90 day fines or a custodial sentence for more than 3 months is imposed (see especially Section 32 BZRG [Act on the Central Federal Register]). In this case, a potential employer may learn of a conviction resulting via penal order.

Penal order proceedings may not be used against juveniles (Section 79 paragraph 1 JGG).

Although the last 10 years have witnessed a decrease in its use, the PPS frequently makes an application for a penal order to be issued. In this context the following question is of particular interest: *How often does the court in fact refuse its approval?* Court proceedings initiated by the court ordering a main hearing are very rare. So the court's control seems to be very slight. Whereas objections by the suspect are more frequent. Court rejection of or a suspect's objection to a penal order result in a main hearing, but not necessarily in a judgement. The courts diversionary options in accordance with Section 153 paragraph 2 and Section 153a paragraph 2 StPO (to which the PPS must agree) are also possible alternatives, and again it is possible that the proceedings are merged with others.

---

[11] Source: Prosecution Statistics, Tab. 2.2., publ. by the Federal Statistical Office Wiesbaden.

[12] Source: Court Statistics, Tab. 2.2, publ. by the Federal Statistical Office Wiesbaden.

Nevertheless the vast majority of all PPS applications result in a penal order being issued. Especially because a court rejection is very rare, the influence of the PPS is significant. Although legally a penal order is a court decision, it can be said that in practice it is a PPS sanction.

Table 4. PPS Applications for the Issue of a Penal Order

	1993[a]		1998[b]		2003[c]	
	Absolute number	%	Absolute number	%	Absolute number	%
(a) Total PPS case-ending decisions	3,355,259	100.0	4,583,228	100.0	4,766,070	100.0
(b) Of which: PPS applies for the issue of a penal order	592,203	17.6	659,368	14.4	603,999	12.7
(c) Court rejection	4,595	0.8 of (b)[d]	7,490	1.1 of (b)[d]	7,634	1.3 of (b)[d]
(d) Suspect's objection[e]	100,779	17.2 of (b–c)[d]	131,155	20.1 of (b–c)[d]	122,540	20.5 of (b–c)[d]

Source: Prosecution Statistics, Tab. 2.2 and Court Statistics, Tab. 2.1, 2.2, publ. by the Federal Statistical Office Wiesbaden

[a] Previous Federal territory including East-Berlin.
[b] Results of (a) and (b) for Hamburg and Schleswig-Holstein are for 1997.
[c] Results of (a) and (b) for Schleswig-Holstein are for 1997.
[d] Once again, the source of figures is varied so the considerations mentioned above are to be borne in mind.
[e] This does not include objections which were later withdrawn by the accused (n=45,915 in 2003).

In 99 % of all penal order applications the prosecution service requests the imposition of a fine; accordingly it would seem that main proceedings are regarded as necessary where a suspended custodial sentence is an option. Nowadays, there is no statistical information available as to which offences are usually dealt with using penal order proceedings. As it is almost exclusively fines which are imposed, however, it is reasonable to assume that offences, for which fines are imposed in far higher proportions than custodial sentences, will often be dealt with using penal order proceedings. This is the case in particular for road traffic[13] and simple property offences.

[13] Until 1997 this presumption can be based on the Prosecution Statistics, Tab. 2.2, publ. by the Federal Statistical Office Wiesbaden. Until that date there was statistical information available concerning this matter: In 1997 the PPS finished 26 % of all road traffic offences by penal order proceedings, in other words 44 % of all penal order proceedings were used for road traffic offences. In 1993 the proportions were 28 % and 43 %.

Finally it can be said that penal order proceedings are an effective means of procedural simplification and for reducing both the PPS and the court workload.

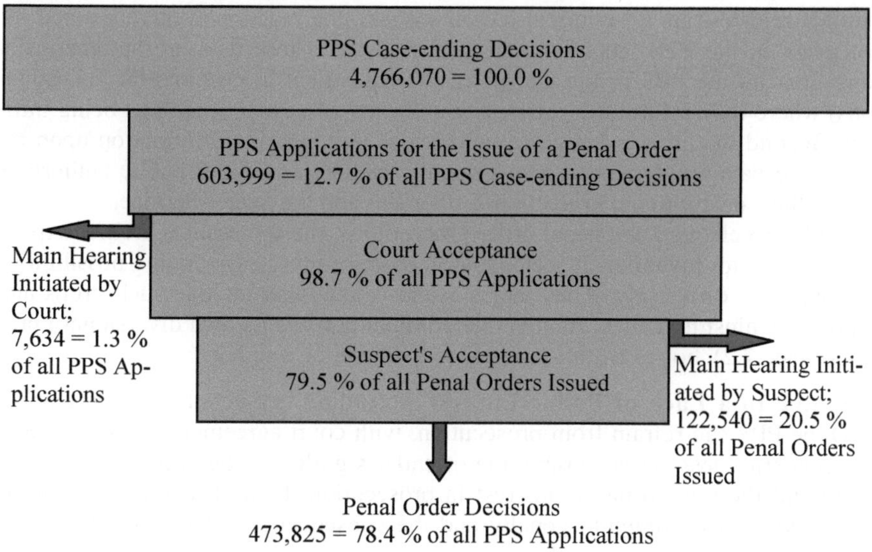

Fig. 1. The flow of penal order applications in 2003

3.3 Cases Dealt with by the Prosecution Service

Cases Ended on Discretionary Grounds

German criminal procedure also provides for alternative case-ending possibilities (drops and diversionary measures). The general provisions of Section 153 paragraph 1 and Section 153a paragraph 1 StPO regulate a drop due to a lack of public interest and conditional disposals.[14]

These provisions enable the PPS to end less serious crime proceedings (Vergehen) on their own initiative in spite of an offence having taken place and a offender becoming known; both practically and normatively this is a PPS decision. Judicial privilege, as secured by the constitution, provides that only a court may impose a sanction however. Thus these drops and disposals are different from the previously described procedural simplifications in this respect: No punishment can be imposed using them. Section 153 paragraph 1 StPO has no actual consequence and Section 153a paragraph 1 StPO leads to the imposition of conditions and instructions; they cannot, however, be enforced against the offender's will. They ex-

[14] Next to these exist e.g. the possibility to drop in accordance to Section 154 paragraph 1 StPO (because of an irrelevant incidental offence) as well as specific regulations found in the BtMG (Narcotics Act) and AO (Tax Code).

press a presumption of guilt, but this is not proved and any consequence is formally not considered a sanction.

Furthermore, unlike the cases described so far, no entry is made into the central criminal register (i.e. no criminal record ensues), the reaction is merely noted for two years in the PPS' central procedural register. These data are automatically transmitted to the PPS or the tax office (its equivalent in criminal tax investigations) where they inform the registering authority of new proceedings being initiated. Beyond that, the investigative authorities only receive information upon request. The data are, however, also generally available to other public authorities such as the Constitutional Protection Authorities and the Secret Service.

Unlike accelerated and penal order proceedings, these measures are not explicitly excluded for juveniles. It seems that in practice these case-ending possibilities are used very differently. Thus tables 5 and 6 may also include such drops and disposals against juveniles. As juvenile criminal law has its own diversionary provisions (see 7.2), however, this is likely to be a limited number.[15]

Drop due to a Lack of Public Interest According to Section 153 paragraph 1 StPO the PPS can refrain from prosecution, with court agreement, if the proceedings concern a less serious crime, the offender's guilt is to be seen as of a minor nature and there is no public interest in prosecution. If the less serious crime is threatened with a minimum penalty and the consequences of the act are minor, court agreement is not required.

It is particularly interesting to note that suspect's agreement is not required and that, under certain circumstances, the need for court approval can be avoided. The PPS can thus drop cases in accordance to Section 153 paragraph 1 StPO without its decision being evaluated in advance or retrospect. A post-facto review by the courts is not used in practice.[16] The PPS is, however, not prevented from reopening the case in the future because Section 153 paragraph 1 StPO does not spend the right to prosecute. But one should not lose sight of the fact that Section 153 paragraph 1 StPO may not have a tangible consequence, but a presumption of guilt remains.

According to the law, this solution is available for all types of cases fulfilling the criteria described. The individual prosecutor is, however, not entirely free in his/her decision. The Länder have issued guidelines concerning Section 153 paragraph 1 and Section 153a paragraph 1 StPO intended to specify the use of diversionary measures and provide for their uniform application. In some Länder guidelines the use of these legal provisions is excluded if the damage caused by property offences exceeds a certain amount. In Hessen i.e. the limit of the accrued damage is € 5, in Lower Saxony, however, € 25. In some cases the type of offences for which Section 153 StPO may be used is defined[17], in others, certain of-

[15] The PPS statistics do not include any information as to whether the drops/disposals in accordance with Section 153 paragraph 1 and Section 153a paragraph 1 StPO were directed against adults or juveniles.

[16] Opposition to this is limited almost exclusively to academic literature.

[17] In Schleswig-Holstein only for property and asset-related offences.

fences are stated for which it may not be used[18]. Limitations are also imposed for certain types of offenders. In general, the provisions may neither be used if it is not to be expected that the offender will feel warned by the proceedings and in consequence not commit further offences in the future, nor if the circumstances of committal mean the act is of a more serious nature or a punishment is regarded as necessary for the public good. Nevertheless, as far as the costs of damage caused are concerned, the guidelines are very different, so that the use of the public interest drop varies between the Länder.

It is not possible to analyse adherence to these regulations statistically. Nor do the statistics provide information as to how frequently the courts refuse to give their approval or in how far this approval can be dispensed with. The statistics merely provide information as to in how many cases the PPS factually ends using Section 153 paragraph 1 StPO.

Table 5. Drops due to a Lack of Public Interest

	1993[a]		1998[b]		2003[c]	
	Absolute number	%	Absolute number	%	Absolute number	%
Total PPS case-ending decisions	3,355,259	100.0	4,583,228	100.0	4,766,070	100.0
Of which: drops due to a lack of public interest[d]	297,995	8.9	420,807	9.2	413,513	8.7

Source: Prosecution Statistics, Tab. 2.2., publ. by the Federal Statistical Office Wiesbaden

[a] Previous Federal territory including East-Berlin.
[b] Results for Hamburg and Schleswig-Holstein are for 1997.
[c] Results for Schleswig-Holstein are for 1997.
[d] Only Section 153 paragraph 1 StPO.

Table 5 shows the proportion of Section 153 paragraph 1 StPO – the median value for 1993–2002 is about 9 %[19]. Placed in relation to the PPS bringing charges (see table 1), this should not be under-estimated: A drop in accordance to Section 153 paragraph 1 StPO is a real exception to the principle of legality, the fundamental principle of German criminal procedure. The PPS only makes more frequent use of an application for a penal order (see table 4 and fig. 1) but, although the penal order is also a simplified procedural form, it is, of course, not an exception to this principle.

Conditional Disposal Section 153a paragraph 1 StPO provides that the PPS can preliminarily forego bringing public charges for a less serious crime, with court (unless this is regarded as unnecessary Section 153a paragraph 1 line 7 in combination with Section 153 paragraph 1 line 2 StPO) and suspect approval, at the

[18] In Lower Saxony for cases of domestic violence because of the inherent public interest.
[19] If one includes drops due to a lack of public interest in accordance to Section 31a paragraph 1 BtMG the proportion would be about 10 % in 2003.

same time issuing conditions and instructions to the suspect, if these are capable of removing the public interest in a prosecution and the gravity of the suspect's guilt does not go against doing so.

Section 153a StPO is different to Section 153 StPO in as far as the prerequisites for a disposal are not so stringent, a form of reciprocation is, however, expected from the suspect; the fulfilment of conditions and instructions. Until these are carried out the forgoing of public charges is only preliminary. If the suspect complies, the disposal is conclusive and, unlike Section 153 paragraph 1 StPO, it is no longer possible to re-open the case. The prosecution as a crime, however, cannot be ruled out if the interpretation as a less serious crime is later found to have been incorrect (see Section 153a paragraph 1 line 5 StPO). Courts do not scrutinise these decisions after the event either. The conditions are clearer due to the need for suspect agreement.

The Länder have also produced individual guidelines for this regulation. Partially they also include a value limit but this varies strongly from Land to Land. The lowest cut-off limit for the use of disposals in accordance with Section 153a paragraph 1 StPO is € 25. In other cases the value is only an indicator of the level of guilt. The use in relation to certain offences is not different to Section 153 paragraph 1 StPO, thus the above description applies. It is increasingly common to prescribe the use of particular conditions and instructions; in particular the requirement that a payment be made, to provide compensation or offender-victim mediation. Statistically one can present the actual number of disposals in accordance with Section 153a paragraph 1 StPO and the primary condition/instruction imposed.

Table 6. Conditional Disposals

	1993[a]		1998[b]		2003[c]	
	Absolute number	%	Absolute number	%	Absolute number	%
Total PPS case-ending decisions	3,355,259	100.0	4,583,228	100.0	4,766,070	100.0
Of which: conditional disposals[d]	175,391	5.2	236,357	5.2	253,132	5.3

Source: Prosecution Statistics, Tab. 2.2, publ. by the Federal Statistical Office Wiesbaden

[a] Previous Federal territory including East-Berlin.
[b] Results for Hamburg and Schleswig-Holstein are for 1997.
[c] Results for Schleswig-Holstein are for 1997.
[d] Only Section 153a paragraph 1 StPO.

Table 6 shows that the PPS uses Section 153a paragraph 1 StPO significantly less often than Section 153 paragraph 1 StPO. One explanation for this might be that less offences are committed which justify a disposal in accordance with Section 153a paragraph 1 StPO. This must not be the case. It may well also be that Section 153a paragraph 1 StPO is a less attractive provision for the PPS. On the one hand, the prosecutor must find out which condition can sensibly be imposed upon the suspect. On the other, compliance with conditions and instructions must be ensured. This also requires PPS work. This is also evident in the type of conditions imposed. In the vast majority of proceedings a payment to a charitable organisation or the treasury is ordered (88.1 % in 2003). This kind of suspect compliance can be easily ensured. Offender-Victim Mediation (OVM) or compensation are ordered much less frequently (OVM: 2.5 % in 2003; compensation: 5.3 % in 2003), even though the guidelines sometimes declare these as having priority. In particular for OVM, this will be due to the complexity of carrying it out.

3.4. Final Remarks about Case-ending Decisions

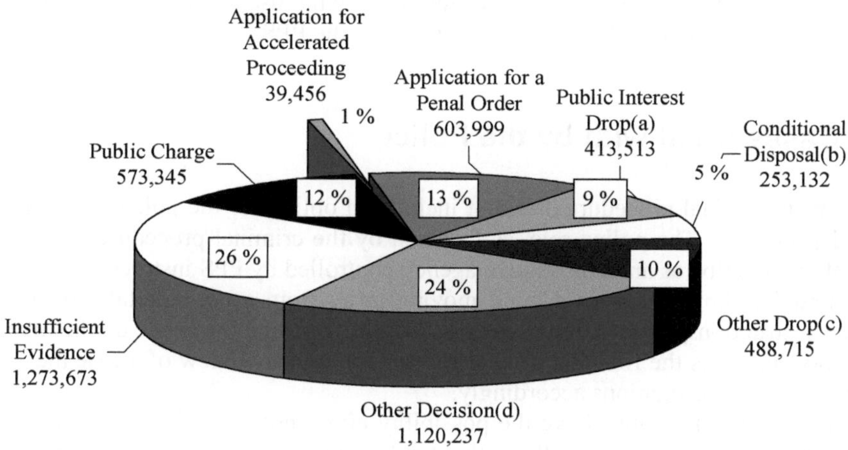

Fig. 2. Cases dealt with by the PPS at the Regional Courts and dealt with by the Amtsanwaltschaften (assistant prosecutor offices) in 2003 (Total number of cases n=4,766,070)

Source: Prosecution Statistics, Tab. 2.2, publ. by the Federal Statistical Office Wiesbaden

[a] Only Section 153 paragraph 1 StPO.

[b] Only Section 153a paragraph 1 StPO.

[c] Especially drops in accordance to Section 45 paragraph 1 (n=95,896); drops in accordance to Section 31a paragraph 1 BtMG (n=64,797); drops because of an irrelevant incidental offence (n=283,182); drops because of a previous question regarding civil or administrative law (n=18,220); drops because of expulsion/extradition (n=22,218).

[d] E. g. including proceedings passed on to other Public Prosecution Offices (n=196,152); to an administrative authority (n=218,244); in connection with another matter (n=249,001); recommendation that private proceedings be brought (n=163,537); also conditional disposals in accordance with Sections 37 paragraph 1 BtMG (Narcotics Act) and 38 paragraph 2 associated with 37 paragraph 1 (n=86), in accordance to Section 45 paragraph 2 JGG (n=96,617) and Section 45 paragraph 3 JGG (n=12,691).

All in all, in Germany the PPS can be seen as making the basic decision as to whether criminal proceedings result in charges being brought or not. If the PPS regards a "court" sanction as necessary, penal order proceedings in particular play an important role. At the start of the period studied they were used significantly more often than the bringing of "normal" public charges (see table 1 and 4). Nowadays both are used in almost the same proportion of cases. It should, however, not be forgotten that PPS influence is far greater in penal order proceedings than in normal ones. As described above, the court can only accept or reject the PPS application. Rejections are exceptional. The application for accelerated proceedings appears not to be a real alternative for the PPS.

If one also considers the cases disposed of by Section 153 paragraph 1 and Section 153a paragraph 1 StPO, one finds that the PPS regards about 14 % of cases as worthy of a reaction, even though not of a sanction. These provisions are intended as an exception to the principle of legality but are not used as such. They appear to be of great importance for relieving pressure on the PPS.

4 Cases Dealt with by the Police

German criminal procedure does not include an option for the police to end cases independently. The police role, as foreseen by the criminal procedure code, ends with its function as an investigative agency controlled by PPS instructions.

Practice, however, sees a trend moving away from a police totally bound by PPS instructions, as defined by law, to a role with strong influence on the investigatory stage. As the first authority to examine and form a view of a case they will direct their investigations accordingly.

First of all the police have the possibility either not to begin or even to break off an investigation informally without informing the PPS. Due to their double role as a crime preventive as well as repressive-prosecutorial agency, the police have considerable defining power in relation to noting relevant behaviour, as well as a great deal of factual discretion. As a rule, it is the police who first learn of potentially sanctionable behaviour.

On the one hand in certain fields of criminal behaviour, like drug offences or some traffic offences, it depends upon police whether offences are detected or not. In this respect the police have a so-called factual opportunity to look for offences and to decide whether to investigate them or not. Minor offences are ignored and the police refer to themselves as the "filter of the prosecution service" (Stock, Kreuzer 1996). On the other hand there are offences which require the victim to press charges or for which a private prosecution is possible, for example simple bodily injury. A few empirical studies carried out during the 70's and 80's indicate that the police tended to privatise and play down the nature of facts during their general investigatory activities, in order to reduce the amount of investigatory work to be done to a manageable level (Kürzinger 1978, Feest Blankenburg 1972).

In this respect policy has now changed; guidelines have been established which require investigation and prosecution in cases of inner familial violence etc.

Another form of police participation in case-ending decisions is their possibility to prepare a case for PPS disposal and to steer the proceedings in the direction they have chosen. In most cases this influence is increased by recommending a drop/disposal to the PPS or anticipating such a PPS decision by carrying out some preparatory action in this direction.[20] Thus one can see that the police assume a far more independent and important role than that legislatively prescribed to them. In cases of less serious crime to ones of medium severity, the police factually not only carry out the investigation but, in choosing how to do so and in performing preparatory work, go a long way to influence the PPS decisions about the procedural steps which follow. In this way, the police have assumed a part of the PPS' tasks and the latter can be described as a type of mere file processing authority for these cases (see below Chapter 6.2).

5 Alternative Procedural Forms

During the 1970's the least serious form of criminal offences (Übertretungen) were almost entirely re-classified as administrative offences and therewith decriminalized by the Offences Against Order Act (OWiG). These are illegal acts, fulfilling legislative conditions which provide for the imposition of an administrative fine.

Primarily, the prosecution and sanctioning of an offence against order falls within administrative organs' competence, and not court jurisdiction (Section 35 OWiG). Which acts are meant and which organ responsible is defined legislatively or by declarations (Rechtsverordnungen) intended to specify the law.

The PPS is a prosecutorial and not administrative organ, can, however, perform such duties if declarations or the law specify it. The police are the active investigatory authority working for the administrative organs in offence against order cases (Section 53 paragraph 1, line 1 OWiG).

There is no specific procedural code for the imposition of administrative fines, according to Section 46 paragraph 1 OWiG the provisions of general criminal procedure apply. Thus the enforcing organs have the same rights and duties as the PPS in relation to criminal offences (Section 46 paragraph 2 OWiG) in as far as the OWiG makes no special provisions. In particular the principle of opportunity

[20] E.g. since 1999 the following procedural model is in place in Saxony to deal with shoplifting and travelling without a ticket in which the police play a decisive role in the decision whether to use the PPS' potential discretionary powers. Where the gain in question does not exceed a value of € 50, the police will inform a first-time offender that they can suggest to the PPS that the case be dropped in exchange for the payment of a certain sum of money see *Sprenger, Fischer* 2000. Further examples of this kind of diversion by the police in Germany can increasingly be found in juvenile criminal law, where individual Länder allow the police to attempt to influence the juveniles using educational discussions and, where these are successful, to effectively pre-empt the PPS' decision to drop the case (see *Lower Saxony*: Gem. RdErl. d. MJ, MK u. MI v. 26.04.1996 u. v. 29.07.1998; *Schleswig-Holstein*: Gem. Erl. d. MJBE, d. IM u. d. MFJWS v. 24.06.1998).

overrides the principle of legality; furthermore, the OWiG does not provide participatory rights. There is no difference between different types of perpetration. Where there are more than one perpetrator, all are regarded as committing an offence against order. Both deliberate and negligent committal is possible. General criminal law only sanctions negligent behaviour where this is expressly legislated for.

An offence against order can be sanctioned by the imposition of an administrative fine and auxiliary consequences. The maximum administrative fine is € 1.000 (500 for negligent committal), the minimum € 5 (Section 17 OWiG). Auxiliary consequences are defined by the specific legislation itself. Thus the Road Traffic Act legislates for the imposition of a driving ban. The authority which issues the letter informing of the offence is responsible for ensuring payment (Section 92 OWiG).

The PPS and court are not involved in the first-instance reaction, but they are responsible for the legal control of notices demanding payment of an administrative fine. The affected person can object to the notice. If the administrative authority does not withdraw the notice after a second examination, it passes the file on to the PPS and the local court. The PPS can then either drop the case or pursue further investigation and then pass the file on to the local court for court proceedings.

Offences against order are only registered as far as they are traffic offences against order in the central traffic register (deleted after 2 years), or defined by the GewO in the central business register (deleted after 3–5 years).

6 Prosecution Service Function in Investigative Proceedings

Legally the investigative stage's primary purpose is to check whether the initial suspicion which caused the PPS to initiate investigation has hardened to provide sufficient suspicion of an offence. In other words the question is as to whether bringing public charges is likely to lead to a conviction. Thus this stage also enables main proceedings to be avoided where suspicion of an offence is unfounded. Alongside this check, where there is initial suspicion, the investigatory stage serves the collection of evidence which will later be used in the main proceedings. The court is excluded from this stage to a large extent. It will only be involved where decisions as to the use of certain measures to secure evidence or other specific investigatory measures are necessary and these must be ordered or carried out by a judge. Involvement will also ensue where the PPS uses its flagranti powers and these must be approved post-facto. Except in urgent cases, the judge will only become active upon PPS request. Due to the statutory provisions which require the PPS to act in order to prepare for the main proceedings and because a case-ending judgement is only then made by the court, one also refers to the investigative stage as mere preparatory proceedings.

The factual importance of the investigative stage has, however, developed further. It is no longer the main proceedings which decide criminal proceedings, but far more the investigative stage which sets decisive posts for its path. This can be seen in the growing number of cases in which case-ending decisions are made out of court or the PPS applies for a penal order to be issued. In such cases, court approval is either unnecessary or reduced to mere formal approval (see above). The investigative stage and the quality of evidence found in it will influence the procedural path and result of the main proceedings; it is therefore a focal point of criminal proceedings.

6.1 Legislative Provisions

The PPS is regarded as the "ruler of the investigative stage", with legal and factual responsibility for this preparatory stage. It is obliged to investigate relevant factual situations where initial suspicion of a criminal offence arises (Section 160 I StPO). It bears responsibility for the correct gathering and the reliability of evidence required for the judicial process. Accordingly, it is exclusively the PPS which decides whether to bring public charges or not once the investigative stage is over (Section 170 StPO). In its function as a prosecutorial authority, the PPS is bound by the fundamental principle of legality (Section 152 StPO). This is, however, broken by certain discretionary provisions (Section 153 onwards, Section 376 StPO) according to which the PPS can refrain from prosecution.

The police are assigned a supporting role in relation to the PPS' activities because the latter has no executing arm of its own. The police are organisationally accountable to the individual Länder's ministries of the interior, but made functionally subservient to the PPS by law as far as the prosecution of offences is concerned. The police have mere preliminary jurisdiction (Section 163 StPO) allowing only measures which cannot be delayed. Having carried these out, they are fundamentally required to inform the PPS of their actions and to pass their records on to the latter so that the PPS can decide how the investigations are to proceed (Section 163 paragraph 2 StPO). The police are also the executing organ during PPS investigations (Section 161 StPO). The law further assigns the PPS auxiliary police officers („Ermittlungspersonen"[21]) with special powers and a closer relationship to the PPS. In practice this difference is of little significance as almost all police officers are made "Ermittlungspersonen". In relation to the prosecution of crimes, the police are viewed only as an organ serving the PPS.

6.2 Factual Police – PPS Relationship

In practice, German criminal procedure is a very different matter. Empirical studies carried out during previous decades have confirmed this (Steffen 1976, Dölling 1987; Stock, Kreuzer 1996). Nowadays the PPS is not the "ruler of the investigative stage" in most cases. In relation to less serious or mass crimes this role has long been assumed by the police. They carry out investigations independently and

---

[21] Until 2004 these officers were called "Hilfsbeamte" instead of "Ermittlungspersonen".

only when these are finished the file is passed on to the PPS which is informed of the case in this way. This picture is confirmed clearly by an analysis of the guidelines issued in the individual Länder to specify legal provisions.

Where there is reason to believe that the PPS will use discretionary case-ending powers or drop the case because no offender is found, the intensity of investigation is reduced so as to provide only for a case-ending decision. Where the offence severity increases, so does the intensity of investigation. PPS involvement is stronger here and at the same time police independence wanes. The PPS is frequently brought into the investigation at an early stage because certain measures which need to be carried out must be ordered by the PPS. Guidelines also require PPS involvement from the very start of the investigation into serious offences.

7 Particular Issues

7.1 Victim Participation

The German Criminal Procedure code has witnessed various changes in recent years to incorporate victim's interests. The most recent reform took place in 2004. The extent of victim participation legally provided for differ according to the seriousness of the offences concerned.

First of all there is a group of offences, the application offences ("Antragsdelikte"), which will only be prosecuted if the victim requests this and which may well be dropped by the PPS with a referral to private prosecution. It will be the case where the prosecutor sees no public interest in prosecution. This happens relatively frequently; in 2003 163,537 cases were dropped with a recommendation of this sort.[22] In these cases the only means of getting the perpetrator punished then lies with the victim. For all of these offences the victim can decide to prosecute without a prior PPS decision. The PPS, however, remains entitled to take over any of these cases up until a judgement is made.

In these cases the victim bears the risk of having to carry court costs if no conviction ensues (studies found this to happen in only 6 % of cases), as well as a potential suit for malicious prosecution. Considering these factors, combined with the need to bring evidence, he or she may have difficulties procuring; it is perhaps not surprising that earlier studies found that only around 10 % of PPS recommendations resulted in a private prosecution being brought. In 2003 the court of first instance decided on 823 such cases (that is 0.5 % of the number of cases referred in that year (n=163, 537) – this absolute number is fairly stable, suggesting that this kind of prosecution has now become very rare indeed).[23]

The victim and close relatives may become joint plaintiffs in proceedings for particularly serious offences. In these cases the victim has the possibility to sug-

[22] Source: Prosecution Statistics, Tab. 2.2, publ. by the Federal Statistical Office, Wiesbaden.

[23] Source: Court Statistics, Tab. 2.1 and Prosecution Statistics, Tab. 2.2, publ. by the Federal Statistical Office, Wiesbaden.

gest a prosecution at pre-trial stage. As a joint plaintiff, the victim has participatory rights in the trial as well as a right to appeal and, in some cases, a right to a lawyer paid for by the state. Even if the victim decides not to participate as a joint plaintiff, this kind of victim has a positive right to be present during trial.

Furthermore the victim may file for joinder proceedings in which s/he applies for civil damages and compensation to be judged in the course of criminal proceedings. These proceedings have been of little importance in practice. In 2003 this occurred in 4,263 of 893,381 cases (0.47 %).[24] One of the main aims of the 2004 law reform was to encourage increased use. Provisions have also been made to encourage consensual agreement on compensation between victim and defendant during the criminal trial (see below Chapter 8.).

Rights to be Informed and to Intervene

The victim also has a number of informational rights which may well trigger participation in the criminal justice process (other than as a witness – the victim's position in this context is not explored here). These have just been strengthened and provide that a victim who applies to be informed must be notified as to the date of main proceedings, of any decision not to bring the case to court, of the outcome of a trial and of any measures involving the deprivation of liberty, i.e. prison, committal, release, relaxation of or holiday from incarceration. A victim who disagrees with a prosecutorial drop or disposal can make a complaint to a superior prosecutor. If a case is dropped for evidential reasons, the victim can initiate proceedings to force a charge in more serious cases. The joint plaintiff victim can appeal against a court decision.

A victim has a general right to a lawyer and to be represented during criminal proceedings. Through his or her lawyer s/he has a right to view case files and to be present at court and prosecutor interviews, provided this does not undermine the investigation. The victim has to cover the costs of this legal representation him/herself.

Criminal justice institutions are now obliged to inform the victim as soon as possible of his/her rights and the means of achieving them (e.g. to explain joinder proceedings), as well as to indicate the potential for support through victim support organisations. Where a court intends to refrain from deciding upon joinder proceedings (meaning that the victim will have to pursue these proceedings before a civil court in separate proceedings), it is obliged to inform the victim as soon as possible and the victim has an immediate right to complain.

The court and PPS are furthermore obliged to consider at all procedural stages whether the case is one suitable for reconciliation between perpetrator and victim and if so, to work towards achieving a conciliatory agreement (Section 155 a, b StPO). They may not do so against the express wishes of the victim. Where conciliation is agreed, both the court and PPS have diversionary powers to drop the case. This will require perpetrator's, PPS` and court's agreement. In practice con-

---

[24] Source: Court Statistics, Tab. 2.1, 4.1, 7.1, publ. by the Federal Statistical Office, Wiesbaden.

ciliation is mostly initiated in the pre-trial stage (90 % of cases in 2002 with the prosecution service playing the decisive role (in 80 % of cases).[25]

Victims of crime have a variety of rights to be drawn into criminal proceedings, but in terms of active participation these are very much focused on the court stage for the most serious offences. The ability to launch private prosecutions should be regarded more as a means to facilitating the exclusion of such cases from public prosecution rather than the inclusion of victims. Whilst the reformed law goes some way to provide for further inclusion of victims in court cases, the vast majority of cases never reach a court and there the victim is largely marginalised with little means of influencing prosecutor decisions.

7.2 Juveniles

One special feature of German criminal law and procedure is that special regulations apply for juveniles. These are provided for in a Code written especially to this end called the Act on Juvenile Courts (*JGG*). The general criminal and criminal procedure provisions apply subsidiarily. The core area of application is to juveniles who are held to be criminally responsible between the age of 14 and 18; it is also used for youths (i.e. offenders between the age of 18 and 21) if their moral and psychological maturity is that of a juvenile or the type, circumstances or motives for the offence were typical of a juvenile short-coming.

Juvenile sanctions and criminal proceedings are marked by an educative purpose. Here, primarily it is not certain behaviour one is concerned with but the offender's personality which forms the heart of proceedings.

The juvenile criminal law provides for special reactions: firstly, educative and disciplinary measures and secondly, youth imprisonment with the possibility of suspension and probation. The imposition of additional legal consequences and measures to reform the offender and protect the public is only possible to a limited extent. Furthermore juvenile criminal proceedings are somewhat different to those conducted in case of an adult perpetrator. Here the general provisions are valid but partly modified:

The Investigative Stage

The investigative stage is basically regulated by the StPO. Differences arise mainly out of Section 43 onwards JGG. Accordingly the investigation of the perpetrator's personality is specified as an object of the investigation. If necessary an expert is to be drawn in to secure this; the courts have specialists to perform this role ("Jugendgerichtshilfe"). There is a juvenile prosecutor; a normal prosecutor assigned to deal with juvenile matters because of special pedagogic abilities (Section 37 JGG). The police also have specially trained personnel for juvenile cases and the youth protection office is often drawn in. The PPS plays a central role.

---

[25] Source: "Täter-Opfer-Ausgleich in der Entwicklung" by Kerner, Hartmann, ed by the Federal Ministry of Justice, Berlin 2005, *www.bmj.bund.de/toa.*

"Normal" Main Proceedings

Normal main proceedings are based on general criminal provisions. Certain special provisions apply, e.g. juvenile criminal proceedings not being public (Section 48 JGG), that the accused can be excluded from the proceedings on pedagogic grounds (Section 51 JGG), as well as the required presence and involvement of the Jugendgerichtshilfe (Section 38 paragraph 2,3 JGG). The proceedings are heard before the juvenile courts which are special departments of the local and regional courts. Court make-up is determined by the seriousness of the offence, or rather the severity of the expected punishment (Section 33 paragraph 2 JGG). Youths are always heard by these courts regardless of whether juvenile or adult criminal law is being applied. The prosecution is represented by a juvenile prosecutor.

Simplified Proceedings

In order to ensure the special nature of proceedings against juveniles, accelerated and penal order proceedings, as well as private and joint-plaintiff prosecutions are not allowed (Section 80 JGG). A special type of simplified procedure is available (Section 76–78 JGG). Proceedings concerning less serious offences for which only a mild sanction is expected can be carried out by the judge without the prosecutor where the latter applies for this to be the case. This procedure is of little importance in practice because the diversionary measures available are used far more frequently.

In 2003 only 7.65 % of all juvenile proceedings ended before local and regional courts were dealt with using such proceedings[26]. Whereas 44.8 % of all juvenile proceedings dealt with by the PPS were ended using Section 45 JGG, the relevant diversionary provision.[27]

Cases Ended by the PPS

The possibility of diversionary measures and therewith informal case-ending possibilities were introduced for juveniles in Germany in 1953 to take account of the fact that committing minor offences can be seen as a normal part of development. Here, the main purpose of such provisions was and is not to reduce the workload, but to avoid a formal court reaction and use the educative effect of informal reactions instead. The general drop/disposal provisions described above also apply to

[26] Proceedings in accordance with Section 76: n=19,336; all proceedings against juveniles ended before local and regional courts: n=252,542 (Source: Prosecution Statistics, Tab. 2.2., publ. by the Federal Statistical Office, Wiesbaden).

[27] Diversionary measures (Section 45): n=205,204; all criminal proceedings dealt with by PPS: n=457,746 (Source: Prosecution Statistics, Tab. 2.2., publ. by the Federal Statistical Office, Wiesbaden). These figures are not exact because, as mentioned above, cases in which the general provisions Section 170 paragraph 2, 153 StPO onwards and 31a BtMG were used against juveniles cannot be determined statistically and thus only those in acc. to the special JGG provisions can be represented here. Figures for Schleswig-Holstein are only available for 1997.

juveniles but are subservient to Section 45 JGG onwards and their educative nature. The latter are wider than those of adult criminal law. They are also available for crimes in so far as the other requirements are satisfied. Section 45 paragraph 1 JGG provides that proceedings can be dropped under the same conditions as those specified by Section 153 StPO without necessitating judicial agreement. The latter is only exceptionally the case when using Section 153 StPO. In acc. to Section 45 paragraph 2 JGG the prosecutor refrains from further prosecution provided certain educational measures are applied. Furthermore a case can be dropped by PPS with Section 45 paragraph 3 JGG with the approval of the court after imposing of certain conditions and instructions on the offender. Decisions of this kind are registered in the educational register to which judicial authorities and youth protection offices have access. These are deleted once the perpetrator has turned 25.

These provisions are subject to steadily increasing use. In 1993 64 % of all cases treated in accordance to the Act on Juvenile Courts were dealt with informally.[28] In 2003 the number already increased to 70 %.[29] That means that only in 30 % off all cases a formal proceeding[30] took place:

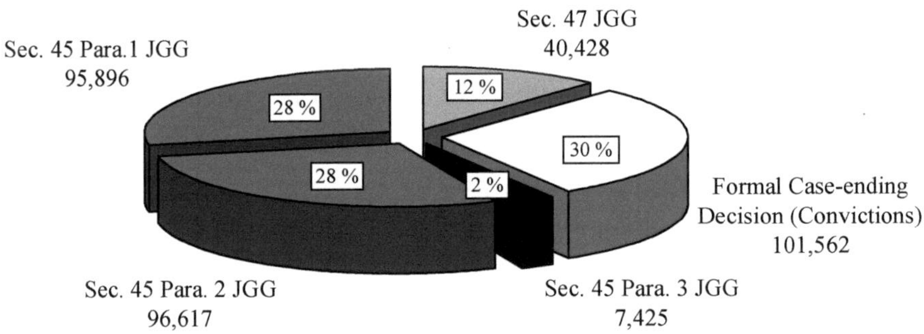

Fig. 3. Rate of Diversions (PPS and Court) in Juvenile Criminal Proceedings 2003[31]

Source: Prosecution Statistics, Tab. 2.2. and Conviction Statistics, Tab. 2.2, publ. by the Federal Statistical Office, Wiesbaden.

---

[28] Informal reactions: all decisions made in accordance to Section 45, 47 JGG.

[29] Source: for the development until 2001 *www.uni-konstanz.de/rtf/kis/index.htm* as well as 2003 Prosecution Statistics, Tab. 2.2. and 2003 Conviction Statistics, Tab 2.2, publ. by the Federal Statistical Office, Wiesbaden.

[30] Formal reaction (convictions): all convicted juveniles including all cases of Section 27 JGG.

[31] The data shown in this figure give only approximate values, because the statistics only include exact data for cases that are treated according to juvenile criminal and procedural law. The number of cases treated by adult criminal law is not included (cases that are dealt with according to Sec. 170 paragraph 2, 153 StPO onwards as well as 31 a BtMG) because differentiation between cases that are committed either by juveniles or adults is impossible. Furthermore results for Schleswig-Holstein are for 1997.

Above all it is the PPS which decides on the use of diversionary measures for juvenile criminal proceedings. Section 47 JGG ensures that the judge has similar options after charges have been brought, but it is rarely used in practice. In 2003 12 % of cases ended in accordance to the diversionary provisions of the JGG were in acc. with Section 47 JGG, i.e. almost 58 % were initiated by the PPS. PPS case-ending decisions out of court play a central role.

Police Participation

Police involvement in PPS diversionary decisions has increased remarkably with a visible trend throughout Germany towards a form of police diversion in juvenile criminal matters becoming apparent. This is the conclusion reached by an evaluation of the guidelines issued in relation to diversionary provisions by the individual Länder. In particular in relation to the PPS decisions to divert in accordance with Section 45 paragraph 1, 2 JGG, one finds tasks assigned to the police which require independent preparation and implementation of diversionary proceedings by which the police effectively anticipate the PPS decision.

The Länder guidelines examined contain provisions as to police involvement in diversionary proceedings in acc. with Section 45 paragraph 1 JGG.[32] The extent of police participation anticipated varied. Almost all regarded the police as making the first decision as to whether a case might be suitable for the application of Section 45 paragraph 1 JGG. Some further increase the police's role by not only stating the right to suggest diversion, but also to try to achieve an educational effect by means of a conversation with the juvenile. Other Länder leave stricter provisions, but assign the police a right of suggestion.

In relation to Section 45 paragraph 2 JGG, again the police are regarded as being the first authority able to make a decision as to the suitability of using the provision. Otherwise there are significant differences. In some cases the police have far-reaching participatory rights with them permitted to try to take influence upon the juvenile or youth as well as upon the PPS decision. In other Länder the police are only given a right to suggest diversion.

8 Current Changes

Currently there are no reform processes taking place specifically to change the PPS role in German criminal procedure. Reform of the investigative stage is frequently called for, however, and some developments are currently evident.

---

[32] All Länder except Bavaria, Mecklenburg-Vorpommern and Bremen could be included in the study. 12 of those remaining (not Hessen) had guidelines concerning diversionary proceedings. For a detailed analysis of all Länder guidelines concerning police participation see Elsner, Reformüberlegungen zur Erweiterung polizeilicher Kompetenzen im strafrechtlichen Ermittlungsverfahren, eine deutsch-niederländisch rechtsvergleichende Analyse in rechtlicher und rechtstatsächlicher Hinsicht, diss. jur. University of Göttingen.

There is a clear trend moving away from the principle of legality towards more powerful and independent prosecuting institutions. This can be seen above all at prosecution service level. Its influence upon prosecution practice in Germany increased clearly during the last decades.

As far as the prosecution – court relationship is concerned, we have already established that the diversionary and penal order procedures, initially intended to be exceptions within German criminal procedure, have long become the norm in relation to mass-crimes (see Chapter 3.4). There is no sign that this trend will change. On the contrary, in order to cope with crimes of this kind, criminal procedure is first and foremost being simplified and speed-up.[33] The proportion of alternative, in particular written, proceedings being used, is continuously increasing, the evidence collection deemed necessary restricted further.[34]

As far as informal case-ending is concerned, this must be viewed as a decisive prosecution service coping instrument. There are frequent calls that the preconditions for use have to be defined more precisely, in order to simplify the prosecution service's work. At the same time greater legal certainty should be provided for in order to direct prosecution service decision-making in individual cases (Horstmann 2002). In consequence this would lead to an increased use and a greater acceptance of this procedural alternative in practice. This in turn leads to the prosecution service gaining decision-making powers previously reserved for the courts.

Furthermore as far as diversionary measures are concerned, an important feature has been introduced: a concluding conversation under PPS leadership in which the possibilities of case-ending agreements, particularly perpetrator-victim mediation and compensation, are to be explored.[35] The PPS is now obliged to offer a conversation of this kind, but the victim and the suspect are free to take part. The main purpose of such a conversation is to encourage open cooperation at an early stage in order to avoid further prosecution.

Besides these legal provisions for more or less independent PPS case-ending decision 2001 saw the introduction of an institutionalized legal and co-operation discussion, without any prescribed procedure, to be considered in order to facilitate case-ending arrangements without a main hearing or a main hearing with reduced evidential requirements.[36]

Reform proposals have also been made in relation to the prosecution service's position in the investigative stage and therewith also concerning its relationship to the police. But all reform proposals to date, from e.g. increasing the PPS' financial and personnel resources to integrating a part of the police into the justice system (inspired by the French police judiciaire) or placing the investigative stage as a

[33] Content of a discussion paper presented by the Federal Government at the beginning of 2004.

[34] The Act to Modernise the Justice System which came into force on the 28.05.2003 expanded the possibilities in the main hearing for a simple reading of evidence gathered at the investigative stage.

[35] The Victim's Rights Reform Act of the 04.03.2004.

[36] The government coalition's priority paper on the reform of criminal proceedings presented in 2001.

whole in police hands, were reconsidered and rejected as impracticable. The current trend moves towards a form of co-operative model: the police should be given far-reaching investigative powers in relation to less serious offences; they should do the whole preparatory work and make suggestion for the PPS decision. However, the PPS control function would have to be secured by the introduction of comprehensive control and reporting obligations.

Reform attempts of this kind are also to be found on Länder level. A number of Länder, like Saxony (as mentioned above), have developed police (subject to PPS approval) diversionary models, applicable to minor crimes, in order to achieve a reduction of case-ending decisions with no consequence, in favour of ones involving a condition in accordance with Section 153a StPO. Increased police involvement in case-ending decisions is regarded as a sensible means to relieve the justice system by using existing resources, in particular due to the contact the police have with suspects in any case. Such models are common in relation to juveniles (see above Chapter 7.2).

References

Brunner R, Dölling D (2002) Jugendgerichtsgesetz Kommentar (11th edn). Beck, München

Dölling D (1987) Polizeiliche Ermittlungstätigkeit und Legalitätsprinzip: eine empirische und juristische Analyse der Ermittlungsverfahrens unter besonderer Berücksichtigung der Aufklärungs- und Verurteilungswahrscheinlichkeit. Bundeskriminalamt (ed), BKA-Forschungsreihe, Wiesbaden

Feest J, Blankenburg E (1972) Definitionsmacht der Polizei – Strategien der Strafverfolgung und soziale Selektion. Bertelsmann Univ.-Verl., Düsseldorf

Heghmanns M (2003) Das Arbeitsgebiet des Staatsanwalts (3th edn). Aschendorff Rechtsverlag, Münster Köln

Horstmann, M (2002) Die Präzisierung und Kontrolle von Opportunitätseinstellungen. Duncker & Humblot, Berlin

Jehle JM (2005) Criminal Justice in Germany: Facts and Figures (5th edn). Federal Ministry of Justice (ed). Forum Verlag Godesberg, Mönchengladbach. Available online: *http://www.bmj.de/media/archive/961.pdf*

Kerner H-J, Hartmann A (2005) Auswertung der bundesweiten Täter-Opfer-Ausgleichsstatistik für den Zehnjahreszeitraum 1993–2002. Federal Ministry of Justice (ed). available online *www.bmj.bund.de/toa.*

Kilchling M (2000) The Role of the Public Prosecutor in Germany. In: Vander Beken T, Kilchling M (eds) The Role of the Public Prosecutor in the European Criminal Justice Systems. VWK, Brussels, pp 73–93

Kissel O, Mayer H (2005) Gerichtsverfassungsgesetz. Kommentar (4th edn). Beck, München

Kühne H-H (2003) Strafprozessrecht. Eine systematische Darstellung des deutschen und europäischen Strafverfahrensrechts (6th edn). Müller, Heidelberg

Kürzinger J (1978) Private Strafanzeige und polizeiliche Reaktion. Duncker & Humblot, Berlin

Meyer-Goßner L (2005) Strafprozessordnung, Gerichtverfassungsgesetz, Nebengesetze und ergänzende Bestimmungen (48th edn). Beck, München

Pfeiffer G (2003) Karlsruher Kommentar zur Strafprozessordnung und zum Gerichtsverfassungsgesetz mit Einführungsgesetz (5th edn). Beck, München
Rieß P (1981) Die Zukunft des Legalitätsprinzips. NStZ: 2–10
Satzger H (2004) Chancen und Risiken einer Reform des strafrechtlichen Ermittlungsverfahrens: Gutachten C für den 65. Deutschen Juristentag. Beck, Bonn
Schlüchter E (1999) Strafprozessrecht (3rd edn). EuWi-Verlag, Thüngersheim
Schroeder F-C (1996) Zur Rechtskraft staatsanwaltschaftlicher Einstellungsverfügungen. NStZ: 319–320
Sprenger W, Fischer T (2000) Verbesserte Verfolgung des Ladendiebstahls – Sächsisches Verfahrensmodell zum Strafgeld. DRiZ: 111–114.
Steffen W (1976) Analyse polizeilicher Ermittlungstätigkeit aus der Sicht des späteren Strafverfahrens. Bundeskriminalamt (ed), BKA-Forschungsreihe, Wiesbaden
Stock J, Kreuzer A (1996) Drogen und Polizei – eine kriminologische Untersuchung polizeilicher Rechtsanwendung. Forum Verlag Godesberg, Bonn.
Weigend T (2004) The Prosecution Service in the German Administration of Criminal Justice. In: Tak P (ed) Tasks and Powers of the Prosecution Services in the EU Member States. Wolf Legal Publishers, Nijmegen, pp 203–222.

The Prosecution Service Function within the Dutch Criminal Justice System

Martine Blom, Paul Smit

1 General

In the Netherlands the Public Prosecution Service (*Openbaar Ministerie)* (PPS) has a central and monopolistic role in criminal proceedings. The prosecutor controls the investigation and only s/he can decide whether to prosecute or not. Non-prosecution can be conditional: this modality is frequently used in the Netherlands. In the near future, this might develop into formal sanctioning by the prosecutor. Since 1999, the PPS is organized into one body, headed by a board of Prosecutors-General, which is answerable to the Minister of Justice. In simple and lighter cases, prosecutor decisions are to a large extent mandated to other institutions such as the police.

1.1 Types of Offences

In the Netherlands there is a legal distinction, defined in the criminal code (*Wetboek van Strafrecht*, Sr), between crimes (*misdrijven*) and infractions (*overtredingen*). However, to understand the Dutch system it is important to categorize differently, which reflects both the Dutch procedural law and the registration practices (on which the Dutch statistics are based) better. This results into the following three categories for all offences:

- Category A: The "Mulder law" (*Wet Mulder*) offences.
  These are the majority of all traffic offences: most speeding offences, parking, traffic light etc. In a legal sense, they can be seen as criminal infractions[1]. However, all offences in this category are handled administratively and do not, except when an appeal is made, have an effect on the prosecution or the court sys-

[1] Although they are not mentioned anymore in the criminal code as infractions they still are called "punishable acts" in the Mulder law.

tem. The total number of Mulder law offences in 2002 was 9,536,864 (input statistics). (Centraal Justitieel Incasso Bureau 2003)

- Category B: All infractions with two exceptions: the "Mulder Law" offences and all economical and environmental infractions.
  Again, many traffic offences (driving without insurance, excessive speeding offences) can be found in this category, but also offences like "travelling in public transport without a valid ticket" or "being drunk and disorderly in a public place". These offences are handled like criminal cases. The main difference with crimes is that, if they come to the court stage, they will be handled (in first instance) in a lower court (*kantongerecht*).
  There are no regular input statistics on the police level for this category. However, the input for the prosecution was 217,732 cases in 2002 (Openbaar Ministerie 2005). From this figure, it could be estimated by using the number of police-*transacties* that were paid and the number of HALT measures imposed, that the police input must have been about 443 thousand (see Chapter 5.1).
- Category C: All crimes and all economical and environmental infractions.
  See Appendix 1 for a listing of all crimes. Also some traffic offences are considered as crime (e.g. driving under influence, leaving the place of an accident). In the first instance, offences in this category will be handled by the "normal" courts (*arrondissementsrechtbank*). There are no special courts for juvenile offenders, but there are special judges for juveniles within the normal courts.
  The number of these offences recorded (police input statistics) in 2002 was 1,422,900.

In Dutch, the categories are called *wet mulderzaken* (A), *kantonzaken* (B) and *rechtbankzaken* (C). Dutch crime statistics almost exclusively refer to *rechtbankzaken* (C).

1.2 Organization and Role of the Police

Since 1993, when a reorganization took place, the police service is divided into 25 police regions. Each region falls under the administrative management of the mayor of the main city (the *korpsbeheerder*) in that region. The police organization as a whole falls under the administrative responsibility of the Minister of the Interior.

The power over the police is divided: the mayor of the local community (more than 450 in the Netherlands) is responsible for maintaining public order; the prosecution service has the authority over police criminal investigations. In order to coordinate the activities of the police, the mayors and the prosecution service come together for regular consultation (the so-called tripartite consultation or *driehoeksoverleg*).

A separate (26th) police force deals with issues at a national level (e.g. national motorway police, central criminal investigations). Besides the police, there are four special investigative agencies for offences, like tax and social security fraud.

Formally, the public prosecutor is the senior investigator in all criminal cases. In practice, the police will deal with the investigation of most criminal cases under general guidelines of the PPS[2]. There is only in the most important criminal cases a direct involvement of the public prosecutor. In addition, some investigations are started on initiative of the prosecutor (e.g. large investigations on organised crime, fraud etc.) Obviously, for these investigations, there is a direct involvement of the prosecutor as well.

When the investigation has ended and an offender has been found, the case (or rather the offender file) must be sent to the prosecution. There are some exceptions which are described in Chapter 5. When no offender is found, the case will be dropped eventually. Actually, since a "police drop" has no legal basis in the Netherlands, it is only a decision (which is made either explicitly or implicitly) not to investigate the case any further, but it is not a formal ending of the case. New evidence could start the investigation again.

The role of the police has changed somewhat in the last 10–15 years. After a Parliamentary Inquiry Committee on Police Investigation in 1996 (Van Traa, 1996) was held, there is more direct PPS supervision of the police in their investigative activities. On the other hand, the police have more possibilities to handle cases themselves (although always under the general authority of the PPS).

By 2002 (end of year), the total number of employees in the police force was 47,964, of whom 34,504 were executive police officers.

1.3 Organization and Role of the Public Prosecution Service

Almost all[3] public prosecutors (*officieren van justitie*) are supervised by a central office (Board of Prosecutors General, or *Parket-Generaal*) led by three to five chief prosecutors. These chief prosecutors fall directly under the political responsibility of the Minister of Justice.

The organization of the PPS (*Openbaar Ministerie*) is directly linked to the courts and follows the geographical division of the Netherlands in 19 districts (*arrondissementen*).[4] For each of the 19 districts there is one prosecution office (*arrondissementsparket*) dealing with cases in the first instance. On a higher geographical level there are five *ressorts*, each consisting of three or four *arrondissementen*. Each *ressort* also has a prosecution office (*ressortsparket*). They handle all appeals. There is no hierarchical link between the *arrondissementsparketten* and the *ressortsparketten*. Both fall under the direct responsibility of the Board of Prosecutors General.

---

[2] Recently, since 2003, there are also guidelines issued from the PPS on how to prioritise investigations or even in some circumstances not to investigate at all.

[3] The exception are the prosecutors at the Supreme Court. They are independent and do not also fall under the authority of the Minister of Justice. And they are appointed for life.

[4] There is also a geographical correspondence with the police regions: each *arrondissement* consists of one or two police regions.

Two separate prosecution offices, with the same powers as the prosecutors at the district level, exist for issues of a national relevance: especially organized crime and special enforcement fields (e.g. frauds, environmental crimes).

The PPS in the Netherlands plays a central and monopolistic role: the prosecutor is responsible for the investigation and decides whether to prosecute, to drop a case against an offender or to deal with the offender himself (disposal with conditions).

This central role does not mean that the prosecutor is directly involved in all individual cases. As shown before, the direct involvement of the prosecutor in the investigative phase is limited to the most serious criminal cases only. As soon as an offender is known, the situation becomes different. With some exceptions that are described in the following chapters the offender file is sent to the prosecution and all further decisions are made by the prosecutor.

The prosecution service is also responsible for the execution of sanctions (Tak 2003). This part of the prosecution activities will not be discussed further here.

There are about 500 public prosecutors. They are recruited in the same way as judges and are appointed directly by the Crown. However, they are not appointed for life and retire at the age of 65.

1.4 Organization and Role of the Courts

In the Netherlands, there are no juries and no lay judges[5]. Only professional judges decide on verdict and punishment. Judges are independent and although there is a central Council for the Judiciary (*Raad voor de Rechtspraak*), this council can not in any way influence the decisions of judges in individual cases.

For each of the 19 districts there is one district court (*arrondissementsrechtbank*). Within such a court, apart from several chambers dealing exclusively with civil cases, the following chambers handle offences (in first instance):

- The single cantonal judge (*kantonrechter*).
  Basically, these are "lower courts" within the district court. Within one district there could be several and they are located in different cities. All category B offences are tried by this judge. They also handle "Mulder Law" appeals, see Chapter 6.
- The police judge[6] (*politierechter*)
  This is a single judge dealing with comparatively minor cases in category C. The police judge may only impose prison sentences not exceeding 12 months[7].

---

5 There are some minor exceptions. In some courts (e.g. a military court) there could be a lay judge, but always as part of a bench where the majority consists of professional judges.

6 Contrary to what the name suggests, this judge has nothing to do with the police. It is a normal judge handling most cases, except for the more serious cases.

7 Until recently this was 6 months.

- The full bench (*meervoudige kamer*)
  The full bench consists of three judges. They deal with the more serious crimes. The decision whether a case is handled by the police judge or the full bench is primarily taken by the prosecutor (by the choice of sentence requested), but also the police judge can decide that a full bench would be more suitable in a specific case.
- The economic police judge (*economische politierechter*)
  This judge will handle almost all economic and environmental offences, both infractions and crimes.
- The juvenile judge (*kinderrechter*)
  Nearly all juvenile crime is treated by a single juvenile judge. This judge also decides if the court session will be open to the public (court sessions with adult offenders are open to the public, with juvenile offenders usually not).

There are five courts of appeal (*gerechtshof*) corresponding with the five *ressortsparketten.* They usually sit in benches of three judges and handle all appeals, both category B and C offences.

There is also a Supreme Court (*Hoge Raad*) where appeals in cassation are held. There is a bench of five (or three) judges.

Within the district courts there are also examining magistrates (*rechter-commissaris*). They have a specific role in the investigative phase, e.g. decide on pre-trial detention, ordering psychiatric examination of the suspect etc.

There are about 1700 judges in the Netherlands, of whom it is estimated that 400 deal with criminal cases. They are appointed by the minister of justice and the Crown for life, but usually retire at 70.

2 The Public Prosecution Service

In this chapter, the organization and role of the public prosecution service (*Openbaar Ministerie*) will be described in more detail. The function of the PPS in investigative proceedings will not be discussed here with here but will be described in Chapter 7.

2.1 Legal Basis of the Prosecution Service

The Public Prosecution Service is part of the judiciary. The organization of the judiciary is regulated in the Judicial Organization Act (*Wet op de Rechterlijke Organisatie*, RO). In 1999 the public prosecution service was reformed. In that year a Board of Prosecutors General was introduced. According to the Code of Criminal Procedure (*Wetboek van Strafvordering*, Sv), this Board is the highest authority for all investigation (Sv art. 140) and prosecution activities and supervises the implementation of a proper prosecution policy by the public prosecution service, and a proper investigation policy by the police. The board may give instructions to the members of the public prosecution service concerning their tasks and powers in relation to the administration of criminal justice and other statutory powers such as supervision of the police (RO art. 130/4). Instructions may be of a general nature (on policy) or of a specific nature (in cases). Prosecutors are legally bound by these instructions (Tak 2003).

Final responsibility (and political accountability) for the PPS lies with the Minister of Justice. He also has the power – within procedural safeguards – to give general or specific instructions to the prosecution service (RO art 127), even in individual cases although this almost never happens in practice.

The main task of the PPS is to administer, by means of criminal law, legal order (RO art. 124). This means that it is responsible for:

- investigating criminal offences (Sv art. 48)
- prosecuting offenders (Sv art. 167 or 242)
- making sure that sentences are imposed properly (Sv art. 553).

2.2 Appointment and Training

Members of the prosecution are not elected but appointed by the Crown (in practice by the minister of Justice). They must have Dutch nationality. There are three ways to become a public prosecutor:

1. By following a special 6-year training path, usually directly after having received a university degree in Law. There is a selection procedure for training. This is the so-called RAIO training (*Rechterlijk Ambtenaar In Opleiding* or "Training to become a member of the Judiciary"). After having completed the training successfully, the candidate will be appointed as assistant prosecutor for one year, after which the actual appointment by the Crown can follow.
2. Persons with a university degree in Law and, at least, four years experience as staff members (or something similar) in a prosecution office may qualify for an appointment as public prosecutor in single chambre sessions.
3. Persons with a university degree in Law and, at least, 6 years appropriate experience outside the prosecution service can be appointed directly.

With some differences, the appointment procedures for judges are the same[8].

2.3 The Decision to Prosecute

After the investigative phase (see Chapter 7), and as soon as an offender is known, the prosecution can start. Or rather, a decision must be made to prosecute or to do something else with the offender. Although this decision lies exclusively with the

[8] Judges are appointed for life (prosecutors are not). In addition, the second option (four years experience as staff member) is not possible for judges.

prosecutor, in practice the actual decision can be made (although always under the authority of the PPS) without active involvement of a prosecutor. There are five main possibilities:

1. For the "Mulder Law" offences (see category A above), there is no involvement of the prosecutor at all, except when the offender decides to appeal (see Chapter 6).
2. For juvenile offenders and then only for specific offences (shoplifting, vandalism etc.) a HALT procedure can be started. Usually this is a kind of working or learning activity. This way the juvenile can avoid prosecution. There is no involvement of the prosecutor. The police will handle this. For a further explanation, see Chapter 8.
3. For many infractions (category B) and for a limited number of crimes (category C), under general guidelines of the Board of Prosecutors General, the police can issue a *transactie* themselves. There is no involvement of the prosecutor.
4. The police can decide not to send the offender file to the PPS. This is sometimes (incorrectly) called a "police drop". See Chapter 5.2. Actually, this decision can also be made on an individual case level by a member of the prosecution, located at a police station. So there can be direct involvement of the prosecution. However, these cases are not registered as prosecution decisions and do not appear in the prosecution statistics.
5. The police send the offender file to the prosecutors office. The prosecutor will now take the decision what to do at the individual offender level.

The options that are open to the prosecution after having received an offender file from the police will be described further in Chapter 4.

2.4 The Role of the Prosecutor in the Trial Phase

When the prosecutor decides to bring an offender before a court, he must present a writ of summons (*dagvaarding*) to the offender. The charge is mentioned in the summons. This charge will be the subject of the court session, and the court can not modify the charge. Under exceptional circumstances the prosecution can alter the charge during the trial.

The prosecution (and the defence) will present the evidence to the court. In most cases, even in many serious cases, this consists of written statements of witnesses and experts, filed by the police or the examining magistrate, which are discussed in the trial. This is why a trial rarely lasts more than a couple of hours.

Examination of the evidence and questioning the accused and, if necessary, the actual questioning of witnesses and experts is primarily done by the court. Afterwards the prosecutor and the defence can ask additional questions, but cross-examination is unknown.

Apart from representing the state, the prosecutor will also take the interests of the offender into account. This way the character of the trial is not purely adversarial (the primary aim of the trial is truth finding) and the interests of the prosecution and the defence are not necessarily conflicting.

After the evidence has been presented and discussed, the public prosecutor makes his closing speech (*requisitoir*)[9]. Part of the closing speech is a request for a specific sentence to be imposed. The judge is not bound by this however: the actual verdict can be lower or higher (Tak 2003).

The role of the prosecutor in the appeal court does not differ from that in the courts in first instance.

3 Cases Brought to Court

The decision to bring a case against an offender before a court is made exclusively by the prosecutor. The only exception is the Mulder Law cases (category A offences). These are described in Chapter 6. Also, both victim and offender can object to decisions made by the prosecutor (see Chapter 8). There are no simplified court proceedings, mainly because the prosecution can in many cases impose a kind of sanction themselves (the *transactie*). This possibility also essentially eliminates the need for a "guilty plea". In the Dutch system the only person to decide on the guilt of an offender is the judge, not the prosecutor or the offender[10].

For various reasons, the number of cases with a court verdict is considerably less than the number of cases brought before the court (as can be seen by comparing the number of verdicts with the figures in table 1). The main reason is that in the trial phase cases against an offender can be combined (*gevoegd*) into one case. See Appendix 2 for a detailed description of the different kinds of *voegingen*.

3.1 Offences Brought before the Cantonal Judge (*kantonrechter*)

These are the *kantonzaken* or category B offences. The prosecutor prepares these cases, decides on the charge and presents them to the cantonal judge. When presented to the court a verdict will always follow. If an appeal is made the prosecutor will present the case at the appeal court (*gerechtshof*). Typically, appeals are made in about 3 % of cases. In 2002 there were 104 thousand court decisions; 100 thousand of these decisions were a guilty verdict with sanction. The most common sanctions were: 92 thousand fines, 10 thousand withdrawals of driver's license and 7 thousand prison sentences. The total number of sanctions is larger than the court decisions, because combinations of sanctions are possible.

---

[9] After the requisitoir the defense lawyer, the prosecutor (again) and the suspected offender are given the opportunity to speak before the court.

[10] But this will change in the near future! See Chapter 9.

3.2 Offences Brought before the District Judge (*arrondissementsrechtbank)*

Also for the *rechtbankzaken* or category C offences the prosecution prepares the case and decides on the charge. In total 146 thousand cases were presented to these courts in 2002, leading to 128 thousand court decisions. In about 8 % of the cases an appeal was made. 11 % of the cases were handled by the full bench, 81 % by the single police judge or by the economic police judge and 8 % by the juvenile judge. On average, the time between the moment a case is presented by the police to the prosecution and the verdict of the court is about 8 months for cases handled by the full bench and 6 months for cases handled by a single judge.

A guilty with sanction verdict was issued in 95 % of the cases. There were 54 thousand prison sentences, 46 thousand fines, 28 thousand community service sentences and 17 thousand withdrawals of driver's licenses.

4 Cases Dealt with by the Public Prosecution Service

A large proportion of the cases presented to the prosecution are handled by the prosecutor in the sense that they do not lead to a writ of summons. In 2002, for *kantonzaken* (category B offences) 32 % of the cases were dealt with by the prosecution, for *rechtbankzaken* (category C offences) this was 42 %[11].

Basically, besides bringing the offender to the court, there are two options for the prosecution. These are to drop the case or to settle the case by means of a *transactie*. A formal sanction by the prosecution is not possible. However, a *transactie* could also be seen as a kind of sanction, although in a legal sense it is not (it does not acknowledge the guilt of the offender and it does not lead to a criminal record).

[11] The lower percentage for *kantonzaken* is due to the fact that for those cases police-*transacties* are used more.

Table 1. Cases Dealt with by the Prosecution Service, 2002 (Thousands)

	Kantonzaken (Category B offences)		Rechtbankzaken (Category C offences)	
Total	209.5	100.0 %	251.4	100.0 %
Unconditional drop	29.9	14.3 %	30.1	12.0 %
of which: Technical	16.9	8.1 %	17.3	6.9 %
Public interest	11.5	5.5 %	10.8	4.3 %
Other	1.5	0.7 %	2.0	0.8 %
Conditional disposal[12]	37.6	17.9 %	75.6	30.1 %
of which: Paying a sum of money	36.9	17.6 %	62.1	24.7 %
Community service	0.2	0.1 %	10.7	4.3 %
Other	0.5	0.2 %	2.8	1.1 %
Brought before court	141.9	67.7 %	145.8	58.0 %

4.1 Drop by the Prosecution

The prosecutor can decide to end further prosecution without imposing any condition. Usually this is done when the prosecutor feels that further prosecution will probably not lead to a conviction (lack of evidence or other technicalities) or when there are reasons of public interest not to prosecute (contrary to the interests of the state or the victim, age or health of the offender, etc.).

The number of prosecution drops has decreased considerably during the last 20 years. This is partly due to a policy change. The *transactie* has to a large extent replaced the drop for reasons of public interest. But also the “police drop“ plays a role here, since many of those cases that used to be sent to the prosecution and would have been dropped there explicitly by the prosecution are now increasingly “dropped“ at the police level. See also Chapter 5.2.

4.2 Conditional Disposals (*transacties*)

The prosecutor can also decide to stop prosecution when certain conditions are met by the suspected offender. This is called a *transactie*.[13] *Transacties* are only possible for offences with a statutory maximum sentence of 6 years or less. This means that for serious crimes such as rape or robbery a *transactie* can not be offered. For the offender, who has to agree to the transaction (if he does not agree, or does not meet the condition, a writ of summons will necessarily follow) this has the advantage that a public trial is avoided and that the *transactie* is not registered in his criminal record.

[12] The number of conditional disposals, where the condition was indeed met by the offender.

[13] In a technical sense, there are also some conditional disposals which are not *transacties*. In table 1 these are included under "Other conditional disposals".

5 Cases Dealt with by the Police

Officially, the police have no discretionary power at all. All police decisions are made under the authority of the PPS, either directly or (in the majority of cases) indirectly. In practice, however, there are some possibilities for the police to influence what happens with an offence.

5.1 "Mulder Law" Offences and *kantonzaken* (Category A and B Offences)

The processing of the 9,5 million "Mulder Law" offences a year is done almost entirely automatically. After the offence is recorded, the details are sent electronically to a special agency handling all these cases, the *Centraal Justitieel Incasso Bureau*, CJIB. After that, the police have no active role in the handling of these offences. Only when an appeal is made (in about 3 % of the cases), the police could be asked to provide evidence.

For the *kantonzaken* (infractions under category B) the first thing to realize is that the detection rate is about 100 %, due to the nature of these offences. So there is always an offender and now there are two possibilities: either the offender is sent to the prosecution (218 thousand in 2002) or the police will give the offender a HALT measure (6 thousand in 2002) or a police-*transactie* (219 thousand in 2002). This decision is made in accordance with general guidelines issued by the prosecution.

5.2 *Rechtbankzaken* (Category C Offences)

With these types of offences the situation is somewhat more complicated. The normal procedure is simple and does not allow the police by themselves to deal with cases: crimes are recorded by the police as soon as they come to their attention and when an offender is found, the file is sent to the prosecution. However, there are many formal and informal ways to deviate from this procedure.

Firstly, in practice, there is a certain freedom for the police to decide whether or not to record a crime. In 2002 the number of experienced crimes (by victims) was estimated to be 5.0 million. 1.7 Million of these crimes were reported to the police and 1.2 million were actually recorded by the police[14] (Van der Heide & Eggen 2005). Apart from some statistical reasons, this difference of 0.5 million is also due to the decision of the police officer not to record a reported crime (e.g. because in his opinion the incident reported is not a crime).

[14] The total number of recorded crimes is somewhat higher: 1.4 million. This number includes also the "victimless" crimes, such as traffic offences, economic offences and drugs crimes.

Secondly, although a suspect is found, a decision can be made not to send him to the prosecution, either by the police themselves or by someone from the prosecution service located at the police station.

The police can do this when they think the suspect is not the offender after all or they feel the evidence is inadequate. Actually what happens is that the case is not dropped, but the offender is not considered as suspect by the police anymore. And probably (but not necessarily) the investigative activities will also stop. However, these are not formal decisions and are not registered anywhere.

When the decision not to send the offender to the prosecution is taken by a prosecutor (or his assistant located at the police station), one could argue that this is a formal decision to drop by the PPS (and both types of drops, technical or public interest, do indeed occur). However, these decisions are not registered as such and therefore do not appear in the prosecution input or output statistics.

Lastly, there are two situations in which the police can impose a sanction themselves, although this is done under general guidelines by the PPS. For juvenile offenders there is the so-called HALT measure, which is explained in more detail in Chapter 8. The number of HALT measures in 2002 was 12 thousand. And, as was the case with kantonzaken, a police-*transactie* is also possible, but for one specific offence (shoplifting) only[15] (9 thousand in 2002).

6 Cases Dealt with by Alternative Procedural Forms

The main alternative procedural form is the administrative handling of almost all traffic offences[16], the so-called "Mulder-law" offences. This procedure is regulated in a special law, the *Wet Administratiefrechtelijke Handhaving Verkeersvoorschriften* (WAHV) or "law on the administrative handling of traffic offences"

The procedure for these offences is as follows:

- Information on the offence is sent electronically by the police to a central agency (CJIB).
- The offender will, within four months from registering the committed offence on, receive a pre-printed giro card requiring payment of a fine from the CJIB. This is done automatically.
- If the offender does not agree, an appeal can be made within six weeks after receiving the fine. The first appeal is to the prosecutor who will reconsider the case. From the 9.5 million cases, there were 360 thousand such appeals and about 40 % of those were granted. A second appeal can be made to the cantonal judge, this was done in 26 thousand cases. Under certain conditions further appeals are also possible to a court of appeal (*gerechtshof*) and/or the Supreme Court.

[15] Until 1/1/2004 a police-*transactie* was also possible for driving under influence (alcohol promillage between 0.53 and 0.80).

[16] In 2002 about 97 % of all traffic offences were "Mulder-law" offences.

- If no appeal was made and if the offender does not pay the fine (after having received two reminders), a collecting procedure is started with various means of coercion. This procedure is completely separated from the original offence and is, in this way, different from not paying a *transactie* (after which a writ of summons follows for the original offence).

Since its introduction in 1990, the WAHV has proven very successful. Despite a high increase in the number of traffic fines imposed, it has considerably reduced the workload for the prosecution and courts. Also, 87 % of the fines were paid before the first reminder (and another 7 % after the first or second reminder).

7 PPS Function in Investigative Proceedings

There are different kinds of investigations mentioned in the Code of Criminal Procedure. A criminal procedure always starts with a police investigation (*opsporingsonderzoek*), usually as soon as the police is aware of the fact that an offence has been committed, e.g. because a victim has reported the offence. After, or in some cases during the police investigation other kinds of investigation can take place if needed: the preliminary judicial investigation (*gerechtelijk vooronderzoek*), the criminal financial investigation (*strafrechtelijk financieel onderzoek*) and the investigation during trial (*onderzoek ter terechtzitting*).

7.1 The Police[17] Investigation

Although formally the prosecutor is responsible for the investigation (Sv art 148), in the majority of cases there is no direct involvement of the prosecutor at all. The primary aim of the police investigation is to find enough evidence against a suspected offender in order to either bring the offender before a court or for the prosecution to make a conditional disposal decision. In many cases, this is never achieved because no suspected offender is found.

In order to gather information, various investigative measures can be used. As long as these methods are not intrusive, the police are very autonomous in using these (although under general responsibility of the prosecutor and within the statutory rules as mentioned in the Code of Criminal Procedure). For these measures cooperation is also needed from the persons involved, e.g. in the case of witness interrogation or search of premises.

As soon as intrusive measures are needed (detention, phone taps etc.) or measures against the will of the persons involved, explicit decisions from the prosecu-

[17] Actually, also other investigative agencies such as the FIOD (for fiscal fraud) can carry out these investigations. The role of the prosecution service however is the same as with police investigations.

tor and/or the examining magistrate (*rechter-commisaris*) are needed[18]. In the case of pre-trial detention, for the first 3–6 days (called police custody) the decision lies with the prosecutor, for the next 10 days (remand in custody) the decision lies with the examining magistrate at the request of the prosecutor. After that, the prosecutor has to make his request to the full bench court for further pre-trial detention. When a search of premises is needed the decision has to be made by the examining magistrate at the request of the prosecutor (request is not needed in the preliminary judicial investigation, see below).

Although the police investigation usually starts when a crime has been committed and this fact has come to the attention of the police, since 2000 the Code of Criminal Procedure (Sv art 132a) gives the police and the PPS the possibility to start an investigation even before there is a "reasonable suspicion that a criminal offence has been committed". According to this new article, in order to be more successful in the fight against organized crime and terrorism, an investigation can also start when there is a "reasonable suspicion that a crime is planned by a group of people".

The end-result of the police investigation consists of written files that may be used as evidence in a trial.

7.2 The Preliminary Judicial Investigation

For more serious cases, where special investigatory measures are needed such as the search of premises against the will of the resident, a preliminary judicial investigation can be initiated by the prosecutor[19]. This investigation is then carried out by an examining magistrate who will take all decisions, also the decision to stop the investigation.

Due to recent changes in the Code of Criminal Procedure the preliminary judicial investigation is less frequent than before. The prosecutor now has more possibilities to initiate investigatory measures himself, such as continuous observation of suspects or infiltration. Also, for some measures that do require examining magistrates permission, such as the search of premises or telephone taps, this permission can also be granted without starting a formal preliminary judicial investigation.

After the preliminary judicial investigation has finished, the decision what to do with the case (to drop, to dispose or to go to the court) lies again with the prosecutor.

[18] There are some exceptions, e.g. in the case of an arrest by the police when caught red-handed. Deprivation of liberty can in this case last 6 hours, extended by 6 hours if necessary, after that a prosecutor decision is necessary.

[19] Also the suspected offender can ask the examining magistrate to use some investigation measures, such as interviewing certain witnesses. This is, however, not a full preliminary judicial investigation.

7.3 The Criminal Financial Investigation

Independent of the other criminal investigations the prosecutor can choose to use a financial investigation[20] in order to determine the financial profit resulting from the crime committed. As part of the measures imposed on the offender when it comes to a conviction for this crime, the offender can be forced to pay an amount of money equal to this financial gain.

The suspected offender does not need to know that a criminal financial investigation has started. Eventually, he has to be informed however, but this can be as late as during trial.

As with the police investigation, for some measures (e.g. confiscation of property) permission from the examining magistrate is needed.

7.4 The Investigation during Trial

The investigation during trial (or final investigation), is considerably different from the other investigations[21]. The initiative to further examining the written files collected during the other investigative stages and to interview additional witnesses and experts lies with the court.
See also Chapter 2.4 for the role of the prosecution during trial.

8 Particular issues

8.1 Victim Participation

The role of the victim in criminal procedures used to be minimal but has been improving during the last years. One of the main characteristics of the Dutch system is the monopoly on prosecution by the Prosecution Service. Private prosecution (by victims, other individuals or companies) is not possible.
However, under certain circumstances and for certain crimes, victims can prevent prosecution: for some crimes, such as insult or libel, or theft between close family members, a victim complaint is a necessary precondition for prosecution.

In addition, when the prosecutor decides to dismiss or dispose of the case, the victim[22] can file a protest against this decision with a court of appeal. After hearing the victim, the court can order the prosecutor to initiate a prosecution. In practice, however, this hardly ever occurs.

---

[20] But permission is needed from the examining magistrate. And a financial investigation is only possible for some (usually the more serious) crimes.

[21] Of course, an investigation during trial only occurs in a minority of the cases, i.e. when the prosecutor decides to bring the case before a court.

[22] Actually this can be done by everyone with an interest in the prosecution of the case. About 1500 appeals are made each year.

Since 1993 the victim can join the criminal proceedings as the injured party in order to get financial compensation from the offender. This can be either a separate decision of the judge, apart from the sanction (in which case the victim is responsible for trying to get the money from the offender) or it can be part of the sanction (in which case the prosecutor takes care of the recovery of the money and the victim receives the money from the state). When joining the case, the victim also gains access to all case files.

Furthermore, since 2005 and for some serious offences only, the victim (or the family of the victim in a homicide case) has the right to issue a statement during trial. Most of the time this is combined with a more broadly introduced possibility of a written "victim impact statement", in which the victim has the opportunity to explain the (emotional) consequences of the crime.

8.2 Juveniles

Juveniles are those who, at the time the offence was committed, were at least 12 and not yet 18 years old. A number of special articles are included in the Criminal Code for them (Sr art. 77d to 77gg), mainly regarding the different kinds of sanctions and measures applicable to juveniles.

A judge can, if he finds reason for this in the severity of the offence committed the personality of the offender or the circumstances in which the offence was committed, apply adult criminal law, but only if the offender was 16 or 17 years old at the time the offence was committed. For the ages 18–21, the judge can decide to apply juvenile law.

If a case against a juvenile is brought before a court, it will always be handled by a special judge, the juvenile judge (*kinderrechter*), either as a single judge or as a part of a full bench. This judge acts also as examining magistrate when decisions on pre-trial detention are needed. Court sessions with juveniles are closed to the public unless the judge decides otherwise.

Sanctions for juveniles are about the same as sanctions for adults, although with a lower maximum. Also, sanctions and measures for juveniles are aimed more strongly at education, reform and reintegration instead of punishment. Detention can not exceed 1 year (for juveniles under 16) or 2 years (for age 16–17). Separate from these sanctions, the judge can impose that the juvenile should go to a special open or closed institution in order to be treated and/ or educated. The duration of this measure is not fixed in advance and can last up to 6 years (2 years, with the possibility of extension for at most 4 years).

As with adults, the prosecution can also decide not to prosecute and to dismiss or conditionally dispose (*transactie*). Besides these options, the police can under certain conditions impose a HALT measure. The advantage for the juvenile offender is that his case will not go to the prosecutor at all. The conditions for the HALT measure are:

1. it must be one of a list of specific offences, such as shoplifting, causing nuisances with fireworks, public property destruction, graffiti etc.,

2. the juvenile has to admit the offence,
3. the juvenile has been to HALT at most only once before and
4. the juvenile has to agree with the HALT measure.

Basically, the HALT measure consists of two parts: a working or learning activity (up to 20 hours) and compensation to rectify the damage done. Sometimes these two can be combined: cleaning the walls that were painted with graffiti. If a HALT measure does not succeed, a report is sent by police to the prosecutor who decides what will be done next.

8.3 The Mentally Disordered and the TBS system

If an offender is mentally disordered the court first has to decide if his mental illness is such that the offender can not be held responsible for his crime. If that is the case, a penalty is not possible, but the court may order that the offender must go to a psychiatric hospital for a period of up to one year.

If (after a psychiatric evaluation) the perpetrator cannot (fully) be held accountable for his or her crime, and the offender is thought to pose a threat to other people or the general public, the court can impose an entrustment order (*terbeschikkingstelling* or TBS). Usually the entrustment order consists of hospital treatment in special institutions and starts – if a prison sentence has also been meted out – after or at the end of the prison sentence. The entrustment order lasts for two years but can be extended if the threat for further criminal behaviour has not been addressed sufficiently. For certain violent crimes this extension can be considerable and effectively lead to incarceration for life. The number of patients in hospitals with an entrustment order has increased from 522 in 1990 to 1,728 in 2004.

9 Current changes

The most important change in the Dutch system will be the introduction of the PPS imposed sanction (*strafbeschikking*) that will replace the conditional disposal (*transactie*). This replacement will probably start in 2007[23] and there will be a certain period where the *transactie* and the *strafbeschikking* will exist next to each other. The main characteristics of the *strafbeschikking* are the following:

- It is a formal sanction which is not imposed by a judge but by the prosecutor. There is no court involvement at all.
- Agreement by the offender is not necessary (as it was with a *transactie*). If the offender does not agree he has to appeal after which his case will probably be brought before the court (of first instance).

[23] The Dutch parliament still has to decide on introduction of the law which makes this possible.

- The offender is explicitly declared guilty and the crime will be added to his criminal record.
- If the offender does not pay in case of a financial sanction, a civil debt collection procedure can be started. This is fundamentally different from not paying a *transactie*, after which a writ of summons follows.
- There are more kinds of sanctions available than for conditional disposals, such as the withdrawal of a driver's license. However, deprivation of liberty is not possible.
- For financial sanctions of more than 2,000 Euro, the offender has to be heard in the presence of a lawyer.
- As with *transacties*, a *strafbeschikking* is only possible for offences with a statutory maximum sentence of 6 years or less.

10 Literature

Centraal Justitieel Incasso Bureau *CJIB Jaarverslag 2002* Leeuwarden, CJIB, 2003
Eggen, A.Th.J. , W. van der Heide (red.)
Criminaliteit en rechtshandhaving 2004; Ontwikkelingen en samenhangen
Den Haag, Boom Juridische uitgevers, 2005
Onderzoek en beleid, nr. 237
Openbaar Ministerie
Kortom: het OM in cijfers 1998–2004
http://www.om.nl (August 5th, 2005)
Tak, P.J.P.
The Dutch criminal justice system; organization and operation
Den Haag, Boom Juridische uitgevers, 2003
Onderzoek en beleid, nr. 205
Traa, M. van (voorzitter)
Inzake opsporing; eindrapport
Den Haag, Sdu, 1996

11 Appendix 1 Classification of Crimes

Standard classification of criminal offences (Source: Statistics Netherlands)
Most recently amended in 2000

1. Criminal Code
Violent crimes, of which
Rape (Article 242)
Indecent assault (Article 246)
Other sex offences (Articles 243 t/m 245, 247 t/m 249, 250, 250bis)
Threat (Article 285)
Serious offence against human life (Articles 287 t/m 291, 293, 294, 296)
Assault (Article 300 t/m 306)

Death or bodily harm ensuing from negligence (Articles 307 t/m 309)
Robbery (Article 312)
Extortion (Article 317)
Property crimes, of which
Falsification offences (Articles 208 t/m 235)
Common theft (Article 310)
Theft preceded by forcible entry (Articles 311–5, 311–4–5)
Other aggravated theft (Article 311)
Embezzlement (Articles 321 t/m 323)
Fraud (Articles 326 t/m 337)
Handling stolen goods and culpably handling stolen goods (Articles 416 t/m 417bis)
Vandalism and public order, of which
Against public order (Articles 131 t/m 136, 138 t/m 151a)
Discrimination (Articles 137c t/m 137g)
General dangerous crimes (Articles 157 en 158)
Against public authority (Articles 177 t/m 206)
Offence against public decency (Article 239)
Vandalism (Articles 350 t/m 352)
Other offences under the Criminal Code

2. Traffic Act, of which
   Drink-driving offences (Article 26)
   Hit and run (Article 30)
   Other offences under the Traffic Act
3. Economic Offences Act, of which
   Environmental hygiene laws
   Other offences under the economic offences act
4. Opium act, of which
   List of illegal substances I
   List of illegal substances II
5. Weapons and Ammunition Act
6. Military Penal Code
7. Other laws

12 Appendix 2 Combining Cases (*voegingen*)

Both, the prosecution and the court can decide to bring several cases against the same offender together (*voegen*) and to handle them as if it is one case. In practice, this will mainly happen with *rechtbankzaken* (category C offences). There are three ways to do this:

1. Adding cases to the "main" case in the writ of summons in order to inform the court.
   This is called a *voeging ad informandum*. This is done by the prosecution. The added offences are not part of the charge and the offender will not be

convicted for them. The idea is to inform the court that the offender had committed also other crimes than the offences he is actually charged with. And the judge may consider these offences when imposing a sentence (if it is obvious that the offender has indeed committed these offences).
The number of the *voegingen ad informandum* has decreased considerably in the last 10 years, from 12 thousand in 1994 to 2 thousand in 2002. In this publication these *voegingen* are statistically seen as public interest drops.

2. Adding cases to the main case in the writ of summons in order to get a conviction.
   This is called a *voeging ter berechting* and is also a prosecutor decision. Now the added offences are part of the charge and a verdict will necessarily follow.
   In 2002 there were about 12,000 *voegingen ter berechting* which is a small decrease compared to the first half of the 1990's. Statistically, the *voegingen ter berechting* are seen as cases brought to court. This way they form part of the output of the prosecution (146,000 in 2002). However, because the cases are combined the actual input for the courts is 12,000 less and is thus 134,000.
3. Combining different writs of summons into one case for the court.
   This is called a *voeging ter zitting* and is a court decision. The effect is the same as the *voeging ter berechting.*
   There were 10,000 *voegingen ter zitting* in 2002. This means that the expected number of court verdicts (the court output) is 10,000 less than the input and is thus 124,000. This is close to the actual court output for 2002, which was 118,000. The difference is due to a certain time lag and other technical and statistical reasons.

The Prosecution Service Function within the Polish Criminal Justice System

Teodor Bulenda, Beata Gruszczynska, Andrzej Kremplewski, Piotr Sobota

1 Introduction

The political transformation, which began in Poland in the late eighties, brought significant social and economic changes, and was a major challenge for the law enforcement and judicial system in Poland. The economic environment, i.e. market economy with free trade and cash turnover, an increased amount of goods and money, as well as legal turnover on the market, which clearly created 'favourable' conditions for an increase in crime. Furthermore, the period showed the weakness of social control and dysfunction of state institutions, which (directly or indirectly) opened the gate for individual and organised crime.

The new political and economic environment called for both: (a) changes in legislation, according to the new needs, as well as (b) the appropriate reaction to any violations of law by the judicial system and law enforcement. Unfortunately, the system changes outpaced the changes in legislation, which contributed – sometimes – to further growth in crime and further challenges to the criminal justice system.

According to the data presented by the Ministry of Justice, between 1993 and 2002 the number of cases filed annually with the public prosecution service increased by 64 % (from 1,033,893 to 1,644,763). The crime rate increased by 71 % in the same period, though the most dramatic growth in crime occurred earlier (in 1990 alone, the crime rate increased by as much as 61 %). It is worth noting that though there were some delays in handling incoming cases by the public prosecution service, they did not exceed 10 % of the inflow, falling to some 7 % lately.

1.2 Penal Proceedings in Poland

Penal Proceedings (For Adults)

They are conducted against perpetrators of 17 years of age and over (exceptionally of 15 years in very serious offence, enumerated in the code). It is the Act of 6 June 1997 – Criminal Procedure Code[1] that forms the basic source of law (CPC).

A criminal procedure is conducted according to the following stages:

- Preparatory procedure,
- Main proceedings (before the I instance court),
- Appeal proceedings (verification before the II instance court),
- Enforcement proceedings (provided under the Executive Criminal Code[2] and Criminal Procedure Code).

In 2002, 1,862,000 criminal and malfeasance cases were filed in the criminal courts. The number of settled cases was 1,788,000 while the number of pending ones was as high as 538,000.

Proceedings in Cases against Juvenile Perpetrators

(In reference to the juvenile delinquents under 18 years of age who demonstrate features of demoralization[3] and those between 13 and 17 years of age who have resorted to punishable acts[4])

As to juvenile delinquents, it is the Act of 26 October 1982 on procedure in cases against juvenile perpetrators[5] that regulates the proceedings.

These are the following stages of proceedings for juvenile cases:

- Verification proceedings,
- Main proceedings (custodian-educational or reformatory procedure),
- Appeal proceedings (verification before the IInd instance court),
- Enforcement proceedings.

In 2002, 121,200 cases were filed related to juvenile perpetrators in the family and juvenile courts. Verification procedures covered 76,800 cases (including 58 000 cases concerning punishable acts). 78,000 cases were settled in verification procedure. 42,800 cases were referred to custodian-educational proceedings (including 30,100 related to punishable acts). 42,900 cases were settled. As to reformatory proceedings, there were 1600 cases filed (and settled).

---

[1] Journal of Laws (JoL) No 89 item 555 as amended.

[2] Act of 6 June 1997, JoL No 90, item 557, as amended.

[3] Demoralization may be exemplified with alcohol abuse, drug taking, flight from home, playing hooky etc.

[4] A punishable act is similar to the offence, however with no element of guilt.

[5] Uniform text: JoL of 2002, No 111 item 109 as amended.

Petty Offence Proceedings

They are conducted in petty offence cases (including petty thefts) – i.e. acts prosecuted under the Petty Offence Code of 1971 – with application of the Act of 25 August 2001 – Petty Offence Procedure Code. Since that year, such cases have been heard by the courts (formerly by the misdemeanour boards – extrajudicial agencies)[6].

The stages of petty offence procedure are as follows:

- Verification operations,
- Proceedings before the court,
- Appeal proceedings,
- Enforcement proceedings.

In 2002, 445,000 petty offence cases were heard before District (Magistrates') Courts[7].

1.3 General Information about Preparatory Proceedings

1. Preparatory proceedings make up one of the stages of Polish criminal procedure, preceding court proceedings.
   The Code of Criminal Procedure of 1997 changed the model of preparatory proceedings by *inter alia* simplifying and accelerating proceedings, the parties' interest guarantee strengthening and equalizing the positions of a suspect and a wronged person in this respect. CPC has also extended the court's share in the preparatory proceedings and the prosecutor's supervision over the operations of other agencies.
2. The purpose of the proceedings consists of: (a) finding out whether an offence has been committed, (b) detection and apprehension of the perpetrator if necessary, (c) examination of the indicted person and making an inquiry at domicile, (d) clarification of the case, including establishment of the wronged persons and extent of damage, (e) collection and securing the evidence for court.
3. There are two forms of preparatory proceedings: (a) an investigation and (b) an inquiry.
   The investigation is conducted in cases of crimes, in cases of misdemeanours committed by judges, prosecutors, police officers, Internal Security agents etc., and in misdemeanours with the decision of a prosecutor. Whereas *the inquiry* is conducted in cases, in which no investigation has been instituted (mostly misdemeanours).
   The inquiry may be carried out by the police or other institutions like Border Guard, Internal Security Agency, Treasury Offices, and Customs' Inspection

6 JoL of 2001 No 106 item 1148 as amended.

7 This is the first full year when the provisions on forwarding the cases related to petty offences to the courts (after the misdemeanor boards were liquidated).

under a prosecutor's supervision for one up to three months if extended by the prosecutor. The investigation is carried out by the prosecutor and by the police (amendment of CPC 2003).

4. A prosecutor is the authority required to conduct preparatory proceedings him/herself or to supervise the same. There is no institution like an investigating judge in Poland. In the court proceedings, a prosecutor plays the role of a prosecuting attorney (as a party to the proceedings).
5. The police are an agency required to conduct inquiry or investigation proceedings as well as other operations ordered by a prosecutor. In their inquiry, they are subordinated to a prosecutor's supervision. The Police may carry out not only inquiry-investigation acts but also operational- and identification actions. Such actions are based on the Police Legal Act. Their operational and identification actions have confidential character and usually precede the preparatory proceeding. The operational actions are beyond the formal proceedings. The prosecutor is not allowed to know these actions and will find no record of them in the files of the cases.
   In prosecution of offences, the Police's rights are also of an extra-procedural character, e.g.: right to wire, to controlled purchase, to watch premises, check a person's identity, detain suspected people, search a person, his/her luggage and cargo.

1.4 Courts in Poland

According to Article 1 § 1 of the Act of 27 July 2001 on Structure of Civilian Courts[8], the following are civilian courts in Poland:

- District Courts,
- Regional Courts,
- Courts of Appeal.

Along with the above mentioned, there are Military Courts[9], Administrative Courts and Supreme Court. As it was explained: Military Courts are the special courts operating in the Armed Forces, but they can adjudge some cases in regarded to persons, who are not members of the Armed Forces[10]. Administrative Courts (Voivodship ones and the Supreme Administrative Court) recognise claims against decisions and orders in administrative law cases. The purpose of the Supreme Court is to ensure uniformity of judicial decisions and adjudication of cassation cases (extraordinary appeal after a judgement becomes valid)[11]. The structure of that court includes also the penal chamber.

[8] JoL of 2001 No 98 item 1070 as amended.

[9] Act of 21 August 1997 "Law on Structure of Court Martial, JoL of 1997 No 117 item 753 as amended.

[10] Jankowski M, Siemaszko A. (1999) Administrative of Justice in Poland. Institute of Justice, Oficyna Naukowa, Warszawa, p. 27.

[11] Act of 23 November 2002 on Supreme Court, JoL of 2002 No 240 item 2052 as amended.

There are particular courts provided for particular kinds of criminal proceedings. Thus:

1. Criminal proceedings take place before the penal courts (the I instance involves District and Regional Courts (for more serious offences), the II instance – Regional ones and Courts of Appeal),
2. Proceedings in juvenile cases are conducted before Family and Juvenile Courts (District Courts – in the I instance, Regional Courts – in the II instance),
3. Petty offence proceedings are heard by the District Courts – (Magistrates' Divisions) – in the Ist instance, by the Regional Courts – in the II instance.

In 2002, the number of penal and petty offence cases in the *District Courts* amounted to 1,535,000. That number included 445,000 petty offence cases. 1,464,000 cases were settled.

300,000 penal cases were filed at the *Regional Courts* (as the court of I instance) in 2002 (282,000 cases in 2001), while the number of II instance cases was 91,800 (92,200 cases in 2001).

The number of cases filed at the *Courts of Appeal* totalled 26,900 cases (growth of 1800 cases in comparison with 2001) and 26,700 cases were settled.

The Supreme Court accepted 7948 cassation penal cases filed, which is 571 more than in 2001.

2 Cases Brought to Court

2.1 "Normal" Cases

After preparatory proceedings are over, a prosecutor submits an indictment to the court and participates in the court proceedings as a party[12] thereto. A prosecutor is by no means „a host" of that stage of proceedings. A prosecutor's role consists in reading the indictment before the court and supporting the same. A prosecutor may also withdraw from the indictment; however it is not binding for the court. His/her part during the trial is to provide evidence as well as question witnesses and accused person.

In the cases prosecuted due to public accusation, it is mandatory for a prosecutor to participate in the trial. Only cases tried under a simplified procedure form exceptions. In certain cases a prosecutor is obliged to take part in the sitting of the court (e.g. while security measures are to be decided – Article 339 § 5 CPC).

When judicial proceedings are closed, a prosecutor, as a public attorney, takes a stance as to the court proceedings and presents his final conclusions as to guilt and punishment.

In 2002 prosecutors filed 391,500 penal cases accompanied by their indictments.

A prosecutor takes part in appeal proceedings through certain legal measures submitted to the Court and is present thereat. As a party to the proceedings, he is vested in ordinary measures of appeal.

In the Polish system of means of review, there are ordinary and extraordinary measures. Appeal and complaint make ordinary measures. The purpose of appeal is to appeal against the Ist instance sentence (i.e. to the District or Regional Court), while complaint serves the purpose of challenging the court decisions and orders excluding issue of a judgement, against a decision on security measure or other acts (like detention, way of searching). A Court of Appeal is the appropriate authority at that stage.

In 2002, the prosecutors appealed against about 21,000 court judgements. Prosecutors' appeals referred to 23,393 people (including 21,145 appeals against judgements of District Courts, and 2248 against Regional Courts' judgements).

Prosecutors also request that the Attorney General appeal for cassation (an extraordinary measure of appeal) to the Supreme Court.

2.2 The Special Instruments Aimed at Simplifying Criminal Proceedings

The *special instruments* aimed to simplify criminal proceedings include:

1. Conditional discontinuance of criminal proceedings;
2. Mediation;
3. A prosecutor's request for passing a judgement without conducting a trial;
4. Voluntary submission to penalty;
5. Simplified proceedings;
6. Penal order proceedings;
7. Proceedings upon private accusation.

The purpose of the above-mentioned procedures is to reduce "normal" criminal proceedings, strict requirements and formality of "normal" criminal proceedings. These procedures include the ones that lead to eliminating a stage of trial and/or a sentence as well as those simplifying the rules of trial course. Some of them are included in the CPC in special proceedings, namely simplified proceedings, proceedings in private accusation cases and penal order proceedings.

Conditional Discontinuance of Penal Proceedings

Table 1. Conditional Discontinuance of Penal Proceedings (Number of PPS Requests in 2000–2002)

	2000	2001	2002	2003
PPS requests	7,091	7,133	7,578	8,223

Conditional Discontinuance of Penal Proceedings breaks a normal course of the preparatory proceedings in this case. Such discontinuance releases the perpetrator from criminal punishment. It is the court that may conditionally discontinue the proceedings, though, in case of preparatory proceedings, upon the prosecutor's request (Article 336 § 1 CPC). The court may order discontinuance of the proceedings provided the guilt and noxiousness of the act are of low degree to society, the circumstances of offence perpetration are unquestionable, the perpetrator is not a persistent offender and may be presumed not to commit an offence again. The penalty faced by the perpetrator due to the imputed offence should not exceed 3 years' imprisonment. However, in the event of positive mediation (e.g. the perpetrator has redressed the injury), this limit is increased to 5 years.

Until 1998, the PPS could conditionally discontinue the investigation. Annually the average number of such drops was about 20,000.

Under the new regulations of 1998, the PPS can only send the proposal of conditional discontinuance to the court (Table 1.).

In 2002, conditionally discontinued penal proceedings, in the I instance courts, was concerned with 37,093 persons.

2.3 Mediation

Table 2. Mediations in 2000–2004

	2000	2001	2002	2003	2004
Total number of mediations	771	786	1,021	1,858	3,569
Number of positive mediations	481	471	597	1,108	2,123

Mediation is not too frequently applied in criminal proceedings, although a high increase is to be observed in the last years. In 2002 there were 1,021 mediations, i.e. a 32 % increase compared to 2000. In 2004 the number of mediations increased fivefold compared to 2000. Mediations ending in agreement (positive mediation) account for almost 60 %.

Mediation is a relatively new instrument in Polish criminal law (Article 23a CPC). A criminal case may be transferred for mediation by a prosecutor in the preparatory proceedings and by the court in the court proceedings. Both the accused and the injured party may request mediation or agree to the same. A mediation procedure should not last longer than 1 month and the time of mediation is not included in the preparatory proceedings.

Positive mediation (reconciliation of the parties: the perpetrator and the victim, injury redressing or reconciliation of the way of redressing) may lead to conditional discontinuance of criminal proceedings and does lead to discontinuance of proceedings upon private accusation (Article 492 CPC).

Positive mediation brings more opportunities with it for conditional discontinuance of proceedings. It may be taken into consideration while deciding on extraordinary mitigation of punishment (Article 60 § 2 PC) as well as on conditional release from serving the full sentence (Article 162 § 1 EPC).

2.4 A Prosecutor's Request for Passing a Judgement without Conducting a Trial

A prosecutor's request for passing a judgement without conducting a trial (Article 335 CPC) is a relatively new institution in the Polish criminal proceedings; it was introduced in 1997. It involves a prosecutor's request for judgement to be rendered without hearing the case included in the charge sheet, provided that the offence described in the charge sheet threat of a penalty of up to ten-year imprisonment. This must be agreed with the accused. Such an agreement also refers to punishment. Then, it is conditioned by the fact that the circumstances of crime commitment have raised no doubts and the goals of the criminal proceedings have been attained.

Recently, prosecutors have been submitting requests for a sentence without a trial more and more often. In 2002, the number of such requests (9,194) doubled compared to 2000. A recent study indicates that some 30 % of cases in which PPS submitted such a request were related to driving motor or other vehicles under the influence of alcohol or drugs12.

2.5 Voluntary Submission to Penalty

Table 3. Voluntary Submission to Penalty in 2000–2004

Voluntary submission to penalty	2000	2001	2002	2003	2004
Number of suspect's applications	25,226	33,285	36,256	42,402	111,522
Number of PPS' requests	4,789	6,222	9,160	18,054	57,484
Number of court's decisions	28,566	36,876	42,242	53,864	137,678

Voluntary submission to punishment (Article 387 CPC) is a new institution, too. It is the opportunity given to the accused to file a request to the court for passing a judgement without hearing of evidence. The accused should submit such a request at the main trial by the time of conclusion of the first hearing of all the persons accused. The accused may do so when being charged with a misdemeanour only, not with a crime. Such a request may be accepted if there are no objections to it on the part of prosecutor or of the injured person, the circumstances under which the offence was committed remain unquestionable and the aims of proceedings have been attained.

Like in the case of prosecutors' requests for sentences without a trial, there are more and more cases when the accused file their petitions for sentences without hearing of evidence. In 2002, there were 36,256 such petitions, i.e. a 44 % in-

[12] Jankowski M, Ważny A.: *Instytucja dobrowolnego poddania się karze (art. 387 k.p.k.) i skazania bez rozprawy (art. 335 k.p.k.) w świetle praktyki. Rezultaty badań ogólnopolskich.* [The practice of voluntary submission to penalty and conviction without a trial. Nationwide study results], photocopied materials, IWS, Warsaw 2005, p.6.

crease compared to 2000. In 2004, the number of such petitions filed by the accused grew to 111,522, i.e. over four times compared to 2000. During the same period (2000 to 2004), the number of prosecutor's requests increased from 4789 to 57,454, that is twelve times.

In 2002, the number of the relevant court decisions grew to 42,242, i.e. an almost 50 % increase compared to 2000. In 2004, the number of such decisions increased five times compared to 2000.

2.6 Simplified Proceedings

The simplified procedure provides for a considerable reduction of criminal proceedings. In a simplified procedure the court hears the cases in which inquiry proceedings have been conducted or when the inquiry was completed in the form of investigation, i.e. when it lasted for more than two months (Article 469 CPC in conjunction with Article 325i CPC). The role of a prosecutor in such proceedings is limited (after 2003 it became even more limited)[13]. It is not only a prosecutor who may appear before the court as public attorney, but also another authorised institution (e.g. Forest Guard or Commercial Inspection). Neither a prosecutor nor another attorney is obliged to participate in trial or at a court sitting. The prosecutor's failure to appear does not impede the course of a trial or sitting (session). In the prosecutor's absence, the indictment is read out by a clerk.

2.7 Penal Order Proceedings

Table 4. Penal Order Proceedings in 2000–2004

	2000	2001	2002	2003	2004
Number of cases	18,860	18,052	17,795	58,530	82,246
Number of objections	4,647	4,349	4,277	13,057	21,338

Penal order proceedings are conducted by I instance court, unless objected to by the accused or the victim. In case of objection, normal proceedings are carried out. In 2002, there were 17,795 requests for instituting penal order proceedings, a slight decrease (by some 5 %) compared to 2000; objections were raised in a quarter of cases. In 2004, the number of penal order proceedings increased four times compared to the annual figures in 2000 to 2002, the objection rate being similar.

2.8 Proceedings upon Private Accusation

Table 5. Proceedings upon Private Accusation in 2000–2004

	2000	2001	2002	2003	2004
Number of incoming cases	21,059	16,655	19,167	18,688	18,278
Number of cases settled	21,389	18,698	18,725	18,698	18,081

[13] Article 17 of CPC.

Proceedings upon private accusation (Article 485 to Article 499 CPC) may be instituted only in cases against private accusatorial offences (like slander, infringement of personal inviolability, slight impairment of body). The proceedings are instituted upon an indictment lodged by the injured person with the court and the rules related to simplified proceedings are then applied thereto, which brings with it the following simplifications in the court procedure:

- An indictment may be in a simplified form (may be limited to identification of the person accused, the act imputed and the evidence making grounds for the indictment);
- May be carried out in the absence of the accused;
- Any break in trial may not be longer than 21 days;
- A trial is preceded by conciliatory session conducted by the court;
- Unjustified absence of the private prosecutor or his/her attorney at the conciliatory session is regarded as dropping the charge, and the court proceedings are discontinued;
- The proceedings are discontinued in the event of reconciliation of the parties.

In the case of offences prosecuted upon private accusation, the state prosecutor shall institute proceedings, or intervene in proceedings previously instituted, if the public interest so requires (Art. 60 §1 CPC).

In 2002, there were 19,167 cases filed with the courts upon private accusation, i.e. a ca. 9 % decrease compared to 2000. In 2004, the number of such cases dropped by a further 5 %.

3 Cases Dealt with by the Prosecution Service

3.1 Sanction

In the criminal proceedings, prosecutors are not authorised to impose penalty or other sanctions on the perpetrator of a forbidden act. Nor do they have such rights in other kinds of proceedings like in petty offence or juvenile cases. As an exception, they may inflict a penalty for breach of order i.e. pecuniary fines up to PLN 3,000 upon a witness, a court-appointed expert, translator or consultant who failed to appear at their call. A prosecutor may also order detention or compulsory appearance of a suspected person (Article 247 CPC) and a witness, sometimes a court-appointed expert, translator and consultant. In the course of preparatory proceedings, a prosecutor may submit a request to the District Court for arresting above said persons for the time of 30 days at utmost (Article 285–290 CPC).

3.2 Conditional Disposal

In the preparatory proceedings, the state prosecutor may prepare and send the request to the court on conditional discontinuance of proceedings, instead of an indictment (see p. 2.3). The state prosecutor may indicate suggested probation period, obligations to be imposed on the accused and a motion regarding supervision[14]. Such a motion should be accompanied with a list of harmed people with their addresses indicated.

3.3 Drop

A prosecutor may discontinue preparatory proceedings upon consideration of the circumstances provided under Article 17 CPC[15].

Article 17 of CPC Criminal proceedings shall not be instituted, or, if previously instituted, shall be discontinued, when:

1. the act has not been committed, or there have not been sufficient grounds to suspect that it has been committed,
2. the act does not possess the qualities of a prohibited act, or when it is acknowledged by law that the perpetrator has not committed an offence,
3. the act constitutes an insignificant social danger,
4. it has been established by law that the perpetrator is not subject to penalty,
5. the accused is deceased,
6. the prescribed statute of limitations has lapsed, or
7. criminal proceedings concerning the same act committed by the same person has been validly concluded or, if previously instituted, is still pending,
8. the perpetrator is not subject to the jurisdiction of the Polish criminal courts,
9. there is no complaint from an entitled prosecutor,
10. there is no permission required for prosecuting the act, or no request to prosecute from a person so entitled, unless otherwise provided by law,
11. other circumstances precluding such proceedings occur.

In 2002, prosecutors discontinued 969,000 cases, including 682,000 due to unknown offenders (70 %).

3.4 Drop „Public Interest"

In the Polish criminal legislation, a public interest principle does not form a prerequisite of absolute or conditional discontinuance of proceedings. A situation that may occur when a prosecutor participates in the private accusatorial procedure is exceptional. A prosecutor may discontinue a procedure against an act under private accusation if he/she finds no public interest in the prosecution being continued.

[14] See: Article 67 PC.

[15] Article 17 of CPC.

4 PPS Structure

The PPS is located in the structure of the Ministry of Justice. The PPS is headed by the Attorney General. The function is exercised – *ex lege* – by the *Ministry* of Justice. The Minister – as Attorney General – controls the prosecutor service in person or through his deputies. One of the deputies holds the position of national prosecutor and is in head of the National Prosecutor's Office.

The PPS consists of the following units:

- National Prosecutor's Office, headed by National Prosecutor
- Appellate Prosecution Offices, headed by appellate prosecutors
- Regional Prosecution Offices, headed by regional prosecutors
- District Prosecution Offices, headed by district prosecutors.

The Prosecution Service – besides the Attorney General (and his deputies) and the National Prosecutor – includes prosecutors of common (public) and military organizational units of the Prosecution Service.

The prosecutors act according to the hierarchical subordination principle, nevertheless, they are self-dependent in performing their statutory duties.

The Law on PPS (1985, Article. 2 of Act of 20 June 1985 on Prosecutor's Offices[16]) constitutes the legal grounds for the PPS.

The Minister of Justice – Attorney General may give specific and general guidelines. These guidelines may also be given by the National Prosecutor, appellate and regional prosecutors, and they are binding. Service instructions and guidelines are passed to the performers in an official way, which means that a superior prosecutor, who gives such service instructions/guidelines, passes them to his direct inferior in hierarchy (according to the scheme: Attorney General → National Prosecutor → appellate Prosecutor → regional Prosecutor → district Prosecutor).

4.1 Appointment and Training

The following is obligatory to become a prosecutor: to receive an M. A. in Law (at university level) and two-and-half-year prosecutor's or judge's training completed with the respective examination. Appointment to the position of legal trainee takes place upon competitive selection. A legal trainee may be a full-time employee or non-employee (nowadays, the majority of legal trainees take their training outside full-time employment). It consists of theoretical and practical training. After examination, a legal trainee may be appointed an assessor and then, having performed his/her duties for a year or so, may be nominated to the post of a prosecutor. Promotion depends on assessment of the assistant's duty performance. There is no system of compulsory training courses for prosecutors and they are carried out as the needs arise.

[16] Uniform text: JoL of 2002 No 21 item 206 as amended.

Table 6. Number of Prosecutors (Full-time Equivalent)

	1993	1998	2002
Public prosecutors and assessors	4,152	5,013	5,082
Trainee	670	448	95*
Total	4,822	5,461	5,177

* This number covers only full time equivalent trainees. Majority of legal trainees take their training outside full time employment.

In 2004, there were 376 prosecution offices, namely 10 appellate, 44 regional and 322 district offices, which employed the force of 5,225 prosecutors, 586 assessors, 156 trainees, 3,754 clerks and 1,422 other employees. A great majority of them (4,970) were employed by regional and district prosecution offices.

According to European Judicial Systems 2002 (CEPEJ), the number of prosecutors in Poland was relatively high, like in other former communist countries. The number of prosecutors per one million of people was 145 in Poland, and was lower than in Latvia (282), Lithuania (251) and Ukraine (211), though higher than in Hungary (138), Slovakia (135) and Czech Republic (105), as well as EU countries, e.g. Portugal (113), Denmark (105), Germany (74) and Sweden (73). Among EU countries, the rate was higher only in Liechtenstein (207), but it is hardly comparable owing to the country size[17].

4.2 Control of PPS Case-ending

The actions undertaken by prosecutors, decisions on discontinuance of preparatory proceedings included, are subject to procedural inspection and official supervision.

Procedural inspection consists in considering complaints submitted by parties to the proceedings as to decisions on discontinuance of preparatory proceedings. That inspection is exercised by a prosecutor directly superior to the one who has taken such a decision. Evaluation is made whether sufficient evidence has been gathered for taking a decision as to the merits of the case and whether the material has been correctly assessed by the prosecutor that decided on discontinuance of the proceedings. The superior prosecutor may reverse the decision challenged and order additional procedural actions. The superior prosecutor's legal views and instructions as to further proceeding, which are included in the content of decision taken up as a superior instance, are binding for inferior prosecutors.

If the superior prosecutor refused to accept a complaint, the latter is passed to the competent court for trying.

An additional measure of procedural inspection of correctness of the decision on discontinuance of preparatory proceedings conducted against a person is to be found in the Attorney General's right to reverse a legally valid decision on discontinuance of proceedings, which is provided under Article 328 CPC if such a dis-

[17] European Judicial Systems 2002. Facts and figures on the basis of a survey conducted in 40 Council of Europe Member States. Council of Europe, Strasbourg 2005, p. 57.

continuance of proceedings is found unjustified. The Attorney General may not exercise that right if the decision on discontinuance of proceedings has been upheld by a court. Then, 6 months after the date upon which the decision on discontinuance of proceedings becomes final, the Attorney General is entitled to reverse it or change it to the suspected person's benefit only.

Official supervision ranges farther as it includes not only the result of preparatory proceedings but also whether the acts performed by a given prosecutor are correct and completed in time. It is a superior prosecutor who exercises such supervision – either *ex officio* or following a complaint submitted by a person concerned or upon request of another authorized institution (like the Commissioner for Civil Rights Protection). Results of such supervision may be limited to the service's affairs (evaluation of the prosecutor's work in the given proceedings). However, they may include procedural instructions (like a request to conduct evidence-oriented operations in order to check the circumstances justifying reopening or resumption of discontinued preparatory proceedings).

There is a system of visiting and inspection performed by a prosecutor of a higher grade. The purpose of visiting or inspection is to find out whether the visited prosecutor's office staff as a whole makes correct decisions, in time, in the course of preparatory proceedings.

Promotion of a given prosecutor depends, to a large degree, on evaluation of his work, which is made in the course of visiting or inspection, as well as of his procedural decisions made or approved, which are evaluated in the course of considering procedural appellate means against his decisions.

A procedural inspection exercised by a superior prosecutor does not refer to the indictments and requests passed to courts. Those actions may be evaluated under the service supervision.

The following are regarded to be flagrant violation by a prosecutor:

1. significant and culpable lengthiness of proceedings,
2. unjustified request for court's imposition of preliminary detention or unjustified decision taken up by the prosecutor in reference to preliminary detention,
3. unjustified decision ending the preliminary proceedings,
4. groundless indictment,
5. evidently wrongful request as to the penalty extent,
6. failure to appeal against an obviously unfair judgement,
7. culpable failure to fulfil a superior's order as to the substance or to keep within strict time boundaries[18].

Such breach of duties may cause a prosecutor to face disciplinary action.

[18] § 59 paragraph 2 of the Regulations of official duties performing in the organizational units of the Prosecution Service (Ordinance of 11 April 1992 of Minister of Justice).

4.3 PPS Jurisdiction and Further Fields of Activity

The PPS is charged with the responsibility to guard the observance of the rule of law and enforcing the prosecution of crimes. A public prosecutor conducts preparatory proceedings in criminal cases and supervises those carried out by the police. He also appears as attorney for the state before courts.

The prosecutors also perform other functions, namely, *inter alia*, they institute civil law actions in criminal cases and may join civil cases to act as auxiliary claimants.

The other duties entail the following:

- appealing to the court against administrative decisions which violate the law,
- coordinating prosecution by other state authorities.

Prosecutor's participation in civil law proceedings is regulated by the Code of Civil Procedure (CCP). A prosecutor may request the institution of proceedings in any case and participate in any pending proceedings if it is, in his/her opinion, required by protection of law and order, citizens' rights and public interest. In non-property cases of family law, a prosecutor may file a suit only in the situations provided under the Act (Article 7 of CCP). A prosecutor may join the proceedings at any stage thereof. There are no connections between him/her and any of the parties. A prosecutor may submit declarations and requests he/she regards purposeful and refer to the facts and evidence to prove them. As soon as a prosecutor reports his/her participation in the proceedings, he/she must be delivered procedural writs, notifications about the time of sittings and trials as well as court judgements. A prosecutor may appeal against any court judgement subject to measure of appeal. The time given to the parties for appeal against the court judgements is binding for the prosecutor, too (Article 60 CCP). CCP provides for notification of a prosecutor about institution of action and time of trials in cases for invalidation of marriage (Article 449 § 1 CCP), denial of paternity or invalidation of fathering a child (Article 457 CCP) as well as of filing a request and of the dates of sittings in cases for taking away a person under parental authority or custody (Article 598^1 § 1 CCP). A prosecutor is obliged to participate in the proceedings for incapacitation (Article 546 § 2 CCP) and take part in the trial referring to recognition of a foreign court judgement (Article 1148 § 2 CCP).

In administrative proceedings, a prosecutor has the right to request a competent public administration institution to institute legal proceedings in order to eliminate unlawfulness (Article 182 of the Code of Administrative Procedure). A prosecutor is entitled to participation at any stage of proceedings in order to ensure lawfulness of the proceedings and settlement of the case as well as to appeal against the final decision if the Code or special provisions provide for resumption of proceedings, declaration of invalidity of a decision, or revocation or change of the same. A prosecutor may participate in any proceedings pending before an administrative court as well as file a complaint, cassation complaint, complaint or appeal for resumption of proceedings if it is, in his/her opinion, required for the protection of law and order, or citizens' or human rights, or public interest. In such an event, a prosecutor has the rights of a party (Article 8 of Act of 30 August 2002 on proceedings before administrative courts).

Activities that are not related to criminal prosecution makes up a small part of prosecutor's duties; nevertheless, as it comes out of the foregoing examples, a prosecutor's role in a civil or administrative procedure is undoubtedly considerable.

4.4 Case flow in PPS in 1993–2004

Table 7. Case Flow in PPS in 1993–2004

	Incoming cases	Total PPS output	Pending cases	Delays (pending cases as % of incoming cases)
1993	1,033,893	1,032,103	87,906	8.5
1994	1,127,738	1,113,923	101,721	9.0
1995	1,210,440	1,206,562	105,599	8.7
1996	1,139,623	1,145,218	100,004	8.8
1997	1,253,613	1,248,873	104,752	8.4
1998	1,298,860	1,291,089	106,332	8.2
1999	1,372,661	1,366,572	112,421	8.2
2000	1,496,432	1,481,925	126,928	8.5
2001	1,651,115	1,643,795	134,248	8.1
2002	1,644,763	1,647,246	131,776	8.0
2003	1,667,556	1,680,090	119,244	7.2
2004	1,696,880	1,699,203	117,133	6.9

These figures present only general statistics and by their very nature do not reflect the actual quality of the PPS output. It is worth noting that following the transformation of 1989 or even earlier in the eighties there was a major change in the types and structure of crime. The police public prosecution service and courts had to face business fraud and group crime (sometimes showing symptoms of organised crime) often of international range. Poland became the first destination and then a connection for organised traffic in drugs, stolen cars, etc. There was also a significant increase in common offences, such as robbery, theft, burglary and theft from car; they were often committed using complex techniques and methods, so sometimes considerable experience and costly technologies were required to apprehend the offenders.

The growing number of investigations/inquiries conducted by the police and public prosecution service led to Polish courts being overloaded with the ever growing number of criminal cases. In the face of these difficulties, legislative and organisational changes were attempted in Poland, the most important reform being the new Penal Code, Criminal Procedure Code and Executive Criminal Code passed in 1997.

5 Cases Dealt with by the Police

5.1 Police Structure

There is only one police force (Policja) in Poland, which operates under the police act of 6 April 1990. They report to the Ministry of Internal Affairs and Administration and are a uniformed and armed force serving society. Their task is to protect the safety of the people and to ensure public security and order (art. 1 of the Police Act). Police units are organized territorially: the Chief Police Headquarters (with Chief Police Commander) provincial headquarters, district headquarters, and local police stations.

In 2004 there were 100,223 policemen employed (including 10,581 women – i.e. 11 %). The police also employed 19,939 civil workers.

5.2 Disposals and Drops

Police may, subject to prerequisites under Article 17 CPC occurring, issue a decision on the discontinuance of an inquiry, which, however, must be approved by a prosecutor. The police may also discontinue proceedings if the particulars acquired in the course of proceedings fail to be sufficient for the detection of a perpetrator. The same right of the police refers to discontinuance of investigation. The police, in principle, conduct inquiry which is characterised by less formality.

The police may neither conditionally discontinue proceedings nor may they file a request to the court for such discontinuance. Such a request, as we have pointed out above, may be submitted by a prosecutor only.

6 Alternative procedural forms

In the Polish penal system alternative procedural forms do not exist. It means that *it* is not possible to resolve the "case" without the court. Every criminal case (when the offender is known) goes through the "chain" – police/PPS and court[19].

[19] Some practitioners consider mediation as "alternative" form.

7 PPS Function in Investigative Proceedings

7.1 Police Competence

Penal Proceeding

An investigation is carried out by the police unless it is carried out by the prosecutor. It is mandatory for the prosecutor to carry out an investigation in manslaughter cases or when it concerns a judge, police officer or a functionary of the Internal Security Agency (Article 309 CPC). If the prosecutor has instituted an investigation, he may charge the police with the proceedings in whole, to a certain extent or with particular actions to be performed (he may not assign the whole investigation to the police if it is mandatory for a prosecutor to carry it out).

In the course of an inquiry, the police perform all and any procedural acts (hearing witnesses and those suspected, inspection, appointment of court experts except psychiatric consultants taking up decisions as to factual proofs and alike). Some of those acts need to be approved by a prosecutor (such as confiscation, searching) or by court (eavesdropping and phone call recording). A decision on ending the proceedings requires a prosecutor's approval.

Police is also entitled to carry out an investigation; however a prosecutor may carry out an investigation instead of the police owing to the importance or complexity of the case.

In the Polish system of criminal proceedings, the Police can gain the competencies reserved for the PPS only in exceptional circumstances (e.g. the need for an urgent search in case of emergency); however, in any such cases they are supervised by a prosecutor (Art. 220 § 3 of the Code of Criminal Proceedings).

The rights of the Police include seeking proofs through operational actions (inquiry at the place of happening and around).

Proceedings in Petty Offence Cases

The Police's powers in petty offence proceedings are considerably wider as it is up the Police to conduct explanatory proceedings, to file requests for punishment to the Magistrates' Courts and to appear before those courts as a public attorney. In certain cases the police officers may inflict fines in the form of tickets namely when:

1. a petty offender is caught *in flagrante delicto* or directly after commitment of the same
2. a police officer finds *absente reo* as an eyewitness that a petty offence has been committed or with a measurement or control instrument and there is no doubt as to the perpetrator[20].

As a rule a fine imposed with a ticket may not exceed the amount of PLN 500 (about Euro 125).

[20] Art. 97 § 1 of Code of Petty Offences Proceedings (CPOP).

A prosecutor has powers to take an active part in petty offence proceedings, however, they are not made use of in practice.

7.2 Prosecutor Service Relationship with the Police

The Prosecutor Service and the police are really independent institutions. In criminal proceedings the police are supervised by the PPS with respect to the investigations and inquiries requested by the latter.

Police immediately notifies the prosecutor of an offence if it is obligatory for the prosecutor to carry out investigation (as opposed to inquiry) in such an offence case. Generally speaking the investigation is obligatory in case of serious offences like manslaughter or when a judge or police officer is a suspected offender (Article 309 CPC). Although regulations do not require it, the police inform a prosecutor about instituting inquiry proceedings by sending a copy of the decision on institution thereof.

The police inform a prosecutor of the occurrence that may prove a serious crime committed against life. A prosecutor carries out inspection of the *locus in quo* and participates in the autopsy of a victim.

District prosecution offices that conduct and supervise the majority of preparatory proceedings are divided into divisions or sections according to *ratione materiae* or *ratione loci* jurisdiction. In practice, in every prosecution office there are divisions (sections) dealing with supervision over inquiries conducted by particular police stations (territorial criterion), divisions (sections) supervising inquiries in more complicated cases which are conducted by the police district headquarters, as well as investigation divisions (sections) (territorial criterion) that conduct their so called "own investigations" and supervising those entrusted to the police in whole or in part.

A prosecutor of the inquiry division supervises an inquiry assigned to him at random as a rule and conducted by the police station under supervision of that particular prosecution office. S/he is also supposed to supervise the procedural activities of the police entity under supervision in broad terms – like proceedings including material evidence.

Cases in the divisions involved in complicated inquiries and investigations are assigned to the prosecutors indicated by their names. A prosecutor's co-operation with the Police is closer in the inquiries and investigations entrusted to the police. All the operations are carried out according to the schedule prepared by the prosecutor. A great many activities (not only those statutorily reserved for the prosecutor's competence) are performed by the prosecutor him/herself (like hearing the victim).

In all proceedings (both in an investigation and in an inquiry) a prosecutor may reserve particular procedural acts for him/herself (like hearing a witness, giving a decision on submission of charges and hearing the suspect).

Re-opening and resumption of discontinued proceedings with the force of law may take place only upon a prosecutor's decision (Article 327 § 1 and 2 CCP).

7.3 Command Chain in Investigations/Guidelines

In the course of preparatory proceedings it is necessary for the police to fulfil the prosecutor's instructions in reference to the particular proceedings. A prosecutor supervising proceedings may:

- get acquainted with the intents of the person carrying the proceedings out, indicate the course of action and give orders in that respect
- request materials gathered in the course of proceedings to be presented to him/her
- participate in activities carried out by those conducting the proceedings, carry them out in person or take over the case for his/her own performance
- make decisions orders or instructions as well as change and reverse the decisions and orders issued by the person conducting the proceedings.

Prosecutor's instructions and guidelines are, as a rule, realized by a police officer conducting proceedings or performing particular tasks. In the event that the police officer fails to satisfy the prosecutor's instructions, the latter may report the fact to the police officer's superior and request disciplinary proceedings against the police officer and the results of the same to be reported to him/her.

It must be stressed that a police officer conducting proceedings is subordinated in a double way: to the prosecutor supervising the proceedings and to his superior. Nevertheless, it is always the prosecutor who finally decides on the course of the proceedings.

7.4 Control/Information

A prosecutor may, at any time, inspect the files of preparatory proceedings conducted by the police. In consequence, there may be instructions and orders given as mentioned above. At any time a prosecutor may request information on the course of proceedings.

7.5 Final Decision

Either the police or prosecutors are to decide on discontinuance of the preparatory proceedings. If such a decision is made by the police it must be approved by a prosecutor.

In the cases, in which an investigation has been conducted, it is a prosecutor who prepares and files his indictment at the court. In inquiry cases, these are filed either by the police or a prosecutor who prepare the indictment. If prepared by the police, such an indictment needs to be approved by a prosecutor.

A request for discontinuance of proceedings due to the perpetrator's non-accountability or conditional discontinuance of criminal proceedings is prepared and filed by a prosecutor.

7.6 PPS Decision Requiring Judicial Approval

In the Polish legal system there are no prosecutor's decisions requiring the court's approval. The only exception is prosecutor's decision concerning telephone taps issued in urgent circumstances (in "normal" circumstances it is the court that issues such a decision).

Prosecutor's decisions ending the preparatory stage of criminal procedures are: refusal to institute preparatory proceedings and, on discontinuance of such proceedings, may be objected to at a court. The court is entitled to cancel such decisions and order the prosecutor to continue preparatory proceedings.

Other prosecutor's decisions which may have a complaint lodged against it to the court are:

- decision concerning the accused's assets freezing,
- decision concerning preventive measures (such as police surveillance and bail),
- decision concerning keeping witness' personal data secret.

8 Particular Issues

8.1 Victim Participation

A victim *ex lege* is a party to the preparatory proceedings. It is also up to the victim whether inquiry or investigation in cases against offences prosecuted upon request is to be instituted. During court proceedings, a wronged person may be a party only on condition that s/he becomes an auxiliary (private) prosecutor or civil law petitioner. When a wronged person is not a party, s/he is entitled to participate in the trial. The Court may also oblige such a wronged person to be present at the trial, in whole or in part, if it is found purposeful (Article 384 § 2 and § 3 CPC).

Until the court examination is started at the main trial, the wronged person may institute a civil law action against the accused (pecuniary claim resulting from offence commitment). In that event a penal court tries such a civil law action along with the criminal case. The prosecutor may either support the action so instituted by the wronged person or, in case of death of the civil law petitioner, institute such an action if required by the public interest (Article 64 CPC).

The wronged person may apply for damage caused to be redressed if no civil law action is instituted (in the event of a serious offence committed against health transport safety and alike) by the time the first hearing at the main trial is finished (Article 49a CPC).

A possible mediation in the course of penal proceedings also depends on the wronged person.

A wronged person, when it is a private person, functions self-dependently and directly in the criminal proceedings. If a minor or incapacitated, a wronged person's rights are exercised by a statutory representative or a person whose constant custody the wronged person is under (Article 51 §2 3 CCP). In any circumstances, the wronged person may act through an attorney.

In the recent years there have been intensified actions intended for implementation of the idea of restorative justice in the criminal policy system. As a result the wronged person's role has increased. It finds expression in the introduction of mediation to penal and juvenile proceedings[21]. Mediation depends on the wronged person in both kinds of the proceedings. A new punitive measure has also been introduced to the Criminal Code i.e. redress of damage (in the case of conviction for an offence of causing death, serious detriment to health, disturbance of health, etc.).

The Ministry of Justice, along with non-governmental organizations, has elaborated and started distributing a Charter of Victim Rights that, *inter alia,* contains a collection of domestic and international regulations related to the rights of crime victims. Within the Commissioner for Civil Rights Protection's Office a Plenipotentiary for Crime Victims has been appointed. In recent years, a number of due steps have been taken by non-governmental organizations, the Plenipotentiary for Crime Victims, Minister of Justice and the Police in order to sensitize the police officers and prosecutors to the victims' problems.

8.2 Particularities in Relation to Juveniles

Juvenile as a Perpetrator

In Poland a traditional model of conduct prevails in juvenile cases, in which the principles of diversion are hardly taken into consideration. Although the doctrine includes a postulate for diversion to be applied to a greater extent, in practice, the justice administration agencies keep resisting. One of the rare solutions in force which might be proof of diversion in relation to juveniles is the possibility that a family law judge can pass the case to the school or a social organization after explanatory proceedings are over.

The role of prosecutor in juvenile proceedings is limited compared to penal proceedings. As we have mentioned above, s/he is a party to such proceedings and at the pre-judicial stage (explanatory proceedings), a prosecutor is by no means a "host" in the case. The role of a host is played by a family judge. Penal proceedings pending make an exception. A juvenile delinquent in penal proceedings must have counsel for the defence appointed by the court. S/he must also have counsel for the defence appointed by the court in proceedings concerning juveniles (where a juvenile comes under the threat of adjudicating his/her placement in a juvenile detention centre).

---

[21] Several non-governmental organizations operating in the line of mediation (like The Polish Centre for Mediation) have been established. The Ministry of Justice has elaborated a list of selected domestic and international regulations related to the role of a victim i.e. Charter of Victim Rights and started promoting it among judges, prosecutors and police officers.

Juvenile as a Victim

Regarding a juvenile being the victim of an offence, his or her rights shall be exercised by the statutory agent. This concerns both, filing a notice of an offence or request for prosecuting and participation in penal proceedings and proceedings regarding juvenile offenders.

Where a juvenile is heard as witness and is under 15 years of age, his/her examination should be conducted, as far as possible, in the presence of a statutory agent or actual guardian. In cases concerned with offences against sexual liberty and decency, a wronged person who at the time of the commission of the relevant offence is under 15 years of age should be heard only once as a rule. The hearing should be conducted by the court with an expert psychologist attending the session (art. 185a § 1 and § 2 of CPC).

8.3 Particularities in Relation to Specific Sub-groups

Women

Women – Crime Perpetrators: In Poland like in other countries the number of female perpetrators is many times smaller than that of masculine ones. According to the court statistics in 2003, the number of female offender was 50,253 while for male offender it was 557,224. There are no differences as to the principles of criminal responsibility and policy of punishment imposed on female and male perpetrators. However, in practice, the justice administration agencies seem to be more tolerant towards women as crime perpetrators – for example, preliminary detention and mandatory penalty of imprisonment is more restrainedly applied in relation to women.

Women – Crime Victims: In the recent years under influence of the State organizations (like Commissioner for Civil Rights Protection and Plenipotentiary for Crime Victims) as well as NGOs (for Women's Rights Center in particular) have undertaken numerous activities to provide crime victims and women in particular with assistance:

- Chief Police Headquarters in agreement with the PARPA (The State Agency for Prevention of Alcohol Related Problems) has elaborated „A blue chart" procedure the purpose of which is documenting the acts of family violation in order to counteract the violation acts more effectively and present them as evidence in the prosecutor's and court's proceedings.
- "La Strada" Foundation Against Trafficking in Women has accomplished an all-over-Poland information campaign to sensitize the officers of the justice administration agencies and uniform service to the problem of extortive prostitution and trading in women.
- As to legislation projects: a bill on counteracting family violation has been presented to the Polish Parliament and the bill contains, *inter alia,* a regulation related to compulsory "isolation of the violent perpetrator" (restraining order).

- As to prophylaxis: the Police has supported numerous NGO's projects serving the purposes of attracting attention to the problem of violence and to the need of prevention of violence in relation to women. The Ministry of Justice takes part in conferences on counteracting violence in the family and efficient sanctioning of the perpetrators thereof.
- Pilot programs have been undertaken within the structure of police and prosecution service in relation to protection of women – rape and violence victims.

Mentally Disordered

Mentally Disordered Perpetrator: If any justified doubts as to the non-accountability of the accused are raised in penal proceedings, the accused must have a defence counsel. The prosecutor or the Court may appoint court experts in order to obtain their expertise on the accused person's mental condition. A psychiatric examination may be connected with observation in a suitable hospital. This is decided by the Court (upon the prosecutor's request).

If it is established that the suspected person has committed a crime under conditions leading to non-accountability and there are grounds for protective measures to be applied, as soon as the investigation is closed, the prosecutor files the case at the Court with his/her request for discontinuance of proceedings and application of protective measures (Article 324 § 1 CPC).

In that situation the prosecutor may not self-dependently discontinue investigations or inquiries, nor may s/he approve a decision on discontinuance of proceedings which was issued by another investigation or inquiry conducting authority.

If necessary, a prosecutor files a request at Court in order to prevent commitment of subsequent acts connected with that person's mental disease, mental handicap or alcohol or another intoxicant addiction (Article 93 and 94 CC), as well as, in order to obtain a court decision as to a protective measure on prohibition of holding certain positions, practicing certain professions, running certain business or driving motor vehicles (Article 99 § 1).

In 2002 the courts applied protective measures against 547 persons upon a prosecutor's request.

It is worth mentioning that a bill was passed in 1994 for the first time in Poland in reference to mental health[22]. Before that time psychiatric treatment (voluntary or compulsory) had been regulated by a basic act (Instruction of the Minister of Health).

Mentally Disorder Victim: There are no legal obstacles for a mentally ill person to take part in penal proceedings. In the case of such a person the laws provide some distinctive features to be taken into account e.g.: where there is a doubt about the mental condition of a witness, the level of his or her mental development, the ability to perceive or reproduce particular circumstances, etc., the court

[22] Act of 19 August 1994 on Protection of Mental Health, JoL No 11, item 355 with amended.

or the public prosecutor may order the witness's examination to be done with the participation of an expert physician or psychologist and the witness has no right to object thereto. Where a mentally ill person is legally incapacitated in penal proceedings then he should be represented by the statutory agent.

However, there is no regulation regarding penal proceedings which would oblige the court to assign counsel for the defence appointed by the court to the wronged mentally ill person. The latter, or his or her attorney, may, however, resort to defence based on "the right of the poor" in order to obtain counsel for the defence appointed by the court.

Foreigners

Foreigner – Perpetrator: The same rules are applied to the foreigners who commit crimes on the territory of Poland as to the Polish citizens. There are few norms referring to the foreigners provided under CPC. These are, *inter alia*, the solutions contained therein:

- The accused foreigner has right to a translation service free of charge, if he/she has no sufficient command of the Polish language (Article § 1 CPC),
- Delivery of the decision on presentation, supplementation or change of charges indictment or appeal able judgement, as well as, those ending the proceedings to the accused (Article § 3 CPC),
- Passing prosecution of a foreigner to the foreign country's competent Governmental agency or acceptance of a foreign country competent authority's request for prosecution of a foreigner (Article 590 § 1 item 4 CPC).
- Delivery of a person hunted for with a European arrest warrant from the territory of Poland in order to conduct penal proceedings or enforcement of sentenced imprisonment or another measure against that person which consists in deprivation of liberty (Article 607k. § 1 CPC) on the territory of another EU member country,
- Delivery of a foreigner sentenced to imprisonment by the Polish Court to the country s/he is a citizen of. It may refer to execution of the protective measure (Article 610 § 1 CPC),
- Extradition of a fugitive in order to conduct penal proceedings against that person or enforcement of the sentenced punishment or protective measure. A prosecutor hears such a foreigner and safeguards the evidence if necessary and then files a request in the case to the Regional Court (Article 602 § 1 and 2).

Foreigners – Victim: The same rules of penal procedure are applied with regard to a foreigner – victim of an offence as those applied with regard to a Polish citizen. If such a foreigner has no command of Polish – an interpreter should be provided. This should also be provided where the translation of a letter (writ) executed in a foreign language into Polish is required or, conversely, where it is necessary to acquaint the defendant with the contents of documents of examination of evidence (art. 204 § 1 p. 2 and § 2 of CPC).

Minorities

Minorities – Perpetrators: An Act on National and Ethnic Minorities and on Regional Language has been in force in Poland since 2005[23]. National and ethnic minorities are not singled out in penal proceedings and the same procedural rules are applied to the offenders originating from minorities as to other ones. Nor is a language of any minority used as the official one in penal proceedings. Therefore, no statistical data exist either on the crimes committed by the representatives of national or ethnic minorities or on the number of penal proceedings conducted against them. The Act on national minorities admits use of the minority language as an auxiliary one only before the commune administration agencies (provided that a given commune satisfies additional conditions like that of at least 20 % inhabitants belonging to the minority).

Minorities – Victims: No special (isolated) rules are applied to members of national or ethnic minorities – both offence victims and perpetrators. The same procedural rules are applied regarding such victims as those regarding all others.

9 Current Changes

9.1 Factual Changes

The system structure of the public prosecutor's office in comparison to the relevant system under socialism as well as the position of the public prosecutor's office amongst state organs have been subjected to essential change. The change regarding the role and position of the public prosecutor's office is based on the act amending the former Constitution (1989) and the amendment of the public prosecutor's office act (1990). In the newly-adopted solution, the General Public Prosecutor's Office does not exist and the Minister of Justice "performs the function" of the Attorney General (i.e. Public Prosecutor General).

In 1993 the system of public prosecutor's offices was adjusted to the system of law courts (appellate public prosecutor's offices were then established whose task was to conduct appeal and annulment proceedings).

The public prosecutor's position was enhanced by the establishment of the National Prosecutor's Office in 1996 as part of the top structure of public authorities. That was another step in adjusting the system of public prosecutor's offices to the structure of law courts. The National Prosecutor then became a deputy General Public Prosecutor. The introduction of the latter institution made it possible for the

[23] Act of 6 January 2005 on National and Ethnic Minorities and on Regional Language, JoL No 17, item 141. Pursuant to Article 1, the Act regulates questions related to preserving and developing cultural identity of national and ethnic minorities as well as preserving and developing a regional language, and the way of realization of the principle of equal treatment of people without regard to their ethnic origin, and determines the objectives and competence of the governmental agencies and territorial self-governments in that respect.

public prosecutor's office to be duly represented in proceedings before the Supreme Court and the Constitutional Tribunal.

The new Constitution of the Republic of Poland of 1997 lacks provisions regarding the rules and role of the public prosecutor's office. The no inclusion there of the rules of procedure of the public prosecutor's office is deemed as an indication of lessening of that institution's importance. Moreover, the dependence of the Attorney General (simultaneously holding the post of the Minister of Justice) from the executive authority provides no guarantee of independence of the public prosecutor's office from purely political influences.

A characteristic feature of the public prosecutor's office in Poland is its centralism, uniformity and hierarchic subordination as basic principles. A debate is now going on in Poland on the necessity to disconnect the public prosecutor's office from the Ministry of Justice.

The public prosecutors are independent in the discharge of their duties prescribed by law. However, limitations stemming from the rule of hierarchic subordination exist. It is because the public prosecutor is bound to follow instructions, directions and orders of his superiors. This limitation is not mitigated by the fact that the public prosecutor may request alteration of any instruction obtained or his exclusion from the performance of the act assigned or involvement in a given case. Such a solution should be deemed inadvisable. It is necessary to provide a legal guarantee and even more so – an actual, procedural guarantee for independence and autonomy of public prosecutors.

It should be acknowledged that the maintenance of the rule of legalism in the Polish system of penal proceedings law is advantageous from the social point of view including the issue of public security protection. This rule affects the number of criminal lawsuits conducted and workload of public prosecutors. Some degree of relief in the public prosecutor's work was the introduction to the CCP in 2003 with the right of the police to conduct inquiries. Up until then the police had a right to conduct investigations only on a given public prosecutor's order.

In order to prosecute criminals effectively new procedural institutions have been introduced such as the control and recording of conversations the anonymous witness, incognito witness and crown witness. Moreover, the police act has been amended by the introduction of new operational means (applied prior to the commencement of penal proceedings) such as: operational control and controlled purchase. Despite initial controversies concerned with the introduction of the above procedural institutions to the Code of Criminal Proceedings those institutions have lately been considered effectual particularly in fighting organized crime.

One of the weak points in the criminal justice system in Poland is the very long duration of penal and court proceedings, which is the reason for the increasing delays. New institutions have been introduced which simplify penal proceedings, i.e. mediation, a prosecutor's request for convicting judgment rendering without conducting a trial and voluntary submission to penalty.

The bodies concerned with penal prosecution and investigation are overburdened by the "doubling" evidential acts in penal proceedings. It is because proceedings before the court involve "repetition" of evidential acts which have earlier been affected in the preparatory proceedings. This is exemplified by repeat examination of witnesses. The rule of procedural directness might be adhered to by examination of witnesses only by the court – including those whose examination was applied for by the public prosecutor.

Characteristic for the Polish system of penal proceedings is the ongoing tendency to adjust procedural solutions to international standards. This regards among other things the guarantee of protection of procedural rights of victims of crimes. That tendency may be exemplified by the importance assigned to justice done by the way of redressing damages and compensational decisions. A national compensational fund is planned to meet that necessity.

Since 1993, upon ratification of the European Convention for Fundamental Freedoms and Human Rights, chances have arisen for the country's citizens to assert their rights before the European Court of Human Rights. Judicial decisions of that court are also of influence on legislative solutions regarding penal proceedings here. E.g., following the judgment in *Kudła v. Poland* (26.10.2001) the right of appeal by litigant parties has been introduced in cases of unjustified protracted ness of proceedings before the court. In Poland, as in other countries, most appeals lodged with the European Court of Human Rights concern violation of the Convention by neglecting the right to immediate and prompt adjudication of the case. It is not without influence upon attempts by both the public prosecutor's office and the courts to liquidate existing protracted ness.

9.2 De Lege Ferenda Proposals

In terms of improving the criminal justice system the following means have to be considered:

- to separate the Attorney General from the Ministry of Justice (and appointing by the Parliament rather than the president)[24];
- to introduce incentive systems (*inter alia* stabilise employment of judges and prosecutors by increase salaries and improvement of working conditions);
- to improve professional skills of prosecutors (training establishment of the Centre for Judge and Prosecutor Training);
- easier access to legal professions for graduates of law schools (especially to the Bar);
- to improve the management of courts and prosecution office (by hiring professional managers, to introduce a two-shift system);
- to establish a special prosecution force to combat organised crime and corruption;
- implement technical improvements (facilities, working conditions, IT systems, etc.);
- to introduce open disciplinary proceedings against public prosecutors.

[24] In a study conducted in 2004 by the Batory Foundation, some 80 % of the prosecutors backed the idea.

The Prosecution Service Function within the Swedish Criminal Justice System

Josef Zila

1 General

The main components of the Swedish judicial system are as follows: the judiciary (*Domstolsväsendet*), the public prosecution service (*Åklagarmyndigheten*), the police and the Swedish prison and probation service (*Kriminalvården*). As far as relations to the government are concerned, all these authorities fall under the Ministry of Justice. However, according to the Swedish constitutional tradition, all of the named parts of the judicial system are independent in relation to the government and they have no relations of subordination among themselves. What is meant by independence in this context is the fact that none of the named authorities may be directly controlled, in individual cases, through orders or instructions issued by the Ministry of Justice. The authorities are obliged to follow the law, but, applying the law, they act independently.

Even if the authorities, that are parts of the judicial system, are independent in the sense mentioned above, the relations within the individual authorities and, consequently, the real content of this independence is very different, with respect to the tasks of each one of the authorities and their structures. The strongest guarantees of independence prevail within the judiciary. The National Court Administration (*Domstolsverket*), which is the central administrative authority subordinated to the ministry of justice, has no possibility to influence the decision practice of the courts. There are strong guaranties of independence for every one of the judges on all levels of the judiciary. On the contrary, the other parts of the judicial system have more or less strict hierarchical structure. This is true especially for the Police organization, as well as the Swedish prison and probation service. The organization of the public prosecution service (PPS) is described in more detail below.

The structure of the most important part of the Swedish judicial system in criminal matters, the Judiciary, is very simple. Basically, all criminal cases start on the lowest level of the system, that is, in the District Courts (*tingsrätterna*). (There are a few exceptions of this rule, which occur very rarely in practice.) All District Courts decisions, except some of the procedural ones, may be appealed to the second instance, that is, to one of the six Courts of Appeal (*hovrätterna*). The decisions of the Courts of Appeal may be reviewed by the Supreme Court (*Högsta Domstolen*). However, the case will be reviewed by the Supreme Court only if this court gives a review permit. All parties in a criminal case, both the PPS and the opposite party, need review permit. There is a category of trivial cases in which an appeal to the Courts of Appeal requires a review permit as well.

There are not any specialized criminal courts in Sweden, for instance for juveniles, or for some category of offences.

The organization and geographical structure of the other elements of the judicial system don't correspond the organizational structure of the Judiciary. For instance, there are 63 District Courts in the country, but only 43 prosecution chambers (the lowest level of the PPS) and 21 police authorities (the lowest organizational level within the police). Whereas the judiciary is organized on three levels (corresponding to the three instances), the police and – since 2005 – also the PPS are structured into two levels.

The Swedish criminal law and criminal procedure law belong, basically, to the family of the European continental law. However, in comparison with the continental countries, the Swedish law shows some specific features.

The main source of the criminal substantial law is the Penal Code (*Brottsbalken*). However, there is a large number of criminal law provisions outside the Penal Code. These provisions are called the *special criminal law*. Any ideology behind the division of the criminal law into these two parts is impossible to find, the division is just a result of the legislative tradition.

What is more important is the fact that there is no categorization of offences (crimes) in Swedish criminal law. All violations of criminal law provisions are *brott*, that is *offences*, or *crimes* (the translation of the notion *brott* varies). It means, for instance, that speeding in road traffic is, legally, the same phenomenon as a murder.

Unlike the majority of European continental countries, in Swedish law no legally defined category of breaches of law outside the criminal law exists, as, for example, *Ordnungswidrigkeiten* in German law. First, approximately, since the 1970-ties, the Swedish legislator introduced a new way of sanctioning some kinds of violations of law outside the criminal law. These sanctions represent a very heterogeneous group. In doctrine, the notion *sanction fees* (*sanktionsavgifter*) have been established for this category of sanctions. Actually, this concerns administrative offences, prevailingly in the field of taxes, customs and some other fields. The procedure concerning this kind of infringements varies. In principle, it is a question about an administrative process. Sometimes, very rarely, the police or the PPS might be engaged, e.g. by sanctioning of illegal parking.

Thus, it is possible to state, in general, that the Swedish criminal law knows only one, unified notion of crime (*brott*), which includes all kinds of violations of the criminal law provisions, regardless of their seriousness.

The necessary instrument of differentiation between the trivial crimes on the one hand and the more serious or complicated crime on the other hand, which makes it possible to handle different kinds of crimes rationally, is criminal procedural law in Sweden. The main source of the criminal procedural law is the Code of Judicial Procedure (CJP) (*Rättegångsbalken*). Like the substantial criminal law, Swedish procedural law differs in some respects from what is usual in the European continental countries.

The most important specific features concerning Swedish procedural law, in comparison with other countries, may be summarized as follows:

- Both the PPS and Police, especially the prosecutors, are entrusted with considerable *judicial powers*, that is, with the powers to impose final sanctions for criminal offences.
- There is no specialization of judges in the criminal and civil matters respectively. In all the three instances, all judges deal with both criminal and civil cases.
- The criminal procedural code in Sweden is common for both criminal and civil procedure. The importance of this fact shouldn't be overestimated, because the distinction between the criminal and civil procedure has been made within the CJP, but a certain influence of this regulation on the nature of the criminal procedure is visible in practice.
- Unlike from a typical continental procedure, the Swedish criminal process has a distinctive adversial character. The judges are considerably less active during trial than, as far as I know, in a number of the European continental countries. In this respect, Swedish criminal procedure resembles the criminal procedure known in the common law countries more closely.

2 Structure of the Swedish Public Prosecution Service

2.1 Organization of the PPS

Since the 1 January 2005, a new organization of the PPS has been launched in Sweden. The PPS is still a hierarchically built organization, but in stead of three levels as before the reform, the new structure includes only two levels. At the top of the organization are the Prosecutor General and his Advice Council. One part of the Office of the Prosecutor General (4 Divisions) represents the second level of the PPS hierarchy, together with 4 Developing Centers. On the first, lowest level of the hierarchy, there are 43 Prosecution Chambers. The organization looks as follows:

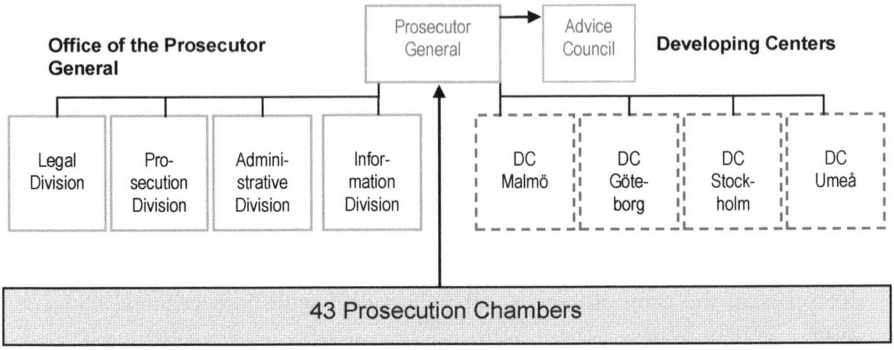

The different divisions, which are parts of the office of the Prosecutor General, fulfill different tasks: the Legal Division deals, among other, with international questions and carries out appeals to the Supreme Court. The Prosecution Division supervises the activities of lower prosecution authorities and reviews decisions of the lower prosecution authorities, which have been appealed by parties. The tasks of the other divisions are described by their names.

The main task of the four Developing Centers is a development of the methods for the prosecution of different types of offences, as well as a supervision of the activity of the Prosecution Chambers. Each of the four Centers focuses on a certain part of criminal law. For instance, the Developing Center located in Stockholm deals with offences against property, narcotic drug offences, tax offences, offences against state security including terror offences, and so on. Other Centers have other fields of activity.

Outside the described organizational structure, a specialized prosecution unit exists, the *Swedish National Economic Crimes Bureau* (*Ekobrottsmyndigheten*). The Bureau is partially subordinated to the Prosecutor General, but has its own budget. The staffs of the Bureau include prosecutors and police officers, as well as a number of specialists from different branches relevant to the with prosecuting of economic crimes. The Chief of the Economic Crimes Bureau has a similar position as the chiefs of the four Divisions belong to the Office of the Prosecutor General.

There is also another kind of special prosecutor in Sweden, the Custom Prosecutors. The Custom Prosecutors deal with minor offences committed in connection with border crossing. The more complicated or more serious custom offences are, however, prosecuted by ordinary prosecutors.

2.2 The Command Chain

The description of the organizational structure of the PPS above is important for an understanding of the hierarchy within the prosecution service as far as the subordination and reviewing of decisions of prosecutors is concerned. The legal regulation of these questions is very fractional and doesn't give any adequate picture of the situation in practice. The only legal provision concerning relations between different hierarchical levels within the prosecution service is Chap. 7 Sec. 5 CJP. Pursuant to this provision, the Prosecutor General, directors and vice-directors of the prosecution authorities (*överåklagare and vice överåklagare*) may undertake the measures that shall be performed by lower prosecutors.

Applied to the hierarchical structure of the Swedish prosecution service, a decision of a prosecutor on the lowest level (Prosecution Chamber) will be reviewed by a superior prosecutor (*överåklagare or vice överklagare*) who belongs to one of the Developing Centers. Which one of the Centers will review a particular decision depends on what kind of offence is concerned. As mentioned above, each of the Centers has a different field of activity.

Also decisions of the Developing Centers, which are results of a reviewing, may be appealed. The Prosecution Division of the Office of the Prosecutor General, which is, formally, on the same hierarchical level as the Development Centers, acts as the third instance.

The command chain from above should go downwards the same way. However, the subordination relations are not quite clear. They are not based on the law, but on internal instructions and practice.

It should be underlined that the description of the command chain, as well as the proceedings reviewing of decisions, concerns *procedural* subordination, that is, the subordination in the frame of the prosecution of offences according to procedural law. As far as administrative subordination is concerned, the role of the chiefs of the individual authorities has to be taken into account.

The supervision of the lower prosecution authorities in general is shared out between the Prosecution Division of the Office of the Prosecutor General and the Developing Centers. It is not quite clear to me how the fields of each of the supervising units are defined.

2.3 The Appointment and Training of Prosecutors

There are following categories of prosecutors in Sweden (Chap. 7 Sec. 1 CJP):

1. the Prosecutor General and Vice Prosecutor General (*Riksåklagare* and *Vice Riksåklagare*);
2. the Director and Vice Director of the Prosecution Service Authorities (*överåklagare* and *vice överåklagare*);
3. the Chief and Vice Chief Prosecutor (*chefsåklagare* and *vice chefsåklagare*)
4. the Chamber Prosecutor (*kammaråklagare*);

The Prosecutors sub 1) and 2) are appointed by the Government, the others by the Prosecutor General. The Government appoints – on the proposal of the Prosecutor General – also the Chief and Vice Chief of the Swedish National Economic Crimes Bureau (see above), who have the same rank as the Director (Vice Director) of the Prosecution Service Authorities. The appointments are not time limited.

The lowest rank in the hierarchy of prosecutors is the Chamber Prosecutor. To be appointed as a Chamber Prosecutor, the following preconditions have to be fulfilled:

1. Master of Law degree;
2. ca 2 year period of service in a law branch (it corresponds approx. to the German "*Referendiat*");
3. 9–12 month education as a prosecutor trainee (*åklagaraspirant*). The last named stage is, actually, an employment form within the Prosecution Service, but the appointment as a Chamber Prosecutor is possible after the mentioned period.

2.4 The Staff of the Public Prosecution Service

On the 31st December 2004, the Public Prosecution Service in Sweden had 1074 employees. 748 persons were prosecutors, the other administrative staff. One of the goals of the reorganization of the PPS which started 2005 has been a reduction of the administrative staff and a strengthening of the operative activity of the PPS. The figures for the end of the year 2004, that is, just before the new organization has been launched, will probably change.

2.5 The PPS Jurisdiction and further Fields of Activity

The prosecution of offences is the main and quite dominating task of the PPS. However, the PPS deals also with some other matters that don't directly concern criminal responsibility, even if they usually have some connection with criminality. For instance, the PPS administrates the prohibition to visit a certain person, the prohibition of carrying on a business, etc. Another important task of the PPS outside regular activity is in its administration of international legal aid in criminal law matters. This kind of activity represents approximately 2 percent of all matters handled by the PPS.

3 Cases Brought to Court

3.1 "Normal" Trial

Both public and private prosecution in court is possible. All offences, except the offences that are expressly excluded, fall within the domain of public prosecution. In practice, only very few offences are prosecuted by private persons. The private prosecution is, consequently, very rare, the public prosecution performed by the public prosecutors is quite dominant in practice. It should be mentioned, in this context, that the injured party, the victim, may, under certain circumstances, institute or take over prosecution in court (see below under section 8.). In such a case, the offence in question is still a publicly prosecutable offence, but the victim acts as a substitute for the prosecutor who has of some reasons refrained from prosecution of the offence. Also this kind of "private" prosecution in court appears very rarely.

According to the procedural law (Chap. 45 CJP), the PPS initiates the prosecution in court by filing a written application for a summons against the person to be charged. The application has to contain, among other things, an exact description of the criminal act, the means of evidence the prosecutor wants to invoke and what s/he wants to prove by each of the means.

The prosecution may not be changed. However, the prosecutor may extend the prosecution against the same defendant by including another act, if the court finds it appropriate. Further, it is not considered to be a change of prosecution, if the prosecutor narrows his action, changes the legal qualification of the act or alleges new circumstances in support of the prosecution. Before the judgment has been announced, the public prosecutor may withdraw the prosecution. He doesn't need consent of the court thereto.

The presentation of evidence is the responsibility of the parties. This rule is applied in that way, that the examination of the defendant, the victim and witnesses is performed by the public prosecutor and defense lawyer respectively. Also other persons may ask questions, especially the victim and its advocate, and, of course, the court. The cross-examination of the defendant, witnesses and experts occurs regularly. The written evidence may be read out by the court, or, if the parties consent to it and there are not any circumstances that prevent it, the written evidence may be taken at the main hearing without being read out.

After the evidence has been presented, the parties may state what they regard as necessary for the summation of their actions. In his plea, the public prosecutor normally proposes a sanction which the court should impose on the defendant if he will be found guilty of the charge. Such a proposal is not required by law, it is just practice.

An important task of the public prosecutor in the main hearing is presentation of the victim's private claim. On the request of the victim, the prosecutor is obliged to prepare and present in the court the private claim of the victim, based on the prosecuted offence, in conjunction with the prosecution. In practice, the private claims presented by the PPS occur in a majority of cases in which such claim comes in question. Normally, the court orders the defendant to pay damages.

Even if the public prosecutor is a party in the proceedings, his activity has to follow the principle of objectivity. It means, among others, that the prosecutor has to present, during whole procedure, both for the defendant aggravating and mitigating circumstances (Chap. 23 Sec. 4).

The public prosecutor may appeal to a superior court, even for a benefit of the defendant. As a rule, the same prosecutor, who has prosecuted the offence in the District Court, continues the prosecution even in the Court of Appeal. The proceedings in the Court of Appeal are, in principle, the same as those in the District Court, the role of the public prosecutor as well.

All parties have the possibility to appeal against the decision of the Court of Appeal to the Supreme Court. However, as mentioned above, the review permit given by the Supreme Court is required. Earlier, all parties needed a review permit, except the PPS. Recently (2004), the law was amended in that way that the PPS (only the Prosecutor General may prosecute in the Supreme Court) needs a review permit as well.

To illustrate, at least partially, the activity of the PPS as far as appeals are concerned, the following table can be presented.

Table 1. The Numbers of Appealed and Changed Judgments of the District Courts 2002

Who appealed the judgment	Number of appealed judgments to the Courts of Appeal	Changed judgments Number	Percent
The sentenced person	4,414	1,392	32
The PPS	585	391	67
Both the sentenced and PPS	952	542	57
Others	287	168	59
Information missing	22	5	23
Total numbers	6,259	2,498	40

(Sources: The Official Statistics of the National Court Administration)

3.2 Simplified Proceedings

It doesn't exist any kind of simplified criminal proceedings in court according to the Swedish law. Once the prosecution in court has been instituted, the proceedings follow the rules mentioned above. However, the fact whether the suspect has confessed to the offence or not, influences presentation of evidence. If the defendant has confessed the offence, the presentation of evidence will be simplified. But it is a matter of fact, not a question of different rules.

4 Cases Dealt with by the Prosecution Service

4.1 Sanctions Imposed by the PPS

As mentioned above, one of the specific features of the Swedish criminal procedure, in comparison with the other systems, is a wide judicial power of the PPS. By means of *penal order* (*strafföreläggande*) (Chap. 48 CJP), the PPS may impose a penalty on the suspects. Any approving of the penal order by a court is not required. Thus, the penal order represents, if accepted by the suspect, a final decision on criminal responsibility and, as such, it is recorded in the criminal register.

The penal order may be issued on condition that:

1. a person is suspect of an offence for which *fines* are included in the range of penalties;
2. the particular offence doesn't deserve a severer penalty than a fine or *conditional sentence* (The *conditional sentence* is a kind of sanction that may be

imposed on the suspect if the offence committed actually deserves imprisonment, but, of different reasons, a sanction which doesn't mean deprivation of liberty still may be applied. That is, the conditional sentence is an alternative sanction to imprisonment.).

Especially the second criterion, which means that the penal order may be based not only on the clear formal criteria as sub 1), but also on expectations in respect of what a probable penalty would be if it had been imposed by court in a trial, manifests the extension of the judicial power of the prosecution service in Sweden.

By means of a penal order, the prosecutor may also decide on a private claim of the victim, if the claim consists of a demand for payment of money or forfeiture of property, if this is motivated by the offence.

If a penal order is submitted to the suspect for approval, the suspect shall be informed that, if the order is not accepted, prosecution may be instituted after the expiration of the period specified. The requirement of an approval of the penal order by the suspect is interpreted in that way, that it is not necessary that the suspect had confessed himself guilty of the offence, but just the fact that s/he has committed the act.

4.2 Waiver of Prosecution

According to Chap. 20 Sec. 7 CJP, the PPS may decide on *waiver of prosecution* (*åtalsunderlåtelse*). The waiver of prosecution means that the PPS refrains from the further prosecution that is bringing the case to court, and stops the proceedings. No other action is taken.

The waiver of prosecution is possible of following reasons: (1) if it may be presumed that the offence would not result in a sanction other than a fine; (2) if it may be presumed that the sanction would be a conditional sentence and special reasons justify waiver of prosecution; (3) if the suspect has committed another offence and no further sanction in addition to the sanction for that offence is needed in respect of the present offence; (4) if psychiatric care or other kinds of special care are rendered.

Further, the prosecution may be waived also in other cases if, with respect to the circumstances, it is manifest that no sanction is required to prevent the suspect-from further criminal activity or the institution of a prosecution is not required for other reasons.

The prosecutor may waive prosecution also during the trial, if it shows circumstances that, had they existed or been known at the time of the prosecution, would have led to waiver of prosecution. However, prosecution may not be waived during trial, if the defendant objects.

A waiver of prosecution may be withdrawn if special reasons so require. Such a special reason could be, for instance, the fact that the suspect has committed another crime. On the other hand, it is not unusual in practice that the waiver of prosecution is applied repeatedly for new offences by the same person.

The institute *waiver of prosecution* has to be distinguished from a simple *drop of prosecution*. Whereas the waiver of prosecution may be applied only if the offence has been cleared up, that is, under such circumstances that prosecution in court could be instituted, the drop of prosecution is used if there are no preconditions for a successful prosecution in court, because of lack of evidence, or the act is not an offence, etc.

The waiver of prosecution is considered to be a successful prosecution of an offence and as such it is recorded in the criminal register.

4.3 Drop of Prosecution

Beside the means of penal order or waiver of prosecution, the PPS may finish proceedings of other reasons.

There are two provisions in the CJP regulating the drop of prosecution at this procedural stage. According to the Chap. 23 Sec. 4, if there is no longer reason for pursuing the investigation, it shall be discontinued. This rule is to be applied by both the PPS and police. The typical situations when "there is no longer reason for pursuing the investigation" are: (1) the prosecuted act is not an offence; (2) the act cannot be proved; (3) there is lack of evidence that the offence has been committed by a certain person. Other thinkable reasons for dropping of prosecution pursuant this provision are, for instance, the fact that the suspect died, the offence cannot be prosecuted because of the time of prosecution has expired, the victim has drawn back the accusation (for certain offences), etc.

This provision doesn't allow the dropping of prosecution for the reason that there is no public interest in prosecuting a particular offence.

The possibility to drop investigation with respect to the public interest follows from of the Chap. 23 Sec. 4a CJP. According to this provision, preliminary investigation may be discontinued (1) if continued inquiry would incur costs not in reasonable proportion to the importance of the matter and, at the same time, the offence, if prosecuted, would not lead to a penalty more severe than a fine, or (2) if it can be assumed that prosecution in court will not be instituted pursuant to the provision on waiver of prosecution, or on special examination of prosecution. Public interest is not named expressis verbis in this provision; however, public interest has to be considered the main ratio of the provision. The decision according to the Sec. 4a may be made by the PPS only, not by the police.

The lack of public interest on prosecution of some offences can be, actually, the reason for non-prosecution by the Swedish law. This issue, however, is not regulated within the procedural law, but the regulation is a part of substantial criminal law. There are a number of descriptions of offences in the Penal Code saying that the particular offence shall be prosecuted only if there is a *substantial public interest* in prosecution. The majority of the crimes of this category are property crimes, but also, for instance, the *negligent causing of bodily injury or illness* and other offences belong to this group.

In practice, this regulation means that prosecutor has discretion power to decide whether the prosecution of an offence will be initiated or not. If the prosecution has been initiated and it appears that the prosecuted offence belongs to this category, the prosecution may be dropped. If a prosecution concerning such an offence has been instituted in court, the prosecutor should state - anyway, in some cases - reasons for the prosecution, that is, he should motivate the existence of the substantial public interest in the particular case.

The following table illustrates the importance of the institutes described above in legal practice. The table shows how many penal orders and waivers of prosecution have been decided by the PPS in relation to the total number of crimes finally prosecuted by the courts, the PPS and the *police.*

Table 2. Number of Offences Finished by the Prosecuting Authorities 2002

All prosecuted offences	Courts: prosecution finished by		Prosecution service: prosecution finished by				Police: prosecution finished by	
	judgments	% of all o.	penal orders	% of all o.	waiver of prosecution	% of all o.	summary fines	% of all o.
342,904	56,772	17	40,112	12	17,591	5	228,429	67

(Sources: The Swedish Official Statistics)

If only prosecution finished by courts and the PPS is taken into account, the number of prosecuted offences in the year 2002 was 114 475. It follows from the table above, that the prosecutors finished 57 703 offences, that is, a little more than 50 percent of all prosecuted offences.

Numbers of penal orders and waivers of prosecution in relation to the other decisions made by the PPS during preliminary investigation follows of the table 3 below. As far as the police prosecution is concerned, see next section.

5 Cases Dealt with by the Police

5.1 Sanctions Imposed by the Police

The police is empowered to impose a sanction on the offender by means of *summary fines order* (*ordningsbotföreläggande, föreläggande av ordningsbot*). (Chap. 48 CJP). The summary fines order is a final decision on criminal responsibility for an offence and is recorded in the criminal register.

According to the law (Chap. 48 Sec. 13 CJP), a summary fine order may be applied to offences punishable by fines, assessed directly, of a set amount, that is, not by day-fines or other kinds of fines. Which particular offences may be punished by the summary fines order, that is, by the police, follows the *Regulation determining which offences may be punished by the police by means of the summary fines*. The Regulation was issued by the Prosecutor General in consultation with the National Police Board.

The Regulation contains a list of offences, as well as the amounts that shall be imposed for each one of the offences on the list. The offences that can be prosecuted in this way are road traffic offences in and offences in connection with board crossing. The more detailed instructions concerning proceedings imposing summary fines by the police have been published by the National Police Board.

The police may impose a penalty for an offence by means of summary fines order only if the offender has confessed to the offence and accepted the summary fines. If the offender has consented to the summary fines, the decision of the police has the same consequences as the judgment of the court and is recorded in the criminal register.

If the offender doesn't consent to the summary fines order, the police hands over the case to the PPS. The PPS may issue a penal order, if the preconditions for it exist, or bring the case to court.

5.2 Refrain from Reporting of the Offence

The police, as well as the PPS, are bound of the principle of legality. It means that the police have to initiate an investigation as soon as there is a reason to believe that an offence subject to public prosecution has been committed.

There is one legal exception to the principle of legality as regards police activity. According to Sec. 9 of the Police Act, a police officer may refrain from his general obligation to report all offences, if the offence in question, in view of the circumstances in the specific case, is of a trivial nature and it is obvious that no other sanction than a fine would be imposed on the offender. Refraining from reporting an offence does, practically, mean that the offence will not be prosecuted.

5.3 Other Ways to Finish the Police Investigation

Even if an offence has been reported, that is, the proceedings according to the Sec. 9 of the Police Act have not been applied, there is still the possibility not to initiate investigation if circumstances occur that would motivate the drop of investigation (see below in this section). In other cases, prosecution has to be initiated. Once initiated, the police investigation can be finished, in principle, in three different ways:

1. The offence has been cleared up and the case is handed over to the PPS for further prosecution.
2. The investigation is dropped; according to the law, the investigation shall be discontinued when there is no longer reason for pursuing it (Chap. 23 Sec. 4 CJP)
3. Before the offence has been completely cleared up, the PPS takes over and continues (or drops) the investigation.

The finishing of investigation as sub a) is the "normal" one.

The wording "*there is no longer reason for pursuing of investigation*" sub b) covers all possible reasons for finishing of investigation at this stage, especially: (1) the act appears not be an offence, (2) it is not possible to prove the offence; (3) it is not possible to prove that a certain person has committed it (the perpetrator is unknown), (4) it becomes apparent that the period for prosecution has expired.

The police have no possibility to drop an investigation because of "public interest", that is, of that reason that the public interest doesn't require prosecution of the particular offence. Even if circumstances appear during investigation, that would have made it possible to apply the institute *refrain from reporting an offence* (see above), it is not allowed to drop the investigation for that reason.

The possibility sub c) should also be taken into account. From the point of view of the police, an investigation is finished when the PPS decides to take over the investigation in a particular case and then either continues it or drops the proceedings.

5.4 Legal Practice

Statistics that would make it possible to analyze the activity of the police as far as the investigation of offences is concerned, are not available. The official criminal statistics contain figures related to the investigative stage of criminal procedure, that is, also to the police investigative activities. However, it is mostly impossible to distinguish if the measures or decisions recorded in the statistics were made by the police or the PPS. It is certain, for instance, that imposition of a summary fine order has to be made by the police, because the PPS doesn't use this instrument (see table 2 above). It is also certain, that drop of investigation according to the Chap. 23 Sec. 4a cannot be decided by the police, because only the PPS is empowered to apply this provision. In other cases, such certain conclusions are difficult to draw.

Another problem is that, in some respects, the official statistics do not seem to be very reliable. For example, the official statistics of the year 2002 (the table concerning data on cleared-up offences) contain a figure on number of *refrains from reporting of an offence* (se above in this section). The figure is 253 decisions under the year. It is hard to believe that the figure corresponds to reality. As a matter of fact, recording of offences which shouldn't be reported appears inconsistent.

6 Administrative Procedural Forms

As mentioned above, in the Swedish legal system, a category of administrative misdemeanors similar to, for instance, *Ordnungswidrigkeiten* in the German law, or *Verwaltungsstrafrecht* as in Austria, has not been developed. It was also mentioned, that, since the 1970-ties, the Swedish legislator has started using of a new kind of sanction for unlawful behaviour outside the criminal law in a legal sense, a so called “sanction fee”. The legal regulation of this kind of unlawful behaviour is unsystematic; it represents typically ad hoc solutions and is rather confusing.

The authorities dealing with these kinds of misdemeanors are administrative bodies. The judicial system in the area of criminal law is, in principle, not engaged. Only in some cases, very rarely, might the PPS or the police might handle such sanctions.

7 PPS Function in Investigative Proceedings

The stage of prosecution between the moment when an offence has been reported and the moment a prosecutor bring the case to a court (*preliminary investigation*) is regulated in the Chap. 23 CJP. More detailed provisions regarding some particular questions are to be found in the *Regulation on Preliminary Investigation.* As far as the police activity is concerned, there is also a number of relevant provisions in the Police Act 1982.

The crucial questions which characterize the type of preliminary procedure in a given legal system are as follows:

1. Who is responsible for the successful investigation at this stage – the PPS or the police?
2. What does the relationship between the PPS and police look like?
3. What decisions may be made by the PPS and the police respectively?

7.1 Who Shall Lead the Preliminary Investigation – the PPS or the Police?

Both the PPS and the police are bound by the principle of legality. According to Chap. 23 Sec. 1 CJP, preliminary investigation shall be initiated as soon as – due to a report or for other reason – there is cause to believe that an offence subject to public prosecution has been committed.

The question who is obliged to initiate preliminary investigation, whether the PPS or the police, is answered by law in the following way:

A decision to initiate a preliminary investigation is to be made either by the police authority or by the prosecutor. If the investigation has been initiated by the police authority and the matter is not of a simple nature, the prosecutor shall assume responsibility for conducting the investigation as soon as someone is reasonably suspected of the offence. The prosecutor shall also take over the conduct of the investigation if special reasons so require. (Chap. 23 Sec. 3 CJP)

This vague legal regulation of the division of competence between the PPS and police leaves, obviously, many questions open. The keyword concerning the decision whether a particular investigation is to be led by the police or the PPS is if the matter is “of a simple nature”.

The issue is regulated more thoroughly in the *Instructions of the Public Prosecution Service concerning the leadership of the preliminary investigation.* The Instructions have been issued by the Prosecutor General *[Riksåklagare]* and made up in consultation with National Police Board [*Rikspolisstyrelse*]. According to the *Instructions*, the offences of "simple nature" should be investigated by the police. The investigation in more complicated cases should be headed by a public prosecutor. Further, a number of different circumstances, enumerated in the Instructions, may cause that the preliminary investigation will be led by the PPS, even if the case is of a simple nature (for instance, the suspected is under 18 years old, the suspected suffers of a mental illness, etc.). The Instructions rules are not compulsory. A detailed agreement concerning division of competence between the police and the PPS is supposed to be reached in a particular case on the local level, that is, between a prosecutor and police authorities. In an appendix to the Instructions, the offences which normally should be considered to be of simple nature are enumerated.

In practice, the question who shall lead investigation in a particular case is often solved rather informally. However, the PPS always has the last word. How the leadership of investigation is divided between the PPS and police as regards the individual offences is shown in the following table (table 3).

By reading the statistics, it should be kept in mind that number of investigations led by the PPS and the police vary also "within" the individual offences. For instance, the average number of investigations of theft led by the PPS is 88,3 %. However, there are certain forms of this offence where investigations led by the police prevail. Generally, it is very difficult to get a clear picture of the criteria concerning the division of competence between the PPS and the police. To put it in other words, the picture of reality is precisely as vague as the legal regulation.

No matter who leads an investigation, whether the police or the PPS, the main responsibility for this stage of investigation lies with the PPS. The PPS may also, whenever it is considered to be appropriate, take over a preliminary investigation led by the police.

Table 3. Leadership of Investigation According to Individual Offences

Offence	Total num. of offences	% of charged suspect	Leader of investigation		% of investing. led by PPS
			Police	Prosecutor	
Murder, manslaughter or assault with a fatal outcome	30	10.0	0	30	100.0
Crimes against creditors	6,241	18.1	14	6,219	99.6
Murder, manslaughter	205	40.0	1	204	99.5
Misuse of office, corruption	3,960	4.2	21	3,939	99.5
Attempt to murder or manslaugter	625	38.2	1	618	98.9
Gross violation of integrity	1,753	38.0	28	1,725	98.4
Rape	1,521	18.3	23	1,497	98.4
Extortion, usury	706	25.9	15	691	97.9
Defamation	5,302	4.1	185	5,117	96.5
Robbery	3,634	50.0	145	3,489	96.0
Gross assault	3,359	48.3	150	3,209	95.5
Crimes involving public danger	1,730	19.7	85	1,645	95.1
Creating danger for another	379	12.4	33	346	91.3
Unlawful threat, molestation	3,6076	22.3	3,354	32,722	90.7
Crimes against public order	1,340	20.5	126	1,214	90.6
Sex. harassment	2,788	33,8	295	2,493	89.4
Breach of data secrecy	185	13,6	20	165	89.2
Causing another's injury	869	13.3	101	768	88.4
Fraud	15,914	33.3	1,856	14,058	88.3
Burglary	17,648	45.9	1,360	15,499	87.8
Others fraudulent crimes	266	18.0	33	233	87.6
Theft of vehicle	12,748	43.0	1,723	11,025	86.5
Assault	36,929	30.2	5,009	31,920	86.4
Embezzlement, other trust crimes	6,504	28.4	885	5,618	86,4
Crimes against liberty and peace	6,480	22.0	1,068	5,412	83.5
Crimes of falsifikation	4,723	33.8	830	3,891	82.4
Tax crimes	8,991	22.9	1,747	7,243	80.6
Receiving	7,172	49.8	1,415	5,756	80.3
Crimes against public activity	14,957	44.3	3,212	11,745	78.5
Perjury and other untruth statment	3,870	14.6	849	3,021	78.1
Causing another's death	281	38.4	67	214	76.2
Smuggling	1,628	41.4	448	1,177	72.
Crime inflicting damages	13,680	36.4	5,270	8,410	61.5
Narcotic drug crimes	38,943	48.7	16,083	22,859	58.7
Petty theft, shoplifting	48,362	38.3	23,784	24,578	50.8
Road traffic crimes	64,129	56.4	54,708	9,420	14.7

(Sources: The Internal Statistics of the PPS)

7.2 The Relationship between the PPS and the Police.

If the police are the leader of investigation, the PPS has no formal powers to give direct orders to the police as to how to run the particular investigation. Only if the leader of investigation is the PPS itself, the law makes it possible for the PPS to require police assistance:

*A prosecutor conducting a preliminary investigation may enlist the assistance of a police authority. He may also direct a police officer to take particular measures in aid of the preliminary investigation when appropriate having regard to the nature of the measure (*Chap. 23 Sec 3 CJP).

This legal situation means that should the PPS consider it necessary to take some measures during an investigation led by the police, the prosecutor has to take over leading the investigation. The problem is, however, that the PPS normally has no insight into investigations led by the police. First when the police has handed the case over to the PPS, can an evaluation of the investigation be made.

Another way how the PPS can get knowledge about an investigation led by the police is if some of the parties (the suspected, the victim or others) complain about decisions made by the police to the PPS. The PPS has, in fact, no power to review or change a decision of the police, unless the PPS take over the leadership of investigation.

The existing legal regulation of the relations between the PPS and the police may cause serious problem in practice, which have already arisen and became a subject for the *Justitieombudsman.* The point is that the PPS and the police are independent organizations with their own budgets. If the PPS asks for police assistance, the PPS actually takes advantage of the financial resources of the police. It has already happened that the police denied the assistance in an individual case referring to the lack of resources. The *Justitieombudsman* has stated that, even if the PPS is empowered to ask the police for assistance according to the law, the prosecution service has no right to force the police to perform the requested measures.

7.3 Decisions During Preliminary Investigation.

If, pursuant to the rules concerning division of competence between the police and PPS, the preliminary investigation shall be led by the police, the same legal provisions are applied as if the investigation were led by the PPS. However, a number of decisions, which come in question during this investigation stage, may be made by the prosecutor only, or by the court.

Only the PPS may make decision on (1) apprehension of the suspect, (2) more extensive search of premises, (3) traveling ban, (4) duty to report himself. Also a drop of investigation because of reasons mentioned in the Chap. 23 Sec. 4a CJP (see sub 4.3) above) may be decided by the PPS only.

Only the court may decide on (1) pre-trial detention, (2) secret camera surveillance, (3) wire-tapping. The decisions of a court may be initiated by the PPS only.

If the PPS has to be involved in an investigation headed by the police, because a decision which only the PPS may make is to be made, two possible situations may arise: either the PPS takes over the investigation, or, after that the decision have been made, the police continues investigation. PPS will decide which of the two proceedings it will choose. A similar situation (that the case is handed over back to the police) cannot arise, practically, if a decision must be made by a court. All decisions that only a court may make (pre-trial detention, camera surveillance and wire-tapping) come in question during the investigation of serious crimes, which are normally led by the PPS.

The next table gives an overall picture of the decisions mentioned above.

Table 4. An Overview over Different Decision Made During the Preliminary Investigation

Category of offences	Apprehensi-on	Report duty	Search of premises	Pre-trial detention	Ban of travelling	Total
Not investigative Measures	71	1	112	24	1	209
Other crimes	15,592	97	6,699	5,902	50	28,340
Offences punis-hable by fines	24		9	7		40
Simple economic Offences	18	1	67	3	3	92
Economic Crimes	127	5	436	57	6	631
Complex economic Crimes	125	3	317	94	10	549
Internationallegal aid	0		8	0		8
Environment Cri-mes	4		85	0		89
Narcotics drug crimes	4,084	5	3,341	1,872	5	9,307
Violent Crimes	7,717	14	3,357	2964	19	40,711
Total	27,762	126	14,431	10,923	94	53,336

(Sources: The Internal Statistics of the PPS)

An important question is who is empowered to review decisions made by the individual authorities, that is, the decisions of the police or prosecutors. This is-suesueis also regulated very fragmentally by the Swedish law and the situation is not quite clear.

As mentioned above, the decision of the police as a leader of investigation cannot be reviewed and changed by the PPS. The PPS is not a supervising authority in relation to the police. If the PPS gains knowledge about a wrong decision of the police, on the bases, for instance, of a complaint by a party, the only possibility to change the decision is to take over leading the investigation. In practice is more usual, however, that the issue will be discussed by the PPS and the police.

When the police have finished investigation and the case has been handed over to the PPS for further prosecution, the PPS may find that the case is not cleared up satisfactorily to facilitate a successful prosecution in court. In such case, the PPS normally takes over the prosecution and asks the police to take the necessary measures in order to complete the investigation. Another possibility is, of course, to drop the investigation.

Not even within the PPS the rules concerning reviewing and, if necessary, changing of wrong decisions are quite clear. The rules of reviewing of prosecutor decisions, which have been appealed by a part, are based on one legal provision (Chap. 7 Sec 2 CJP) saying that "*The Prosecutor-General and the regional prosecutors may themselves take on an assignment that would otherwise be the responsibility of a subordinate prosecutor.*" On the base of the provision, the following practice has been developed:

1. All decisions of prosecutors during investigation may be reviewed by a superior prosecutor, either on the basis of a complaint of a party, or on his own initiative.
2. If the reviewed decision is found wrong, the further proceedings depend on the circumstances of the particular case: the proceedings may be continued by the same prosecutor, who has made the wrong decision, or another prosecutor is appointed, or the superior prosecutor takes over the case and continues the investigation himself. There is no legal regulation of this issue.

7.4 Final Decision in the Preliminary Investigation

A final decision in the investigative stage may be made either by the police (if the police acts as the leader of investigation) or by the PPS.

The police may:

- impose a sanction on the offender by means of a summary fine order (see sub V. above). In this situation, no real investigation takes place;
- drop investigation according to the Chap. 23 Sec. 4 ("*When there is no longer reason for pursuing the investigation, it shall be discontinued.*");
- hand the case over to the PPS to further prosecution, if the offence has been successfully cleared up.

The PPS may:

- impose a sanction on the offender by means of penal order (see above);
- waive the prosecution (see above);
- decide to bring the case to court;

- drop the prosecution according to Chap. 23 Sec. 4 or 4a (see above)

(Both the police and PPS, when an offence has been reported, may decide not to initiate prosecution.)

It should be added that none of the possible decisions of the PPS requires judicial approval.

How the individual decisions are used in the PPS practice is shown by the following table.

Table 5a. The Structure of the PPS Decisions During Investigative Stage

Offences / Decisions	Invest. not initiated	Dropped 23:4a	Dropped other reasons	Offence not proved	Not prosecuted in court	Other decisions	Prosecution in court	Penal order	Waiver of prosecution	Total
Traffic offences	72	1,622	1,085	1,926	472	7,777	38,606	11,729	5,154	68,443
of which drunk driving	1	366	354	431	100	1,882	11,162	4004	500	18,800
Intentional homicide	18	2	387	38	2	62	321	0	0	830
of which completed	5	0	97	4	0	14	80	0	0	200
Assault	1,304	1,514	3,6338	5,544	492	6,733	23,691	746	317	76,679
of which more serious forms	10	16	1,022	172	30	175	1,391	0	5	2821
of which leastserious form	1,294	1,498	35,316	5,372	462	6,558	22,300	746	312	73,858
Rape	34	1	1,080	47	1	80	278	0	0	1,521
Less serious form of sex. har.	41	65	1,157	107	28	128	706	39	9	2,280

(Sources: The Internal Statistics of the PPS)

Table 5b. The Structure of the PPS Decisions During Investigative Stage

Offences / Decisions	Invest. not initiated	Dropped 23:4a	Dropped other reasons	Offence not proved	Not prosecuted in court	Other decisions	Prosecution in court	Penal order	Waiver of prosecution	Total
Robbery	4	21	801	97	15	174	1,096	0	2	2,210
Mugging/bag snatching	0	2	47	21	4	39	209	2	2	326
Theft	436	4,804	13,026	5,147	674	10,088	32,301	7,956	4,356	78788
of which: of a motor vehicle	32	546	2,607	894	98	1,883	5,062	34	244	11400
of which: Burglary	60	1,052	2,427	1,708	162	2,332	8,717	68	369	19037
of which domestic burglary	5	69	636	154	19	215	906	3	7	1892
of which Shoplifting	0	2,476	609	1,184	312	4,317	13,826	7,670	3,420	35283
Drug offences	22	1,957	3,716	1,562	456	5,721	18,996	4,154	2,455	39039
of which trafficking	0	12	247	74	17	249	674	210	37	1520
of which posses. and pers. use	14	1,862	2,520	1,171	411	4,969	15,991	3,890	2375	33204
Total	1,931	9,988	57,637	14,489	2,144	30,802	116,204	24,626	12,295	270,127

(Sources: The Internal Statistics of the PPS)

Table 6. The Structure of the PPS Decisions During Investigative Stage (in percent)

Offences / Decisions	Dropped 23:4a	Dropped other reasons	Offence not proved	Not prosecuted in court	Other decisions	Prosecution in court	Penal order	Waiver of prosecution	Total
Traffic offences	2,4	1,6	2,8	0,7	11,4	56,4	17,1	7,5	99,9
of which drunk driving	1,9	1,9	2,3	0,5	10,0	59,4	21,3	2,7	100,0
Intentional homicide	0,2	46,6	4,6	0,2	7,5	38,7	0,0	0,0	97,8
of which completed	0,0	48,5	2,0	0,0	7,0	40,0	0,0	0,0	97,5
Assault	2,0	47,4	7,2	0,6	8,8	30,9	1,0	0,4	98,3
of which more serious forms	0,6	36,2	6,1	1,1	6,2	49,3	0,0	0,2	99,6
of which least serious form	2,0	47,8	7,3	0,6	8,9	30,2	1,0	0,4	98,2
Rape	0,1	71,0	3,1	0,1	5,3	18,3	0,0	0,0	97,8
Less serious form of sex.	2,9	50,7	4,7	1,2	5,6	31,0	1,7	0,4	98,2
Robbery	1,0	36,2	4,4	0,7	7,9	49,6	0,0	0,1	99,8
Mugging/bag snatching	0,6	14,4	6,4	1,2	12,0	64,1	0,6	0,6	100,0
Theft	6,1	16,5	6,5	0,9	12,8	41,0	10,1	5,5	99,4
of which: of a motor vehicle	4,8	22,9	7,8	0,9	16,5	44,4	0,3	2,1	99,7
of which: burglary	5,5	12,7	9,0	0,9	12,2	45,8	0,4	1,9	88,4
of which domestic bur.	3,6	33,6	8,1	1,0	11,4	47,9	0,2	0,4	106,2
of which shoplifting	7,0	1,7	3,4	0,9	12,2	39,2	21,7	9,7	95,8
Drug offences	5,0	9,5	4,0	1,2	14,7	48,7	10,6	6,3	99,9
of which trafficking	0,8	16,3	4,9	1,1	16,4	44,3	13,8	2,4	100,0
of which posses. and use	5,6	7,6	3,5	1,2	15,0	48,2	11,7	7,2	100,0
Total	3,7	21,3	5,4	0,8	11,4	43,0	9,1	4,6	99,3

8 Particular issues

8.1 Victim Participation

The injured party, the victim, has a relatively strong position in Swedish criminal procedure. The main rights of the victim provided by law are as follows:

When a prosecutor has instituted a prosecution, the victim may support the prosecution. The victim may also appeal to a superior court. The victim has the position of a party in the trial if s/he takes civil action in connection with the prosecution.

If the victim has reported the offence and the PPS has decided not to initiate prosecution in court, or if the prosecution in court has been withdrawn, the victim may initiate prosecution in court or take over the prosecution, respectively.

More importanly, practically, is the obligation of the PPS to prepare and present in court the victim's action in conjunction with the prosecution, provided that the private claim is based on the investigated offence and the victim has notified the PPS that s/he desires to have the private claim to be connected with the prosecution.

As regards certain offences, especially the violent ones, the victim has the right to counsel.

There are no statistics on disposals concerning to what extent victims take advantage of their rights. On the basis of experience, it seems that the right to initiate or take over a prosecution in court is applied very rarely. On the other hand, the counsel for victims of violent offences are appointed regularly. Also victim's actions based on private claims are successful in the great majority of cases.

Generally, it is possible to state that, at present, the position of victim in criminal procedure has became much stronger than it was twenty years ago, when Swedish criminal policy started to focus on this issue.

8.2 Particularities in Relation to Juveniles

The Code of Judicial Procedure doesn't contain any special provisions as far as the prosecution of juveniles is concerned. Such provisions are provided by a special law, *The Law with special provisions concerning prosecution of young offenders*. The main differences in comparison with the prosecution of adults can be summarized as follows:

- Investigation of the offences committed by juveniles (up to 18 years of age) must always be led by a prosecutor, if the possible sanction is imprisonment more than six months.
- The leader of the investigation shall make contact with the social authorities and the personal situation of the young offender shall be investigated thoroughly.
- The penal order and waiver of prosecution may be applied more extensivly than for adults.

The law also contains some special provisions concerning the investigation of offences committed by children less than 15 years of age.

8.3 Peculiarities in Relation to Specific Sub-groups

There are no special provisions which regulate prosecution of some specific groups in society differently, except the prosecution of persons who don't reside in the country that is mainly foreigners. Such persons may be placed in pre-trial detention regardless of the nature of the offence if there is a reasonable risk that they will avoid legal proceedings or a penalty by fleeing the country. For more trivial offences committed by this category of persons, for instance shop-lifting, a special kind of proceedings has developed in practice. The suspect shall deposit a sum of money in Sweden, corresponding to the expected fines, and then the person is allowed to leave the country. The following prosecution is run in absence of the suspect. It is difficult to find a legal basis for this kind of proceedings.

The prosecution of offences against women or minorities follows the regular legislation. Both the offences against women and minorities, so called "hate-offences" are given priority. That is, however, an issue of criminal policy, not an issue of law.

9 Current Changes

As was already mentioned, the PPS in Sweden went through extensive reorganization. The present organization was launched in January 2005. The main target of reorganization was strengthening the operative activities of the PPS. According to the proposal for the new organization, the administrative personal of the PPS should be reduced with ca 40 percent and the resources saved moved over to operative activity. At present it is too soon for evaluation of whether the target was reached or not.

In the long-term perspective, one of the most visible tendencies concerning the position of the PPS in the judicial system is the fact, that judicial powers of the PPS have been considerably widened. The *penal order* was introduced in Swedish law in the year 1948. At that time, the penal order could be issued for offences punishable only by fines, if the sanction imposed by the penal order was not severer than 20 day-fines. Step by step, the preconditions for issuing penal orders have been widened. At present, the penal order may be used for all offences which have fines in the range of sanctions (alongside imprisonment), there is no limitation of the number of day-fines which may be imposed, and by means of the penal order even a *conditional sentence* may be imposed that is, an alternative sanction which is used if the act deserves imprisonment but the imprisonment can still be avoided. Similarly, the possibility of waiving the prosecution has become more and more extensive.

This development is understandable with respect to the necessity of increasing effectiveness of the prosecution, especially for minor criminality. However, a discussion of more principal issues, e.g. if it is appropriate to entrust the executive authorities with such powers, would be desirable. The question is not only about process economy, but also about guarantees against thinkable misuse of powers.

Besides the principal issues just mentioned, the Swedish legal regulation of some aspects of the preliminary investigation is surprisingly vague and fragmental. What should be regulated in a much more definite way is the division of competences – and relationship alltoghter – between the PPS and the police. It seems that the regulation of today may function only if the two authorities reach an agreement. However, as has already become evident in practice, an agreement between those two independent organizations is not easy to reach if there is lack of resources.

It seems also that the reciprocal independent position between the police and the PPS results in the PPS not having sufficient insight in the prosecuting activity of the police. A co-operation between the PPS and the police exists, however, the Swedish *Justitieombudsman* has stated several times that, in his opinion, the police has dropped or not initiated investigation in cases in which the prosecution was clearly motivated. It was obvious that the PPS had no knowledge about the cases.

Another issue which deserves clear and unambiguous regulation are the rules for reviewing decisions within the PPS. It might be that the rules developed in practice work. However, nobody outside the organization can understand how.

If an overall conclusion concerning the investigation stage of the Swedish criminal procedure may be drawn – the conclusion which is based not only on the facts mentioned in this report, but also on everyday experience – it is as follows. The characteristic feature of legal regulation of the investigative stage of criminal procedure, as well as the relations between the two main actors in this area, the PPS and the police, is a strong pragmatism in solution to the given issues. This means that the PPS and also the police fulfill their tasks, in general, satisfactorily. However, the lack of clear and distinct regulation of a number of important questions may cause individuals who come into contact with this machinery to have difficulties in maintaining their rights.

During the final stage of drafting of this national report, an expert opinion of a committee appointed by the Minister of Justice has been published (*A New Allocation of Tasks and Responsibility between the Police and Public Prosecution Service. Swedish Public Reports (SOU) 2005:84*). The task of the committee was to work out a basic structure for the relationship between the PPS and the police during crime investigation, and, if necessary, to propose legislative measures in order to improve the co-operation between these authorities, as well as to improve the effectiveness of the criminal procedure. Thus, the expert opinion concerns the central issues that have been discussed in this report. The expert opinion fully confirms the conclusions drawn above; the proposals presented by the committee are dominated by a strong pragmatic approach to the solutions of the tasks posed by the Ministry of Justice.

The main points of the expert opinion concerning the topics of this report can be summarized as follows:

- As mentioned above (Chap. 7.1), according to existing law, the leader of investigation is either the PPS or the police. The police may lead the investigation if the case is "of a simple nature". The Committee proposes that the police should lead investigation to a larger extent than today. This should be achieved by changing the wording of the law in such a way that, in the future, the PPS shall lead investigation only if the case is a very extensive one or of a complex nature. The purpose of this proposal is to create preconditions for possible concentration of the higher qualified staff on the more complicated and serious cases.

- In future, the police should also take over the investigation of offences committed by juveniles less than 18 years of age. Today, only the PPS may lead the investigation of such cases.
- In Chap. 7.2 some problems of co-operation between the PPS and the police concerning resources have been mentioned. The Committee suggests an amendment to the existing relevant provision, providing that the police shall partition off resources for activities led by the PPS.
- The Committee proposes that the Police Authorities should have powers to issue *penal order* in the future, in principle in the same way as the PPS does today, except the possibility to impose *conditional sentence* (see Chap. 4.2.) above). The main motive of the proposal is a "considerable improvement of the effectiveness of the investigation", because the PPS, instead of just formally dealing with cases handed over by the police, could focus on cases that really need the PPS's capacity.

The expert opinion contains a number of other proposals, which are important, but concerning some detailed questions of the activities of the PPS and police. On the other hand, some questions important from the point of view of *legal security*, for instance the rules of reviewing of decisions made during the investigation, are not discussed in the expert opinion.

It should be added that the expert opinion represents the first step in Swedish legislative procedure. It means that the proposals submitted may be and probably will be changed. They illustrate well the direction of the development in this area in Sweden.

References

The list of the laws and other official materials used in the Report

Rättegångsbalken (1942:740)
(The Code of Judicial Procedure)

Förundersökningskungörelse (1947:948)
(The Regulation on Preliminary Investigation)

Lag (1964:167) med särskilda bestämmelser om unga lagöverträdare
(The Law with special provisions concerning prosecution of young offenders)

Polislagen (1984:387)
(The Police Act)

Riksåklagarens föreskrifter (1999:178) om ordningsbot för vissa brott
(The Regulation of the Prosecutor General determining which offences may be punished by the police by means of the summary fines)

Åklagarmyndighetens föreskrifter och allmänna råd om ledning av förundersökning i brottmål. Åklagarmyndighetens författningssamling 2005:9.
(The Instructions of the Public Prosecution Service concerning the leadership of the preliminary investigation in criminal procedure. PPS Collection of Regulations 2005:9.)

Åklagarmyndighetens utvecklingsplan 2005–2007
(Public Prosecution Service Development Plan 2005–2007)

Åklagarmyndighetens årsredovisning 2002, 2003, 2004.
(Public Prosecution Service Annual Reports 2002, 2003, 2004.)

The internal statistics of the PPS 2002

Domstolstatistik 2002
(The Official Statistics of the National Court Administration)

Kriminalstatistik 2002
(The Swedish Official Criminal Statistics)

En ny uppgifts- och ansvarsfördelning mellan polis och åklagare. Statens offentliga utredningar 2005:84.
(A New Allocation of Tasks and Responsibility between the Police and Public Prosecution Service. Swedish Public Reports (SOU) 2005:84).

Part III

Appendix

Contents of the Questionnaire*

Chapter I: Offence Definition

General Overview: Which reaction forms are available for which offence types in your country?

I.1. Are all offences defined as criminal?

I.2. Does the state respond to all known offences by formal criminal proceedings?

I.3. Are all offences to be met by a penal sanction?

I.4. Please provide details of what the offences named below are defined as and how they are dealt with

I.4.a. Illegal parking is a…

I.4.b. Exceeding the speed limit is a…

I.4.c. Driving under the influence of alcohol, without causing danger or an accident is a…

I.4.d. Driving under the influence of alcohol and causing danger to road traffic (driving recklessly) is a…

I.4.e. Driving recklessly/dangerously (without influence of alcohol) is a…

I.4.f. Special forms of theft are…

I.4.g. Possession of a small amount of cannabis/hash for personal use is…

I.4.h. Travelling with public transport without a ticket is a…

I.4.i. Begging in a public place is…

I.4.j. Being „drunk and disorderly" (being drunk and causing a nuisance) in a public place is…

I.4.k. Prostitution is a…

I.4.l. Other offence, namely…

---

* The complete questionnaire including all categories of answers can be found via internet *www.kriminologie.uni-goettingen.de/pps*.

Chapter II: Investigative Stage

The Police in the investigative stage

II.1. Please describe briefly the police service in your country

II.1.a. Is there only one police organisation with all divisions (ultimately) responsible to one ministry (the ministry of the interior)?

II.1.b. Please describe police service organisation including its hierarchy, i.e. who sets policy, provides resources, defines how these are to be used etc.?

II.1.c. Where there is more than one kind of police, how are they different? Is, e.g., one police responsible only for a particular type or group of offences?

II.1.d. In how far does a judicial structure (PPS, Ministry of Justice etc.) have influence on the police forces? Is there a police force which is factually controlled by these institutions?

II.2. Are there alternative investigatory agencies, e.g. customs, tax and financial authorities etc.?

II.2.a. If yes, what offences do they deal with?

II.2.b. If yes, what happens to the case?

Chapter III: Control by PPS in the investigative stage

III.1. What is the organisational relationship between PPS and police?

III.2. Does the prosecution service have legal powers to direct police investigations?

III.2.a. If no, does it direct the police anyway?

III.2.b. Is the PPS considered to be „in charge of" investigating offences?

III.3. How does the PPS direct investigations generally? Can PPS issue general guidelines and instructions as to…

III.3.a. Are these guidelines legally binding?

III.3.b. How well are they observed in practice?

III.3.c. Is there a disciplinary procedure to sanction police disobedience of such general guidelines?

III.3.d. Does the PPS in fact issue such general guidelines?

III.3.e. How often?

III.4. When are the police required by law to inform the PPS about a case for the first time?

When do the police actually report a case to the PPS?

III.5. Which cases does the PPS leave entirely in police hands including the decision to drop/dispose (in so far as police are empowered to do so)?

III.6. Which cases does the PPS leave entirely in police hands until the investigation is completed, but insist on being involved in all decisions beyond that?

III.7. In which cases does there tend to be a moderate level of PPS involvement in the investigative stage, e.g. because PPS advice needed or permission for certain measures required etc.?

III.8. In which cases is the PPS involved in a case from the very beginning of the investigation?

III.9. PPS becomes actively involved in the investigative stage (if yes, please describe):

III.9.a. To allow certain measures?

III.9.b. To allow pre-trial detention?

III.9.c. To guide police evidence collection?

III.9.d. To be present during interrogation/statements or to interrogate/hear suspect?

III.9.e. To be present during interrogation/statements or to interrogate/hear victim?

III.9.f. To be present during interrogation/statements or to interrogate/hear witnesses?

III.9.g. To co-ordinate and plan investigation (with police command)?

III.10. Is the type of offence for which PPS should/can take charge of and how far (and which the police can deal with relatively independently) regulated in any way, e.g. by guidelines?

III.10.a. Who decides this/ issues such guidelines?

III.10.b. Are there guidelines instructing what kind of measures are appropriate in a "typical" investigation into types of offences?

III.10.c. If yes, who issues such guidelines?

III.10.d. If this is regulated regionally, is there significant regional variation? Please give examples

III.11. Which actions require the police (or PPS where head of the investigation) to seek whose approval (normally in advance where there is no time pressure/emergency)?

III.12. Are there emergency or „in flagranti" police powers (meaning that police can exercise powers they usually need permission for because, e.g. there is time pressure or danger that a suspect may destroy evidence etc.)?

III.13. Which powers does this apply to in what circumstances?

III.14. Are there any actions the police may never take without the prior approval described above?

III.15. Where the police use emergency/ in flagranti powers and this requires post-facto court approval what happens if the court finds that the action was not justified and therefore illegal?

III.16. Does the PPS have some means (other than disciplinary proceedings etc.) of influencing the police?

III.17. Do police and PPS work together in any other fields than investigation?

Police duty to report/hand on cases/information at the end of the investigative stage

III.18. Is there a general principle of legality at police level?

III.19. As far as offences not taken directly to court by the police are concerned: Are the police obliged to hand a case on where the offender is known?

III.20. Do they do so in practice?

III.21. When (at what stage in the proceedings) do the police hand a case over?

III.21.a. Is there a legal provision as to when the police should hand a file over to the PPS?

III.21.b. When is the file (and responsibility for a case) actually handed over?

III.22. Is there a mechanism for the PPS to check the cases not handed on where the police are obliged to hand on?

III.23. How often are such powers actually used? Does this actually take place?

III.24. How do systems manage an agreement between the police and the PPS to decide what should/should not be handed on?

III.25. Can the police hand a case over to an agency other than the PPS? (Please answer for cases involving adults only)?

III.26. Does this agency then make the decision whether to prosecute?

III.27. Are there any alternative systems which deal with offences (as we have defined these before) i.e. are there alternative institutions, e.g. for specific sections of society like the military?

III.27.a. Is there an alternative police?

III.27.b. Is there an alternative court?

III.27.c. If yes, which section of society and what offences do they deal with?

III.27.d. Does the PPS become involved in any way?

III.27.e. If yes, please describe

Chapter IV: Police Competence

IV.1. What happens to a case when police investigation is ended?

IV.2. Can the police take cases to court?

IV.2.a. If yes, what types of cases can the police take to court?

IV.2.b. For which offences can the police bring a case straight to court?

IV.2.c. How is this regulated?

IV.2.d. If by guidelines, who issues these?

IV.3. What kind of proceedings do the police use?
If the police can decide between different procedural forms, does the PPS have any influence on which form they chose?

IV.4. Does the PPS have any way of influencing such cases (other than giving approval where this is required)?

IV.5. Is there discretion/ a principle of expediency/opportunity at police level?

IV.5.a. Can the police decide to drop a case on grounds of insufficient evidence?

IV.5.b. If yes, for what types of cases can the police do this?

IV.5.c. Can the police to this for all offences?

IV.5.d. How is this regulated?

IV.5.e. If by guidelines, who issues these?

IV.5.f. Does the PPS have any other way of influencing such cases (other than giving approval where this is required)?

IV.5.g. Can the police drop a case on public interest grounds?

IV.5.h. If yes, is/does this…?

IV.5.i. If yes, for what types of cases can the police do this?

IV.5.j. Can the police to this for all offences?

IV.5.k. How is this regulated?

IV.5.l. If by guidelines, who issues these?

IV.5.m. Does the PPS have any other way of influencing such cases (other than giving approval where this is required)?

Unknown Offenders

IV.5.n. Where there is no known offender, who makes the decision no longer to look actively for an offender?

IV.5.o. Can the police dispose of cases?

IV.5.p. If yes, is/does this…?

IV.5.q. If yes, for what types of cases can the police do this? E.g. where evidential deficiency very clear e.g. because there are no witnesses, or witnesses are not prepared to testify

IV.5.r. Can the police do this for all offences?

IV.5.s. How is this regulated?

IV.5.t. If by guidelines, who issues these?

IV.5.u. Does the PPS have any other way of influencing such cases (other than giving approval where this is required)?

IV.5.u. Where there is no known offender who makes the decision no longer to look actively for an offender?

IV.6. Can the police end a case by a fixed penalty (defined by a catalogue)? E.g. fine 50 Euros for driving < 20 Km/Hour above the speed limit

IV.6.a. If yes, what kind of fixed penalty can they give?

IV.6.b. If yes, for what types of cases can the police do this? (E.g. where evidence very simple)

IV.6.c. For which offences can the police do this?

IV.6.d. How is this regulated?

IV.6.e. If by guidelines, who issues these?

IV.6.f. Does it lead to a record of any sort? IV.7. Can the police end a case with a consequence, e.g. a kind of sanction or criminal record?

IV.7.a. If yes, what kind of consequence can arise?
IV.7.b. If yes, for what types of cases can the police do this? E.g. first-time offender, where police officer decides this is sufficient to deter the suspect from further offences in the future
IV.7.c. Can the police to this for all offences?
IV.7.d. How is this regulated?
IV.7.e. If by guidelines, who issues these?
IV.7.f. Does the police need PPS or court approval to do this?
IV.7.g. Must the suspect agree to a consequence of this type?
IV.7.h. Is this considered an admission of guilt?
IV.7.i. Does it lead to a record of any sort?
IV.7.j. If yes, is this a conviction?
IV.7.k. Who has access to this record at a later stage?
IV.7.l. What usually happens if the suspect refuses to agree?
IV.7.m. How often does a suspect not agree?
IV.8. Where the police require approval/agreement from another institution, how is this reached?
IV.8.a. Where approval/agreement, how often is approval refused?
IV.8.b. Or if possible, provide data (%) of cases in which approval is not given on one or more years

Chapter V: Unknown Offenders and Police Output

V.1. What happens if the offender is unknown?
V.2. Is PPS approval necessary?
V.3. Does PPS have any means of ensuring police are not just making decision not to investigate certain types of crime?
V.4. Please provide police in and output data
V.4.a. Police drops - offence related (statistics)
V.4.b. Police disposals - offence related (statistics)
V.5. Where there are input and output (i.e. between reported and recorded crime) statistics at police level, is there a significant difference between the two?
V.6. Are there, excluding the police, alternative prosecutorial agencies which take cases to court or make a decision not to do so?
V.6.a. If yes, what offences do they deal with?
V.6.b. Can such institutions drop on discretionary grounds?
V.6.c. Can they impose conditions or sanctions?
V.6.d. What kind of?
V.6.e. Please provide statistics of cases dealt with by such institutions

Chapter VI: Prosecution Stage: Input

VI.1.	Can the PPS itself initiate an investigation?
VI.1.a.	If yes, on what basis?
VI.1.b.	If yes, how often does it do so?
VI.1.c.	If possible, please provide data on how many cases were initiated by the PPS in one or more year/s
VI.2.	Can the victim report an offence directly to the PPS?
VI.3.	Once a case has been received by the PPS (file handed on), can a prosecution be stopped at this stage by any other body/ person ?
VI.3.a.	Where a stop is possible, is this limited in any way? (e.g. victim can stop proceedings in certain types of offences because his/her agreement is a pre-condition.)
VI.3.b.	How often does this happen?
VI.3.c.	If possible, provide data for one or more year/s as to how often this happens
VI.4.	Must the PPS consider any other factors when making the decision whether to prosecute?
VI.5.	What happens if the PPS does not consider/ is not seen to have considered such factors?

Examining Magistrates

VI.5.a.	Is there an examining magistrate alongside the PPS?
VI.5.b.	What is the relationship between PPS and the examining magistrate?
VI.6.	Who can refer cases to him/her?
VI.7.	In what kinds of cases does the examining magistrate become involved?
VI.7.a.	What is his or her function/role in such cases?
VI.7.b.	What role does the PPS (still) play in proceedings in which an examining magistrate is involved?
VI.8.	Can the examining magistrate decide to drop a case?
VI.8.a.	If yes, on what grounds?
VI.8.b.	With a condition?
VI.8.c.	Can the examining magistrate drop without PPS agreement?
VI.8.d.	If yes, can the PPS appeal against this decision?
VI.9.	Examining Magistrate Level (statistics)
VI.10	PPS input statistics

Chapter VII: Prosecution Decision-making

VII.1.	On what grounds can the PPS drop a case?
VII.1.a.	If these tests are defined by guidelines, who issues these?

VII.2. Where a case is dropped, what records are kept?
VII.2.a. Who has access to these?
VII.2.b. How often are they referred to in future investigations?
VII.3. Where court approval is required, how often is it not granted?
VII.4. Where cases can be re-opened, under what circumstances?
VII.4.a. How often does this happen?
VII.5.a.i. Who has a mechanism to force the PPS to charge?
VII.5.a.ii. Who has a mechanism to attempt to force a public trial?
VII.5.a.iii. How often are these used?
VII.5.b. Can the PPS refer a case for private prosecution (in combination with dropping the public case)?
VII.5.c. Can anyone other than PPS (or victim where PPS refers a case for private prosecution) prosecute a case?
VII.5.d. How often does this happen?
VII.5.e. If possible, provide data on how many such alternative prosecutions took place in one or more year/s
VII.6. Where the PPS wants to end a case what options does it have?
VII.6.a. Please answer the following questions separately for all potential disposals the PPS can use (penal order/ conditional disposal (no conviction)/ drop (public interest)
VII.6.b. Is an admission of guilt necessary for this kind of solution?
a) If yes, is this recorded?
b) Where?
c) If there is a record, who has access to this record in the future?
VII.6.c. Whose consent is required for the disposal?
VII.6.d. Where a suspect refuses to give his consent and it is necessary for a PPS disposal suggestion what will happen?
a) When suspect's consent is required, how is this gained?
b) How often is consent refused?
c) Please provide data on how often an offer was refused/order was appealed against in one or more year/s
VII.6.e. If necessary, how does the court give its consent?
a) Can the court alter the proposed disposal? I.e. impose a different condition than PPS suggests?
b) How often does the court refuse its consent?
c) Please provide data on how often a proposal was refused in one or more year/s
VII.6.f. Where victims consent is required, how is this gained?
a) How often does the victim refuse consent?
b) Please provide data on how often consent was refused in one or more year/s
VII.6.g. Does this kind of disposal lead to a conviction/record?
a) Where is this recorded?
b) Who has access to this record in the future?

VII.6.h. What are the limits to the use of this kind of disposal? (e.g. offences for which it may not be used) Please also state where these are defined (legislation, guidelines)
a) Are any patterns visible in the use of this type of discretion in relation to particular offences or offence types? Please consider in particular (and provide definitions)
b) Or types of offenders? Please consider in particular
c) Law allows us for…
d) Penal order is used to deal with... (Please state the proportion of penal orders used to deal with the following: e.g. petty theft: 1/3 of penal orders issued are a reaction to petty theft)

VII.6.h.e. The following make up (please provide proportion) of penal order, e.g. 90 % of petty thefts are dealt with by penal order

VII.6.i. Which conditions/sanctions are usually imposed by this procedure?

VII.6.j. Are any measures in place to ensure uniform use of discretionary PPS powers?

Transparency and Accountability

VII.7. In which form is a decision to drop or dispose of a case laid down?
VII.7.a. This note is recorded…
VII.7.b. Who has access to this at a later stage?
VII.7.c. Who is informed of the decision?
VII.8. Prosecution output (statistics)

Chapter VIII: Court Stage

VIII.1. What is the PPS' role in preparation for and during trial?
VIII.2. How is evidence presented during trial?
VIII.3. Who decides what information should be given to the court?
VIII.4. Where a judge or magistrate has conducted interviews before the trial, is this evidence presented differently?
VIII.5. Are there quicker procedural paths at the court stage? E.g. accelerate proceedings

VIII.5.a. Name of procedural alternative:_________
a) If PPS has decided to/applies to use alternative proceedings, is the court legally required to check that the requirements for such proceedings are fulfilled?
b) Does the court do so thoroughly in practice?
c) If the court agrees with the procedural form, but disagrees on contents (e.g. type or severity of punishment applied for) can it simply change an element?
d) Can any party insist on normal proceedings?

e) Which sanctions can be given after such proceedings?
f) In how far do the PPS/police influence these proceedings?
g) Does a guilty plea alter the trial procedure? If yes, how?
h) How often does the court disagree with the use of alternative proceedings?
i) If the police prepare but the PPS formally makes the application to court, how often does the PPS not follow the police's recommendation?
j) How often is this procedural alternative used?
k) Where possible, please provide numbers for one or more years
l) How does this form of proceedings vary from „normal" proceedings?
m) Who provides the court with information in theses cases?
n) Where another body decides what evidence to bring, does the court have any means to get additional evidence and does it do so in practice?
o) Can a trial take place without the defendant?
p) Under what circumstances?
q) In what form is the charge made?
r) Can these effectively be seen as the decision of the institution which prepares them because the court usually agrees to the proposal made?
s) Can cases be joined at the court stage?

Normal Proceedings

VIII.6. Can a trial take place without the defendant?
VIII.6.a. Under what circumstances?
VIII.7. Who decides what to charge a suspect with?
VIII.7.a. Can the court change the original legal evaluation the PPS makes of the offence committed (the charge it brings, e.g. manslaughter instead of murder)?
VIII.7.b. If no, what happens where the charge is incorrect?
VIII.7.c. If the court can change a charge, how often does this happen?
VIII.7.d. Are there any mechanisms to form and safeguard correctness of charge?
VIII.7.e. Does the accused make a guilty/innocent plea upon which court decides?
VIII.7.e.i. What effect does an admission of guilt have?
VIII.7.f. Is plea-bargaining forbidden?
VIII.7.g. Are there signs that the PPS may reduce the seriousness of a charge due to concessions of the suspect, in particular in exchange for a guilty plea?
a) Is this regulated in any way?
b) Are there signs that suspect co-operation with the PPS can lead to only a part of the potential charges being brought?

c) Is this regulated in any way?

VIII.6.h. Where a person is accused of several offences can the PPS drop the others because the most serious is being prosecuted?

England & Wales only

VIII.7.i. Who decides which mode of trial to use?
VIII.7.j. If the PP - does the court have the power to correct a mistake?
VIII.7.k. How often does it actually do so?
VIII.7.l. Where there is doubt as to which court has jurisdiction over the case, who decides which court to bring it to?
VIII.7.m. On what basis is this decision made?
VIII.7.n. Is there any indication that offenders are charged with lesser offences in order to avoid higher court jurisdiction?
VIII.8. Does the PPS suggest a sentence?
VIII.8.a. Where the PPS suggests a sentence, in how far does this influence the court?
VIII.8.b. How often does the court not impose what the PPS requested?
VIII.8.c. Can the PPS appeal against a verdict?
VIII.8.d. How often does the PPS appeal against a verdict?
VIII.8.e. Can the PPS appeal against a sentence?
VIII.8.f. How often does the PPS appeal against sentence?
VIII.8.g. Please describe briefly the PPS' appeal possibilities and the court structure for criminal cases
VIII.9. Does a trial have to end with a verdict?
VIII.10. How long do proceedings last?
VIII.10.a. Is information available as to how long special procedural forms take in comparison?
VIII.10.b. Is any information available on how long proceedings ended at PPS level last?
VIII.11. Court output (statistics)

Chapter IX: Prosecution Service's Legal Role

IX.1. Is the PPS regarded as an objective body, i.e. working to find all incriminating and exonerating evidence?
IX.1.a. Do any legal obligations arise from this? When?
IX.1.b. Considering the powers the PPS has in the investigative stage (see above), what rights do the defence (suspect or his/her legal representation) have? Mechanism, e.g. to stop a search or assets being frozen, the right to be present when witnesses are interviewed, a possibility to insist on certain investigative steps being taken etc.

a) What means are there for a suspect/the defence to gain access to case information (in particular the file) where the PPS refuses this?
b) What means are available for a suspect/the defence to force certain alternative investigative steps where the PPS refuses this?

IX.1.c. What consequences are available when an individual prosecutor makes a mistake?
a) How often are such mechanisms (and which ones) actually used? What usually happens?
b) Where figures are available, how often have such consequences been implemented?
c) What mechanisms are in place to ensure an individual PP is dealing with cases as desired?

IX.2. Is the PPS only active as the step between investigation and court within the procedural administration of criminal law? i.e. only role is a s a law enforcement agency

Chapter X: Control of the PPS and Individual Public Prosecutor (PP) Decisions

X.1. What legal basis does the PPS have?

X.1.a. What is the PPS?

X.1.b. In how far is this reflected in reality? How independent is the PPS?

X.2. Which PPS activities have a formal legal basis, which are laid down in guidelines or other form? Where legislation is concerned please name it, where guidelines or other mechanisms are concerned please name them and state who issues these

X.3. Apart from government decisions anchored in legislation, how is general PPS policy determined, by whom?

X.4. What forms of political control are in place outside of the PPS hierarchy to ensure PPS performs this role?

X.4.a. Does this/do these institutions only become active upon a complaint by an interested party in an individual case?

X.4.b. Can a citizen make a more general complaint, e.g. against a certain PPS policy?

X.4.c. Is the PPS required to report regularly to this (or one of these, if so, please state to which one) institution(s)?

X.4.d. Does an institution of this kind have powers to inspect the PPS?

X.4.e. Can any other body inspect the PPS?

X.4.f. If yes, which one?

X.4.g. What form does an inspection take? - i.e. at what level does it occur, what methods are used, etc.?

X.4.h. What is inspected?

X.5. Is the PPS answerable to a ministry?

X.5.a. If yes, is this the formal head of service?

X.5.b. Can an external ministry/member of government issue general instructions (guidelines) to the PPS?
X.5.c. Can an external ministry/member of government issue case-specify instructions to the PPS?
X.5.d. Can another political figure issue case-specific instructions to the PPS?

Internal Control

X.6. Please describe PPS structure
X.6.a. Please provide details of prosecution service manpower (full-time equivalent)
X.6.b. Cases dealt with per head of lawyers and paralegals per year (in as far as available)?
X.6.c. What qualifications are necessary to become a PP?
X.6.d. What is the average age or age group of a PPS employee?
X.6.e. What is the average age of employees entering the service?
X.7. In how far can an individual prosecutor be given instructions in relation to a particular case? By whom?
X.8. Does the individual PP have any possibilities to resist/appeal against a case-specific instruction?
X.9. How are cases distributed within the system?
X.10. Do any other factors influence a PP's work strongly?
X.10.a. Are some of the measures/options available to a prosecutor to deal with a case much easier or quicker than others? Which ones, e.g. Mediation is likely to involve more work than a penal order?
X.10.b. If certain measures are valued more highly than others in an evaluating system, does this reflect the actual (more or less) work involved? Where necessary, please explain the system
X.11. Are there any more general influences on PPS work, e.g. media?
X.12. Who finances the PPS? Is there any possibility to put pressure on the PPS as a whole through budgeting?
X.12.a. Who decides how to distribute resources within the PPS? It is interesting to know in how far a level of the service may have flexibility in the distribution of resources and so, in how far it might be able to bring pressure to bear on prosecutors, who dispose of cases in a way it does not approve of. Additional certain options, e.g. mediation, may only truly be available where extra resources are provided
X.12.b. Is there flexibility within the PPS budget?
X.12.c. If yes who decides on distribution?

Chapter XI: Juveniles

XI.1. What is the age of criminal responsibility?
XI.1.a. What is the age of full (adult) criminal responsibility?
XI.1.b. Is there a group between juveniles and adults? How is this group treated differently?
XI.1.c. Do any factors other than age influence how juveniles are treated?
XI.2. Are there status offences for juveniles (ones which adults cannot commit)?
XI.3. If a juvenile commits an offence defined as criminal for an adult, is this also regarded as criminal for a juvenile?
XI.4. If juveniles committing offences are not regarded as criminal are they dealt with within the criminal justice system?
XI.5. If they are regarded as criminal, how are juveniles/young people treated differently in law?
XI.5.a. If they are dealt with by a different court, which one?
XI.5.b. What happens in practice?
XI.5.c. If there is variation or where juveniles are not regarded as criminal etc., are juveniles included in police and other criminal justice statistics?
XI.5.d. If no, are there independent statistics for juveniles?
XI.6. Who leads an investigation into such offences?
XI.7. Who investigates such offences?
XI.7.a. What happens to the case when the investigation is complete?
XI.7.b. Who decides whether to prosecute or not?
XI.8. Where different institutions are involved; who transfers cases/ensures that cases are transferred to them?
XI.8.a. Where different institutions are involved, where do they liaise with the criminal justice system?
XI.8.b. Where different courts take over, are these fully responsible for all cases?
XI.9. If juveniles are treated differently, this is true for…
XI.10. Is it possible to use simplified/accelerated proceedings?
XI.11. Are these the same as for adults?
XI.12. What sentences are available?

Diversion

XI.13. Can any other body than a court drop a case?
XI.14. What is necessary for a case to be dropped? E.g. Where guilt is presumed but not regarded as serious. Do the same circumstances apply as for adults?
XI.14.a. What conditions are necessary?
XI.15. Juvenile disposals (statistics)
XI.16. Are these decisions recorded?

XI.17 Who has access to these at a later stage?

Chapter XII: Victims

XII.1. What rights does a victim have according to the law?

XII.1.a. If the victim has a right to appeal against discretionary decisions to drop/dispose, can s/he do so fast enough to prevent a conditional disposal becoming legally binding (e.g. because suspect has fulfilled condition)?

XII.2. What information must be given to the victim by the PPS according to the law/guidelines?

XII.2.a. Is any information usually or often provided which the law does not prescribe?

XIII. Basic Principles

What basic principles dominate criminal procedure law? – Please comment on the definitions provided below (presumption of innocence; principle of officiality/ legality; immediacy; public trial; decision on guilt only made by a judge; guilt established only by a judge).

List of Authors

Aubusson de Cavarlay, Bruno,
Centre de recherches sociologiques sur le Droit et les Institutions pénales (CESDIP), Ministère de Justice/CNRS, 43 Boulevard Vauban, F-78280 Guyancourt (Paris), France.
Bruno Aubusson de Cavarlay, research director at the CNRS, works at the Center for Sociological Research on Law and Penal Institutions (CESDIP,Guyancourt, France) on criminal statistics and the functioning of the criminal justice system and is member of the experts group "European Sourcebook of Crime and Criminal Statistics".

Blom, Martine, mw. Dr.,
Ministry of Justice, Research & Documentation Centre, P.O. Box 2031, 2500 EH The Hague, Netherlands.
Martine Blom is currently employed at the Research and Documentation Center (WODC) of the Ministry of Justice in the Netherlands. Her main research areas are registered and self-reported juvenile delinquency, delinquency of ethnic minorities and recidivism.

Bulenda,Teodor, Dr.,
Warsaw University IPSiR, Chair of Criminology and Criminal Policy, ul. Podchorazych 20, 00-721 Warsaw, Poland.
Dr. Teodor Bulenda is a senior lecturer at the Institute of Social Prevention and Resocialization of Warsaw University. He is also a senior specialist at the Office of the Commissioner for Civil Rights Protection (the Polish Ombudsman) in Poland and member of the Polish Section of the International Commission of Jurists and the Polish Society of Criminology.

Elsner, Beatrix,
Academic assistant, Göttingen University, Faculty of Law, Department of Criminology, Platz der Göttinger Sieben 6, 37073 Göttingen; Germany.
Beatrix Elsner is a qualified academic assistant at the Abteilung Kriminologie at the Law Faculty of the University of Göttingen. She has recently finished her doctoral thesis focusing on the legal and factual relationship between the prosecution service and police during criminal investigations in the Netherlands and Germany.

Grusczynska, Beata, Dr.,
Warsaw University IPSiR, Chair of Criminology and Criminal Policy, ul. Podchorazych 20, 00-721 Warsaw, Poland.

Dr. Beata Gruszczynska is a senior lecturer at the Institute of Social Prevention and Resocialisation of Warsaw University, and the Head of the Criminal Statistics and Research Division of the Institute of Justice in Poland. She is an expert on evaluation of the efficiency of justice for the Council of Europe, a member of the expert group "European Sourcebook of Crime and Criminal Justice Statistics" as well as a member of the Polish Society of Criminology and the European Society of Criminology.

Jehle, Jörg-Martin, Prof. Dr.,
Göttingen University, Faculty of Law, Department of Criminology, Platz der Göttinger Sieben 6, 37073 Göttingen, Germany.
Prof. Jörg-Martin Jehle holds the chair for Criminology and Criminal Law at the Law Faculty of the University of Göttingen and is managing director of the Institute of Criminal Law and Justice and head of the department for criminology. He is the former director of the Federal Center for Criminology, Wiesbaden, member of the Board of the Scientific Association of German, Austrian and Swiss Criminologists (NKG) and member of the experts group "European Sourcebook of Crime and Criminal Justice Statistics".

Kremplewski, Andrzej,
Warsaw University IPSiR, Chair of Criminology and Criminal Policy, ul. Podchorazych 20, 00-721 Warsaw, Poland.
Andrzej Kremplewski is a lecturer at the Department of Criminology and Criminal Policy at the Institute of Social Prevention and Rehabilitation of Warsaw University. He is an associate of the Helsinki Foundation for Human Rights in Poland, Member of Polish Society of Criminology and the Polish Section of International Commission of Jurists.

Lewis, Christopher, Prof. Dr.,
Portsmouth University, University House, Winston Churchill Avenue, Portsmouth, UK/ Hampshire, PO1 2UP, Institute of Criminal Justice Studies, UK
Chris Lewis was Assistant Director of Research at the British Home Office until May 2003 when he joined Portsmouth University as a senior research fellow to research on serious crime and and diversity in Britain and study comparative justice systems. Recent British work includes research with firearms offenders and an application of modelling techniques to gun crime: a review of diversity statistics: a diversity impact assessment of the new British prosecution charging system: and a study of an undercover police operation. Comparative analyses include this comparison of prosecution systems in Europe, two spells as a World Bank consultant on the administration of Kenya justice systems: collecting information and statistics on volume and organised crime within Europe: and comparing UK and Japanese justice systems.

Peters, Julia,
Academic assistant, Göttingen University, Faculty of Law, Department of Criminology, Platz der Göttinger Sieben 6, 37073 Göttingen; Germany.
Julia Peters is a qualified academic assistant at the Abteilung Kriminologie at the

Law Faculty of the University of Göttingen. She is currently working on her doctoral thesis focusing on prosecutorial negotiating case-ending powers available in France and Poland, guilty pleas in England & Wales and what can be drawn from them for the developing German legal regulation.

Smit, Paul,
Ministry of Justice, Research & Documentation Centre, P.O. Box 2031, 2500 EH The Hague, Netherlands
Paul Smit is a senior researcher at the Research and Documentation Center (WODC) of the Ministry of Justice in the Netherlands. He specializes in cross-national comparisons of crime and sentencing statistics. Also, he is involved in homicide research in the Netherlands and member of the experts group "European Sourcebook of Crime and Criminal Justice Statistics".

Sobota, Piotr,
The Office of the Commissioner for Civil Rights Protection, Biuro Rzecznika Praw Obywatelskich, Al. Solidarnósci 77, 00-090 Warszawa, Poland
Piotr Sobota is a senior specialist at the Office of the Commissioner for Civil Rights Protection (the Polish Ombudsman) in Poland. His work is focused on the protection of citizens` rights and freedoms within the criminal justice system. From 1987 – 1993 he worked as a public prosecutor. He is currently working on his doctoral thesis concerning the Ombudsman's cassation appeal powers.

Wade, Marianne, Dr.,
Göttingen University, Faculty of Law, Department of Criminology, Platz der Göttinger Sieben 6/ Max-Planck-Institute for Foreign and International Criminal Law, Günterstalstr. 73, 79100 Freiburg i.B., Germany.
Dr. Marianne Wade is Referentin in the European Criminal Law section of the Max-Planck-Insitute for International and Foreign Criminal Law in Freiburg, Senior Researcher at the Abt. Kriminologie at the University of Göttingen and a fellow of the Gottlieb-Daimler and Karl-Benz Stiftung. Her main research areas are surveillance, comparative and European criminal law.

Zila, Josef, Dr.,
Stockholm University, Faculty of Law, 106 91 Stockholm, Sweden
Josef Zila is associated professor in criminal law at the Faculty of Law, Stockholm University. He is currently engaged in a research project concerning child abduction in Sweden. His main research areas are sentencing principles and rules in criminal law, as well as topics of criminal law theory. In criminal procedural law, his focus is on existing investigative methods.